To Nikky
with many thanks
for your hard work
with gratitude
Andrew (and Harriet)
Sept 16.

A MIRROR FOR MAGISTRATES IN CONTEXT

This is the first essay collection on *A Mirror for Magistrates*, the most popular work of English literature in the age of Shakespeare. The *Mirror* is analysed here by major scholars who discuss its meaning and significance, and assess the extent of its influence as a series of tragic stories showing powerful princes and governors brought low by fate and enemy action. Scholars debate the challenging and radical nature of the *Mirror*'s politics; its significance as a work of material culture; its relationship to oral culture as print was becoming ever more important; and the complicated evolution of its diverse texts. Other chapters discuss the importance of the book as the first major work that represented Roman history for a literary audience, the sly humour contained in the tragedies, and their influence on major writers such as Spenser and Shakespeare.

HARRIET ARCHER is a Leverhulme Early Career Fellow at Newcastle University, working on a book-length project called 'New Poets: Writing and Authority in 1570s England' and an edition, with Paul Frazer, of Norton and Sackville's *Gorboduc* for the Manchester Revels Plays Series. She completed her DPhil on the *Mirror for Magistrates* and textual transmission at Christ Church, Oxford, in 2013. Her research interests include sixteenth-century historiography, modes of authorship, and the early modern reception of ancient and medieval culture.

ANDREW HADFIELD is Professor of English at the University of Sussex. He is the author of several studies of early modern literature and culture including *Shakespeare and Republicanism* (2005) and *Edmund Spenser: A Life* (2012), both of which were awarded prizes. He is currently writing a study of lying in early modern England funded by the Leverhulme Trust and is co-editing the Works of Thomas Nashe, funded by the AHRC. He is vice-chair of the Society for Renaissance Studies and is a regular reviewer for the *Times Literary Supplement* and the *Irish Times*.

A MIRROR FOR MAGISTRATES IN CONTEXT

Literature, History, and Politics in Early Modern England

EDITED BY

HARRIET ARCHER and
ANDREW HADFIELD

CAMBRIDGE
UNIVERSITY PRESS

CAMBRIDGE
UNIVERSITY PRESS

University Printing House, Cambridge CB2 8BS, United Kingdom

Cambridge University Press is part of the University of Cambridge.

It furthers the University's mission by disseminating knowledge in the pursuit of education, learning and research at the highest international levels of excellence.

www.cambridge.org
Information on this title: www.cambridge.org/9781107104358

© Cambridge University Press 2016

This publication is in copyright. Subject to statutory exception and to the provisions of relevant collective licensing agreements, no reproduction of any part may take place without the written permission of Cambridge University Press.

First published 2016

Printed in the United Kingdom by Clays, St Ives plc

A catalogue record for this publication is available from the British Library

Library of Congress Cataloguing in Publication Data
Names: Archer, Harriet, 1986– editor. | Hadfield, Andrew, editor.
Title: A mirror for magistrates in context : literature, history and politics in early modern England / edited by Harriet Archer and Andrew Hadfield.
Description: New York : Cambridge University Press, 2016. |
Includes bibliographical references and index.
Identifiers: LCCN 2016016072| ISBN 9781107104358 (hardback) |
ISBN 9781107505827 (paperback)
Subjects: LCSH: Mirrour for magistrates. | English poetry–Early modern, 1500–1700–History and criticism. | Literature and history–Great Britain–History–16th century. | Great Britain–Politics and government–1485–1603.
Classification: LCC PR2199.M53 M57 2016 | DDC 821/.3–dc23
LC record available at https://lccn.loc.gov/2016016072

ISBN 978-1-1071-0435-8 Hardback

Additional resources for this publication at www.cambridge.org/9781107104358

Cambridge University Press has no responsibility for the persistence or accuracy of URLs for external or third-party internet websites referred to in this publication, and does not guarantee that any content on such websites is, or will remain, accurate or appropriate.

Contents

List of illustrations	*page* vii
List of contributors	viii
Acknowledgements	xii
List of abbreviations	xiii

Introduction: *A Mirror for Magistrates* and early
modern English culture   1
Harriet Archer and Andrew Hadfield

PART I   A MYRROURE FOR MAGISTRATES (1559–1563)

1 A Renaissance man and his 'medieval' text: William Baldwin
   and *A Mirror for Magistrates*, 1547–1563   17
   Scott C. Lucas

2 'A miserable time full of piteous tragedyes'   35
   Paul Budra

3 Tragic and untragic bodies in the *Mirror for Magistrates*   53
   Mike Pincombe

4 Reading and listening to William Baldwin   71
   Jennifer Richards

5 Bibliophily in Baldwin's *Mirror*   89
   Angus Vine

PART II   LATER ADDITIONS (1574–1616)

6 'Hoysted high vpon the rolling wheele': Elianor
   Cobham's *Lament*   109
   Cathy Shrank

v

7	Romans in the mirror *Paulina Kewes*	126
8	'Those chronicles whiche other men had': *Paralipsis* and Blenerhasset's *Seconde Part of the Mirror for Magistrates* (1578) *Harriet Archer*	147
9	Richard Niccols and Tudor nostalgia *Andrew Hadfield*	164
10	A mirror for magistrates: Richard Niccols' *Sir Thomas Overburies Vision* (1616) *Michelle O'Callaghan*	181

PART III   READING THE *MIRROR*: POETRY AND DRAMA

11	Rethinking absolutism: English *de casibus* tragedy in the 1560s *Jessica Winston*	199
12	'They do it with mirrors': Spenser, Shakespeare, Baldwin's *Mirror*, and Elizabethan literature's political vanishing act *Bart van Es*	216
13	'Most out of order': Preposterous time in the *Mirror for Magistrates* and Shakespeare's histories *Philip Schwyzer*	231

Select bibliography   246
Index   250

Illustrations

1 William Baldwin's printer's device, *The Canticles or Balades of Salomon* (London, 1549; STC 2768), sig. n4v.   *page* 19
2 Johann Froben's printer's mark, Erasmus, *Nouum Instrumentu[m] omne* (Basel, 1516; Pitts Theological Library 1516 BIBL B.), sig. Ff8r.   20

Contributors

HARRIET ARCHER, Newcastle University
Harriet Archer is a Leverhulme Early Career Fellow at Newcastle University, working on a book-length project called 'New Poets: Writing and Authority in 1570s England'. She completed her AHRC-funded DPhil on the *Mirror for Magistrates* and its transmission at Christ Church, Oxford, in 2013, and is revising her thesis for publication as *Unperfect Histories: the* Mirror for Magistrates, *1559–1610*. Her research interests include sixteenth-century historiography, modes of authorship, and the early modern reception of medieval culture; she is the co-editor, with Paul Frazer, of a critical edition of *Gorboduc* (Manchester Revels Plays Series, forthcoming), and has written on Holinshed and the Middle Ages; Chaucer, Spenser and Luke Shepherd; and John Higgins and marginalia.

PAUL BUDRA, Simon Fraser University
Paul Budra is Professor and Chair of English at Simon Fraser University. He teaches Shakespeare and early modern literature and has published articles on Renaissance literature and contemporary popular culture. He is the author of A Mirror for Magistrates *and the* de casibus *Tradition* (University of Toronto Press, 2000) and *Shakespeare Early and Late* (Simon Fraser University Library, 2016). He is the co-editor of the essay collections *Part Two: Reflections on the Sequel* (University of Toronto Press, 1998), *Soldier Talk: Oral Narratives of the Vietnam War* (Indiana University Press, 2004), *From Text to Txting: New Media in the Classroom* (Indiana University Press, 2012), and *Shakespeare and Consciousness* (Palgrave, 2016).

BART VAN ES, St Catherine's College, Oxford
Bart van Es is Professor of English Literature at Oxford and a Fellow of St Catherine's College. His research interests include sixteenth- and seventeenth-century historical prose and poetry, the writing of Edmund Spenser, and the reception of classical texts in the early modern period.

He is the author of *Spenser's Forms of History* (Oxford University Press, 2002), *Shakespeare in Company* (Oxford University Press, 2013), and *Shakespeare's Comedies: A Very Short Introduction* (Oxford University Press, 2016), and editor of *A Critical Companion to Spenser Studies* (Palgrave-Macmillan, 2005). Amongst other articles and book chapters he has contributed the chapter 'Spenser and History' to *The Oxford Handbook of Edmund Spenser*, ed. Richard McCabe (Oxford University Press, 2010) and the chapter 'Historiography and Biography' to *The Oxford History of Classical Reception in English Literature*, eds. Patrick Cheney and Philip Hardie (Oxford University Press, 2015).

ANDREW HADFIELD, University of Sussex
Andrew Hadfield is Professor of English at the University of Sussex and visiting Professor at the University of Granada. He is the author of a number of works on early modern literature, including *Edmund Spenser: A Life* (Oxford University Press, 2012); *Shakespeare and Republicanism* (Cambridge University Press, 2005, paperback 2008); *Literature, Travel and Colonialism in the English Renaissance, 1540–1625* (Oxford University Press, 1998, paperback, 2007); *Spenser's Irish Experience: Wilde Fruyt and Salvage Soyl* (Oxford University Press, 1997); and *Literature, Politics and National Identity: Reformation to Renaissance* (Cambridge University Press, 1994), which contains a chapter on *A Mirror for Magistrates*. He was editor of *Renaissance Studies* (2006–11) and is a regular reviewer for the *Times Literary Supplement*.

PAULINA KEWES, Jesus College, Oxford
Paulina Kewes is a fellow and tutor in English Literature at Jesus College, Oxford and a Fellow of the Royal Historical Society. She has published widely on early modern literature, history, and politics. Her books include *Authorship and Appropriation: Writing for the Stage in England, 1660–1710* (Clarendon Press, 1998) and, as editor or co-editor, *Plagiarism in Early Modern England* (Palgrave Macmillan, 2003), *The Uses of History in Early Modern England* (Huntington Library, 2006), *The Oxford Handbook of Holinshed's Chronicles* (Oxford University Press, 2013), *Doubtful and Dangerous: The Question of Succession in Late Elizabethan England* (Manchester University Press, 2014), and *Literature of the Stuart Successions* (forthcoming, 2017).

SCOTT C. LUCAS, The Citadel
Scott C. Lucas is a professor of English Literature at The Citadel, the Military College of South Carolina. He is the author of the monograph

A Mirror for Magistrates and the Politics of the English Reformation (University of Massachusetts Press, 2009) and of other works on early modern English literature, history, and culture. Recent articles and book chapters have appeared in *The Huntington Library Quarterly, Review of English Studies, The Oxford Handbook of Holinshed's* Chronicles and *Catholic Renewal and Protestant Resistance in Marian England*. He is currently preparing a critical edition of William Baldwin's *A Mirror for Magistrates*, the editions of 1559 and 1563, for Cambridge University Press.

MICHELLE O'CALLAGHAN, University of Reading
Michelle O'Callaghan is Professor of Early Modern Literature at the University of Reading. She is author of *The 'Shepheards Nation': Jacobean Spenserians and Early Stuart Political Culture* (Oxford University Press, 2000), *The English Wits: Literature and Sociability in Early Modern England* (Cambridge University Press, 2007), and *Thomas Middleton: Renaissance Dramatist* (Edinburgh University Press, 2009). She is the co-editor, along with Alice Eardley, of *Verse Miscellanies Online* (http://versemiscellaniesonline.bodleian.ox.ac.uk/), and is currently working on a monograph on the early printed poetry miscellanies.

MIKE PINCOMBE, Newcastle University
Mike Pincombe has written a number of notes and articles on various authors connected with the mid-Tudor *de casibus* tradition: Cavendish, Baldwin, Ferrers, Sackville. He is Professor of Tudor and Elizabethan Literature at Newcastle University.

JENNIFER RICHARDS, Newcastle University
Jennifer Richards is Professor of Early Modern Literature and Culture at Newcastle University. She is completing a new monograph, *Voices and Books in the English Renaissance: A New History of Reading*, which was supported by a Leverhulme Trust Major Research Fellowship and an AHRC Network Grant. She is general editor with Andrew Hadfield, Joe Black, and Cathy Shrank of *A New Critical Edition of the Complete Works of Thomas Nashe*, 6 volumes (Oxford University Press, 2020), and editor of the journal *Renaissance Studies*.

PHILIP SCHWYZER, University of Exeter
Philip Schwyzer is Professor of Renaissance Literature at the University of Exeter. His books include *Shakespeare and the Remains of Richard III* (Oxford University Press, 2013), *Archaeologies of English Renaissance Literature* (Oxford University Press, 2007), and *Literature, Nationalism, and Memory in Early Modern England and Wales* (Cambridge University

Press, 2004). His current projects include a study of sites of memory in England and Wales, and an investigation of 'Shakespeare and the Anglo-American Way of Death'.

CATHY SHRANK, University of Sheffield
Cathy Shrank is Professor of Tudor and Renaissance Literature at the University of Sheffield. Her publications include *Writing the Nation in Reformation England, 1530–1580* (Oxford University Press, 2004) and essays and articles on various sixteenth- and early seventeenth-century topics, including language reform, civility, travel-writing, cheap print, and mid-sixteenth-century sonnets. She is the co-editor, with Mike Pincombe, of *The Oxford Handbook of Tudor Literature, 1485–1603* (Oxford University Press, 2009). Current research includes writing a monograph about non-dramatic dialogues, funded by a Leverhulme Major Research Fellowship, and editing *Shakespeare's Sonnets* and *A Lover's Complaint* for the Annotated English Poets series. She is one of the General Editors of the *Oxford Works of Thomas Nashe*.

ANGUS VINE, University of Stirling
Angus Vine is Lecturer in Early Modern Literature at the University of Stirling. His research interests include sixteenth- and seventeenth-century history writing, antiquarianism, the works of Francis Bacon, manuscript culture, and history of the book. He is the author of *In Defiance of Time: Antiquarian Writing in Early Modern England* (Oxford University Press, 2010) and of a number of articles on early modern manuscript and textual culture. He is also one of the editors of *The Oxford Francis Bacon* and *The Oxford Traherne*. He is currently completing a monograph on miscellanies, manuscripts, and the organisation of knowledge, and a co-edited collection of essays on Shakespeare and authority (Palgrave, 2017).

JESSICA WINSTON, Idaho State University
Jessica Winston is Associate Professor of English at Idaho State University. Her research focuses on the literary culture of the English legal societies, the Inns of Court, in the early modern period, and the Elizabethan reception of the tragedies of the ancient Roman playwright and philosopher Seneca. She has recently finished editing *Elizabethan Seneca: Three Tragedies* (with James Ker), which is part of the MHRA's Tudor and Stuart Translations Series, and her monograph *Lawyers at Play: Literature, Law, and Politics at the Early Modern Inns of Court, 1558–1581* (Oxford University Press) was published in 2016.

Acknowledgements

This volume began its life as 'Fame and Fortune: the *Mirror for Magistrates*, 1559–1946', a conference organised by Harriet Archer in 2012. The editors are very grateful to all participants at the conference; those not represented by the chapters below include Jane Griffiths, Gillian Hubbard, Andy Kesson, Anthony Martin, Kavita Mudan Finn, Meredith Skura, and Matthew Woodcock. We would also like to thank James McBain and the staff at Magdalen College, Oxford, for hosting us, and the Society for Renaissance Studies and the Royal Historical Society for their financial backing. Thanks are also due to David Norbrook and Emma Smith for their support of the project along the way. At Cambridge University Press, we are grateful to Sarah Stanton, Emma Collison, Isobel Cowper-Coles, Rosemary Crawley, and Sarah Starkey for their assistance, and our anonymous readers for their suggestions and enthusiasm, and at Out of House Publishing to Helen Flitton and Nikky Twyman for helping us bring the text together.

Abbreviations

ANQ	*American Notes and Queries*
EHR	*English Historical Review*
ELH	*English Literary History*
ELR	*English Literary Renaissance*
EMS	*English Manuscript Studies*
HLB	*Huntington Library Bulletin*
HLQ	*Huntington Library Quarterly*
JBA	*Journal of the British Academy*
JNR	*Journal of the Northern Renaissance*
JWCI	*Journal of the Warburg and Courtauld Institutes*
LC	*Literature Compass*
MLQ	*Modern Language Quarterly*
MLR	*Modern Language Review*
MP	*Modern Philology*
NQ	*Notes and Queries*
ODNB	*Oxford Dictionary of National Biography*
OED	*Oxford English Dictionary*
P. & P.	*Past and Present*
PQ	*Philological Quarterly*
RD	*Renaissance Drama*
RES	*Review of English Studies*
RQ	*Renaissance Quarterly*
RS	*Renaissance Studies*
SAQ	*South Atlantic Quarterly*
SEL	*Studies in English Literature, 1500–1900*
SP	*Studies in Philology*
SQ	*Shakespeare Quarterly*
SS	*Spenser Studies*

STC	*Short Title Catalogue of Books Printed in England, Scotland, & Ireland and of English Books Printed Abroad*, ed. A. W. Pollard et al., 3 vols. (London: Bibliographical Society, 1976–91).
TAPA	*Transactions of the American Philological Association*
TC	*Textual Cultures*
TL	*Translation and Literature*
TLS	*Times Literary Supplement*
TRHS	*Transactions of the Royal Historical Society*

Introduction
A Mirror for Magistrates *and early modern English culture*

Harriet Archer and Andrew Hadfield

It is frequently acknowledged that the large, diverse, constantly evolving literary project *A Mirror for Magistrates* was a text that shaped the contours of Tudor and early Jacobean literature. Even so, beyond the enthusiasms of a few specialists eager to discuss the work with each other, the substance of the *Mirror* has largely been ignored. The assumption made is that, while it did exert a profound influence on readers and writers, it was the wrong sort of influence, one that is better ignored and left to a dark corner of academia. E. M. W. Tillyard, writing in the 1950s, could not understand why the *Mirror*'s 'execrable verse', 'however alien to modern taste and however poor as poetry by enduring standards', was so enthusiastically received by Elizabethan readers, while C. S. Lewis's judgement made over sixty years ago still stands for readers and non-readers alike:

> No one lays down the *Mirror* without a sense of relief. An immense amount of serious thought and honest work went into its composition and it remains, with Tottel, the chief poetical monument of the Drab Age. Like Tottel it did useful work in re-establishing metrical regularity, but in many other respects its influence on succeeding poets was mainly bad. It encouraged that taste for heavily doctrinal history in verse which is partly responsible for [Michael Drayton's] *Mortimeriados* and *Polyolbion*.[1]

The *Mirror* performs a bit of useful work in sorting out clumsy and flawed poetry, but it is hard to imagine a reader, even one hostile to Lewis, turning voluntarily to the *Mirror*, especially when there are so many other exciting and colourful works on offer in the period. After all, who, apart from specialists, really cares about metrical regularity?

The *Mirror* does not feature in many histories of sixteenth-century literature and, when it does, it is often a single poem, Thomas Sackville's 1563 'Induction', which is considered worthy of mention; nor does it appear on undergraduate or graduate courses in English departments.

Although its influence on Shakespeare is noted – albeit with reluctance – the edition which he actually would have read, John Higgins' compilation of 1587, is usually eclipsed by the editions recent scholars have thought best repay critical attention, those of 1559–63, and any references are generally relegated to the appendices of only the most extensively informative editions of Shakespeare's works. Despite the sustained popular interest in the Tudors, it is hard to imagine a television presenter explaining that the *Mirror* played a vital role in making Elizabethan literature as exciting and diverse as it is thought to be, or William Baldwin appearing in a costume drama or a Philippa Gregory novel. We should note, however, that with the rise of environmental concerns the historical poet Michael Drayton's verse chorography *Poly-Olbion* (1612) has generated far more interest as a poem that predicted many later disasters, in particular the destruction of Britain's forests.[2] Times do change.

The *Mirror* presents difficulties for contemporary readers not inclined to read narrative poetry after the rise of the novel transformed the literary landscape two centuries later. Comprising almost one hundred individual tragedies at its greatest extent, its sheer scale and tangled bibliographical history make getting to grips with the work a daunting undertaking. Nor do readers generally enjoy what they think of as its didactic judgements, monotonous tone and repetitive plot structure. However, as the chapters in this collection, especially those of Jennifer Richards and Mike Pincombe, demonstrate, it is not at all clear that we should always take the apparent judgements of the *Mirror*'s narrators at face value, nor should we assume that what looks like the truth is actually the truth. The *Mirror*, in all its various manifestations, is a far more challenging and complicated work than is generally assumed.

A brief overview of the *Mirror*'s publishing history provides some idea of its bewildering complexity and its role in establishing the literature of the English Renaissance.[3] The *Mirror* was, it seems, the brainchild of the printer John Wayland, who was keen to capitalise on the success of John Lydgate's *The Fall of Princes*, a fifteenth-century poem of 36,000 lines which detailed the tragic fate of a long list of virtuous and badly behaved monarchs, establishing the vogue in England for Boccaccian *de casibus* tragedy – stories of those who descend into misery and desperation after happiness and success, following the rotation of Fortune's wheel.[4] At some point in the mid-1550s Wayland asked William Baldwin, an assistant in the fugitive Edward Whitchurch's print shop, who had already built up a significant reputation as a writer at Edward VI's court, to oversee the project, planning to continue Lydgate's classical tragedies using subjects from

English history. Baldwin, a learned humanist and man of many roles, as Scott C. Lucas's chapter in this volume demonstrates, assembled a team of writers – although only the name of George Ferrers is recorded – who worked through the histories and chronicles they had to hand to produce a series of tragic poems depicting the falls of the great. Read aloud by the poets, it would be as if these historical figures appeared to the assembled writers as ghosts, warning others not to make their mistakes and so share their unpalatable fates. The innovative feature of the edition was the interconnecting prose prefaces which recorded dialogues between the writers about the content, style, and presentation of the orations they had just witnessed.

The snappily titled *Memorial of Suche Princes as Since the Tyme of King Richard the Seconde, have been Unfortunate in the Realme of England*, which was to be printed alongside Wayland's latest imprint of *The Fall of Princes*, was suppressed at the instigation of the Lord Chancellor, Bishop Stephen Gardiner, a sign of its seditious potential in light of the changes inaugurated by Mary I's Catholic regime. After Mary's death in November 1558 a new, revised version was printed in 1559 by the prolific and canny Thomas Marshe, but this did not contain the full text of the 1555 *Memorial*. In 1563 a second edition of the sanitised *Mirror* was produced, which contained more tragedies almost certainly derived from the suppressed *Memorial*, although Baldwin's supposed death from the plague in 1563 prevented him from overseeing the collection's publication any further. It is an indication of its popularity that a third revised edition appeared in 1571, followed by versions under the title *The Last Part of the Mirror for Magistrates* in 1574, 1575, and 1578. This last iteration contained two new tragedies (one mentioned in the 1559 edition's table of contents); a further edition of 1587 added yet more. Alongside the main collection, a series of spin-offs appeared: written by the poet, editor, translator, and Somerset vicar John Higgins, *The First Part of the Mirror for Magistrates* (1574) used material from Geoffrey of Monmouth's *History of the Kings of Britain*, and the chronicles of Grafton and Stow, to extend the *Mirror*'s narrative back to the foundation of Britain by the Trojan, Brutus. The soldier-poet Thomas Blenerhasset, discussed in Harriet Archer's chapter, produced *The Second Part of the Mirror for Magistrates* (1578) while he was stationed on Guernsey, containing twelve tragedies also derived from British/English history from the conquest of Caesar to the Norman Conquest, an anomalous addition to the *Mirror* canon ostensibly composed as a private exercise, and printed in Blenerhasset's absence. The 1587 edition, printed by Thomas Marshe's son Henry, and edited by Higgins, added a series of histories of Roman figures, a significant development in the collection's historical and geographical scope which inaugurated a new phase in the reception of Roman history in England, as Paulina Kewes argues in her chapter. In 1610 Richard Niccols, the subject of the chapters by Andrew Hadfield and Michelle O'Callaghan, brought together almost all the tragedies published so far, omitting the prefaces so that the work became a poetry anthology, perhaps with encouragement from his printer, Felix Kingston, who had inherited the rights to the *Mirror* franchise.

Evidently the product of an efficient and opportunistic succession of Renaissance printers, who navigated the rough political terrain of the sixteenth and early seventeenth centuries to extend and exploit the collection's huge commercial success, the *Mirror*'s knotty bibliography has not fared so well at the hands of modern editors. Last printed more or less in full in 1815, edited by the antiquary, Joseph Haslewood, who also produced early scholarly versions of Thomas Tusser's *Five Hundred Points of Good Husbandry* (1810), George Puttenham's *Arte of English Poesie* (1811), and William Painter's *The Palace of Pleasure* (1813), the *Mirror*'s modern reception has been dominated by Lily B. Campbell's edition of Baldwin's *Mirror* (1938), and the so-called *Parts Added to the* Mirror for Magistrates (1946). Campbell pre-empted much of the New Critical antipathy towards the *Mirror*'s verse, and her particular bias against the later additions (and complete exclusion of Niccols' additions from the canon) has persisted into the twenty-first century. Sherri Geller was one of the first scholars to draw attention to the deficiencies of Campbell and her predecessors' bibliographical approaches, including in particular the gradual downgrading of Baldwin's prose frame, both in terms of readerly appreciation and typographical appearance, over the course of repeated editorial resettings.[5] As Geller observed, the framing narrative had been transformed over the centuries from the main substance of the work to a paratext, subordinate to the inset tragedies. The recalibration of the relationship between these two aspects of the *Mirror*, its verse histories and prose links, has provided much of the critical interest for modern readers, as the historiographical and aesthetic doubts of the poets are restored as a central focus.[6] It also allows us to begin to interrogate more sensitively the evolution of the *Mirror* corpus as Higgins and Niccols co-opted, adapted, and excised Baldwin's narrative of composition. A work that has a history this involved and complex clearly absorbed the imagination of a large number of readers and writers over a significant period of time. Shakespeare, Spenser, and Sidney (who singled out the *Mirror* as 'meetly furnished of beautiful parts') are only the most obvious examples of writers who learned from and engaged with the

Mirror.⁷ If we want to understand Tudor and Stuart literature we have to face up to the *Mirror*'s pervasive influence, as the chapters by Bart van Es and Philip Schywzer demonstrate.

Understanding of the period has moved on and developed since Lewis rather unkindly labelled the *Mirror* the very epitome of the Drab Age. Critics and scholars are now able to debate the significance of the *Mirror* and are taking different positions and emphasising different aspects of the work in their evaluation of its undoubted significance, hardly surprising given its complex and varied nature. Much criticism of the *Mirror* has developed out of the recognition that the work exists as an interesting qualification of the ubiquitous genre, *Speculum Principis*, a mirror for princes, which advised aspiring and actual kings and rulers how they should govern, providing them with a series of ideal cases and examples to inspire them and disastrous actions and attitudes to warn them. A part of the sixteenth-century tradition derived from the Erasmian model of the education of princes, internalised to such a degree by the end of the century that the fates of contemporary figures were recycled as moral *exempla*, James VI of Scotland was tutored in the late 1560s and early 1570s by the great French-schooled Scottish humanist, George Buchanan (1506–82), who terrified the young prince with interminable stories about the awful fates of bad kings, which haunted him into old age.⁸ The title, *A Mirror for Magistrates*, signals a significant shift in emphasis, with the focus moving from the prince to the governing class, 'magistrate' being a wide-ranging term in early modern England, including all governors from lowly Justices of the Peace in shires, to powerful first ministers advising the monarch. The work, therefore, as has long been recognised, targets a substantial readership, which would not only have helped its sales, but also hints at an attempt to spread the language of politics more widely. For many readers the *Mirror*, certainly in its early editions under the guidance of William Baldwin, was a radical work, eager to tap into the contemporary inclinations of political discourse by placing heavy emphasis on the need for governors to govern fairly and wisely and stressing their responsibility to the people just as the republican Buchanan argued was the duty of a future king like Prince James. It is a moot point whether the *Mirror* is a work inspired by humanist teaching that sought to train governors to rule well; a republican – or republicanesque – work, emphasising the rights and duties of active citizens who need to govern wisely; a commonwealth work which emphasised the same virtues as integral to a unified and interconnected body politic; or an old-fashioned treatise based on the conciliarist tradition, most famously expressed by Marsilius of Padua, placing emphasis on the interconnectedness of society and the need for councils to achieve consensus between rulers and people. The *Mirror* was manipulated in different directions by its various editors, each responding to a particular aspect of the text, such that its stance is constantly shifting.

Scholarly interest in the *Mirror* was reinvigorated in the 1980s and 1990s by the text's promise as a site of oppositional political engagement. Lawrence D. Green and Paul Budra recognised a polyphony of dissenting voices, destabilising the work's reputation as a repository for conservative moral teaching in line with recent revisionist studies of other monumental Tudor texts.[9] In addition to the hubbub of authorial voices who put forward the *Mirror* tragedies and argue over questions from the true sequence of historical events to the decorous matching of aesthetics to subject matter, including, according to various editions of the text, Baldwin and Ferrers along with key literary names of the period Thomas Chaloner, Thomas Churchyard, Thomas Phaer, Thomas Sackville, John Dolman, and other anonymous collaborators, the historical figures themselves do not agree on the political stance of the complaint collection. Neither do they offer a satisfactory consensus on historical causation, or the role of divine retributive justice.[10]

In contrast to Budra's emphasis on the text's polyvocality, Scott C. Lucas outlines a structured case made cumulatively by the *Mirror*'s tragedies which, he argues, consistently reinforces the key role of resistance theory in Elizabethan political counsel.[11] Contributors to this volume disagree about the extent to which the *Mirror*'s transgressive potential has been overplayed, and elsewhere Pincombe has called for readers to reject the seductive narrative of resistance which stems from the *Mirror*'s early suppression for, we can only suppose, political reasons.[12] What is radical about Baldwin's *Mirror*, though, is its scepticism regarding the historical claims which underpin the political *status quo*, and its acknowledgement of oral and written texts' vulnerability to misuse – examined by Vine and Richards's chapters in this volume, and elsewhere.[13] As Lucas demonstrates in his monograph on the *Mirror*'s reformist politics, Baldwin and Ferrers consult and then repeatedly deviate from historical accounts provided by historians of late medieval England who populated the Edwardian intellectual landscape, such as Edward Hall.[14] Hall's *Union of the Two Noble and Illustrate Famelies of Lancastre and Yorke* (1548) provided the *Mirror* authors with a recent chronological template for their selection of tragedies, and the treatment of a discrete dynastic conflict, while the popular abridgements of Grafton and Stow offered models for bite-sized heteroglossia, within a tense and heavily ideologically inflected historical battleground.[15]

As David Womersley notes, 'Protestant religion and Elizabethan historiography cannot be pulled apart', and the collection's ambivalence and irreverence towards temporal rulers and their chroniclers is part and parcel of Baldwin and Ferrers' serious religious faith, which shaped their rewriting of English foundational stories.[16] Far from the worthy 'doctrinal history' Lewis postulates, historical narrative and moral guidance are now commonly understood as only two of a broad selection of their concerns, in amongst legal reform, political opposition, literary experimentation, affect, and the instigation of learned debate, while providential history is only one model promulgated by the capacious and intellectually active compendium.[17]

Spanning the reigns of three live English monarchs, in addition to the deceased rulers who populate its pages, the *Mirror*'s development offers us a window onto a tumultuous period of early modern history as well as its authors' perspectives on the nation's past. Jim Ellis saw the text as perfectly placed to interrogate the early modern transition from feudal to capitalist property relations, manifested in its poetry's violent mutilation of physical bodies – a view Pincombe re-evaluates below.[18] Elsewhere, Philip Schwyzer has read the *Mirror*, and in particular the early collections of orations compiled by Baldwin and Higgins, as a product of the closing off of dialogue with the dead inflicted by the Chantries Acts – a loss of which both the radical evangelical Baldwin, and the conformist clergyman Higgins would have approved, but which nonetheless radically reconfigured contemporaries' access to their island's ghosts.[19] Schwyzer suggests that where souls in purgatory had been served by the prayers of the living until the practice was legally done away with, the *Mirror*'s speakers served their listeners by offering moral advice. As the *Mirror*'s complex evolution progressed up to the end of the sixteenth century and beyond, this dynamic was reversed once again as successive editors placed ever greater emphasis on the collection's commemorative role. It is possible to contextualise the work's expansion among the other monumental historiographic enterprises of the age, like John Foxe's *Acts and Monuments* (1570) and Raphael Holinshed's *Chronicles of England, Scotlande and Irelande* (1577), texts which also reached back – during the 1570s and in multiple subsequent iterations – into the nation's prehistory. Like the *Mirror*, Foxe and Holinshed's composite histories elided a sweeping chronological approach with intensifying shades of didacticism, and exerted new, sceptical methodological pressure on text extracted from medieval source material. Like the *Mirror*, too, these volumes were quickly pushed to the brink of obsolescence by imminent changes in antiquarian and interpretative techniques, print technologies, and cultural taste, but represented a brief but thoroughly striking Elizabethan efflorescence.[20] To dismiss the *Mirror*'s historiographical function is to sideline a huge part of its early modern appeal, and the seemingly limitless appetite of Elizabethan and Jacobean readers for epitomes and verse retellings of chronicle history on and off the stage.[21] The chapters which follow hold this facet of the compilation's purpose in tension with the diverse additional motivations which directed the *Mirror*'s development.

It is not just the *Mirror*'s historical content, of course, instantly recognisable from canonical late Elizabethan historical drama, but more significantly its modes of historiography which were so hugely influential in the second half of the sixteenth century. Where criticism has focused predominantly on the *Mirror*'s adaptation of Lydgate's vernacular *de casibus* format in this regard, as Winston, van Es, and Schwyzer demonstrate in Part III of this volume its literary impact was far more wide-ranging. The *Mirror* itself was produced in its own cultural crucible, drawing not only on Lydgate's model but also on vibrant new forays into satire, tragedy, and prose fiction, to say nothing of the anthology culture instigated by Tottel's *Miscellany* and promoted in large part by the *Mirror* itself. Instead of the 'metrical regularity' Lewis claims these works encouraged, the *Mirror* and its various recensions saw all kinds of formal experimentation ranging far beyond the rhyme royal stanza with which it has come to be so closely associated. As Archer's chapter notes, Thomas Blenerhasset's *Second Part of the Mirror* (1578) was hardly a reiteration of a tired aesthetic product with a 'medieval' flavour, but instead a bold statement of poetic innovation, which hitched Blenerhasset's mischievous interpolation to the mid-century metrical experiments of George Gascoigne, Thomas Phaer, and George Turberville. Sackville's contributions to the 1563 edition were held up into subsequent centuries as examples of surpassing literary skill, and Spenser and Shakespeare drew not just on the *Mirror*'s historical subject matter and verse chronicle structure but also its idiom and imagery, its forensic focalisation and interiority. The female complaint form may have been the *Mirror*'s most commercially successful export, as Churchyard's Jane Shore spawned rivals by Daniel, Drayton, and numerous others.[22] But the construction of Martin Marprelate, and the volatile horde of imitative prose satirists who followed in the 1580s and 1590s, can also trace their heritage back to the playful personae and irreverent humour that Pincombe identifies from the earliest editions of the *Mirror*, itself inherited, he suggests, from the classical Menippean tradition. Meredith Skura has also identified the *Mirror* as one of the most significant but unrecognised contributors to 'the prehistory of autobiography', as well as drawing on a rich tradition of fictions in prose and verse, from Chaucer's *Canterbury Tales* to More's *Utopia*.²³

This volume seeks to open out debate on the *Mirror* at all stages of its history, and to read its various iterations in their contexts. The following chapters do not intend to explore each of these contexts exhaustively, but rather to showcase the ways in which the *Mirror for Magistrates* may illuminate, and be illuminated by, current scholarly debates. Part I investigates the significance of the first edition of the *Mirror*, overseen by William Baldwin and – probably – George Ferrers, and printed by Thomas Marshe in 1559. This is the edition which has received most critical attention, and against which the *Mirror*'s later expressions have been judged, but these chapters seek to approach 'Baldwin's *Mirror*' from a series of new angles. For Richards, it is the debate within the *Mirror* that we have been neglecting, failing to listen to the text and imagine it existing within a primarily oral culture where sound was a more important sense than sight. For Richards, the *Mirror* does not simply acknowledge debate but actively encourages it, providing the reader with a series of open-ended stories that mean different things to different readers. Her argument places great emphasis on the prefaces to the tales and the material that links the poems – all of which was removed in 1610, signalling an end to this dimension of the project. The poems are often based on commonplaces – pieces of easily extractable wisdom which Baldwin had collected elsewhere in his enormously popular *Treatise of Moral Philosophy*, first printed in 1547 – which are then challenged, refigured, rethought, and questioned in the debates they inspire within and beyond the boundaries of the text. Pincombe also wonders whether we have misread the *Mirror* and taken it far too seriously, missing its humour, and therefore its literary qualities, in the process of transforming it into a serious political work of counsel. Like Richards he places great emphasis on the connecting material as well as the tragedies, and wonders whether the *Mirror* should be thought of in terms of the history of satire rather than just the advice-to-princes tradition. When both chapters are read alongside Scott C. Lucas's reminder of the range and variety of William Baldwin's achievement as the most significant writer at the court of Edward VI, it becomes clear that our understanding of the *Mirror*'s position within a so-called Drab Age of English literary achievement needs to be revised.

Angus Vine makes a similar claim but pursues a different route, asking readers to think more about the significance of the bibliographical nature of the early editions of the *Mirror*. For Vine, the *Mirror*'s bookishness signals a dialogic character, a tension between 'a confidence in the historical authority of the written and printed word' and an anxiety that 'histories are themselves subject to the same quirks, unreliability, and doubtfulness as oral testimony' (p.102). While Richards hears a noisy work full of uncontrollable sound, Vine reads a confusing text that can never convince the reader of its own authority.

Paul Budra is also eager to reorient the ways in which we read the *Mirror*. His chapter argues that we have not paid enough attention to the affect of the work, the ways in which it emotionally engages readers who witness the terrible downfall of so many unfortunate figures. Budra, too, is sceptical of arguments that the work had a coherent agenda given the number of writers involved in its production. He argues that, rather than imagining that their readers should understand a particular political message, the authors of the tragedies wanted them to feel the cruel and unstable nature of life on earth and concentrate on the afterlife.

The next section of chapters explores the Elizabethan and Jacobean adaptations of the work, finding much more to admire in these versions than many earlier critics have discovered. Cathy Shrank, in a dense and historically informed reading of George Ferrers' 'Elianor Cobham's lament', finally added to Baldwin's set of medieval tragedies as late as 1578, wonders whether readings that have seen the work as unified have missed its challenging variety and diversity. In a chapter which complements Vine's in Part I, she argues that the poem brings together different versions of the truth and deliberately does not provide an overall judgement, a symptom of Ferrers' 'fascination with conflicting or disputed versions of history' (p.123). Harriet Archer's chapter, in an argument which parallels Pincombe's new reading of Baldwin, argues that the much maligned Thomas Blenerhasset was a far more interesting – and less serious – poet than his detractors have claimed. Archer suggests that we have overlooked the subtlety and playfulness of Blenerhasset's writing and not been alive to his particular use of the trope of *paralipsis* – claiming to want to skate over an unimportant issue and so drawing attention to it – a potent use of irony, most famously exploited by Mark Antony in his oration over the body of Julius Caesar in Shakespeare's play. Like Baldwin, Blenerhasset was keen to exploit the ironic possibilities of the form's metatextual framing narrative, and unwilling to tie up the loose ends of historiographical uncertainty, instead requiring the reader to understand his writing and so draw his or her own conclusions. Paulina Kewes offers a similarly revisionist reading of John Higgins' *Mirour* of 1587, and his earlier *First Parte* (1574/5). Kewes argues that Higgins is another undervalued author and editor, drawing on the political resonances of the Galfridian legend and Roman history to adapt the *Mirror* for the crisis that faced the monarchy in 1587 after the trial and execution of Mary, Queen of Scots. Higgins' text explores the language of treason as he asks his readers to think about the complicated loyalties that were precipitated after the Roman conquest of Britain. His text cannot be read allegorically; rather, readers have to work hard to understand how his ancient British and Roman histories might apply to England in the perilous late 1580s.

Andrew Hadfield and Michelle O'Callaghan debate the merits of Richard Niccols, the Jacobean editor of the collected *Mirror* versions, and author of his own additional set of complaints, *A Winter Night's Vision*. Hadfield sees Niccols as a pioneering but limited poet, inferior in literary imagination to Baldwin and Blenerhasset, but understanding the project of the *Mirror* well enough to be able to update it for a new audience and so warn them of the military threats that were facing their effeminised country under the disappointing leadership of James I. Niccols cannot really be seen as the writer who killed off the *Mirror*; rather, he prolonged the life of a significant body of work. O'Callaghan concentrates on another complaint collection by Niccols, *Sir Thomas Overbury's Vision* (1616), written in the wake of the sensational trial of Frances Howard and Robert Carr for Overbury's murder, a scandal which defined the political character of the court in the last years of James's reign. For O'Callaghan, Niccols has adapted the 'mirror language' to good effect, proving himself to be a flexible and resourceful writer as he exposes a corrupt and degenerate court.

The final three chapters cast their nets wider to look at the influence of the *Mirror* on Elizabethan and Jacobean writing, in particular focusing on Shakespeare, the major writer most obviously connected in the public imagination to the *Mirror*. Jessica Winston examines how the work shaped the development of English tragedy from the 1560s, focusing especially on the ways in which it is shown to have been read and imagined in Jasper Heywood's *Troas*, Sackville and Norton's neo-Senecan *Gorboduc*, Alexander Neville's *Oedipus*, and George Gascoigne and Francis Kinwelmersh's *Jocasta*, to conclude that the language of the fall of princes had an important anti-absolutist thrust in reminding readers that they needed to recognise political responsibility when it took place and exercise it if they upheld positions of power, however humble. Bart van Es shows how the language and imagery of the *Mirror* had a profound influence on both Edmund Spenser, the most celebrated English poet of the 1590s, and Shakespeare's history plays. Both *The Faerie Queene* and *Richard II* have pivotal scenes that are based on seeing in and through a mirror: Spenser represents Merlin's prophetic glass as a device that can tell the future, while Shakespeare has the deposed king realise his identity as a tragic figure when he finally looks at himself and thinks about what might have been. Philip Schwyzer shows how the complicated art of prophecy enables Shakespeare to stage his history plays in what he calls 'preposterous' time, having them return to the past in a double sense, as the characters look forward to a future that the audience knows has already passed. Characters, notably Richard III, are able to demonstrate an 'uncanny foreknowledge', one that we know is trumped by our superior knowledge of history. Shakespeare recognised the *Mirror*'s profound late sixteenth-century impact and learned a great deal from the work about dialogue, characterisation, irony, the representation and significance of history, and the unrelenting nature of causation. Modern-day scholars of Renaissance literature and culture would do well to follow his example.

A note on the text

As editors we have not sought to impose uniformity on the contributors, and readers will encounter different editions of the *Mirror* in the chapters. Given the range of editions which exist, from Baldwin's original project to Lily B. Campbell's two modernised edited versions, with so many additions, deletions, reorderings, and rewritings in between, it would be invidious to impose unity when so many of the arguments in the chapters depend on the specific context of particular versions. Accordingly, each contributor has used the edition most appropriate for their chapter.

Notes

1. E. M. W. Tillyard, '*A Mirror for Magistrates* Revisited,' in Herbert Davis and Helen Gardner, eds, *Elizabethan and Jacobean Studies* (Oxford: Clarendon Press, 1959), p.10; C. S. Lewis, *English Literature in the Sixteenth Century, Excluding Drama* (Oxford University Press, 1973, rpt. of 1954), p.246.
2. 'The Poly-Olbion Project' (http://poly-olbion.exeter.ac.uk/) (accessed 8.9.15); Jonathan Bate, *The Song of the Earth* (London: Macmillan, 2011), pp.224–5.
3. See also Elizabeth M. A. Human, 'House of *Mirrors*: Textual Variation and *The Mirror for Magistrates*', *LC* 5:4 (2008), 772–90.
4. On Wayland, see H. J. Byrom, 'John Wayland – Printer, Scrivener, and Litigant', *The Library*, 4th ser., 11 (1931), 312–42; *ODNB* entry by Elizabeth Evenden; on *The Fall of Princes*, see Derek Pearsall, *John Lydgate* (London: Routledge, 1970), pp.223–54.
5. Sherri Geller, 'Editing under the Influence of the Standard Textual Hierarchy: Misrepresenting *A Mirror for Magistrates* in the Nineteenth- and Twentieth-Century Editions', *TC* 2:1 (2007), 43–77.

6 See Sherri Geller, 'What History Really Teaches: Historical Pyrrhonism in William Baldwin's *A Mirror for Magistrates*', in Peter C. Herman, ed., *Opening the Borders: Inclusivity in Early Modern Studies* (University of Delaware Press, 1999), pp.150–84.
7 Sir Philip Sidney, *A Defence of Poetry*, J. A. Van Dorsten, ed. (Oxford University Press, 1966), p.64.
8 Roger A. Mason, 'George Buchanan, James VI and the Presbyterians', in Roger A. Mason, ed., *Scots and Britons: Scottish Political Thought and the Union of 1603* (Cambridge University Press, 1994), pp.112–37, at p.122. See also Aysha Pollnitz, *Princely Education in Early Modern Britain* (Cambridge University Press, 2015); Alexandra Gajda, *The Earl of Essex and Late Elizabethan Political Culture* (Oxford University Press, 2012), p.2.
9 See Lawrence D. Green, 'Modes of Perception in the *Mirror for Magistrates*', *HLQ* 44:2 (1981), 117–33; Paul Budra, A Mirror for Magistrates *and the* de casibus *Tradition* (University of Toronto Press, 2000); Annabel Patterson, *Reading Holinshed's Chronicles* (Chicago and London: University of Chicago Press, 1994).
10 See William Peery, 'Tragic Retribution in the 1559 *Mirror for Magistrates*', *SP* 46:2 (1949), 113–30; Frederick Kiefer, 'Fortune and Providence in the *Mirror for Magistrates*', *SP* 74:2 (1977), 146–64; Allyna E. Ward, 'Fortune Laughs and Proudly Hovers: Fortune and Providence in the Tudor Tradition', *The Yearbook of English Studies* 39:1/2 (2009), 39–57.
11 Scott C. Lucas, "Let none such office take, save he that can for right his prince forsake': *A Mirror for Magistrates*, Resistance Theory and the Elizabethan Monarchical Republic', in John F. McDiarmid, ed., *Monarchical Republic of Early Modern England: Essays in Response to Patrick Collinson* (Aldershot: Ashgate, 2007), pp.91–107.
12 Mike Pincombe, 'William Baldwin and *A Mirror for Magistrates*', *RS* 27 (2013), 183–98.
13 Donald Jellerson, 'The Spectral Historiopoetics of the *Mirror for Magistrates*', *JNR* 2:1 (2010), 54–71; Harriet Archer, 'The *Mirror for Magistrates*, 1559–1610: Transmission, Appropriation and the Poetics of Historiography', unpublished doctoral thesis (University of Oxford, 2012).
14 Scott C. Lucas, A Mirror for Magistrates *and the Politics of the English Reformation* (Amherst: University of Massachusetts Press, 2009), see especially pp.71–2, 92–3, 97, 104, 164.
15 See Scott C. Lucas, 'Hall's Chronicle and the *Mirror for Magistrates*: History and the Tragic Pattern', in Mike Pincombe and Cathy Shrank, eds, *The Oxford Handbook of Tudor Literature, 1485–1603* (Oxford University Press, 2009), pp.356–71.
16 David Womersley, 'Against the Teleology of Technique', *HLQ* 68:1–2 (2005), 95–108, at pp.102–3.
17 See Jennifer Richards, 'Transforming *A Mirror for Magistrates*', in Margaret Healy and Tom Healy, eds, *Renaissance Transformations: The Making of English Writing, 1500–1650* (Edinburgh University Press, 2009), pp.48–63;

Jessica Winston, '*A Mirror for Magistrates* and Public Political Discourse in Elizabethan England', *SP* 4 (2004), 281–400; Paul Budra, 'The *Mirror for Magistrates* and the Politics of Readership', *SEL* 32:1, 'The English Renaissance' (1992), 1–13.

18 Jim Ellis, 'Embodying Dislocation: *A Mirror for Magistrates* and Property Relations', *RS* 53 (2000), 1032–52.

19 Philip Schwyzer, *Literature, Nationalism, and Memory in Early Modern England and Wales* (Cambridge University Press, 2004), ch. 4, 'Ghosts of a Nation' (pp.97–125).

20 Alexandra Gillespie and Oliver Harris, 'Holinshed and the Native Chronicle Tradition', in Ian W. Archer, Paulina Kewes, and Felicity Heal, eds, *The Oxford Handbook of Holinshed's* Chronicles (Oxford University Press, 2013), pp.135–52; D. R. Woolf, 'Genre into Artifact: The Decline of the English Chronicle in the Sixteenth Century', *The Sixteenth Century Journal* 19:3 (1988), 321–54.

21 See D. R. Woolf, 'From Hystories to the Historical: Five Transitions in Thinking about the Past, 1500–1700', in Paulina Kewes, ed., *The Uses of History in Early Modern England* (San Marino, CA: Huntington Library, 2006), pp.31–68.

22 Richard Danson Brown, ' "A Talkatiue Wench (Whose Words a World hath Delighted in)": Mistress Shore and Elizabethan Complaint', *RES* 49 (1998), 395–415; Bart van Es, 'Michael Drayton, Literary History and Historians in Verse', *RES* 59:239 (2007), 255–67.

23 Meredith Skura, *Tudor Autobiography: Listening for Inwardness* (University of Chicago Press, 2008), pp.73, 80.

PART I

A myrroure for magistrates *(1559–1563)*

CHAPTER I

A Renaissance man and his 'medieval' text
William Baldwin and A Mirror for Magistrates, *1547–1563*

Scott C. Lucas

Many scholars have approached William Baldwin's *A Mirror for Magistrates* as a late medieval text, an unexpected flowering of fourteenth- and fifteenth-century literary art in the mid-Tudor age. Critics who characterise the work in this manner have traditionally decried its medieval elements as great liabilities. In what was perhaps the earliest twentieth-century study of the *Mirror*, J. W. Cunliffe described the work as medieval in its aim and thus 'medieval in its monotony'. Echoing Cunliffe, C. S. Lewis later influentially declared the *Mirror* to be an artistic failure, chiefly because it was composed 'under the disastrous, late medieval influence of "tragedy" (as Chaucer's Monk understood it)'. Whereas in 1936 Willard Farnham saw some new styles of thought appearing in the text, Richard Harrier dismissed the *Mirror* forty years later as a 'backward looking work', while Lawrence Green cast its contributors as men hopelessly wedded to an outmoded, medieval 'way of thinking which outlived its ability to make sense of the world'. Stuck in the past as they were, Green argued, the authors' antiquated habits of thought inevitably 'created more problems than they solved when applied to the needs of Renaissance England'.[1]

The debt of Baldwin's two *Mirror* editions (1559, 1563) to the traditions of English medieval literature is, of course, undeniable. *A Memorial of Suche Princes* (1554), the first version of *A Mirror for Magistrates*, was designed as a specifically British continuation of John Lydgate's fifteenth-century *Fall of Princes* (c.1431–9); the poems of the *Memorial* and Baldwin's *Mirror* editions focus exclusively on historical personages of the fourteenth and fifteenth centuries; and most of the *Memorial–Mirror* tragedies were composed in the 1550s, a period marked by strong interest in the great literature of England's medieval past. It is no surprise that many interesting critical engagements with the *Mirror* in recent years have come from medievalists who approach the literary heritage of the text as a source of strength rather than a liability, and who examine the work in the larger context of sixteenth-century England's continuing fascination with enduring moral and political topics and its attraction to what for many remained vibrant medieval literary forms.[2]

While the compiler and guiding genius of the *Memorial* and the first two *Mirror* editions, William Baldwin (d. 1563), is best known by scholars for a work composed in the medieval literary tradition, Baldwin himself was unmistakably the intellectual product of the European Renaissance, an ardent admirer of humanist learning and Renaissance verse forms. Baldwin's allegiance to the Northern Renaissance movement was of a distinctive kind, however. Unlike many of those who promoted the 'rebirth' of classical learning by demonising the literature and thought of the Middle Ages, Baldwin betrays no belief in a radical split between England's medieval literary legacy and the new intellectual ideals that had seized the imagination of his sixteenth-century contemporaries. Baldwin filters his attraction to Renaissance humanist endeavour through long-standing English literary traditions, and he approaches the task of continuing Lydgate's century-old *Fall of Princes* assigned to him by his Marian print-master John Wayland not as an endeavour at odds with the beliefs he champions in other works but as a valuable means of advancing them. Moral instruction, conveyance of wisdom to the people, and the enrichment of English art and language: all of these were pursued by Lydgate and continued by Baldwin in Lydgate's *de casibus*-tragedy form but with 'Renaissance' innovations. Far from backward-looking, Baldwin's *Mirror* maintained a living tradition of poetry writing in mid-Tudor England that he and his fellow *Mirror* authors deftly turned to Renaissance ends.

The intellectual principles to which Baldwin committed himself in the years leading up to the creation of *A Memorial of Suche Princes* are most concisely expressed in a single work: not a text *per se* but a communicative artefact, the highly symbolic woodcut printer's mark he had carved for his self-printed *Canticles or Balades of Salomon* (1549) (see Image 1). As Leslie Hotson first observed, Baldwin explicitly modelled his new device on that of the celebrated Basel printer Johann Froben[3] (see Image 2). Baldwin chose to emulate Froben's mark for two principal reasons: to associate himself as a printer-author in readers' minds with the sort of humanist texts Froben published, as well as to communicate in emblematic form a sense of the intellectual projects he most strongly embraced.

While Johann Froben is best known today among English-literature scholars as the printer of the elegant third edition of Sir Thomas More's *Utopia* (1518), in his own time Froben enjoyed greatest fame as the principal publisher of that guiding light of the Northern Renaissance, Desiderius

Image 1 Printer's mark of William Baldwin, from William Baldwin, *The Canticles or Balades of Salomon* (London, 1549). Folger STC 2768, sig. n4v. Reproduced by permission of the Folger Shakespeare Library, under a Creative Commons Attribution Share-Alike 4.0 International Licence.

Erasmus.[4] It is difficult to underestimate the influence of Erasmus on the course of sixteenth-century European letters. Erasmus, more than any other scholar of his time, spread the humanist call to return to original sources for learning, whether in establishing proper texts for the study of scripture and patristic writings or for discovering the wisdom of pagan classical authors, many of whose works had been lost for centuries to the readers of Western Europe. Erasmus was also one of the most important figures behind the drive for a new eloquence in Latin letters, a project he advanced both by composing handbooks describing the art of beautiful

Image 2 Printer's Mark of Johann Froben, from Erasmus, *Nouum Instrumentu[m] omne* (Basel, 1516). Pitts Theological Library 1516 BIBL B., sig. Ff8r. Reproduced by permission of the Pitts Theological Library.

writing and by modelling such writing through his own finely crafted prose style. Finally, no other author of his time was more closely associated with the power of print to disseminate learning to the widest possible audiences. Through partnerships with a host of skilled printers, most notably Aldus Manutius in Venice and Johann Froben in Basel, Erasmus was able to bring long-lost and long-corrupted ancient texts to readers in forms close to their first versions. He complemented these editorial endeavours with a multitude of original publications on an array of topics, enthusiastically using the medium of print to convey his words to every Western European land.[5]

Baldwin began his literary career when Erasmian ideals were at perhaps the height of their influence in England, and he eagerly embraced Erasmus's intellectual goals. As scholars have long noted, Baldwin consciously modelled his first substantial work, *A Treatise of Morall Phylosophie* (January 1548), on Erasmus's writings, basing its sections in large part on Erasmus's oft-printed collections *Apophthegmatum Opus, Adagia,* and *Parabolae sive Similia*. In his next publication, *The Canticles or Balades of Salomon* (1549), Baldwin presented a poetic rendering of the Song of Songs in the manner of an Erasmian paraphrase, providing his readers not only with a versified rendering of the text but also with the original scripture passages on which he drew and his own commentaries on them.[6] Baldwin concluded this work with his newly created printer's mark, so reminiscent of Froben's own, to signal clearly the ties between his own writings and the great Erasmian productions of Froben's press that inspired them.

It is likely that the specific Froben device Baldwin chose to emulate was of particular importance to him for its presence in the Erasmian work with which it was most widely associated. Evidence suggests that Froben employed the mark upon which Baldwin chose to model his own only over the course of two years, 1516 and 1517. The device appeared during that time, however, in the single most famous and important publication to come from his press, Erasmus's epochal Greek New Testament with Latin translation, the *Novum Instrumentum* (1516). Erasmus's *Novum Instrumentum* was a watershed in the European study of scripture. It provided readers with a new Latin text of the Christian Bible more clear and more accurate than that of the Vulgate, and through its success it proved triumphantly to those who embraced it the value of Erasmus's call to recover and restore original textual sources, the famous exhortation to return *ad fontes*.[7]

Nearly as significant in the eyes of English reformers, the *Novum Instrumentum* first brought to readers Erasmus's inspiring plea for all Christians to engage in the direct study of the gospel, a call he makes in the exhortatory essay 'Paraclesis' that prefaces this edition. There, Erasmus urges that the Bible be translated into every contemporary language and disseminated so widely that even farmers, weavers, and the 'lowliest women' might have unmediated access to the good news of Jesus Christ. Notably, Erasmus calls for lay people not just to read scripture, but to sing it. Baldwin answered Erasmus's twin appeals for the dissemination of God's word among the people and the singing of scriptural song in the very work in which his printer's device appears, *The Canticles or Balades of Salomon*, a text that brought the Song of Songs before a wide reading audience and in a host of poetic forms conducive to singing.[8] Through his version of the mark by which Froben concluded the *Novum Instrumentum*, Baldwin could connect his *Canticles* with the very work that helped to inspire so many English scripture translators to bring God's word in compelling form to the people of England.

Baldwin also made this Froben device of 1516–17 the basis of his own for the specific symbolism he found within it, symbolism Baldwin then shaped to match more precisely his personal intellectual commitments. The serpent-entwined wand Froben took as his insignia calls forth thoughts of the Roman god Mercury, a figure whose caduceus stood in the Renaissance as a symbol of eloquence, wisdom, and the literary arts, as well as an emblem of concord and peace, of formerly opposed entities joined in harmonious coexistence.[9] Just what opposing elements its viewers are to understand as being joined in concord Froben indicates through the polyglot mottos that surround his mark. The Greek and Hebrew texts are Biblical: the Greek quotes Matthew 10:16, 'Be wise as serpents and innocent as doves', while the Hebrew reproduces Psalm 125:4, 'Do good, O Lord, to those who are good, and to those who are upright in their hearts'. The Latin phrases, by contrast, are from the pagan classical tradition. The first, '*prudens simplicitas*', translates as 'wise simplicity' and is taken from one of Martial's most famous epigrams, 10.47, an epigram that Baldwin included in its entirety in his *Treatise of Morall Phylosophie*. The phrase '*amorque recti*', finally, translates as 'and love of the right' and derives from Martial's epigram 10.78.[10]

The mix of Old Testament, New Testament, and classical texts with which Froben surrounded his caduceus indicates the harmony humanists in general and Erasmus in particular had sought to achieve between the seemingly antithetical traditions of Biblical wisdom and ancient learning. Froben's three tags reflect also the ideal of trilingual endeavour, Erasmus's belief that all scholars should learn Latin, Greek, and Hebrew in order to search out the wisdom of Biblical, patristic, and classical texts in their original forms. Indeed, the snakes and the dove of the device convey not only a pictographic image of Christ's exhortation to wisdom and simplicity quoted in Greek above and below them but also an allegory of the Erasmian scholarly ideal, showing the Judaeo-Christian dove – a symbol of peace in the Old Testament (Genesis 8:11) and a form of the Holy Spirit in the New (Matthew 3:16) – resting comfortably in concord with Mercury's classical serpents.

For his own device, Baldwin artfully reshaped key elements of Froben's symbolic mark. To stir thoughts of Erasmus's call in 'Paraclesis' for the universal dissemination of scripture, Baldwin adds an open book to his design, an image meant to suggest the Bible and, in its elevated position, the superiority of God's word over all other learning. He similarly places a dove spread-winged above his Bible to evoke thoughts of the Holy Spirit brooding over the text, reminding viewers both of scripture's divinely inspired creation and his conviction that to read the Bible is to engage directly with the Holy Spirit.

Below his representation of the word of God, Baldwin places in banderoles the wisdom of the ancients, the subject, of course, of his *Treatise of Morall Phylosophie*. Erasmus first praised the adage '*nosce te ipsum*' (know thyself) in his exceedingly popular *Enchiridion Militis Christiani* (1501), asserting there that the great men of antiquity uniformly 'iudged al plenty of wysdom to be shortly co[m]prehe[n]ded in this lytel sentence | that is to wyte | yf a man knowe himselfe'.[11] In his *Adagia*, he promotes both '*nosce te ipsum*' and '*ne quid nimis*' (nothing to excess) as maxims of particular value, and he draws readers' attention to the relation of these sayings to pagan prophecy, noting that they are Latin translations of two of the three apophthegms carved above the entrance to the temple housing Apollo's oracle at Delphi. They were put there, Erasmus explains, because they were deemed 'maxims worthy of the god'.[12]

In his device, Baldwin emphasises these sayings' connection to Apollo and classical prophecy by placing beneath them a rendering of the Delphic tripod, the shallow raised cauldron in which the priestess of Apollo would sit as she delivered her divine messages.[13] Baldwin meant his Delphic tripod to evoke thoughts of the god of poets, Apollo, and also, through its juxtaposition with the Bible and Mercury's wand, the possibility of Christian inspiration in the pagan world, a subject that deeply fascinated him. In the *Treatise*, Baldwin proclaims the legendary philosopher, prophet, and ruler Mercurius Trismegistus (also known as Hermes Trismegistus) to be the most excellent of all the learned ancients. His remarkable learning, Baldwin declares, indicates his receipt of inspiration from the true God, a prophetic power the Lord himself granted to Mercurius to interpret divine will and thus to teach a form of Christian doctrine long before Christ's birth. Baldwin revives the subject of Mercurius in the *Canticles*, in which he expresses his profound hope that God will grace England's monarch and Supreme Head Edward VI with the same sort of prophetic power to discern divine intentions that he earlier bestowed on Mercurius.[14]

Baldwin's words on Mercurius reveal the surprising depth of his commitment to the 'new learning'. Although some have questioned Baldwin's true adherence to humanist ideals, owing to the fact that he culled many of his classical maxims for the *Treatise* not from original texts but from the medieval collection *Dictes and Sayings of the Philosophers* (1477), Baldwin draws verbatim for his account of Mercurius in the *Treatise* on an indisputably humanist source, Marsilio Ficino's 1463 essay 'Argumentum', showing the range of his reading in learned Latin works.[15] The use and misuse of claims to prophecy and secret wisdom would continue to fascinate Baldwin in subsequent writings, whether in the satire of *Beware the Cat* or in the tragedies 'Owen Glendour' and 'George, Duke of Clarence', in *A Mirror for Magistrates*. While he was a man devoted to classical learning and intrigued by the idea of ancient prophecy, Baldwin is nevertheless careful in his device to indicate that he holds pagan wisdom to be only second to the teachings of scripture. To that end, he places his symbol of the word of God at the very top of his insignia, he adds extra doves to Froben's single fowl so that they outnumber the pagan snakes, and he associates himself above all with Christian tradition rather than that of the pagan era by placing his favourite personal motto, 'Love and Lyve', directly under the Bible.[16]

Baldwin also adapts the frame of Froben's mark by replacing its surrounding three multilingual tags, which he could have had his woodcut-maker carve into his device, with a single English one. His use of English alone in his device's frame – and as the principal language in all of his known writings – signals his commitment to disseminating learning and advancing literary art principally among the speakers of his own tongue. Baldwin will pursue Erasmus's ideal of eloquence, his printer's mark implies, but it will be a *vernacular* eloquence, one made for a specific people in a specific land.

The cultivation of rhetorical beauty was, of course, a key part of the Erasmian humanist endeavour. In the sixteenth century, many English writers lamented the alleged crudeness of their own language, viewing Chaucer as the only poet before their time to have written beautifully in the mother tongue. In the mid-Tudor period, two men came to be particularly celebrated for bestowing a new, Renaissance-inspired eloquence on English verse, Sir Thomas Wyatt and Henry Howard, styled Earl of Surrey. Although the bulk of their writings enjoyed only limited circulation before publication of Tottel's *Songes and Sonettes* in 1557, Wyatt's enrichment of the English language was proclaimed in print by two texts in the early 1540s, Surrey's 'Wyat Resteth Here' – the only Surrey poem published during its author's lifetime – and John Leland's *Naeniae in Mortem Thomae Viati*. For his admirer Surrey, Wyatt possessed 'a Hand that taught, what might be saide in rime| That refte Chaucer, the glorye of his wytte'; for Leland, Wyatt's skill in English verse proved him the equal even of Italy's most revered vernacular poets Dante and Petrarch. Elsewhere in *Naeniae*, Leland hails Surrey as Wyatt's poetical heir, and he proclaims 'Wyat Resteth Here' to be worthy of the great Chaucer himself.[17] Both Leland's and Surrey's words imply what many of their time believed: that the mid-Tudor period showed promise of developing into an age of eloquence in English letters of a sort not seen since the days of Geoffrey Chaucer.

In his own writings, Surrey eagerly followed Wyatt's artistic leads, particularly Wyatt's experiments in Italian sonnet forms. Whereas the elder poet explored many sonnet styles over the course of his life, Surrey settled into one in particular, the fourteen-line, pentameter sonnet structure of his own devising that rhymed abab cdcd efef gg. The appeal to writers of Baldwin's age and beyond of this clever and compact form may be seen in the thousands of Surreyan sonnets written in the Tudor and Stuart periods, each in adherence to Surrey's concise, sophisticated design.

Tellingly, it was precisely this Renaissance-inspired verse form that Baldwin chose for his first published work. Many scholars have observed that Baldwin's commendatory poem affixed to Christopher Langton's *Very Brefe Treatise … of Phisick* (April 1547) is the first known printed sonnet of any kind in English. Baldwin's use of this form indicates his familiarity with at least some of Surrey's unpublished verse, a familiarity further indicated by Baldwin's inclusion of Surrey's translation of Martial's epigram 10.47 – one of the very Martial poems from which Froben chose to quote in his printer' device – in *A Treatise of Morall Phylosophie*. His admiration for Surrey's art apparently continued throughout Edward VI's reign, as evidenced, so Frederick Tromley argues, by Baldwin's employment of 'Wyat Resteth Here' as a basis for the third section of his memorial to England's lost young monarch, *The Funeralles of King Edward the Sixt* (July 1553).[18]

It would at first seem odd for Baldwin to take for a piece of commendatory verse a sonnet form that Surrey employed chiefly in his courtly love poetry. It is important to note, however, that Surrey himself authored a commendatory sonnet, one that would have appealed forcefully to Baldwin's deep loves for vernacular eloquence, Biblical translation, poetry, and classical learning. This is Surrey's 'The Great Macedon', a poetic commendation of Wyatt's psalm paraphrases. Whether or not he ever saw Wyatt's psalms before their publication in late 1549, Surrey's admirer Baldwin could have encountered this eloquent manuscript sonnet in praise of them and thus understood the sonnet form to be one particularly suited to commendation. Surrey's poem ends with a bold assertion of the admonitory function of Wyatt's psalms. They are texts

> Where rulers may see in a mirrour clere
> The bitter frute of false concupiscence:
> How Iewry bought Vrias death full dere.
> In princes harts Gods scourge imprinted depe,
> Ought them awake, out of their sinfull slepe.[19]

One may only wonder if Baldwin recalled these lines in 1559, as he chose 'A Mirror for Magistrates' to be the title for his newly re-edited *Memorial of Suche Princes* and presented the text to England's officers as one in which, 'as in a loking glas, you shall see (if any vice be in you) howe the like hath bene punished in other heretofore, whereby admonished, I trust it will be a good occasion to move you to the soner amendment'.[20]

It was the Renaissance man William Baldwin who in 1554 turned his interests in humanist learning and vernacular eloquence to a text explicitly modelled on a work from England's medieval literary past. While he recalls some reservations in the *Mirror* about accepting the daunting task his print-master John Wayland had assigned to him, Baldwin never betrays any sense of the familiar humanist distaste for vernacular art created before the advent of the 'new learning'. Instead, Baldwin and his fellow contributors only speak with tones of respect for Lydgate's fifteenth-century poetic rendering of Giovanni Boccaccio's fourteenth-century *De casibus virorum illustrium*. Given Lydgate's reputation in the earlier sixteenth century, this is not fully surprising. Although modern scholars have long tended to denigrate Lydgate as an unappealing epitome of late medieval dullness, many in the early and mid-Tudor periods celebrated him as a master of English verse. For Stephen Hawes, whose *Pastime of Pleasure* (c.1505) Baldwin saw through Wayland's presses immediately before printing the *Fall-Memorial* volume, Lydgate was the preeminent poet of English eloquence. In his *Conversion of Swearers* (1509), Hawes insists that 'my good mayster Lydgate',

> The eloquent poete and monke of bery
> Dyde bothe contryue| and also translate
> Many vertuous bookes to be in memorye
> Touchynge the trouthe well and sentencyously.

In the *Pastime of Pleasure*, Hawes specifically commends the *Fall of Princes* to readers as a work of great moral value:

> Of the fall of Princes, ryght wofully
> He did endite, in all piteous wise
> Folowyng his auctoure, Bocas rufully
> A ryght great boke, he did truely compryse
> A good ensample, for vs to despyse
> This worlde so full, of mutabilitie
> In whiche no man, can haue a certaintie.

Even John Skelton (or, more precisely, his speaker in *Philip Sparrow*), while judging Gower and Lydgate as unable to equal Chaucer's high example, nevertheless must admit of the latter poet that 'no man can that amend | Those maters that he hath pende'.[21]

Mid-Tudor devotees of Renaissance aesthetics could find much to admire in Lydgate's medieval verse. In the course of introducing a new, classically derived vocabulary for the 'better vnderstanding of good authors' in his *Schemes and Tropes* (1550), the humanist rhetorician and Erasmus translator Richard Sherry finds space to praise 'the most excellent monumentes of our au[n]cie[n]t forewriters, Gower, Chawcer and Lydgate'.[22] Later, despite adding his voice to the humanist dismissal of England's late medieval period as a disastrous age when 'al good letters were almost aslepe', Robert Braham honours John Lydgate as a poet who somehow escaped the literary sinkhole of his time. During the 'dercke and unlearned' period of the fifteenth century, Braham writes, the story of Troy's fall was,

> by the diligence of Iohn Lydgate a moncke of Burye, brought into our englyshe tonge: and dygested as maye appere, in verse[; whose travail] as well in other his doynges as in this hathe wythout doubte so muche preuayled in this our vulgare language, that hauynge his prayse dewe to his deseruynges, may worthyly be numbred amongest those that haue chefelye deserued of our tunge.

Despite his nearly wholesale condemnation of medieval English literature elsewhere in the preface to his edition of Lydgate's *Troy Book*, Braham can still present the author of the *Fall of Princes* as a poet worthy of respect even by the strongest partisans of Renaissance aesthetic innovations.[23]

To have his sense of the appropriateness of Lydgate's medieval form to the English Renaissance confirmed, Baldwin need go no further than the prologue to book 8 of the *Fall of Princes*. There, Lydgate portrays none other than Francis Petrarch, revered humanist, master of the Italian sonnet form, and the very inventor of the idea of a 'Renaissance' in European letters, as coming before his fatigued narrator 'Bochas' (Boccaccio) to encourage him to continue in the creation of morally instructive *de casibus*-tragedy narratives. Petrarch exhorts Bochas to persist in writing in order to benefit humankind, just as revered classical authors and the prophets of the Bible did before him. The purpose Petrarch identifies for Bochas's endeavour precisely comports with Baldwin's principles: the 'forthering of vertue' through writing so that the 'fyne of our labour be yeue [*given*] to Christ Iesu'.[24]

In accepting Wayland's charge to continue Lydgate's poem, however, Baldwin and his fellow *Memorial* authors did not limit themselves to creating a mere imitation of the *Fall*. Instead, they augmented their work with elements expressive of their attachment to humanist inquiry and Renaissance poetics.[25] Baldwin artfully creates space for such matter by eschewing the primarily univocal 'envoys' with which Lydgate divides his tragic tales and replacing them with prose links conveying, first, conversations among the poets of the 1554 and 1559 publications and, later, discussions among the 'frendes and furderers' who gathered to listen to the tragedies added to the 1563 *Mirror*. These multivocal passages allow Baldwin and his associates opportunities to explore a range of topics related to history, political theory, moral philosophy, and art. Thus, in the prose link following the poem 'Jack Cade', one of the authors does not merely laud the destruction of the rebel Cade portrayed in the tragedy but uses Cade's example to dwell on the uncomfortable claim that God often uses devilish acts to achieve righteous ends. The prose section following Baldwin's 'Mowbray', similarly, records the authors' recognition of problems in English history writing, detailing the poets' encounter with the contradictory claims made by the chroniclers Robert Fabyan and Edward Hall concerning the 1399 dispute between Thomas Mowbray and Henry Bolingbroke. In the face of the chroniclers' irreconcilable statements, Baldwin expresses his and his fellow authors' humanistic desire that the matter be investigated and the truth once and for all be discovered, either by the royal heralds or by learned men willing to seek out (in the manner of Erasmus's exhortation of classical and Biblical scholars to return *ad fontes*) the primary sources of Richard II's reign – Ricardian 'recordes and registers' – in order to recover missing historical truth.[26]

In the 1563 *Seconde Parte* of the *Mirror*, Baldwin portrays the gathered auditors as at times engaged with concerns similar to those raised in the 1559 prose links. Nevertheless, these men most often respond to the tragedies they hear as works of art, weighing them in accordance with the developing aesthetic ideals of their time. Their considerations of the poems' forms, metres, language, clarity, and adherence to decorum place their literary-critical assessments far beyond those found in the most famous medieval frame narrative portraying listeners passing judgement on compositions they have just heard, that of Boccaccio's *Decameron*.

The *Mirror* authors also express humanist and Renaissance interests in the tragedies themselves, creating poems that, as a consequence, often range far from simple moralised presentations of tragic careers. Thus, the author of 'Henry VI' devotes much of his tragedy's opening to a lengthy consideration of the general causes of worldly events; the composer of 'Worcester' offers criticism of Fabyan and Hall (and, by extension, of the whole medieval chronicling tradition) for their refusal to determine precisely the origins of historical occurrences; and William Baldwin turns the initial stanzas of 'Owen Glendour' to a detailed assertion of the humanist credo that virtuous behaviour rather than high birth is the mark of the true gentleman. In the *Seconde Parte*, Thomas Sackville expands boldly on the *Mirror* authors' inherited Lydgatean form by supplying a long poetic induction for his 'Henry, Duke of Buckingham', and he and Baldwin both embellish their contributions to this edition with aspects of ancient learning, guiding readers to interpret the events of medieval England through a host of classical sentences, images, and allusions.[27]

For all this, however, Baldwin ever strives to keep his and his fellows' guiding aim to be that of Lydgate's *Fall*, the 'forthering of vertue'. It is this imperative that leads the authors ultimately to put aside consideration of the Mowbray–Bolingbroke question, since further investigation would distract them from their collection's primary purpose, 'to diswade from vices and exalte vertue'. It is this same overriding goal, furthermore, that provides the licence by which several of the poets choose, despite their expressed concerns for truthfulness in English history, freely to alter the historical source material they draw on for their tragedies, so that they might 'mirror' the specific behaviour of contemporary magistrates in politically pointed, topically evocative exemplary admonitions.[28]

To strengthen the admonitory force of their tragedies (and, with it, their poems' literary complexity), Baldwin and his fellow authors work to augment the affective power of Lydgate's *de casibus*-tragedy form. They do so by borrowing once again from humanist practice, modifying Lydgate's convention of having chiefly Bochas narrate the tales of the ghosts who appear before him to having the fallen spirits themselves describe their lives and tragic ends. This alteration allows the authors to create eloquent, emotionally charged, and highly personal speeches for their historical figures to deliver, a humanist historiographical strategy derived from classical tradition and practised most notably in early Tudor England by Sir Thomas More in his *History of King Richard III*.[29] Making the ghosts rehearse their own tragic errors and utter their own words of warning extends a feeling of immediacy to their admonitions, creating a sense of continuity between the figures of the medieval past and the readers of the sixteenth-century present, the men and women on whose behalf the ghostly speakers insist they return from the dead to speak. If humanists often expressed their dream of having the ancients speak to the present, the *Mirror* authors, through the rhetorical figure of *prosopopoeia*, fulfil a similar desire through their crafting of personal confessions for some of the best-known figures of medieval British history. The combination of humanist historiographical practice and the poets' talents in vernacular eloquence results in a powerfully compelling literary form for the *Mirror* tragedies. It is this dramatic and affective mode of presentation that the authors hoped would both rationally and emotionally spur readers to examine their own lives and thus fulfil one of those ancient maxims Baldwin held most dear, *nosce te ipsum*, 'know thyself', the only starting point for true ethical change.[30]

It was William Baldwin, Renaissance man, who oversaw the combination of a tried-and-true medieval genre with Renaissance aesthetic and intellectual innovations, all put into the service of political and moral correction. The result was a literary achievement that remained almost constantly before the public, from its first publication in 1559 until its last reissue in 1621. Its unique synthesis of old and new, furthermore, quickly provided inspiration for numerous other poets, who sought to create tragedies of their own in its distinctive style. Far from outdated or backward-looking, Baldwin and his fellow *Mirror* authors' joining of what many of their time saw as the best of the English medieval literary tradition with the best of Renaissance innovation ensured that their work would remain a source of fascination for more than sixty years of Tudor and Stuart readers.

Notes

1 J. W. Cunliffe, '*A Mirror for Magistrates*', in A. W. Ward and A. R. Waller, eds, *The Cambridge History of English Literature* (Cambridge University Press, 1908), p.192; C. S. Lewis, *English Literature in the Sixteenth Century, Excluding Drama* (Oxford: Clarendon Press, 1954), p.240; Willard Farnham, *The Medieval Heritage of Elizabethan Tragedy* (Berkeley: University of California Press, 1936), pp.271–93; Richard Harrier, 'Invention in Tudor Literature: Historical Perspectives', in Edward Mahoney, ed., *Philosophy and Humanism: Essays in Honor of Paul Oskar Kristeller* (New York: Columbia University Press, 1976),

p.386; Lawrence Green, 'Modes of Perception in the *Mirror for Magistrates*', *HLQ* 44.2 (1981), 121.
2 See, among others, John Thompson, 'Reading Lydgate in Post-Reformation England', in A. J. Minnis, ed., *Middle English Poetry: Texts and Traditions* (Woodbridge: York Medieval Press, 2001), pp.181–209; Paul Strohm, *Politique: Languages of Statecraft between Chaucer and Shakespeare* (Notre Dame University Press, 2005), pp.109–32; Nigel Mortimer, *John Lydgate's 'Fall of Princes': Narrative Tragedy in its Literary and Political Contexts* (Oxford University Press, 2005), pp.266–77; Alexandra Gillespie, *Print and the Medieval Author* (Oxford University Press, 2006), pp.213–25. See also Paul Budra, A Mirror for Magistrates *and the de casibus* Tradition (University of Toronto Press, 2000), a study that explores the influence of the *de casibus*-tragedy tradition on the *Mirror* but intriguingly complicates the familiar medieval–Renaissance divide by treating *de casibus* tragedy as an Italian-Renaissance rather than as a medieval genre (p.15).
3 William Baldwin, *The Canticles or Balades of Salomon* (London, 1549; *STC* 2768), sig. n4ᵛ. Leslie Hotson, *Shakespeare by Hilliard* (Berkeley: University of California Press, 1977), p.40. Hotson mistakenly compares Baldwin's mark not to one of Johann Froben's devices but to a piece created several years after the elder Froben's death for his son Hieronymous. Nevertheless, Hotson's general point still holds, since both Frobens employed the motif of the caduceus and dove upon which Baldwin based the central part of his own mark.
4 From 1513 until his death in 1527, Froben was Erasmus's close friend and most-favoured printer. For Froben's life and his relationship with Erasmus, see Peter Bietenholz and Thomas Deutscher, eds, *Contemporaries of Erasmus*, 3 vols. (University of Toronto Press, 1985), 1, pp.60–3.
5 Studies of Erasmus, his influence, and his artful self-presentation in his works include Johan Huizinga, *Erasmus and the Age of Reformation* [1924], trans. Frederik Hopman (New York: Harper, 1957); Roland Bainton, *Erasmus of Christendom* (New York: Charles Scribner's Sons, 1969); and Lisa Jardine, *Erasmus: Man of Letters* (Princeton University Press, 1993). For Erasmus's profound influence on mid-Tudor English letters, see James McConica, *English Humanism and Reformation Politics* (Oxford: Clarendon Press, 1965).
6 William Baldwin, *A Treatise of Morall Phylosophie* (London, 1547 [i.e. Jan. 1548]; *STC* 1253); W. F. Trench, 'William Baldwin', *Modern Quarterly of Language and Literature* 1.4 (1898), 260; D. T. Starnes, 'Sir Thomas Elyot and the "Sayings of the Philosophers"', *Studies in English* 13.1 (1933), 13–18. Baldwin refers to Erasmus's paraphrases in the dedicatory epistle of the *Canticles*, sig. A2ᵛ.
7 W. J. T. Kirby calls the release of the *Novum Instrumentum* 'arguably the most consequential of all publishing events of the sixteenth century' (*Persuasion and Conversion: Essays on Religion, Politics, and the Public Sphere in Early Modern England* [Leiden: Brill, 2013], p.101).
8 Erasmus, 'Paraclesis', in John C. Olin, ed., *Christian Humanism and the Reformation* (New York: Harper and Row, 1965), p.101; Baldwin, *Canticles*, sig. A3ᵛ.

9 Heinrich Plett, *Rhetoric and Renaissance Culture* (Berlin: Gruyter, 2004), p.509; Douglas Brooks-Davies, *The Mercurian Monarch: Magical Politics from Spenser to Pope* (Manchester University Press, 1983), p.34; Stephen Gaukroger, *The Uses of Antiquity* (Dordrecht: Reidel, 1991), p.7. Mercury is said to have encountered the two snakes of his caduceus fighting and to have brought them to harmonious living through the power of his staff (William Stahl, *Martinus Capella and the Seven Liberal Arts*, 2 vols. [New York: Columbia University Press, 1977], 1, p.44).

10 'Printer's Device of Johan Froben: *Nouum Instrumentu[m]*', *Digital Image Archive*, Pitts Theological Library, Candler School of Theology, Emory University www.pitts.emory.edu/dia/detail.cfm?ID=93, accessed 15 May 2015. The author of this description suggests Statius' encomium to his father in *Silvae*, book 5, as the origin of '*amorque recti*'; Martial's epigram to the virtuous Macer, however, is the more likely source.

11 Erasmus, *A Booke Called in Latyn Enchiridion Militis Christiani, and in Englysshe the Manuell of the Christen Knyght*, trans. William Tyndale (London, 1533; *STC* 10479), sig. C7^v. Baldwin was well acquainted with the *Enchiridion*, to which he alludes in the dedicatory epistle of the *Canticles* when he mentions Erasmus's praise for the early Church father Origen (sig. A2^r).

12 Erasmus, *Adagiorum Opus* (Basel, 1526), pp.219–21; Erasmus, *The Adages of Erasmus*, ed. William Barker (University of Toronto Press, 2001), pp.96–100. Baldwin had already employed '*ne quid nimis*' as one of his personal mottos in the preface to the *Treatise* (Baldwin, *Treatise*, sig. A7^r).

13 Hotson, *Shakespeare*, pp.41–2.

14 Baldwin, *Treatise*, sig. B3^v; Baldwin, *Canticles*, sig. A3^r.

15 Curt Bühler, 'A Survival from the Middle Ages: William Baldwin's Use of the *Dictes and Sayings*', *Speculum* 23.1 (1948), 76–80; J. S. Gill, 'How Hermes Trismegistus was Introduced to Renaissance England: The Influence of Caxton and Ficino's "Argumentum" on Baldwin and Palfreyman', *JWCI* 47 (1984), 222–5. William Caxton printed Anthony Woodville, Earl Rivers's, translation of the *Dictes and Sayings* in 1477, and this translation served as an important source for Baldwin's *Treatise*. Baldwin would later adopt the voice of Earl Rivers in the opening poem of the *Seconde Parte of the Mirrour for Magistrates* (1563).

16 The placement of 'Love and Lyve' in this mark would seem to add support to Mike Pincombe's suggestion that the motto is Baldwin's shortened form of 'Love and live the gospel', a phrase promulgated by the prolific evangelical author Thomas Becon (Mike Pincombe, '"Love and Live": The Source and the Significance of William Baldwin's Motto', *NQ* 57.3 [2010], 341–6).

17 Henry Howard, Earl of Surrey, *An Excellent Epitaffe of Sir Thomas Wyat* (London, 1543?; *STC* 26054), sig. A1^v; John Leland, *Naeniae in Mortem Thomae Viati* (London, 1542; *STC* 15446), sigs A2^r, A3^v. The *STC* dates the *Excellent Epitaffe* as '1545?', but the topicality of Wyatt's death in October 1542, Leland's reference to 'Wyat Resteth Here' in *Naeniae*, and the fact that the same woodcut of Wyatt found in *Naeniae* appears the *Excellent Epitaffe* would suggest that the *Excellent Epitaffe* appeared in the months following

Naeniae and not in later years. 'Wyat Resteth Here' was released anonymously, with two poems by other men on general subjects following it in the *Excellent Epitaffe*; there is no indication that Surrey had any hand in the production of this work.

18 Christopher Langton, *A Uery Brefe Treatise ordrely declaring the Pri[n]cipal Partes of Phisick* (London, 1547; *STC* 15205), sig.[+1^v]; Baldwin, *Treatise*, sig. Q1^v; Frederick B. Tromly, 'Two Tudor Epitaphs: Surrey on Wyatt; Baldwin on Edward VI', *ANQ* 12:2 (1973), 24–5.

19 Henry Howard, Earl of Surrey, 'Praise of Certaine Psalmes of Dauid, Translated by Sir T. W. the Elder', *Songes and Sonettes, Written by the Right Honorable Lorde Henry Haward Late Earle of Surrey, and Other* (London, 1557; *STC* 13861), sig. D4^v.

20 Lily B. Campbell, ed., *The Mirror for Magistrates* (Cambridge University Press, 1938), pp.65–6.

21 Campbell, ed., *Mirror*, pp.68–70; Stephen Hawes, *The Conuercyon of Swerers* (London, 1509; *STC* 12943), sig. A1^v; Hawes, *The Historie of Graunde Amoure and La Bel Pucell, Called the Pastime of Plesure* (London, 1554; *STC* 12950), sig. F4^r; John Skelton, *Here After Foloweth the Boke of Phyllyp Sparowe* (London, 1545?; *STC* 22594), sig. C4^v.

22 Richard Sherry, *A Treatise of Schemes and Tropes* (London, 1550; *STC* 22428), sigs A1^r, A2^v–3^r. Baldwin was well enough acquainted with Sherry to suggest his presence as one of Gregory Stremer's interlocutors in his prose fiction *Beware the Cat* (Baldwin, *Beware the Cat by William Baldwin: The First English Novel*, ed. William Ringler and Michael Flachmann [San Marino: Huntington Library, 1988], p.16).

23 John Lydgate, *The Auncient Historie and Onely Trewe and Syncere Cronicle of the Warres Betwixte the Grecians and the Troyans*, ed. Robert Braham (London, 1555; *STC* 5580), sig. [A2^r]. Baldwin was responsible for printing this text in Wayland's shop. Although future *Mirror for Magistrates* printer Thomas Marshe's name and place of business (The Prince's Arms) appear in the colophon, Marshe was a bookseller at this point in his career and not a printer (Peter Blayney, *The Stationers' Company and the Printers of London, 1501–1557*, 2 vols. [Cambridge University Press, 2014], 2, pp.784, 979–82). The 95-millimetre textura type employed for the body of the text is identical to that used in the Wayland edition of the *Fall of Princes* (*STC* 3178).

24 Lydgate, *The Tragedies, Gathered by Jhon Bochas of All Such Princes, as Fell from Theyr Estates* (London, 1554; *STC* 3178), sig. Aa1^{r-v}. On Petrarch as the source of the idea of a 'renaissance' of learning after the medieval period, see Charles Nauert, *Humanism and the Culture of Renaissance Europe* (Cambridge University Press, 2006), pp.19–21. In describing the encounter between 'Bochas' and Petrarch, Lydgate follows his poem's source, Boccaccio's prose *De casibus virorum illustrium*, as filtered through Laurent de Premierfait's expansive French translation of it.

25 The four known mid-Tudor authors of *A Memorial of Suche Princes* and the 1559 *Mirror* were all men of learning who held humanist interests. In addition

to Baldwin, they are the antiquarian and legal scholar George Ferrers; the neo-Latin poet and Erasmus translator Sir Thomas Chaloner; and the humanist nobleman Henry, Lord Stafford, who owned an extensive library of continental humanist texts, including many of Erasmus's publications. For these men, see Scott C. Lucas, A Mirror for Magistrates *and the Politics of the English Reformation* (Amherst: University of Massachusetts Press, 2009), pp.35–49; Scott C. Lucas, 'Henry Lord Stafford, "The Two Rogers", and the Creation of *A Mirror for Magistrates*', *RES* (forthcoming).

26 Campbell, ed., *Mirror*, pp.110, 178–9, 243. For a study of the multivocal function of the prose links, see Jessica Winston, '*A Mirror for Magistrates* and Public Political Discourse in Elizabethan England', *SP* 101.4 (2004), 381–400.

27 Campbell, ed., *Mirror*, pp.120–2, 198–9, 212–15, 298–358.

28 Campbell, ed., *Mirror*, p.110; on the poets' frequent changes to their historical sources in order better to admonish magistrates against acts the authors saw as politically immoral, see Lucas, A Mirror for Magistrates *and the Politics of the English Reformation*.

29 Charles Ross, *Richard III* (Berkeley: University of California Press, 1981), p.xlii. Ross notes that More devotes about one third of his *History of Richard III* to the often dramatic speeches he invents for his characters (pp.xxvii–viii). More's *History* was available to the *Memorial-Mirror* authors through its wholesale inclusion in Edward Hall's chronicle. The authors may also have been influenced by the work of another poet famous for his combination of medieval and Renaissance interests, Sir David Lindsay, whose first-person *de casibus*-tragedy *The Tragical Death of Dauid Beato[n]* was translated from Lowland Scots and printed by Baldwin's friend John Day in about 1548 (*STC* 15683).

30 Campbell, ed., *Mirror*, pp.65–6.

CHAPTER 2

'A miserable time full of piteous tragedyes'

Paul Budra

The fifth poem in the 1559 edition of *A Mirror for Magistrates*, composed and read by 'one of the cumpany' (p.110)[1] of gathered writers, is that of King Richard II who was, according to the title of his entry, 'for his euyll gouernaunce deposed from his seat, and miserably murdred in prison' (p.111). In the prose paratext that follows the poem, William Baldwin, the coordinator of the *Mirror* writing collective, says 'Whan he had ended this so wofull a tragedy, and to all Princes a ryght wurthy instruction, we paused: hauing passed through a miserable time full of piteous tragedyes' (p.119). After the pause, Baldwin and his collaborators continue their search through the chronicle histories of England for tragic tales, turning to the reign of Henry IV for 'what Piers were fallen therin', but they pass over a number of them because 'their examples were not much to be noted for our purpose' (p.119). Baldwin then addresses his companions: 'What my maysters, is euery man at once in a browne study, hath no man affeccion to any of these storyes? you minde so much sum other belyke, that these do not moue you: And to say troth there is no speciall cause why they should' (p.119) (a brown study is a mood of deep thoughtfulness or melancholy). Baldwin himself goes on to tell the story of 'Owen Glendour' who led the Welsh revolt against Henry IV beginning in 1400 and is best remembered as the self-important and mystical character in Shakespeare's *Henry IV Part 1*.

All the poems up to this point have been called by the team of writers tragedies or they have been described as containing a 'tragicall example' (p.110), concerning a 'tragicall matter' (p.181), or as portraying a 'tragicall person' (p.154). In total the word 'tragedy' or some variation on it appears 16 times in the 1559 edition of the *Mirror*. The word 'fall', used to denote a tragic decline in fortune, appears 15 times. But the story of Glendower is not described using any variation on the word 'tragedy'. He is merely one of 'fortunes owne whelpes' (p.119). The next three poems, which depict the fates of Henry Percy, Richard Earl of Cambridge, and Thomas Montague,

35

also avoid the use of any variation of the word 'tragedy'. Following those comes the story of James I of Scotland, who is described as a 'tragicall person', but next is the story of William de la Pole, Duke of Suffolk (one of the powers behind Henry VI). The *Mirror* collaborators are positively gleeful at the recounting of his non-tragic death: 'Every man reioyced to heare of a wicked man so maruaylously well punished' (p.170). The title of the next poem, the story of the populist rebel Jack Cade, makes no bones about its intent: that rebel 'was for his treasons and cruell doinges wurthely punyshed' (p.171). No tragedy here. After Cade, the following six poems are described in one way or another as tragic. The final poem in the 1559 edition, the story of King Edward IV, does not use the word 'tragedy', though given its title – 'How king Edward through his surfeting and vntemperate life, sodainly died in the mids of his prosperity' (p.236) – one might expect it would.

Is there a meaningful pattern here? A couple of thoughts emerge: the first non-tragedy-labelled story is told when the writers move from the reign of Richard II to Henry IV. Was the reign of Richard II the problem? Did the ascension of Henry IV to the throne mean that the fates of great men would no longer be tragic? Had England put that 'miserable time' behind it? Well, perhaps: none of the tales that take place during the reigns of Henry IV and Henry V are labelled as tragic and there are only two under each of those monarchs. On the other hand, there are three non-tragic tales (and six tragic) under Henry VI. The authors do acknowledge a monarch can have an impact: when the collaborators are finished with the reign of Richard II, Baldwin notes 'the reyne of Henry the fourth ensued, a man more ware & prosperous in hys doynges although not vntroubled with warres both of outforth and inward enemies' (p.119). Henry VI gets his own tragedy and the preceding paratext explains 'king Henrye him selfe was cause of the destruction of many noble princes, being of all other most vnfortunate him selfe' (p.211). A second possibility: perhaps the tragic or non-tragic status of the *Mirror*'s ghosts is unrelated to the times and is instead linked to the nature of the protagonists' character and crimes. Were certain of these people so malevolent that their demises could only be called just retribution rather than tragedy? Well, some of them, yes. The worthy punishment of Jack Cade makes that clear. But some of persons in the poems that *are* labelled tragic are just as bad: John Clifford, whose ghost is described as appearing headless, 'for his straunge and abhominable cruelty, came to as straunge and sodayne a death' (p.192). John Tiptoft, Earl of Worcester (known in his time as the Butcher of England), came to his end 'for cruelly executing his princes butcherly commaundements' (p.197). And, on the other side, Thomas Montague, the Earl of Salisbury, was a military commander under Henry V who 'in the middes of his glory, was chaunceably slayne with a piece of ordinaunce' at Orleans, an event depicted by Shakespeare in 1.4 of *Henry VI Part 1*. It is not described as a tragedy by the *Mirror* collective but as a 'straunge aduenture' that befalls a 'good erle' (p.154) though according to Baldwin the recounting of that adventure had an impact on the collective of writers: it 'drave vs al into a dumpne' (p.154).

If Baldwin and his collaborators were making a statement about the nature of tragedy and history, critics have not been able to agree on what it was, but then critics have not been able to agree on the argument of the *Mirror* as a whole. Scott C. Lucas has contended that *A Mirror for Magistrates* and its suppressed earlier version, *A Memorial of suche Princes*, is 'topically allusive in form and politically interventionary in purpose' and that its authors were Protestant evangelicals responding to their oppression under Marian magistrates by offering a re-evaluation of key events and personalities in the reign of Edward VI, most notably those surrounding the disgraced Edward Seymour, through a recounting of the lives of earlier disgraced or tragic historical characters.[2] For Jessica Winston, on the other hand, the book, especially in its later editions, 'presents and fosters a public conversation about governance'.[3] Andrew Hadfield places the book in the context of nation building, calling the *Mirror* 'a self-proclaimed *nationalistic* project, of the sort Sidney encouraged in the "Exordium" of his *Apologie* and mapped out in the "Digression"'.[4] Mike Pincombe, on the other hand, believes that the *Mirror* reflects questions of social class and that its editor, William Baldwin, 'was not worried about the implications of any radical politics in the *Mirror* ... He was worried about the possibility of offending individual members of the present aristocracy by getting the facts wrong about their ancestors'.[5] In fact, he argues 'Baldwin tries to depoliticize *A Mirror for Magistrates*'.[6] For Jim Ellis, the *Mirror* displays an 'obsession with the effects of social mobility. The alienated ghosts of the text may bear witness to more than simply their crimes: they are bearing witness to a shift in their society's relation to property and the trauma that such a shift might cause.'[7] I would like to come at this discussion from another direction. I want to understand not what William Baldwin and his collaborators intended the *Mirror* to *mean*, but how they intended it to *feel*. Was there an emotional effect that the *Mirror*'s writers were striving for when they assembled their poems in this complex, multivalent text? And how was their understanding of tragedy tied to that emotional agenda?

Only a few critics have addressed the question of the affective rhetoric of the 1559 *Mirror*. Lucas asserts that the tragic poems are 'political acts in themselves, uniquely effective – because affective – attempts to rewrite the recent political past and to alter the political future'.[8] This is part of his argument that the *Mirror* authors sought to exonerate Seymour, 'to "rewrite" the dismal legacy of his time in power; and to lead readers to indict those men and women whom the authors hold to be truly to blame for the manifest disasters that afflicted the "good Duke" of Somerset'.[9] His reading is based primarily on the tragedies of 'Edmund Duke of Somerset', 'Humfrey Duke of Gloucester', and 'Thomas of Wudstocke', only the last of which appears in the 1559 edition. Lucas has a second main argument that is more germane to the first edition of the *Mirror*, the 'presentation of admonitory exempla designed to lead Marian magistrates to eschew ongoing or anticipated political practices to which the *Memorial* authors were opposed'.[10] Indeed, Lucas argues that four of the first five of the tragedies in the *Mirror* sought to 'alter the political behavior of Marian England's highest officers, moving them to eschew courses of action that the authors feared would lead the country to injustice, tyranny, and even civil war'.[11] He focuses on the tragedies of Robert Tresilian, Lord Mowbray, and Richard II – written by George Ferrers, William Baldwin, and Thomas Chaloner respectively – and demonstrates how they were written, early in Queen Mary's reign, as a direct comment upon what the evangelical community saw as the corruption of Marian magistrates specifically as it was manifest in the 1554 trial of Sir Nicholas Throckmorton, evangelical and Parliamentarian. The emotions that Lucas emphasises derive from the first of these two arguments: 'sorrow for the loss of all that was promised by Seymour's rule over the nation … a mix of fierce anger and bitterness – anger directed at those who Ferrers believes unjustly drove Seymour to his death and bitterness of Ferrers' haunting knowledge that Seymour's own personal failings in the wake of his deposition helped to hasten his destruction'.[12] Yet this 'painful project' also offers 'a modicum of consolation', and pity for the fallen Seymour.[13]

Jennifer Richards has traced the emotional agenda of the *Mirror* across numerous editions and has argued that those critics who have dismissed the later editions of the book as sentimental in comparison to the original edition 'miss the emotiveness of the early tragedies, as well as its authors' collective concern with the process of interpretation and the role this plays in the remaking of its argument'.[14] She argues 'the experience of reading the tragedies in 1559 raises more problems than a moral frame can resolve because the tales are affecting. A crucial question that arises from this observation is how it influences our understanding of the *Mirror* as political writing. Indeed, is it still a political work?'[15] Richards ties much of the *Mirror*'s emotional power to its use of *prosopopoeia*, writing in a persona, and focuses her attention on the sympathy the text evokes and how that emotion evolves across the long publishing history of the book.[16] *Prosopopoeia* was a exercise that schoolboys undertook in Tudor grammar schools and it was recognised as having innate emotional power:[17] 'literary prosopopoeia learns from rhetoric an interest in what is involved for the performer of the voice, how that performer can become absorbed in the role he plays, can only move his audience by moving himself'.[18] Most of Richards' argument, in fact, is about the later editions of the *Mirror*; so, for example she contends that 'John Higgins's *The first parte of the Mirour for magistrates* (1574) makes sympathy a comfortable part of our reading experience.'[19] But she recognises 'the tension between judgement and rhetorical affect that was already an issue in the 1559 *Mirror*'.[20] At the same time, she argues that Baldwin and company were cognizant of the power of emotion in argument: 'From the beginning its authors were concerned with the way in which rhetorical affect influences the interpretation of moral examples, and this informs the development of its argument'.[21]

Were they? I wonder if both Lucas and Richards are assuming more cohesion, both in literary form and rhetorical affect, than the 1559 *Mirror* provides. Let us start with the literary form. The frontispiece of the 1559 edition of the book promises tales of declining fortune: 'A MYRROVRE For Magistrates. Wherein may be seen by example of other, with howe greuous plages vices are punished: and howe frayle and vnstable worldly prosperitie is founde, even of those, whom Fortune seemeth most highly to fauour'. This synopsis points directly to the *de casibus* tragic tradition. The *Mirror* was modelled as an English-history-based extension of Lydgate's *Fall of Princes*, itself a loose translation of Laurent de Premierfait's French adaptation of Boccaccio's *De casibus virorum illustrium*.[22] I have argued in the past that those books set out to make a teleological argument through the rhetoric of accumulation. Boccaccio, and Lydgate after him, collected an extraordinary number of stories to demonstrate though exhaustive induction the rise-and-fall pattern of history.[23] Boccaccio did not consider his work a tragedy (the few times he uses the word he does so figuratively, not as a literary genre designation): it was a collection of moral histories that gained teleological weight through concatenation.[24] Boccaccio's 'overriding purpose for telling them, as stipulated in his Preface, is to illustrate not the workings of Fortune (a misnomer for Providence) but the judgements of God on famous men and women, in order to persuade the eminent persons of his own day to reform their wicked ways'.[25] Sympathy for the fallen was not necessary, so the histories need not be 'piteous'.[26]

Lydgate *did* use the word 'tragedy' and aligned the form with a specific emotional effect. He 'biwailles' stories that are 'pitous & lamentable| And dolorous to writen & expresse' (1:6308–9).[27] But he was not the first English author to recognise Boccaccio's moral histories as having a tragic structure and, as a result, an implied emotional register: that was Chaucer. In *The Monk's Tale*, one of the most popular of the *Canterbury Tales* in the fifteenth century, Chaucer aligned the accumulative *de casibus* form with tragedy.[28] As the Monk says, 'Tragedie is to seyn a certeyn storie,| … Of hym that stood in greet prosperitee,| And is yfallen out of heigh degree| Into myserie, and endeth wrecchedly' (VII: 1971–97).[29] Further, he recognised that tragedy is supposed to evoke sympathy: the Monk will 'biwaille' his tragedies. The Knight and Host who interrupt the Monk's tale do not complain about its tedium, but sadness. The Knight says, 'I seye for me, it is a greet disese,| Whereas men han been in greet welthe and ese,| To heeren of hire sodeyn fal, allas!' (VII: 2771–73). The Host concurs: 'and als of a tragedie …| It is for to biwaille ne compleyne| That that is doon, and als it is a peyne' (VII: 2783–86). No wonder that in the preface to the *Fall of Princes*, Lydgate describes Chaucer as 'That whilom made full pitous tragedies' (1: 248).

The *de casibus* form, then, entered the sixteenth century with two traditions: one was that of Boccaccio, who held the figures in his moral history up for inspection and criticism if not simple reproof.[30] The second was from Chaucer, who categorised the accumulated stories of the *de casibus* tradition by their narrative arc rather than moral purpose, calling them tragedies and expecting them to invoke sympathy. Lydgate, whose *Fall of Princes* was the immediate model for Baldwin and the other writers of the *Mirror*, oscillates between Boccaccio's censoriousness and Chaucer's pity, between historical exemplum and piteous tragedy, but leans towards the latter. For Lydgate, 'Tragedy deals primarily with the sudden fall of great men, and it gives rise to lamentation. If the men are innocent of wrongdoing, then Fortune or some human enemy gets the blame. If the men are sinful and deserve to fall, then they are blamed, but there is still room for lamentation.'[31] Baldwin, then, inherited a split tradition and so, in the 1559 edition of the *Mirror*, as we have seen, twelve of the poems are referred to as somehow tragic, while seven of the poems make no reference to tragedy. Baldwin and his collaborators lament the deaths of some of the figures they impersonate, but not all: witness Cade.

But there was another model of tragedy that was emerging and may have had an influence on Baldwin and his colleagues' understanding, and therefore application, of the word 'tragedy' and its emotional impact: dramatic tragedy. For Boccaccio and Lydgate, this was not an issue; dramatic tragedy for them was an extinct and not well understood performance art. Chaucer seems to have had no knowledge whatsoever of ancient drama.[32] But Baldwin and his collaborators were writing on the cusp of what would become one of the greatest explosions of drama in world history and several of them were active dramatists: Baldwin wrote plays for the 1552–53 court Christmas season. Ferrers, who contributed to the early editions of the *Mirror*, acted as Lord of Misrule at the courts of Henry VIII and his son. Thomas Sackville, responsible for the 'Induction', perhaps the most famous poem in the *Mirror* (1563 edition), would go on to co-write *Gorboduc; Or, Ferrex and Porrex*, first performed in 1561/2. That play has been called the 'first real English tragedy'.[33] The *Mirror* authors were thinking at least in part dramatically. In the poem of Thomas, Duke of Gloucester, Thomas says: 'Thus hoysted so high on Fortunes wheele,| As one on a stage attendying a playe,| Seeth not on whiche syde the scaffolde doth reele,| Tyll tymber and poales, and all flee awaye' (p.94). For a more explicit dramatic reference, we have to turn to the 1563 edition of the *Mirror* (also edited by Baldwin). In it Henry, Duke of Buckingham, delivers this speech:

> In place of whom, as it befel my lot,
> Like on a stage, so stept I in strayt way,
> Enioying there but wofully go wot,
> As he that had a slender part to playe:
> To teache therby, in earth no state may stay,
> But as our partes abridge or length our age
> So passe we all while others fyll the stage. (p.319)

A number of the poems in the *Mirror* are presented in a fashion that feels dramatic: the ghost is described or is given a specific setting.[34]

The great Elizabethan tragedies were written after the Baldwin editions of the *Mirror* were published and the critical commentaries on drama, and especially tragedy, by Sidney, Lodge, Gosson, and Puttenham were in the future. There was no permanent theatre in London when the *Mirror* went to press. Where, then, would Baldwin, his colleagues, and their readers have got their ideas about dramatic tragedy? The standard answer has been Seneca, who is mentioned in the *Mirror* by the ghost of Henry Percy, Earl of Northumberland: 'O Morall Senec true find I thy saying,| That neyther kinsfolke, ryches, strength, or fauour| Are free from Fortune' (p.132). Seneca was staged intermittently at Trinity and Queen's Colleges,

Cambridge, from 1551 (though not at Oxford until 1591) and other neoclassical tragedies written in Latin and Greek were performed at Cambridge and Oxford Universities from the 1540s.[35] The first printed English translation of a Seneca play was Jasper Heywood's version of *Troas*, which came out the same year as the *Mirror*. So Seneca was in the air, but it was not all about Seneca. As Howard B. Norland tells us,

> The principal guide to the study and composition of tragedy was Horace's *Ars poetica* as supplemented by sixteenth-century commentaries. Especially important were Badius's elaboration of Horace's concept of decorum published in several editions of the *Ars poetica* and elaborations of Horatian theory by Scaliger and Giraldi Cinthio … By contrast, Aristotle's tragic theory appears to have had very little influence on Elizabethan commentators.[36]

Indeed, according to Norland, Boccaccio and Lydgate were more important to the early Elizabethan concept of tragedy than Aristotle. And since Boccaccio and Lydgate were best known to the English audience of the mid-sixteenth century through the *Mirror*, Baldwin and his crew were, in effect, helping shape Elizabethan tragedy for the stage, but it was a form of tragedy that was not structured to generate or purge pity and fear in the Aristotelian tradition. It was, rather, tragedy designed, as Irby B. Cauthen Jr says of *Gorboduc*, to 'reinforce the moral element'.[37]

The *Mirror* is not entirely a collection of tragedies. It is also a narrative of the process of assembling those tragic monologues and much of its rhetorical affect is determined by the prefatory prose material and paratexts. As many critics have noted, Baldwin's preface to the book makes clear his political thesis: 'the goodnes or badnes of any realme lyeth in the goodnes or badnes of the rulers' (p.64). Indeed, Baldwin's direct address to officeholding readers is polemic: 'here as in a loking glas, you shall see (if any vice be in you) howe the like hath bene punished in other heretofore, whereby be admonished, I trust it will be a good occasion to move you to the soner amendment' (pp.65–6). Those punishments, Baldwin makes clear, are the providence of God: 'God can not of Iustice, but plage such shamles presumption and hipocrisy, and that with shamefull death, diseases, or infamy' (p.65). The tone is rueful, righteous, and perhaps angry, but in the following address to the reader Baldwin dilutes his theme, first by promising to focus on Fortune rather than God as the agent of retribution for bad officers – 'to shew the slyppery deceytes of the waueryng lady, and the due rewarde of all kinde of vices' (p.68) – and, second, by narrowing the scope of the vices discussed. The first tragedy is that of Robert Tresilian, which stands as a warning to 'all of his authorytie and profession, to take heed of wrong Iudgementes, mysconstruyng of lawes, or wrestyng the same to serue the princes turnes' (p.71). However admonitory the tragedy may have been for Marian judges, to the casual reader its message may have only been applicable to lawyers and the tone of the introductory paratext is as much nationalistic as it is condemnatory, with Ferrers arguing that 'our nacion' has as many 'myserable princes' as does Italy (p.69).

The next paratext, the one before the tragedy of the two Mortimers, does not pick up on the themes of punishment by Fortune or providence. One of the writing collective admits that the biography he has to hand 'be not greatly appertinent to our purpose' (p.81) but decides to go ahead with the tale because 'I thynke it woulde be wel to obserue the times of men' (p.81). The paratext before the tragedy of Thomas of Woodstock is brief and recounts Ferrers' argument that 'there are many wurthy to be noted, though not to be treated of' (p.91). It is only with the paratext before the tragedy of Mowbray that Baldwin returns to the ostensible theme of the *Mirror*: warning officers against vice. He has Mowbray 'admonysh all Counsaylers to beware of flattering princes, or falsely enuying or accusyng theyr Peregalles' (p.101). In the following paratext an historical digression on the facts surrounding the Mowbray–Bolingbroke confrontation requires Baldwin to remind his company of their purpose, 'which minde onely to diswade from vices and exalte vertue' (p.110). This works briefly – the tragedy of Richard II is deemed 'to all Princes a ryght wurthy instruction' (p.119) – but the paratext before the tragedy of Henry Percy is a lengthy digression on historical facts surrounding the reign of Henry IV. The same is true of the next two paratexts, the ones before Richard Earl of Cambridge and Thomas Montague. The latter leads to the speculation that 'This Earle is neyther the first nor the last whom Fortune hath foundered in the heyth of their prosperitye' (p.154), harkening back to a line in the preface: 'sum haue for their vertue been enuied and murdered, yet cease not to be vertuous' (p.67). The writers lament his 'wofull destynye' (p.154) but it is not until the paratext before the tragedy of Jack Cade that the writers come back to the ostensible argument of the book, 'howe notably God dysposeth all thinges' (p.170). This is picked up at length in the following paratext, where God's judgement on rebels is confirmed – 'whosoever rebelleth agaynst any ruler either good or bad, rebelleth against GOD' (p.178) – but soon the writers are discussing historical facts and Baldwin himself is nodding off. The remaining six paratexts are dominated by discussion of historical detail and speculation on the dangers of a divided kingdom. If the tragedies in the 1559 *Mirror* are, in Lucas's words, 'political exempla profitable for magistrates', the authors of the book seem to have largely forgotten the fact by the end of their day of writing.[38] The righteous emotions of Baldwin's preface become lost in the minutiae of dynastic politics.

It is not only authorial digression that complicates the rhetorical purpose of the paratexts of the 1559 *Mirror*. Sherri Geller has convincingly argued that the critical attention that has traditionally favoured the poems rather than the paratexts is the result of editorial decisions made in the nineteenth and early twentieth centuries, decisions that drew readers' attention to the monologues and away from the prose. She contends that the original editions of the book demonstrate that the prose paratexts were not merely a framing device for the tragedies. In fact, 'Baldwin's versions seek to destabilize the textual hierarchy in order to inspire in the reader an equal sense of obligation toward the frame and the complaints' (p.181), creating a more complex reading experience.[39] In her interpretation the paratexts should be read as a 'pseudo-nonfiction' that 'needs to be situated in the context of other early modern pseudo-nonfictional frames, such as those in Medwall's *Fulgens and Lucres*, More's *Utopia*, Baldwin's *Beware the Cat*, and other early modern English writings that play with meta-textuality.[40] So when Baldwin claims to fall asleep in the paratext before the tragedy of Richard Plantagenet and have a dream of 'a tall mans body full of fresshe woundes, but lackyng a head', he is parodying the standard medieval dream-vision framing device.[41] If Geller is correct, then the original reading experience of the *Mirror* must have been complex indeed. Aside from whatever sympathy the tragic stories themselves might evoke, this 'pseudo-nonfiction' frame seems aimed at more intellectual pleasures: appreciation and perhaps awe at the innovation and originality of the authors; contentment at recognising the traditions being overturned; amusement at the wit with which it is being done. Certainly simple emotional engagement – the sort of sympathy that Richards describes in the later editions of the *Mirror* – would be qualified by the disruption of narrative illusion.

There are further complications of that illusion. Critics of the *Mirror*, for the most part, talk unproblematically of the monologues of the ghosts. But, of course, there are no ghosts in book: there are only poets performing as the ghosts of the historical dead and addressing their complaints to William Baldwin. In a few cases the oration is prefaced with an exhortation to imagine the appearance of the ghost – 'And therfore imagine *Baldwin* that you see him al to be mangled, with blew woundes, lying pale and wanne al naked vpon the cold stones in Paules church, the people standing round about him, and making his mone in this sort' (p.111) – but for the most part the poet in question just delivers his speech. It is *Baldwin* who has to imagine that he is seeing ghosts.[42] Readers of the *Mirror*, then, are distanced from what sympathy the ghosts' lamentations might elicit because they are not allowed to simply engage with the fiction of a spectral visit: 'The introductions emphasize the person in the frame who is about to recite a complaint, the person who, in complete control, offers his historical research as "what I have noted".'[43] But it is not always so clear; at times the paratexts that follow the poems confuse the status of the 'ghosts': 'Often Baldwin treats them (albeit with a wink) as if they were real. After impersonating the ghost of Richard Plantagenet, for example, Baldwin continues his frame narrative by saying, "Whan stout Richarde had stoutly sayd his mind," rather than "When I had finished reading".'[44]

Philip Schwyzer raises another issue about the monologues. Critics of the *Mirror* have tended to talk about the ghosts, or, more accurately, the impersonation of the ghosts by the members of Baldwin's collective, as if ghosts were unproblematic entities. That is, they have tended to discuss the historical person that the ghost figures forth, or paid attention to the details of the ghosts' confessions of sin or admonitions to its listeners, but not to the complex cultural status of the ghosts themselves. As Schwyzer demonstrates, while later editions of the *Mirror* present what might be called 'classic ghosts', that is disturbed souls returned from the grave, the fervent Protestants in Baldwin's company avoid identifying them as such. 'Instead, betraying an anxiety born of recent controversies, Baldwin and his interlocutors repeatedly go out of their way to insist that these are not real people at all. They are merely – like Simone Martini's painting of Laura – artist's renderings.'[45] Wary of the supernatural, the evangelical writers of the *Mirror* made their ghosts, despite occasional headlessness, unthreatening and remarkably passive. They do not seek the 'ease and grace' that Horatio offers the ghost of Hamlet's father. It seems 'Departed souls cannot return to this world except in poetry, there is nothing the living can do to benefit them, nor can they do anything to help the living beyond providing awful examples of fortune's inconstancy', though 'with each new edition of the *Mirror* the dead speakers become more like the ghosts of Catholic tradition', a process that begins as early as the 1563 edition.[46] There would have been no culturally established emotional reaction – not fear, awe, or denial – for the strange literary ghosts of the 1559 *Mirror*.

The final factor we should address is the delayed publication of the *Mirror*. The emotions that Lucas both mentions and implies, emotions generated by a community of evangelical authors reeling from the failure of their once hopeful cause under Edward IV and smarting from the repression and corruption they experienced under Mary, are anger, regret, sorrow, and condolence. They are the emotions of a group that has seen its hopes dashed and is trying to rationalise defeat. But all of these emotions must have been at least partially denuded of their original power when the *Mirror* was finally published in 1559. In the words of Lucas, 'By that time the immediate topical "moment" of these tragedies had passed, and it was for this reason that Baldwin offered the newly titled *Mirror for Magistrates* to Elizabethan officers not as a text engaged specifically with the concerns of Mary's early reign but as a collection of more general political exempla profitable for magistrates of any period.'[47] While the authors may still have felt bitterness and anger at both the failure of the Seymour Protectorate and the corruption of Marian magistrates, in 1559 there was a new Protestant queen on the throne. Those tragedies directed at rehabilitating the reputation of the Edward Seymour Protectorate and castigating those Marian judges who had manipulated the laws of the land in response to the Queen's personal agenda, while not empty of meaning or bite, would have been at least in part de-fanged. As mentioned, only one of the three tragedies that directly comments on Seymour even makes it into the 1559 edition.

Given all of the above, it may be entirely unrealistic to expect that the authors of the 1559 *Mirror* had any emotional agenda for their book or cohesive understanding of tragedy as a literary form with a specific affective rhetoric. It was a collection of nineteen poems by nine different authors and 'there is no indication that the authors intended the seemingly universal statements offered at the beginnings and ends of their tragedies to apply to anything other than the specific poems in which they are found'.[48] On the other hand, Lucas notes that the authors 'were members of a specific group – the shaken, defeated, and generally silenced evangelical community living in England in the first years of Mary I's reign'.[49] The community of 'like-minded evangelical authors', had ties to each other and they are represented in the prefatory material as a randomly assembled group only to 'deflect suspicions about the collaborative nature of the project'.[50] They were colleagues, and perhaps friends. With the possible exception of Thomas Churchyard, they were university educated and, as we have seen, several of them had experience in the dramatic arts. And more, the work, first as the *A Memorial of suche Princes* and then as the *Mirror*, was the creative invention of William Baldwin, who acted as the main author, editor, and, perhaps, printer.[51]

The work was shaped by Baldwin, right down (if Lucas is correct) to the choice of the frontispiece woodcut of the first suppressed edition.[52] The *Mirror* would be forever associated with his name. The relative homogeneity of the collective of writers, their shared political and religious agenda, as well as the shaping hand of their editor, Baldwin, at least raises the possibility of an intentional emotional agenda. That does not mean that they had a specific, or at least not doctrinaire, idea about tragedy, history, or the emotional impact of literary forms. But they may have had an eye to the broader emotional power of the book. With that in mind, I'd like to turn to what is probably the least discussed part of the 1559 *Mirror*: the last tragedy.

The title of the final tragedy of the 1599 edition, 'How king Edward through his surfeting and vntemperate life, sodainly died in he mids of his prosperity', seems to promise a tragedy of immoral life, but this is not what the poem delivers. While the ghost of Edward implies a life of dissolution – 'I had ynough I helde me not contente' (p.237) – his gravest sin seems to be the extravagance of fortifying existing architectural structures and building some new ones: 'I amended Dover on the mountayne hye,| And London I prouoked to fortify the wall' (p.237). Theologically, the poem is less than coherent: 'What ordeyned God to be terrestriall,| Without recourse to the earth by nature?' (p.236) asks Edward before going on to blame 'Lady Fortune' with her 'sugred lyppes' (p.237) for granting him victory in England and the throne. But emotionally the poem is one of the most focused in the collection. The bulk of its seven twelve-line stanzas are a *memento mori* lamentation. Edward elaborates on the theme of inevitable mortality, the vanity of pride, and the capriciousness of fortune. He tells the reader 'Saynt Barnard therof nobly doth treat,| Saying a man is but a sacke of stercory' (p.238), and then invokes the passing of great men from both the classical and Old Testament traditions: Alexander, Samson, Solomon, and Absalom. The poem even hints at the dance of death motif as Edward tells us Lady Fortune 'toke me by the hand and led me a daunce' (p.237). The last stanza is one of the most explicitly Christian in the 1559 *Mirror*: '*In manus tuas domine* my spirite vp I yelde,| Humbly besechyng the o God, of they grace' (p.239). Each stanza ends with the line '*Et ecce nunc in pulvere dormio*', 'behold, now I sleep in the dust', which derives from Job 7:21.

This is, of course, the only poem in the collection that is not by one of the eight authors that Baldwin has assembled for the project. It is, rather, by John Skelton, who died in 1529. In the penultimate paratext its inclusion is presented as a matter of convenience. The writing collective is about to break up for the day as 'nyghte was se nere cum that we could not conveniently tary together any longer' (p.235). George Ferrers proposes reassembling in a week's time but, before they do, 'an other' says they should end their 'daies labour with the same oracion which mayster Skelton made in his name, the tenour wherof so farre as I remember, is this' (p.235). But his memory is selective. The title given to Skelton's poem in its first printed edition, 'On the Death of the Noble Prince King Edward the Fourth', is a long cry from the *Mirror*'s 'vtemperate life' but it was clearly this version, printed by Richard Lant in 1545, that the *Mirror* contributor had to hand (or memory) because the Lant version is seven stanzas long. Other editions add another stanza, a stanza that, interestingly, actually makes the case for an 'vntemperate life':

> I see well they live that double my yearės:
>> Thus dealéd this world with me as it list,
> And hath me made, to you that be my peerės,
>> Example to think on, had I wist.
> I storéd my coffers and alsó my chest
> With taskės taking of the commonalty;
>> I took their treasure, but of their prayerės missed;
> Whom I beseech with pure humility
> For to forgive and have on me pity:
>> I wás your king, and kept you from your foe.
> I would now amend, but that will not be,
>> *Quia, ecce, nunc in pulvere dormio.*[53]

Now, If Lucas is correct about the Protestant politics behind the composition of the *Mirror* and its suppressed predecessor, *A Memorial of suche Princes*, it seems odd that the writing collective would end their book with a saint-invoking poem written by a Catholic subdeacon, deacon, and priest with a 'deep and abiding hatred of the new Lutheranism'.[54] It seems especially odd, since the version of the poem that the authors seemed to know is the one missing the details of royal intemperance that would provide evidence for their argument about the necessity for righteousness in rulers. They do not even describe the tale or its protagonist as tragic. We can speculate that Baldwin simply wanted to finish the collection with as little fuss as possible and so grabbed a poem that was close enough in form (a monologue delivered by a deceased ruler) that he could fit it in. But I would like to entertain another possibility: perhaps Baldwin used the poem to close the book because of its affective rhetoric.

The poem, with its repetition and injunction to 'behold' the deceased, invokes the *De contemptu mundi* tradition (from a poem attributed to 'Saynt Barnard', Barnard of Cluny) that informed the tragic teleology of the *de casibus* tradition. It harkens back to Lydgate, Chaucer, and Boccaccio. At the same time, given its placement in the *Mirror*, it suggests what Scott L. Newstok has called 'the poetics of epitaphic closure', a fashion in Tudor and Stuart literature to include epitaphs in various forms of discourse.[55] Newstok explains the prevalence of this device as 'a textual response to the dissolution of Catholic memorial practices', but Baldwin may have been interested in the poem's tone of utter contrition, its sombreness, its piety, and its invocation of that vision of earthly ephemerality which was at the foundation of the *de casibus* tragic vision of history.[56] It is the most epitaphic poem in the 1559 *Mirror* and it closes the book with a note of pious melancholy that feels like an intentional affective strategy.

Any attempt to trace a coherent emotional effect or agenda through the 1559 *Mirror* is challenged by the complexity of the form of the text, the delay in its publication, its self-referential use of literary tradition, the bifurcated tradition of *de casibus* tragedy it inherited, as well as the nascent dramatic tragedy which it helped form, the nature of its ghosts, and its sometimes rambling paratextual material. Whether this radical heterogeneity is the product of the contingencies of publication and group authorship or an intentional aesthetic decision, we will never know, but it is clear that any attempt to fit the first edition of the *Mirror* into a specific affective agenda must either offer a very narrow reading of this multivalent text or interpret it with the hindsight that the later editions offer: while the 1563 *Mirror* offered a sustained critique of the Protectorate of Edward Seymour, only the most sensitive reader would have recognised the allusion to that fallen Protestant hero in the 1559 edition. Similarly, only readers of the later editions of the *Mirror* would have been predisposed to think of the *Mirror* as a book that generates sympathy; the authors of the first collection seem not to have considered many of their tales tragic, much less empathy-provoking. Let us remember what Baldwin said to his companions just before the Glendower monologue: 'you minde so much sum other belyke, that these do not moue you: And to say troth *there is no speciall cause why they should*' (p.119, emphasis added). But Baldwin and his friends did promise to demonstrate 'howe frayle and vnstable worldly prosperitie is founde', and their choice of a last poem suggests they wanted their readers to feel, and not just understand, the weight of miserable time.

Notes

1. All references to the various versions of the *Mirror* cite *The Mirror for Magistrates*, ed. Lily B. Campbell (Cambridge University Press, 1938). Page numbers are given in parentheses.
2. Scott C. Lucas, A Mirror for Magistrates *and the Politics of the English Reformation* (Amherst: University of Massachusetts Press, 2009), p.3.
3. Jessica Winston, 'A *Mirror for Magistrates* and Public Political Discourse in Elizabethan England', *SP* 101:4 (2004), 381–400, at p.397.
4. Andrew Hadfield, *Literature, Politics and National Identity: Reformation to Renaissance* (Cambridge University Press, 1994), p.84.
5. Mike Pincombe, 'William Baldwin and *A Mirror for Magistrates*', *RS* 27:2 (2011), 183–98, at p.195.
6. Pincombe, 'Baldwin', p.184.
7. Jim Ellis, 'Embodying Dislocation: *A Mirror for Magistrates* and Property Relations', *RQ* 53:4 (2000), 1032–53, at p.1033.
8. Lucas, *Mirror*, p.17.
9. Lucas, *Mirror*, p.69.
10. Lucas, *Mirror*, p.172.
11. Lucas, *Mirror*, p.175.
12. Lucas, *Mirror*, p.106.
13. Lucas, *Mirror*, p.107.
14. Jennifer Richards, 'Transforming *A Mirror for Magistrates*', in Margaret Healy and Thomas Healy, eds, *Renaissance Transformations: The Making of English Writing (1500–1650)* (Edinburgh University Press, 2009), pp.48–63, at p.49.
15. Richards, 'Transforming', p.56.
16. In fact, the device employed in the *Mirror* is *eidolopoeia*, in which the speaker puts words in the mouths of the dead; *prosopopoeia* designates the impersonation of a fictional character, while *ethopoeia* refers to the impersonation of another living person.
17. See Ursula Potter, 'Performing Arts in the Tudor Classroom', in Lloyd Edward Kermode, Jason Scott-Warren, and Martine Van Elk, eds, *Tudor Drama before Shakespeare, 1485–1590: New Directions for Research, Criticism, and Pedagogy* (New York: Palgrave, 2004), pp.143–65, at p.152.
18. Gavin Alexander, 'Prosopopoeia: The Speaking Figure', in Sylvia Adamson, Gavin Alexander, and Katrin Ettenhuber, eds, *Renaissance Figures of Speech* (Cambridge University Press, 2007), pp.97–112, at p.102. Guyda Armstrong makes the case that Boccaccio achieved similar emotional effects by having the ghosts talk to him in the third person (*The English Boccaccio: A History in Books* [University of Toronto Press, 2013], p.38).
19. Richards, 'Transforming', p.58.
20. Richards, 'Transforming', p.58.
21. Richards, 'Transforming', p.48.

22 See Armstrong, *English Boccaccio*, pp.23–91, for a detailed account of the changes wrought to the *de casibus* tradition as it passed from Boccaccio, through Laurent de Premierfait, and Lydgate.
23 See Paul Budra, A Mirror for Magistrates *and the de casibus Tradition* (University of Toronto Press, 2000), p.18.
24 See Henry Angsar Kelly, *Chaucerian Tragedy* (Cambridge: D.S. Brewer, 1997), p.23.
25 Kelly, *Chaucerian Tragedy*, p.11.
26 For a discussion of fortune and providence in the precursors to the *Mirror*, see Budra, *Mirror*, pp.45–51. The word 'fortune' appears 83 times in the 1559 *Mirror*; the word God, 94.
27 All citations of *Fall of Princes* are from Henry Bergen's edition: *Early English Text Society*, Extra Series, nos 121–4 (London: Oxford University Press, 1924–7), 4 vols. Book and line numbers are given in parentheses.
28 See Larry Scanlon, *Narrative, Authority, and Power: The Medieval Exemplum and the Chaucerian Tradition* (Cambridge University Press, 1994), p.219.
29 All references to Chaucer cite *The Works of Geoffrey Chaucer* 2nd ed., ed. F. N. Robinson (Boston: Houghton Mifflin, 1957).
30 Though Armstrong has argued that Boccaccio's use of ghostly monologues 'created by the present-tense narrative and the urgency … creates a kind of enforced empathy in the reader, an effect amplified by the skilful narratorial presentation of the characters' (*English Boccaccio*, p.38).
31 Kelly, *Chaucerian Tragedy*, p.175.
32 See Kelly, *Chaucerian Tragedy*, p.57.
33 Irby B. Cauthen, Jr, 'Introduction' to Thomas Sackville and Thomas Norton, *Gorboduc or Ferrex and Porrex*, Regents Renaissance Drama Series (Lincoln: University of Nebraska Press, 1970), pp.xi–xxx, xiii.
34 See Budra, *Mirror*, p.75.
35 Howard B. Norland, *Neoclassical Tragedy in Elizabethan England* (Newark: University of Delaware Press, 2009), pp.19, 46–7.
36 Norland, *Neoclassical Tragedy*, p.19.
37 Cauthen, 'Introduction', p.xix.
38 Lucas, *Mirror*, p.200.
39 Sherri Geller, 'Editing Under the Influence of the Standard Textual Hierarchy: Misrepresenting *A Mirror for Magistrates* in the Nineteenth- and Twentieth-Century Editions', *TC* 2:1 (2007), 43–77, at p.50.
40 Geller, 'Editing', p.56.
41 Geller, 'Editing', p.181.
42 See Geller, 'Editing', p.53.
43 Geller, 'Editing', p.47.
44 Meredith Skura, '*A Mirror for Magistrates* and the Beginnings of English Autobiography', *ELR* 36:1 (2006), 26–56, at p.40.
45 Philip Schwyzer, *Literature, Nationalism, and Memory in Early Modern England and Wales* (Cambridge University Press, 2004), p.107.

46 Schwyzer, *Literature*, pp.108, 115.
47 Lucas, *Mirror*, p.200.
48 Lucas, *Mirror*, pp.10–11.
49 Lucas, *Mirror*, p.15.
50 Lucas, *Mirror*, p.54.
51 See Lucas, *Mirror*, p.54.
52 Lucas, *Mirror*, p.55.
53 John Skelton, *The Complete Poems of John Skelton, Laureate*, ed. Philip Henderson (London: J. M. Dent; New York: E. P.Dutton, 1959), p.2.
54 Nan Cooke Carpenter, *John Skelton* (New York: Twayne, 1967), p.34.
55 See Scott L. Newstock, 'Elegies Ending "Here": The Poetics of Epitaphic Closure', *Studies in the Literary Imagination* 39:1 (2006), 75–100.
56 Newstock, 'Elegies', p.75.

CHAPTER 3

Tragic and untragic bodies in the Mirror for Magistrates

Mike Pincombe

In the year of millennium, 2000, Jim Ellis, musing on mutability, and on the decline in the popularity of the *Mirror for Magistrates* since the Renaissance, asked: 'what did the Elizabethans find so fascinating about this poem that the rest of us have been missing?'[1] His answer is surprising. It is not its 'overt moralizing', though that is what we might have expected. After all, this is what medieval readers found so fascinating about the text the *Mirror* was originally intended to continue: John Lydgate's *Fall of Princes*.[2] But no: Elizabethan readers were captivated by 'its fascination with the mutilated bodies of its subjects, and its compulsive return to the spectacle of the body in pieces'.[3]

My chapter will take up Ellis's point and reanalyse his mutilated bodies from a different perspective. I shall argue that the *Mirror* does indeed contain several examples of dismembered corpses, but that these may be better explained in terms of an artistic response to a formal problem, in fact, to the most significant problem posed by the *Mirror* to its compiler, William Baldwin. In a word, the descriptions of damaged and otherwise dysfunctional bodies throw light on the difficulty of inserting the tragedies of the *Mirror* into its more or less realistic prose frame. Baldwin says that the poets gathered to write the *Mirror* determined at their first conference that the tragedies should be delivered as quasi-theatrical performances, and it is in the problem of making these performances convincing that the problem lies. For this reason, I shall restrict the scope of this chapter to the bodies described in the very earliest texts in the sequence: the 1554 *Memorial* and the 1559 *Mirror*. In 1563, Baldwin abandoned this scenario for something more plausible, though the descriptions of mangled corpses still survive to some extent here and in later versions of the text. For Baldwin, the problem was not only technical, but also tonal. I shall argue that he could never take the idea of a talking cadaver quite seriously, so that 'tragic bodies' tend to turn into 'untragic bodies' at several points in his narrative.

Let us start with the basic critical problem of imagining how the company of poets are meant to imagine the 'speakers' of the tragedies, by which I mean the fictional characters they impersonate. The quality of *headlessness* will be a very useful focus here, since it seems to have provoked the most difficulty in terms of plausible representation. William Delapole, Duke of Suffolk, is our model example. There is no doubt that the historical Suffolk lost his head; the detail is in all the history books. The *Mirror* Suffolk – our 'speaker' – follows the chronicles in this respect, and he mentions the fact to Baldwin in his first lines:

> Heavy is the hap whereto all men be bound,
> I mean the death, which no estate may fly.
> But to be banished, headed so, and drowned
> In sink of shame from top of honours high,
> Was never man so served, I think, but I. (p.162)

There is no doubt, then, that this Suffolk *was* beheaded. But does that mean that he *is* headless? In other words, does the anonymous performer of this tragedy, the impersonator of Suffolk the speaker, expect the other poets to imagine that he, the poet, is headless when he plays the part of the fallen prince? He does not say so, for, as scripted by Baldwin in the prose, he only mentions that Suffolk suffered a 'notable death' (p.161).

This makes sense in terms of the fiction of the earliest texts, in which the tragedies are improvised as performances by the poets gathered together to compose a sequence of exemplary monologues spoken by fallen princes (and also some commoners). When the character who is about to launch into his performance says that Suffolk's death is 'notable', he means that it fulfils the key condition for inclusion in the sequence: *notability*. Indeed, the example must be *notably* notable. Less remarkable examples are to be discarded, whilst others are given the full 'tragic treatment'. As 'master Ferrers' says early on in the day: 'there are many worthy to be noted, though not to be treated of' (p.91). Many are called, but few are chosen. But there is absolutely no mention of a headless body here in the prose. Only in 1571 was it revised so that the poet now says that Suffolk was 'beheaded the first day of May, *anno* 1450, and the dead corpse thrown up at Dover upon the sands' (p.161n). But, even here, the other characters in the fiction are still not asked to imagine or suppose that they see a decapitated man 'appear' in front of them to make his moan.

And, of course, Suffolk does not truly *appear* to the members of the company. There are *no* 'apparitions' and, even more emphatically, *no* 'ghosts' in these early versions of the *Mirror*.[4] In the frame fiction, there is only one man asking seven other men to use their imaginations so that his impersonation of the tragic subject may sound – and perhaps even *look* – more impressive. The most we can say is that Baldwin and the other characters are asking their audiences to shut their eyes, as it were, and 'see' Suffolk or any of the other tragic speaker-subjects 'appear' in their imagination. As soon as the character performing the tragedy of Suffolk says, in the person of the fictional nobleman, that he has been beheaded, so – perhaps – the imagination of the audience represents the image of the dead duke as headless.

By the same token, however, they may also 'see' Suffolk drenched in sea-water, at least, at the poem's close, where he says his body was thrown in the sea. In fact, Suffolk says at the start that he has been 'drowned | In sink of shame', which is perhaps a hint towards his final destination. And in 1571, the poet indirectly invites his audience to see Suffolk's headless body washed up on the beach. Yet critics never mention this detail of the drowned corpse, though it is surely much easier to imagine the performer as drowned than as decapitated. Headlessness has a certain *cachet*, it seems, amongst the mighty dead. Yet there is also something slightly fantastical, even humorous, about the idea of a headless body that is still able to deliver its mournful message, for it lacks the organs of thought and speech: *ratio et oratio*. We do not notice, perhaps, if we simply read the tragedies by themselves (as many critics do); but once they are placed within the frame, they start to look differently, especially when the poets remark on how their performances should be seen by the others.

Recent work on the *Mirror* has insisted that we should pay much more attention to the frame, and to treat it on an equal footing with the tragedies.[5] I would add that the prose also functions as a kind of commentary on the poems, and especially on their status as a kind of dramatic monologue. Once we take the fiction set out in the prose seriously, then we must try to imagine the complaints as performances before an audience. And then we have to ask ourselves how we are to imagine the poets imagining the performer who impersonates an 'apparently' headless speaker. It is not easy – and this is why critics tend to head for either the prose or the verse parts of the *Mirror*. When we read the work as it requires to be read, that is, continuously, then the discontinuity between its prose and verse parts becomes more evident. There is a difference in the level of seriousness in the *tone* of the prose and verse parts, with the prose feeling almost light-hearted in comparison with the gloomy moralising of the tragedies. Even the tragic bodies described in the prose take on a slightly grotesque aspect. Meredith Skura is perhaps the only critic to have really appreciated the *un*seriousness of the prose in this respect. She says of Baldwin's prose: 'his descriptions of the dead are almost mischievously ghastly'.[6] *Mischief* seems exactly the right word here. It is not as if Baldwin is really using these mutilated bodies to make any seriously satirical point about the futility of ambition, and so on; rather, he is playing with the conventions of grisly literary horror. And given the pleasure we take in the elusive and yet pungent wit and humour Baldwin displays in *Beware the Cat*, it is puzzling that we should not recognise – perhaps even *expect* – elements of this same ironical genius in the proses of the 1559 and 1563 versions of the *Mirror*. But that is what I shall argue in the pages that follow.

The tonal disjunction set up by prose and verse in the *Mirror* is what produces the effect of the 'tragic body' and its mischievous partner, the '*un*tragic body'. Let me say straight away that I am aware that there is a vast corpus of literature on 'the body', even though this is the only acknowledgement of it that I am able to give in this short chapter. The 'tragic body' I have in mind here is the one that Aristotle was surely also thinking of in his admittedly all too brief and ambiguous remarks on *pathos* in the *Poetics*. Aristotle says that there are three parts to the tragic plot: *peripeteia*, *anagnōrisis*, and *pathos*. In S. H. Butcher's translation, Aristotle defines a *pathos* as 'an act involving destruction or pain, for example deaths on stage and physical agonies and woundings and so on'.[7] The problem with this definition is that very few Greek tragedies show deaths and woundings and so on 'on stage'; and it has been recently argued that the key phrase *en tōi phanerōi* should really be translated as 'in the open', 'or "before the eyes" or "vivid" in a primary rhetorical, rather than literal, sense'.[8] The gory description of a murder reported in a messenger's speech would thus count quite as much as a *pathos* as if we actually saw the murder committed on stage. In this case, the *pathos* may be defined in terms of the rhetorical figure of *evidentia*: 'the vividly detailed depiction of a broadly conceived whole object ... through the enumeration of (real or invented) observable details'.[9] Thus, we might adapt Butcher's translation of Aristotle's *pathos* as 'Scene of Suffering' to 'image of suffering', in order to permit non-theatrical interpretation of the term. The 'tragic body', then, is the body as it is represented in a *pathos* of this kind. The *Mirror* poet-performers describe tattered and battered bodies as vividly as they can in order to produce a rhetorically affective image of the imaginary speaker-subject of the tragic complaint they are about to deliver.

The first example of this kind of *pathos* in the 1559 *Mirror* is found in the prose that introduces the tragedy of Sir Roger Mortimer. The anonymous character who is about to deliver it says: 'I will take upon me the personage of [Sir Roger Mortimer], who full of wounds, miserably mangled, with a pale countenance and grisly look, may make his moan to Baldwin as followeth' (p.81). Here, again, there is no direct invitation to suppose or imagine a body; but surely that is what the character intends his audience to do. In some way, they have to *not* see or *un*see the performer and to see instead an image of the tragic body of the fictional speaker. However, the precariousness of the connection between prose and verse is worth noting. The description here is not directly keyed into the tragedy. Mortimer certainly tells us that he died violently at the hands of Irish kerns: 'fro my corpse my life they rent asunder' (p.88). His forces fared no better: 'all my helps in pieces they to-hew;| Our blood distained the ground as drops of dew' (p.88). In short: 'I was destroyed' (p.89). But the details of the *pathos* have been invented by Baldwin, not by the anonymous author of Mortimer's tragedy.

But what of the '*un*tragic' body'? I have used this unfamiliar adjective to express a certain ambivalence in some of the descriptions to be found in the 1559 *Mirror*. An example is Baldwin's own tragedy of the Duke of Clarence, and the prose introduction which he himself penned for it. Clarence, notoriously, was drowned in a butt of malmsey, and Baldwin's treatment of the duke's death stays true to this detail of history. Baldwin's Clarence relates how his brother Richard and his henchmen finished him off in prison: 'they bound me, whether I would or no,| And in a butt of malmsey standing by,| New-christened me, because I should not cry' (p.233). The tone of these lines is difficult to gauge. Clarence means (probably) that his murderers drowned him so that he should not reveal Richard's villainy by his protests; but the comparison of being drowned in a vat and being christened at the font creates a witty sense of distance between the act and its telling, a cool retrospective humour which is very far removed from the passionate outcry Clarence may have made when his assailants laid hands on him in the last minutes of his life.

There is a similar uncertainty of tone in the way Clarence introduces himself to Baldwin-the-Listener, where Clarence apologises for his delivery:

> though unneth [*with difficulty*] I utter speedy speech,
> No fault of wit or folly maketh me faint,
> No heady drinks have given my tongue attaint
> Through quaffing craft. Yet wine my wits confound,
> Not which I drank of, but wherein I drowned. (p.220)

This is the only time in the 1559 *Mirror* where one of the speakers comments on the way he sounds. Several speakers show they are aware of the situation in which they 'appear' to Baldwin by more than merely mentioning his name; but this is the only time that one of them draws attention to his own 'performance'. Another opportunity for such comment is provided but not exploited by the tragedy of the Earl of Salisbury, who died of wounds to the face: 'A pellet [*piece of cannon-shot*] came and drove a mighty flake| Against my face and tare [*tore*] away my cheek' (p.152). Salisbury might also have had difficulty speaking, but, for some reason, Baldwin treats him with much greater respect than Clarence. The poets are moved to a 'dump' at the recital of Salisbury's tragedy, so Baldwin can hardly make fun of him. Yet that is what he seems to do in the case of Clarence. There is even an olfactory element in his 'apparition': 'my wine bewrays me by the smell' (p.221). Baldwin is meant to be able to *smell* Clarence's presence! And the element of the grotesque is confirmed by the way in which Baldwin introduces his own performance in the preceding prose, where he says to others: 'ye shall hear what I have noted concerning the duke of Clarence, … who, all to-bewashed in wine, may bewail his infortune after this manner' (p.219). (And we think back to the drowned Duke of Suffolk at this point.)

Clarence's is what I call an '*un*tragic body'. It looks as if it might *almost* pass as a tragic body, as the subject of a *pathos*, or 'image of suffering', and yet the tone of the description seems too light-hearted. It is not as if this body has turned into a *different* kind of body, such as a 'comic body', or a 'grotesque body'; it is just that the text seems to be sending out mixed generic signals. The aesthetic effect is one of a slight interruption of tone, as if we halt for a moment in puzzlement, before proceeding, still slightly unsure of what is happening. In that respect, the untragic body produces an 'affect' which is peculiarly undefinable – and this may be one reason why critics have generally failed to recognise its presence in the *Mirror*.

The untragic body is hard to identify with real confidence in the 1559 *Mirror*, so we shall dwell on one example in some detail: Baldwin's tragedy of Owen Glendower. As it happens, we can draw on the single leaf from the main text of the 1554 *Memorial* that has survived. Here, Baldwin relates how, after 'master Chaloner' had ended his 'woeful … tragedy' of Richard II, the poets paused, as if for breath, 'having passed through a miserable time full of piteous tragedies' (p.119). They considered the potential of a group of conspirators early in the reign of Henry IV, but passed them over, 'because their examples were not much to be noted for [their] purpose'. Then Baldwin comes across Owen Glendower, and he says to the 'silent company':

> Owen Glendower, since he is a man of that country whence, as the Welshmen bear me in hand, my pedigree is descended, although he be but a slender prince, yet rather than he should be forgotten, I will tell his stale for him under the privilege of Martin Hundred; which Owen, coming naked out of the wild mountains, like the image of Death in all points, his dart only excepted, so sore hath famine and hunger consumed him, lamenteth his infortune after this manner. (p.119)

In the *Memorial* text, there is a blank line, then the title: 'How Owen Glendower, seduced by false prophecies, took upon him to be prince of Wales, and was by Henry, then prince thereof, chased to the mountains, where he miserably died for lack of food'. (Note that these words are not presented as having been *spoken*. They are an entirely *literary* interpolation in the narrative, like chapter headings.) Then there is another blank line, and the tragedy follows, set out in two columns of verse. The first stanza reads:

> I pray thee, Baldwin, sith thou dost intend
> To show the falls of such as climb too high,
> Remember me, whose miserable end
> May teach a man his vicious life to fly.
> O Fortune, Fortune! Out on her, I cry!
> My body and fame she hath made lean and slender,
> For I, poor wretch, am starved Owen Glendower. (pp.120–1)

All of this was written by Baldwin, as we may suppose that he supplied the titles to all the tragedies. In other words, here we have a prose–title–poem sequence in which the poem *may* have been written after the prose, instead of the other way around, which must be the case with the poems known to have been written by other men than Baldwin. Here, then, we may expect a greater degree of continuity between the parts. But it is not so.

First of all, let us note that Baldwin-the-Character introduces his about-to-be-improvised tragedy of Glendower with a description of the tragic subject's body. It is naked, and it is skeletally thin. So it is interesting to hear the sly remark that Glendower is 'but a slender prince'. In the context, the word *slender* is being used here to mean that Glendower's claim to princedom 'lacked substance'. But Glendower was also physically 'slender' because he starved to death, looking like the 'image of Death', when he finally expired. Indeed, Glendower comes close to making exactly this same punning point himself in his outcry against Fortune: 'My body and fame she hath made lean and slender,| For I, poor wretch, am starved Owen Glendower'.

Glendower is not inviting us to smile at his misery, but I cannot help feeling that Baldwin is presenting his 'image' of Glendower as more grotesque than horrifying. The others are supposed to imagine him as like the image of Death 'in all points', which would make him a terrifying figure indeed; but this description is immediately qualified by the phrase 'his dart only excepted', which renders the comparison far less impressive. After all, it is not so much Death we have to fear as his dart, which is what actually kills us. Despite all this, the tragedy of 'Owen Glendower' *is* perfectly serious. As with all the others, it is mainly taken up by telling the story. But the narrative is interspersed with a pervasive moralisation of events and, less frequently, punctuated with rhetorical devices which are intended to raise the level of narration to that of tragic speech. For example, Glendower's complaint against Fortune – 'O Fortune, Fortune! Out on her, I cry!' – is typical of the 'Apostrophe to Fortune' that leads the list of the formal features of 'dramatic lament' marshalled by Wolfgang Clemen as characteristic of Tudor stage-tragedy.[10] At one level, then, the idea seems to be that the speaker is overwhelmed by powerful emotions, effectively, by a surge of physical agitation which interrupts an otherwise rational speech. So it is that Glendower starts by talking quite calmly to Baldwin, but, as soon as he mentions and remembers his own 'miserable end', he is overcome by emotion. His body takes over – and this is where we come closer to the idea of a tragic body actually manifested *en tōi phanerōi* by speech. Glendower does not have to show us his wounds to prove that he is a subject of tragic status. He can display his psychosomatic pain and torment in a *pathos* which is produced *by speech alone*.

Glendower's outcry is an example of what ancient rhetoric calls *exclamatio*, listed as the first of the 'emotive figures' by Quintilian. These figures occur, he says, when we (he means: 'we orators') 'pretend we are angry, happy, frightened, surprised, grieved, indignant, desirous of something or the like'.[11] In the case of the *Mirror*, the speaker is the poet-performer; and the same interesting and difficult questions arise as to the way in which Baldwin expected his readers to imagine the fictional characters of the poets behaving as they recited and listened to their tragedies. How does Baldwin-the-Performer 'play' his part? Heinrich Lausberg, who follows Quintilian in making *exclamatio* the ring-leader of the emotive figures, defines it as: 'the expression of emotion by means of isolated, intensified *pronuntatio*'.[12] By *pronuntatio* is meant 'the realisation of the speech by speaking and making accompanying gestures'.[13] In other words, *exclamatio* occurs when the speech becomes suddenly more *physically* intense, by means of a cry or a clenched fist. Are we – the readers – invited to 'imagine' Baldwin acting in this way?

For most critics, the title serves to cut off the tragic monologue from the frame narrative, so the question does not really arise. But if we are interested in the relation between the verse and the prose parts of the *Mirror*, then it is a question which must be pondered at the general level. Some critics do recognise the fact that the tragedies become *prosopopoeiae* when they are read as part of the prosimetrical whole. Donald Jellerson writes thus of the anomalous case of the response to Salisbury's tragedy: 'The more effective the prosopopoeia, the greater the sense that the poet is possessed by the spectre and dispossessed of his own intention'.[14] However, the point of *prosopopoeia*, according to ancient theory, is that the speaker is *not* 'possessed by the spectre', but that he is in control of his own *fictio personae*.[15] More useful, to my mind, is Jennifer Richards's sceptical attitude to the affect produced by *prosopopoeia*. She gently – but correctly – admonishes Scott C. Lucas for being 'taken in' by the manipulative rhetoric of the speech given to the Earl of Worcester, whom Lucas calls an 'anguished ghost'.[16] But his anguish, she says, is just as likely to be simulated as actually experienced.

The prosopopoeic character of Glendower's complaint is complicated yet further by his recourse to *apostrophe*. At one point, Glendower, prompted by his reflections on Fortune's dalliance with the over-confident, cries out to an invisible addressee: 'How saist thou, Henry Hotspur? Do I lie?' (p.128). From a rhetorical point of view, this is an emotive figure. Here is Lausberg on *apostrophe*: 'it is the expression, on the part of the speaker, of a pathos ... which cannot be kept within the normal channels between speaker and audience'.[17] Glendower's audience is Baldwin, whom he addresses in the first line of his speech. But here he suddenly 'turns away' from Baldwin (Greek *apostrephein* means 'to turn away') and addresses the absent Henry Hotspur, his former ally, moved by the power of his grieving memory of Hotspur's valour: 'thou right manly gavest the king a field| And there was[t] slain because thou wouldst not fly' (p.128). Glendower's *pathos* – the Latin equivalent is *affectus*, the modern 'affect' – overpowers him and distracts him from the task in hand. Or so he would have us believe. Or so Baldwin-the-Performer would have us believe. And, of course, in the fiction of the frame, in taking on the person of Glendower, Baldwin is actually 'speaking' to himself! As Philippe Lejeune asks in a more specifically theatrical context (la Berma acting in *Phèdre*): 'who is saying *I*?'[18]

It is easy to see why critics tend to smooth over or flatten out the almost unimaginable narratorial contortions involved in the presentation of the 1554 *Memorial* and the 1559 *Mirror*. No wonder Baldwin opted for a much simpler frame, *sans* charades, for the 1563 edition of the text. But the original 'theatricalised' version of the frame fiction is so complex that we can understand why Baldwin might not have taken it too seriously. At the end of 'Glendower', after he has stepped from the role of the performer back to that of the narrator-author of the frame fiction, he says to the reader: 'When starved Owen had ended his hungry exhortation' (p.131). Can we help but smile?

I have argued above that the treatment of the tragic body in these early versions of the *Mirror for Magistrates* ranges from the genuinely tragic to a description or performance which is perhaps not tragic at all. Now I shall suggest that the tendency to slip towards the untragic is actually predominant, and that this is because almost all of the instances of such descriptions and all of the performances are from the pen of William Baldwin. Here I would risk the speculation that Baldwin got the idea of the tragic body from elsewhere than his own imagination. Ellis does not really consider this possibility, other than compare Glendower with its chronicle sources. But certain literary-generic traditions no doubt play their part, and other individual poets had introduced the lacerated bodies of their tragic speakers before Baldwin and his friends sat down to write the old *Memorial* in 1554.

For example, they may have known of Sir David Lindsay's *Tragical Death of David Beaton, Bishop of St Andrews*. An anglicised version of this poem by Robert Burrant was printed in 1548 by John Day, with whom Baldwin seems to have had some connection as a fellow printer.[19] Early one morning, says Lindsay:

> I took a book, to occupy the time;
> Where I found many a tragedy and story
> Which John Bochas had put in memory,
> How many a prince, conqueror and captain
> Were dolefully deposed from their reign.[20]

Then, as he read through one lugubrious story after another: 'Right suddenly, afore me did appear | One [*a*] wounded man, abundantly bleeding | With visage pale, and with a deadly cheer'. It is Cardinal Beaton, who has come to tell his tragic tale to Lindsay in the absence of the Italian *Urvater*. 'Right sure I am, were John Bochas alive, | My tragedy at length he would descrive'.

There is also a strong similarity between Lindsay's *mise en scène* and the description of the Duke of York and his young son, the Earl of Rutland. York's tragedy is another one of those which is performed by Baldwin himself, and, as usual, it is Baldwin who wrote the words which he places in his own mouth as the narrator of the preceding prose. As with the prose before Glendower, the company of poets are somewhat wearily making their way through a tract of history full of death and disaster, this time, the period of the Wars of the Roses. Baldwin-the-Narrator explains that he was so tired that he fell asleep, and in a dream saw two ghastly figures before him. In any case, this is a triumph of Baldwin's imagination, which, stimulated by the 'tragical matter' of the fields and fields of 'noblemen slain' that he read about in the chronicle, 'brought [him] such a fantasy':

> a tall man's body, full of fresh wounds, but lacking a head, holding by the hand a goodly child, whose breast was so wounded that his heart might be seen, his lovely face and eyes disfigured with dropping tears, his hair through horror standing upright, his mercy-craving hands all to-bemangled and all his body imbrued with his own blood. (p.181)

The boy is depicted at the moment of his death at the hands of Lord Clifford, whose tragedy follows, and who confesses the murder: 'I am the same that slew duke Richard's child,| The lovely babe that begged life with tears' (p.193). Rutland is frozen in the traumatic moment of his death. Likewise, the state of York's body is also just as it was at the moment of his death: headless. The two figures can genuinely 'appear' to Baldwin in this state, because anything can happen in a dream.

Not surprisingly, Baldwin was impressed. He says that he gazed at the apparitions, and turned his head away when, 'through the ghastfulness of this piteous spectacle, I waxed afeard' (p.181). Do we not see here an analogue of the *phobos kai eleos* – fear and pity – that Aristotle thought the appropriate responses to tragedy, and thus to the 'image of suffering' involved in the *pathos*. It is almost as if Baldwin were demonstrating that he could 'do tragedy' if he were to be granted the right occasion, not the fantastical format of the *Memorial* and the 1559 *Mirror*.

The idea that reading about tragical matters should inspire the reader to produce a tragical poem is presumably what is meant to explain the way in which the tragedies of the 1559 *Mirror* were composed. And this is to some extent the case, for all of the tragedies are written for performance at a level of high seriousness. But the light-hearted way in which the characters generally treat the tragedies they themselves compose and perform to each other is suspicious. They comment on technical matters, and on historical points, but they remain untouched by the *pathos* that the speakers of the tragedies seem to be striving to excite in them.[21] These performances simply fail. Only one poem seems to move them. After hearing the 'strange adventures' of the Earl of Salisbury, the poets fall 'into a dump, inwardly lamenting his woeful destiny' (p.154). But they are brusquely brought back to the task in hand: ' "To what end", quoth one, "muse we so much on this matter?" ' If Baldwin means them as a model of reception, then we would have to assume that he makes very little claim to the affective power of the poems he composed or collected.

Yet even in the intensely pathetic description of York and Rutland, there is perhaps a little mischief. When Baldwin turned away his head, he says: 'methought there came a shrieking voice out of the weasand-pipe [*wind-pipe*] of the headless body'. Are we to take this seriously? It is hard to be sure. It is a striking image, certainly, and its seems to have appealed to Baldwin, for the poet of the tragedy of Lord Clifford emulates it in the following prose:

> as you thought you saw and heard the headless duke speak thorough [*through*] his neck, so suppose you see this lord Clifford all armed save his head, with his breast-plate all gore blood running from his throat, wherein an headless arrow sticketh, through which he saith thus. (p.191)

Once as tragedy, the second time as farce. Clifford's voice has to squeeze its way through a hole in his neck already occupied by a (headless!) bolt. And it is not even as if the other poets *have* seen and heard the Duke of York speak through his weasand-pipe, for the description is delivered by Baldwin-the-Narrator to the Reader, not Baldwin-the-Character to his fellow poets.

Even with the freedom afforded by dreams and visions, the idea that a headless torso should actually speak seems to have been difficult to imagine. The figure of Lord Rochford, in George Cavendish's contemporary *de casibus* sequence, the *Metrical visions*, likewise speaks *sine capite*. His oration ends: 'Behold here my body, but I have lost my head'.[22] To me this sounds a little frivolous, as if Rochford has merely mislaid his head, so blandly does he draw attention to the extraordinary figure he must present to Cavendish. There is a similar awkwardness in the (verse) prologue to the tragedy of the decapitated Irenglass in John Higgins' *First Part of the Mirror for Magistrates* in 1574. When Irenglass's body appears before Higgins-the-Dreamer, and the poet must prepare himself to write his tragedy, he says: 'speech of headless men doth pass my skill'.[23] His spirit-guide, Morpheus, touches the corpse with his mace: 'And suddenly an head on shoulders pight [*placed*]'. It reads like a conjuring trick. There is a definite problem of representation here, I think.[24]

But a more seriously imitated model for Baldwin's tragic body may have come from closer to home than Lindsay's tragedy of Beaton. One poem which must have given Baldwin particular food for thought when it arrived was Chaloner's 'Richard II'. In the 1559 edition, where Chaloner's identity is suppressed, the anonymous character who is about to perform Richard's complaint introduces himself as its speaker thus:

> imagine, Baldwin, that you see him all to-bemangled, with blue wounds, lying pale and wan, all naked upon the cold stones in Paul's church, the people standing round about him, and making his moan in this sort. (p.111)

Here we have a good example of the way Baldwin's prose elaborate details he found in the poem handed in to him by another poet. Chaloner's Richard says nothing of St Paul's church, which is a detail added from the chronicles by Baldwin, probably taken from Fabyan's Chronicle.[25] Chaloner's source seems to have been Froissart, who relates in his own chronicle how Richard's corpse was displayed in Cheapside: 'thither came in and out mo [*more*] than 20,000 persons, men and women, to see him where as he lay his head on a black cushion, and his visage open'.[26] We note also that the description given by the anonymous performer of the tragedy of the Earl of Warwick also asks the others to help them 'see' Warwick in St Paul's:

> And therefore imagine that you see this earl lying with his brother in Paul's church in his coat armour, with such a face and countenance as he beareth in portraiture over the door in Paul's, at the going down to Jesus Chapel fro the south end of the choir stairs, and saying as followeth. (p.205)

Baldwin's imagination seems to be pointing in the direction of a different *mise en scène* than the room where the poets meet here, too. The *ekphraseis* are so similar that one even wonders if he at one point had an alternative scenario in mind.

John Higgins seems to have been thinking in the same direction with the crypt-like scene of his encounter with the ancient British dead in *The First Part*. Like Lindsay and like Baldwin, in the dream episode of the 1559 *Mirror*, Higgins' imagination is fired by tragical matter when he reads *A Mirror for Magistrates*. He sleeps and dreams that Morpheus guides him to a 'goodly hall | At the end thereof there seemed a duskish aisle'.[27] From this aisle stagger the dead, many mutilated, as is the first of them, Albanact: 'A person tall, wide wounds in breast that bare [*bore*]'.[28] The strange meeting in a subterranean setting is also used by Thomas Sackville in his own abortive *Mirror* sequence. Sackville sends his dream-visionary avatar, with Sorrow as guide, down into the Virgilian underworld. This is where he meets the Duke of Buckingham, and would have met many others in the same place if he had continued with his project. Morpheus takes Richard Robinson, in a dream, to listen to the complaints of the fallen in an intriguingly Dantesque Hell in *The Reward of Wickedness* (1574). In fact, any place connected with the final resting place of the dead would serve rather well for this kind of frame-narrative. But a church full of tombs is a very good location, and it certainly appealed to the fifteenth-century French poet, Georges Chastelain, when he located *Le Temple de Bocace* in just such a setting.[29] Here, too, we see another glimpse of a road not taken by the *Mirror* – or not *yet* taken.

Chaloner's 'Richard II' may also have nudged Baldwin in the direction of the untragic body. In Froissart, we learn that there were different responses to the sight of Richard's body:

> Some had on him pity, and some none, but said he had long ago deserved death. Now consider well, ye great lords, kings, dukes, earls, barons and prelates, and all men of great linage and puissance. See and behold how the fortunes of this world are marvellous and turn diversely.[30]

Now Richard II to Baldwin:

> Behold my hap. See how the seely rout
> Do gaze on me and each to other say:
> 'Lo, how the power, the pride, and rich array
> Of mighty rulers lightly fade away.
> The king which erst kept all the realm in doubt
> The veriest rascal now dare check and lout.
> What mould be kings made of but carrain clay?
> Behold his wounds, how blue they be about,
> Which, while he lived, thought never to decay.' (p.112)

There is no pity here. The 'seely rout' look on dispassionately and repeat what Chaloner had read in Froissart. They are 'philosophical' in that they calmly generalise a moral maxim from the case in hand. But they still envisage mockery from the 'veriest rascal'.

Now let us compare two much more sharply contrasted attitudes towards the *pathos* of the wounded corpse. The first is a serious treatment of dismembered and mutilated bodies *en masse*: William Patten's *Expedition into Scotland of the Duke of Somerset* (1548). The text is particularly interesting in this respect, as it mentions the activities of Chaloner and Ferrers, both of whom took part in the campaign. After the rout of the Scots at Musselburgh, the field was full of carnage:

> dead corpses, lying dispersed abroad, some their legs off, some but hought [*wounded*] and left lying half-dead, some quite thrust through the body, others the arms cut off, divers their necks half asunder, many their heads cloven, of sundry the brains pashed [*bashed*] out, some other again their heads quite off, with a thousand other kinds of killing.[31]

As Patten notes, this is a 'pitiful sight', and one, moreover, which Baldwin may have 'seen' if he had read this book by a friend of his friends.

Now we turn to Lucian's *Menippus*, a Greek satirical dialogue from the second century AD, in which the Cynic philosopher of that name visits the underworld and inspects the state of the dead. A fragmentary text of an early English translation of this text contains part of the philosophical anti-hero's description of his journey to the underworld, where he finds himself on Charon's ferry amongst a crowd of men who seemed to have come 'from some battle or field'.[32] Their bodies are in pieces: 'Some lacked the head, some lacked the ear, | The thigh was stricken off of another; | He lacked one member, he lacked another'. The tone here is neutral; but it is still perhaps slightly disquieting to think of these mutilated bodies, so similar to those described with tragic seriousness by Patten, quietly lined up in Charon's ferry like passengers on a boat trip.

Menippus, of course, is the founder of the so-called 'Menippean satire'. In its simplest form, Menippean satire is a mixture (*satura*) of prose and verse – just like the sequence of texts published as *A Mirror for Magistrates* between 1559 and 1587. In Lucian, the incorporation of lines of epic and tragedy into colloquial prose is used to make sport of the pompousness of the former. For example, at the start of *Menippus*, the hero lards his speech with scraps of Euripides and has to be asked to stop by his interlocutor: 'O thou tragedian [*tragōidōn*], I pray thee heartily, | Leave off thy versifying [*tōn iambeiōn*], | Speak … openly and plainly'.[33] The abrupt transitions from tragic verse to colloquial prose in the *Mirror* also provide occasions for this kind of stylistic irony. But Menippean satire is also genuinely satirical, in that it mocks at pretensions to grandeur of all kinds. Menippus reports how he sees great tyrants in the underworld reduced to cobbling shoes, or selling fish, or giving lessons in grammar. As for the passengers on Charon's boat, they are headed for the pile of bones that is the final destination of the great as well as the small. Menippus reports sardonically: 'It was not at all easy, though, to tell them apart, for all, without exception, become precisely alike when their bones are bare'.[34] We might also note that there is a tragic version of the same *topos* in Patten: 'there found we our horses slain, all gored and hewn, and our men so ruefully gashed, and mangled in the head specially, as not one by the face could be known who he was'.[35]

It is but a step from Menippus's philosophically superciliously attitude towards the great and the powerful to the less emphatic mischief of Baldwin's attitude to some of the imaginary speakers of the 1559 *Mirror*. These speakers routinely confess to ambition in their earthly existence; and we might note how the spirit of emulation still drives some of them. Suffolk, for example, still wants to be top, even it means being at the very bottom: 'Was never man so served, I think, but I.' The speakers all want to be *recognised*. Yet all of them are so similar, precisely because they are *all* ambitiously emulative. When the speakers are impersonated by the performers, they are made even more unrecognisable by the fact that they do *not* appear to the company of poets, but must be represented by means of a *pathos*. And, even here, Baldwin seems to have been mischievously attracted to distinguishing between the images of the corpses so represented by extreme or eccentric details, such as squeaking wind-pipes or the smell of wine.

Do we take the *Mirror for Magistrates* too seriously? Or, to put it another way: Do we neglect its unserious elements? I think we do; and it is because we have not yet fully grasped the work – in its original form – as a prosimetrical totality. In fact, the *Mirror* has suffered the same fate as some of its subjects: it has been *dismembered*. When we study the tragedies in isolation from the prose, they look very serious indeed. But when we restore them to their proper places in the work as a whole, they start to look a little less serious. The effect is similar to that which might be produced by surrounding a sober portrait of some stern-faced magistrate with a frame carved with frolicking nymphs and smiling satyrs. This is all Baldwin's doing, of course, and one wonders what his collaborators must have thought of the way their poems were handled in the old *Memorial* and *Mirror*. And we, too, should wonder about the significance of Baldwin's playful and puzzling format.

Notes

1 Jim Ellis, 'Embodying Dislocation: *A Mirror for Magistrates* and Property Relations', *RQ* 53 (2000), 1032–53, at p.1033.
2 For the readership of *The Fall of Princes*, see A. S. G. Edwards, 'Selections from Lydgate's *Fall of Princes*', *The Library* (5 ser.) 26 (1971), 337–42.

3 Ellis, 'Embodying Dislocation', p.1033.
4 See Sherri Geller, 'Editing Under the Influence of the Standard Textual Hierarchy: Misrepresenting *A Mirror for Magistrates* in the Nineteenth- and Twentieth-Century Editions', *TC* 2 (2007), 43–77, at pp.51–5.
5 See Geller, 'Editing Under the Influence', and Jessica Winston, '*A Mirror for Magistrates* and Public Political Discourse in Elizabethan England', *SP* 101 (2004), 381–400.
6 Meredith Skura, '*A Mirror for Magistrates* and the Beginnings of English Autobiography', *ELR* 36 (2006), 26–56, at p.40.
7 Aristotle, *Poetics*, ed. and trans. S. H. Butcher (1895; 4th ed. London: Macmillan, 1925), p.43 (1452b).
8 Elizabeth S. Belfiore, *Tragic Pleasures: Aristotle on Plot and Emotion* (Princeton University Press, 2014), p.136.
9 Heinrich Lausberg, *Handbook of Literary Rhetoric: A Foundation for Literary Study*, ed. David E. Orton and R. Dean Anderson, trans. Matthew T. Bliss Annemiek Jansen, and David E. Orton (Leiden: Brill, 1998), § 810.
10 Wolfgang Clemen, *English Tragedy Before Shakespeare: The Development of Dramatic Speech*, trans. T. S. Dorsch (London: Methuen, 1961), pp.226–7.
11 Quintilian, *The Orator's Education*, ed. and trans. Donald A. Russell (Cambridge: Harvard University Press, 2001), 9.2.26.
12 Lausberg, *Handbook*, § 809.
13 Lausberg, *Handbook*, § 1091.
14 Donald Jellerson, 'The Spectral Historiopoetics of the *Mirror for Magistrates*', *JNR* 2 (2010), 54–71, at p.65.
15 Quintilian, *Education*, 9.2.27.
16 Jennifer Richards, 'Transforming *A Mirror for Magistrates*', in Margaret Healy and Tom Healy, eds, *Renaissance Transformations: The Making of English Writing (1500–1650)* (Edinburgh University Press), pp.48–63, at p.55, citing Scott C. Lucas, '"Let none such office take, save he that can for right his prince forsake": *A Mirror for Magistrates*, Resistance Theory and the Elizabethan Monarchical Republic', in John F. McDiamid, ed., *The Monarchical Republic of Early Modern England: Essays in Response to Patrick Collinson* (Aldershot: Ashgate, 2007), pp.91–107, at p.97.
17 Lausberg, *Handbook*, § 762.
18 Phillipe Lejeune, 'The Autobiographical Pact', trans. R. Carter, in Tzvetan Todorov, ed., *French Literary Theory Today: A Reader* (Cambridge University Press; Paris: Editions de la Maison des Sciences de l'Homme: 1982), pp.192–222, at p.198 (translation slightly modified).
19 See the chapter by Scott C. Lucas in this volume.
20 David Lindsay, *The Tragical Death of David Beaton, Bishop of St Andrews* (1548: *ESTC* 15683), image 15.
21 See Mike Pincombe, 'William Baldwin and *A Mirror for Magistrates*', *RS* 27 (2013), 183–98.
22 George Cavendish, *Metrical Visions*, ed. A. S. G. Edwards (Columbia: The University of South Carolina Press for The Newberry Library, 1980), p.41.

23 John Higgins, *The First Part of the Mirror for Magistrates*, in *Parts Added to the Mirror for Magistrates by John Higgins and Thomas Blenerhasset*, ed. Lily B. Campbell (Cambridge University Press, 1946), pp.1–349, at p.209.
24 Cavendish almost solves the problem with the last of his speakers, Lady Jane Grey, who, though headless, manages to communicate her story 'by signs, without words' (*Metrical Visions*, p.130).
25 Robert Fabyan, *Fabyan's Chronicle* (1533: *ESTC* 10660), image 358.
26 Jean Froissart, *The Third and Fourth Book of Sir John Froissart of the Chronicles of England*, trans. John Bourchier, Lord Berners (1525: *ESTC* 11379), image 333.
27 Higgins, *Mirror*, pp.43–4.
28 Higgins, *Mirror*, p.46.
29 See Henry Ansgar Kelly, *Chaucerian Tragedy* (Cambridge: D. S. Brewer/ Boydell & Brewer, 1997), p.262.
30 Froissart, *Chronicle*, image 333.
31 William Patten, *The Expedition into Scotland of the Most Worthily Fortunate Prince, Edward, Duke of Somerset* (1548: *ESTC* 19476.5), image 105.
32 Lucian, *Menippus*, trans. anon. (1534: *ESTC* 16895), image 3; cf. *Menippus; or: The Descent into Hades*, in *Lucian*, trans. A. M. Harmon (London: Heinemann/ New York: G. P. Putnam's Sons, 1925), iv, pp.71–110, at p.91.
33 Lucian, *Menippus* (1534), image 1; (1925), p.75.
34 Lucian, *Menippus* (1925), p.97.
35 Patten, *Expedition*, image 113.

CHAPTER 4

Reading and listening to William Baldwin
Jennifer Richards

William Baldwin is a man of a mystery. It is easier to say what we don't know about him than what we do. We don't know when he was born, nor are we sure when he died: 'in or before 1563', says the entry in the *ODNB*.[1] We don't know where he was from, although it is possible that he was of Welsh descent. We don't know where he went to school; nor do we know if he went to university. 'Baldwin may have supplicated the regents of Oxford University in 1533 for a degree and entered service as a schoolmaster', says John N. King, although he quickly adds that 'this too cannot be confirmed'.[2]

Yet, the few things we do know about him have been enough for Scott C. Lucas to build a picture of the literary strategies of this most popular of mid-Tudor writers. It is thought, for instance, that he worked as a corrector for the Reformation printer Edward Whitchurch, who, with Richard Grafton, oversaw the publication of the Matthews Bible (Antwerp, 1537) and the printing of the first edition of the Great Bible (1539) and the first editions of *The Book of Common Prayer* (1549, 1552), as well as ABCs and catechisms for children.[3] We also know that when Whitchurch retired, perhaps to avoid persecution under Mary I in 1553, as Lucas proposes, that Baldwin continued to work in the same shop for its new owner, 'a scrivener named John Wayland, a religious conservative who enjoyed the favour of Mary's government'.[4] We know this if we read Baldwin's account of the origins of this work in one of the prefaces, 'A Briefe Memorial of sundrye Unfortunate Englishe men', to his best known print publication, *A Myrroure for Magistrates* (1559), alongside John Wayland's note on his publishing plans, 'The Prynter to the Reader', in John Lydgate's translation of *The Fall of Prynces* (1554), to which the original *Myrroure* was meant to be appended.[5]

Baldwin's professional life during a decade of political and religious turmoil, the 1550s, goes some way to explain the difficulties of the *Myrroure*, a text which, as Lucas rightly observes, has been all but abandoned by literary critics who find it lacks a clear sense of purpose.⁶ Indeed, the *Myrroure* is a complex work. For a start, the 1559 edition, to which I turn at the end of this chapter, has two prefaces, likely written by Baldwin at different times, and these orientate the reader in different ways. The first is dedicated 'To the nobilitye and all other in office', and it makes the *Myrroure* a work of admonition, leading with a memorable moral-political saying, which is marked with inverted commas (diples) in the margin: 'Well is that realme governed, in which the ambicious desyer not to beare office.'⁷ The second, titled 'A Briefe Memorial', perhaps surviving from the suppressed earlier edition (1554–5), emphasises instead that this is a 'multivocal collection'.⁸ Each one of its nineteen tragedies is spoken in the first person by a different fallen 'magistrate', composed by one of seven collaborators. One of these collaborators is already known to us: Baldwin. The only other collaborator who is named in this preface is George Ferrers, and he is quoted at length proposing that they should begin where John Lydgate's *The Fall of Prynces* left off, 'whiche was about the ende of king Edwarde the thirdes raigne'.⁹ Other names are revealed in later editions, including Thomas Chaloner, the translator in 1549 of Erasmus's mock-oration, *Moriae Encomium*, and the author of Richard II's narration, which I will discuss later.

Lucas offers one way of making sense of this 'multivocality'. The sympathies of Baldwin, an 'evangelical editor', he explains, lie with Whitchurch, who was 'a leading producer of evangelical literature' during the reign of the King Edward VI (1547–53).¹⁰ His convictions, he proposes, were unknown to the more conservative Wayland, although they were apparently known to Stephen Gardiner, who suppressed the first edition of a *Myrroure*, titled *A Memorial of suche Princes, as since the tyme of kyng Richard the seconde, have been unfortunate in the Realme of Englande* (c.1554–5). It is during this difficult period, Lucas surmises, that Baldwin learned how to become a covert controversialist. He established 'two contexts for reading the *Memorial* tragedies, one overt but actually deflecting and misleading, and the second much less widely interpretable but highly significant for the intended audience to whom it spoke'. In short, Baldwin sought to mislead Marian magistrates while communicating to evangelical readers his commitment to the '"godly" ideals of Edward VI's reign' and 'his support for free expression of potentially uncomfortable political commentary in print'.¹¹

Literary scholars have long acknowledged Baldwin's confessional identity, and there is convincing evidence to suggest that he became a minister in or shortly before 1559.¹² It is also clear that the *Myrroure* is a political work, although in what way is less obvious, because the two prefaces point us in different directions.¹³ Lucas has done more than any other recent scholar to try to think through Baldwin's possible religio-political allegiances, and his insights are suggestive. The claim that Mary I's judiciary is being covertly criticised in the first tragedy of Robert Tresilian by Ferrers seems right to me.¹⁴ He also makes an interesting case to support the idea that the tragedy of 'Humfrey Duke of Gloucester', intended for the 1554 edition but not printed until 1578, was meant to reflect on the protestant hero Edward Seymour, Duke of Somerset.¹⁵ Yet, all the same, there are a few additional details we could add to our portrait of Baldwin to inform our reading of his work, including of the *Myrroure*.

Indeed, there is one other verifiable detail, the likelihood that Baldwin was employed as an actor, a deviser of entertainments and a propmaker at court during the Christmas season of 1552/3 under the Master of the King's Pastimes, Ferrers. This detail is documented in the Revels Accounts for this Christmas period, and it is also written into Baldwin's anti-Catholic fiction, *Beware the Cat* (1570; 1584; ms. 1553). Its preface explains the 'real' context for this fabulous tale thus: 'Baldwin' (G.B. in the text) and Ferrers heard the tale from Master Streamer while they were organising Christmas interludes for King Edward VI.¹⁶ Might this detail lead us to a simpler explanation of the *Myrrour*'s multivocality? I suggest that it would; it reveals a Baldwin who is more playful and more knowledgeable about rhetorical affect than does the one-dimensional version of him as an underground reformer.

There is more that we might add to flesh out this portrait. It is not known if Baldwin went to university, but he certainly would have gone to grammar school, and it is there that he would have learned his craft both as a writer and a performer of multivocal texts. Education in the Renaissance, like the medieval period, was oral. We might do well to imagine Baldwin engaging in the reading activities designed to help him become a fluent reader, writer, *and* speaker of Latin: matching emotions to types of voice; varying the intonation and the meaning of Latin sentences as he pronounced them; uttering 'every dialogue' that he was asked to read – whether by Aesop, Terence, or Virgil – in a 'lively' fashion as if he 'were the persons which did speake in that dialogue'. We might also imagine him putting this knowledge to use in Latin written exercises like 'prosopopoeia', 'a certaine Oracion made by voice, and lamentable imitacion, upon the state of any one', which he may also have been asked to perform 'as if *ex animo* in good earnest, with all contention and vehemencie'.¹⁷

Finally, we might imagine him honing these skills in English outside the schoolroom not just in the entertainments organised by Ferrers, but also in Whitchurch's print shop, one of the places, I have already noted, where the performance scripts for the new liturgy were printed. As a corrector he would have read these texts aloud as they were prepared for the press.[18] And as a reformer, he would have welcomed the Prayer book's new emphasis on listening *and* understanding. For too many years, Thomas Cranmer complained in its preface, the church service in England was read in Latin so that the people 'heard with their ears only: and their hearts, spirit and mind have not been edified thereby'.[19] Baldwin's interest in performance would have carried over to secular works too. Since he was employed by Wayland in 1554, he likely also read aloud some of Lydgate's *The Fall of Prynces*. If he did, he surely would have noted the effect of the tragic narrations on the poet who penned them. In the final narration, the historical moment at which Baldwin's *Myrroure* takes over, we read that King John of France tells the tale of his defeat by King Edward III to 'Bochas', as well as Lydgate's comment on this. The latter thinks Boccaccio has shown too much 'affection', overlooking John's faults: 'Of right witnesse every croniculer| Should in his wrytyng make no exception,| Indifferently convey his matter| Nor be perciall of none affection'.[20]

I sketch out this particular soundscape of Baldwin's day-to-day to take more account of a feature of his writing to which he so insistently draws our attention, and which we just as insistently ignore: its vocality. By 'vocality' I don't mean only that Baldwin is experimenting with the speaking voice in writing. Rather, I mean that he imagines the effect of writing when it is enlivened by the speaking voice. Baldwin foregrounds this in the *Myrroure* in the frame between the tragedies in which the collaborators are represented responding to the tales they have heard. It is not that this feature is ignored by scholars, but it is not sufficiently noted. It should be the starting point of any reading because it complicates how we make its moral-political content meaningful.[21] To help to make this dramatic feature of the *Myrroure* more central to how we read it, I begin with one of Baldwin's earlier writings in which his concern with the voice cannot be ignored, *Beware the Cat*.

The visible voice of Beware the Cat

I am not the first to notice that William Baldwin is preoccupied in his fiction with reading as oral and aural as well as visual. We only have to recall the scene-setting of *Beware the Cat* to recognise 'the fluidity between aural and visual experiences of texts' for Baldwin.[22] This oral tale is first told in a bedchamber. Four men, George Ferrers, his astronomer Mr Willot and divine, Master Gregory Streamer and G.B. [Gulielmus Baldwin] are at court at Christmas. 'Baldwin', and Ferrers have been employed to organise the Christmas interludes for the King. In a conversation with Streamer, 'Baldwin' makes clear his objection to one of the planned interludes, 'Esop's Crowe', dismissing the conceit because he does not think it is 'Comicall to make either speechlesse things to speeke: or brutish things to common reasonably'. Indeed, he goes further, arguing that it is 'uncomely … to bring [animals] in lively parsonages to speake, doo, reason, and allege authorites out of authours'. Yet, Streamer holds 'the contrary parte', and he promises to share with the company the tale we are about to read: his encounter with cats who could speak.[23]

The tale 'Baldwin' transcribes is very odd. There is a rambling opening, which locates Streamer in a friend's house in St Martin's Lane and, more specifically, 'in a Chamber hard by the Printing house' where he is busy correcting the proofs of his 'Greeke Alphabets'.[24] Streamer tells his companions at the fireside of the noise that cats are making outside his chamber at night-time. This prompts one of the company to tell an Irish tale of the death of the king of the cats, Grimalkin, and of the strange behaviour of one kitling when she heard the news. There are other tales that follow, all of which are considered as proof either that cats have reason or, on the contrary, that they can be bewitched. This discussion prompts Streamer to listen again later that night, noting the variation in the cats' miaows, and this leads him to prepare a magical potion to purge his ears so he can understand what they are saying. The potion is successful. It turns out that Streamer is right: the cats are communing with each other. They have gathered for the trial of Mouse-slayer, who has refused to mate with Catch-rat, so breaking one of the holy laws of cats: that females are forbidden 'to refuse any males not exceeding the number of x. in a night'.[25] In her defence, Mouse-slayer is required to declare her life since 'kitling hood' so her judges can 'perceive how I behaved me'.[26]

Odder still is the way the tale is shared with us. It is spoken by Streamer, who is in turn recalling the stories told by many other incidental speakers, including Mouse-slayer. These tales have been transcribed by 'Baldwin', who aims to make the collection look more 'book like' by adding marginal glosses, prefatory material, and a moralising epigraph, and by organising the rambling story into three chapters or orations.[27] If you happen to read it in William Ringler's and Michael Flachmann's modern spelling edition of 1988 – as most scholars do – rather than in the only surviving early print edition of 1584, or the 1847 manuscript transcription of the now lost first edition of 1570 held in the British Library, then you read it through yet another editorial frame and set of assumptions.[28] Add to this the fact that in the fiction the text is described as being in a state of revision; that is, the manuscript is being prepared for print. 'Baldwin' asks the dedicatee, John Young, to pass the manuscript to Streamer so he can 'peruse it before the printing, and amend it if in any point I have mistaken him'.[29] Rachel Stenner summarises the position that the reader finds herself in thus: she is reading a 'still unprinted document, a manuscript representation of an oral tale, that has been sent to its originator for checking and correction before going to press'.[30]

The interplay between these three different modes of communication – speech, writing, print – makes this a challenging work, and indeed it is hard to identify a clear line of argument. It is only recently, I would suggest, that we have recognised this. *Beware the Cat*, John N. King wrote confidently in 1982, is an attack on Catholicism and its 'oral traditions'. 'Baldwin's written texts', he argues, 'which are labelled by Streamer as "hearsay", are more tangible than the bewildering oral tradition' the latter offers 'by way of firsthand experience and "proof"' that cats can talk.[31] More than two decades later, though, it is accepted that Baldwin is challenging the authority of the written word as well, and that communication is his theme. Baldwin shows no confidence whatsoever, Thomas Betteridge argues, in the 'power' of writing or print to 'carry a radical reforming message throughout the country'.[32] Meanwhile, Stenner suggests that 'writing by hand' is just as much one of this work's 'objects of satire': the handwritten text, she observes, can be put 'to suspect uses'.[33] Jane Griffiths is a little more optimistic. She focuses on the marginal glosses, noting that, though they appear to be 'a diligent printer's attempt to make his text more accessible to the reader', in fact they reveal 'Baldwin's' 'inability to discriminate'. The disjunction between text and gloss, however, is designed to make us independent and critical readers.[34]

All of these literary scholars, though, quietly assume a silent reader. In so doing, they overlook an additional complication: the possibility that the text – manuscript or print – is read aloud, or, if it is not actually read aloud, then that the reader projects aurally onto the text.[35] The possibility either way is signalled in 'The Epistle Dedicatory'. 'Baldwin' acknowledges that he is aware that its dedicatee, John Young, had really wanted Ferrers to report the story to him, and he modestly recognises that he cannot match his skill as a storyteller. Still, he believes that he has represented Streamer's speaking voice in his prose, boasting that 'I dout not but that he and M[aster]. willot shal in the reading think they hear M[aster]. Streamer speak, and he him self in the like action[n], shal dout whether he speaketh or readeth'.³⁶ It is not just Streamer's voice, however, that we are being invited to 'hear', but the voices of the cats and many other shady characters. Meanwhile, 'Baldwin's' unease with *prosopopoeia* – the technical term for making 'speechlesse things to speeke' – is passed onto us.

The voice is one of the central themes of *Beware the Cat*. We are asked not just to read a series of oral tales and to imagine a sociable oral culture – gentlemen sitting at the fireside telling each other stories – but also to think about the 'voice' as a mode of communication and a means to interpretation. The catalyst for the story is the noise of cats on adjacent rooftops. Their miaowing is so melodious that Streamer is led to believe they are speaking to one another:

> they observed no Musicall cordes neither Diatessero[n], Diapente, nor Diapason, and yet I ween I lye, for one Cat groning as a Beare dooth, when Doges be let slip to him, throwled out so lowe and loud a base, that in comparison of an other Cat which crying like a yung Childe squeiled out the shriking treble: it mought be wel counted a double Diapason.³⁷

Streamer is intrigued. He finds a room with a window overlooking the rooftop so he can hear and see the cats. He identifies a large grey cat, 'the cheef', and a second cat (Mouse-slayer) who 'mewed continewally', declaring 'some matter'. 'I was straight caught with such a desire', he admits, 'to knowe what she had said: that I could not sleep of all that night, but lay devising by what meanes I might learn to understand them'. He decides to make a potion to clear his ears, and discovers a recipe in the section 'Si vis voces avium intelligere' (if you wish to understand the voices of birds) in Albertus Magnus's *De virtutibus animalium*.³⁸

With the help of this recipe, he makes pills for his ears to sharpen his hearing so that he can distinguish between noise which, he explains, is created by the moving air of 'dead' things like 'windes, waters, trees, carts, falling of stones', and voices, which are the 'breth of living creatures'.³⁹ These pills in turn embody the physical voice in several ways. The ingredients include the organs of voice and hearing, the 'tungs' and 'eares' of various animals,⁴⁰ the power of which has been released by the 'breath' of Streamer, who says the following magic/nonsense words aloud as he kills them: '"Shavol swashmeth, gorgona liscud"'.⁴¹ Streamer explains that he then 'fryde' the pellets 'in good oyle olife' – a detail I always enjoy – 'and layd the[m] hot to mine eares', keeping them in place 'til nine a clock at night, which holpe exceedingly to comfort my understanding power'.⁴² He immediately hears 'a loud voice' crying 'what Isegrim', and rightly deduces that this is one of the cats speaking.[43] Thereupon he is overwhelmed by the noises he can hear within a radius of one hundred miles until he has the good sense to stop his ears, at which point he can settle down to listen.

Baldwin is clearly sceptical of the power ascribed to the voice. Having Streamer pronounce the nonsense words '"Shavol swashmeth, gorgona liscud"' is not enough; 'Baldwin', the listening reader, must diligently add in the margin this superfluous note: 'Albertus saith if a man when he prepareth any Medicin tell alowde why he maketh it: it wil be of more force.'[44] The satire no doubt is directed at Catholicism and its 'oral traditions', just as King proposed. The bawd's tale – and the tales related in the first oration – are reminiscent of late medieval stories that attribute supernatural properties to voice, like the 'well known tale of a mother', recalled by C. M. Woolgar, who carelessly cursed her daughter because she had displeased her. The mother's spoken words – 'Þe Deyvl com on Þe' – had 'a literal effect', Woolgar notes, 'her passion reflecting that of her soul, speaking directly to the Devil', who then spirited the daughter away.[45] Yet, Baldwin's object of satire is not *only* medieval or Catholic oral traditions. We should remember that the anti-Catholic pronouncements in *Beware the Cat*, of which there are many, are made by a fool, Streamer, and his naïve auditor, 'Baldwin'; and we should also recall that the attribution of special powers to the voice had its Reformation equivalents. Defenders of the established church like Richard Hooker would eventually complain that the Puritans set too much store by 'accidentals': voice and gesture.[46]

Baldwin's awareness of the voice, I suggested earlier, would have been a product of his training, his working life, and his Protestantism. We need to take account of the fact that he would have been trained to think about vocal affect at school, and that he was committed both as a reformer *and* printer to the production of texts that understood that salvation was dependent on aural comprehension. Yet the voice is a tricky means to comprehension, not just because of the risk of mishearing but also because it communicates emotion. One of the ways that Baldwin alerts us to this latter danger – and trains us to be discriminating listening readers – is by exploring the effects of *prosopopoeia* on the reader inside and outside his fiction.

Prosopopoeia, the 'speaking figure' as Gavin Alexander calls it, helps us to understand 'the creation of character', and it involves, in its most basic form, 'a simple trick of grammar that personifies something inanimate'.[47] It's a useful term for literary scholars to know because it helps us to distinguish clearly between the author and persona when we are reading. Yet, *prosopopoeia* is also a figure of address, one that 'happens', Gavin Alexander acknowledges, citing Quintilian, 'when readers perform the voices that writers have created'.[48] (On this view, all reading aloud in the first person is *prosopopoeia*.) The figure is the same but the focus is now on the reader, not the author, and on the act of voicing rather than silent reading. The effect of the figure also changes. When someone – a real reader *or* a character in a text – performs the voice of a character created by a writer, the relationship between the persona and the speaker (or singer) is blurred. Often this blurring is usefully revealing. So Alexander cites the example of Desdemona singing the words of the jilted maid Barbary in Shakespeare's *Othello*: ' "The poor soul sat sighing by a sycamore tree." ' When she sings these words she identifies with the maid. Here, the 'possibility of sharing emotion and experience', Alexander argues, is 'both therapeutic and heuristic; the performer discovers something about herself by comparing her identity to that of another, and by putting on a mask is able to express herself more eloquently than by remaining in her own person'.[49] Yet sometimes the blurring between speaker and persona is confusing, even troubling; for instance, when the voice the reader breathes life into belongs to an untrustworthy narrator.

We are given a very good example of the dangers of *prosopopoeia* in Baldwin's third oration: Mouse-slayer's recollection of a double conversion, which Streamer overhears. The first is the transformation of a virtuous, married lady into a cat. This is an elaborate fiction told by a bawd – and recounted by Mouse-slayer – that succeeds in persuading another virtuous wife 'to co[m]it whordome'.[50] This second act of conversion involves several different kinds of performance and lots of tears to soften the lady's heart: the tears of the bawd who pretends that it is her daughter who was turned into a cat; the weeping daughter-cat (Mouse-slayer, who has been fed a heavy dose of mustard, causing her to cry); and the tears of the lady once she has read a fake letter handed to her by the bawd. It is this letter, shared by the illiterate bawd, which breaks the lady's resolution so that she agrees to fulfil her suitor's 'lust'.

I would suggest that to understand this moment of conversion – how it is that an unquestionably virtuous lady becomes a whore – we need to understand the letter not only as a literary artefact or document but also as an example of performed *prosopopoeia* that blurs the distinction between the reader (the lady) and the speaker (the fake rejected lover). The letter is an 'Oracion made by [the] voice' of the fake unrequited lover. Indeed, it represents his voice visibly, substituting for his physical presence. It is full of the 'aural' patterns that 'speak' to an addressee: 'Cursed be the woful time wherin mutuall loove first mixed the masse of my miserable carcasse.

Curssed be the houre that ever the fatall destinies have ought for me purveyed...'⁵¹ Meanwhile, the curse/prayer he pronounces is voiced outside the letter too. 'I besech (I say) the just Gods', he writes, 'that eyther they chaunge that honest stony hart or els disfigure that faire merciless favour'. Two days later a mysterious 'voice', the origin of which is uncertain, 'cried a lowd, ah flinty hart repent thy crueltie', and the daughter is indeed disfigured. My point is that it is this letter, 'read' by the lady, possibly silently, aurally projecting on to the page or, just as likely aloud since Mouse-slayer is eavesdropping, that initiates her conversion from faithful wife to adulteress. On reading it, this lady seems to discover 'something about herself': her cruelty. In fact, she only thinks she does because she has identified with the fake hard-hearted daughter *and* the fake suitor. When she returns the letter to the bawd, she does so 'with much to doo to with holde her swelling tears', expressing sorrow equally for both the daughter *and* the suitor.⁵²

It is not just the lady in the story who is confused by what she reads; however, nor is it only the act of performing that proves complicating. A silent reading that fails to recognise 'voice' is also susceptible. The difficulty of this work is the way in which one voice blurs into another: Streamer's voice is also Mouse-slayer's, which is also the lady's, which is also the fake lover's. All of this is transcribed by 'Baldwin', who tries – not entirely successfully – to bring some order to this multivocal tale, making it look 'book like'. One of the ways he does this is by adding a gloss to key points and moral sayings for the reader. Often the gloss is helpful. Who can disagree with one of the notes on the bawd's tale: 'Evil communication confoundeth good vertues'? This is – or surely should be – the moral of the tale we have just read. However, most of the time 'Baldwin's' gloss is downright misleading, and it adds to the confusion of voices. Indeed, 'Baldwin' often seems oblivious to who is speaking, and, as he transcribes and then edits further, all voices blur into one. Above the marginal note I have just noted is another: 'All extremities are to be forsaken'.⁵³ In this instance, the saying is excerpted from a speech whose source is the bawd, and she is persuading the virtuous lady that committing adultery is a moral action. How did it come to pass, I ask, that 'Baldwin', so sceptical of *prosopopoeia* at the start of Streamer's tale, obligingly marks the sayings that are uttered by the bawd (and Mouse-slayer) in the passage below?

> Whereupon I gather that though God would have us keep our faith to our husbands yet rather then any should dye for our sakes, we should not make any conscience to save theire lives. For it fareth in this poi[n]t as it doth in all other: for as all extremities are vices: so it is a vice, as apeereth plainly by

the punishment of my daughter to be to extream in honesty, chastety, or any other kinde of vertue.⁵⁴

Finally, this conundrum is shared by the actual reader of the text. Let's suppose that you read the text aloud, or imagine that you are doing so. After all, 'Baldwin' did boast in his preface that he thinks he has caught Streamer's speaking voice in the text, declaring that the reader may well 'dout whether he speaketh or readeth'. You may indeed share this 'dout' if you attend to the vocal cues on the page of the 1584 edition, printed by Edward Allde, from which I have been quoting. Among these cues I include the text's phonetic spelling: 'throwled' sounds more 'lowe' and 'base', I suggest, than the modern substitution 'trolled' (sang).⁵⁵ We also have 'corde' without the 'h', 'yung' without the 'o', 'dout' without the 'b', and a sounded 'w' in 'continewally' as well as a double 'oo' to lengthen 'do' and a final 'e' to lengthen 'talke' or 'speeke'. (The 'e' at the end of a word, the schoolmaster Richard Mulcaster argues in his discussion of English spelling, lengthens the sound of the vowels in the middle of a word.)⁵⁶ I also include the text's punctuation, added by a compositor in Allde's print shop, which we know was attentive to the pointing of play texts.⁵⁷ In this edition of *Beware the Cat*, it is the use of the colon to prompt a dramatic pause that I would draw to your attention. We can see how this works in the following sentence delivered by the bawd: 'Within two dayes after my sonne in law her husba[n]d dyed sudainly, and within two dayes after as she sate heer with me lamenting his death: a voice cried alowd, ah flinty hart repent thy crueltie, and immediately (o extreme rigor) she was chaunged as you now see her.'⁵⁸ This dramatic pause, followed by a shorter pause or comma after 'alowd', allows for a shift in voice as the real reader breathes life into the curse by reading it aloud.

What is so curious about *Beware the Cat* is that there is no way we can avoid being implicated in this multivocal text. Nor can we ignore the fact that our judgment is being clouded just like 'Baldwin's'. This is what is so brilliant about Baldwin's writing: he makes the reader think about how she is being acted on as she reads aloud (or imagines that she is doing so). This is the same conundrum, I now want to argue, that Baldwin explores in a collection of tragic histories written a year after *Beware the Cat*, and which was printed in a 'lightly revised' form in 1559, *A Myrroure for Magistrates*.⁵⁹

A Myrroure for Magistrates (1559)

The 1559 *Myrroure* has two prefaces, both written by Baldwin, probably at different times. Each of them indicates a different way of reading the work, the one silently and studiously, the other aloud. In the first preface, dedicated 'To the nobilitye and all other in office', Baldwin proposes that the purpose of the work is moral-political, and we are advised to 'reade & marke' the *Myrroure*'s tragic narratives as admonitory examples, noting that bad governors have not 'escaped infamy'.[60] Some Renaissance readers did read the *Myrroure* in this way. In one edition, held by the Bodleian Library, wise sayings are either underlined or highlighted with a trefoil in the margin.[61] However, in the second preface, titled 'A Briefe Memorial', Baldwin tells us more about the inception and composition of the work and suggests a different way that it might be read. He relates that he carried to the first meeting of the *Myrroure*'s collaborators a copy of Lydgate's *The Fall of Prynces* and that all present agreed that they would have to start afresh since, with Lydgate dead, the 'unfortunate' would need a new listener to 'make their mone' to. He also tells us that they agreed that this new listener should be 'Baldwin' himself:

> To make therfore a state mete for the matter, [the collaborators] al agreed that I shoulde usurpe Bochas rowme, and the wretched princes complayne unto me: and tooke upon themselves every man for his parte to be sundrye personages, and in theyr behalfes to bewayle unto me theyr grevous chaunces, hevy destinies, & wofull misfortunes.[62]

This second preface, it is often noted, draws attention in a way that the first preface does not to the unusual dramatic frame that connects the tragedies, in which the collaborators comment on what they have heard.[63] I agree, although I would also note that what it draws attention to first and foremost, and uniquely, is the idea that the fallen protagonists will 'bewayle ... theyr grevous chaunces, hevy destinies, & wofull misfortunes' in the first person to Baldwin. Each narrative, that is, is delivered orally by its author so that what we are reading – aloud or silently – is imagined as a live performance. In short, the tragedies are an example of what Neil Rhodes calls 'speech-writing' and the Tudor schoolmaster, Richard Rainolde, 'eidolopoeia': an oration 'when a dedde manne talketh'. (This is one of the sub-genres of 'ethopoeia' or *prosopopoeia* discussed by Rainolde.)[64] Once we note this, it is difficult to read the *Myrroure* as straightforwardly admonitory. There is no point in marking a wise saying in the margin, even when we are explicitly invited to do so, unless we also take account of who is saying it and why, and think about how their 'mone' affects us.

I will consider one paradigmatic example, although I pick up the broader implications of this way of reading the *Myrroure* in my conclusion.

My example is the tragedy attributed to Chaloner titled 'Howe kynge Richarde the seconde was for his evyll governaunce deposed from his seat, and miserably murdred in prison'. From its title, it would seem to be an admonitory tale, and indeed it is full of wise sayings. The speaker Richard II addresses 'Baldwin' directly, asking him to 'paynt' his 'vicious story' so that others might learn from it.[65] Richard dutifully details the vicious things he did while alive. He listened to 'false Flatterers' rather than wise counsellors; he embezzled money raised from his over-taxed subjects; he was a glutton, living high on the hog; and he overindulged in 'Venus pleasures'. In the annotated copy held by the Bodleian Library, the following sentences – all of them wise – are dutifully underlined:

> Shame sueth sinne, as rayne drops do the thunder.
>
> A king can never imagine ought so bad
> But most about him will perfourme it glad.
>
> And whan a man is falne in froward fate
> Still mischeves light one in anothers pate:

The last four lines of the final stanza are marked with a trefoil in the margin:

> Thus lawles life, to lawles deth ey drawes.
> Wherfore byd Kynges be rulde and rule by right,
> Who wurketh his wil, & shunneth wisedomes sawes
> In flateries clawes, & shames foule pawes shal light.[66]

If we take the advice of Baldwin's first preface then this tragedy must be read as admonitory. Considering the time of its composition, we might suppose that the advice given was originally intended for Mary I, although by 1559, when Mary was long dead, it would have offered a more general message for anyone taking up office.[67] Yet difficulties with this reading remain. How easy is it for us to take Richard II's admonition from the grave when we are listening to him, or rather to 'one of the cumpany', Chaloner, who has elected to 'say sumwhat *for* king Richard' (my italics), and who invites 'Baldwin' to 'imagine … that you see him al to be mangled, with blew woundes, lying pale and wanne al naked upon the cold stones in Paules church'?[68] It is not just that Richard II is a compromised moraliser because of the way he lived his life. We hear this moral tale from the 'mouth' of a sympathiser who makes this usurped king both self-pitying and, I would also suggest, pitiable.

Richard II does not just confess his crimes, reminding us what happens to ambitious men unsuited to high office; he also blames those whom he knows have betrayed him. Chaloner – a master of *prosopopoeia*, as his translation of *Moriae Encomium* attests – allows Richard II's 'voice' in the text to change almost imperceptibly, so that we move from a confession, in which the speaker lists his failings, to a complaint focused on this speaker's sense of betrayal. There is another turn in the story that places Richard II's treacherous servants centre stage. They were later 'Abhorde' by the usurper Henry Bolinbroke, leading them to attempt to reinstate Richard II, only to discover how hard this is: 'Thinges hardly mende, byt may be mared amayne'.[69] It is this self-interested rebellion that leads Henry Bolingbroke, now Henry IV, to despatch 'a traytrous knight … Who *causeles* kild me there agaynst all lawes' (my italics).[70] Is this murder a just punishment or an injustice without cause?

We can see just how confusing this admonitory tale is if we look more closely at the sentences highlighted in the Bodleian Library copy as well as the fictional frame which records the views of the collaborators. This reader, whoever he or she was, has noted the moral advice of the tragedy in its last four lines: that kings should be ruled by 'right'. However, other annotations signal that this reader is taking a different admonition from the mouth of King Richard: that a ruler cannot trust his servants, and that the turning of fortune's wheel is unstoppable (so one can't get back up again easily). It is as if this reader is unsure whether Richard II is the perpetrator or the victim, and this confusion, I suggest, is shared by the collaborators *in* the fiction. Having listened to this 'so wofull a tragedy', as one of them puts it, the collaborators pause to reflect on what they will do next, since they have 'passed through a miserable time full of piteous tragedyes'. What is striking is that they have been rendered a 'silent cumpany', unable to choose the next story to tell. Have they been cast in 'a browne study', 'Baldwin' asks? Have they no 'affeccion' to any of the stories he proposes? We are a long way from the intention of the *Myrroure*, as set out in the first preface.

To explore this privileging and problematising of affect, I have considered Chaloner's tragedy of Richard II as a paradigmatic example. In reading this tragedy in this way, it has not been my intention to argue that it is neither moral nor political. The commonplace that a king should be ruled by the law is just that: a commonplace. There is no reason to assume that Baldwin would have demurred from this conventional view. What I am suggesting, however, is that a moral and political reading involves much more than the marking of particular content and 'sentences'. It also involves a heightened sensitivity to affect, to the ethos and pathos of a speaker, judged against the life he or she lived. This means 'listening' to

Richard II critically, judging what he says alongside the tragedies of his servants. It also means being aware of the effect of the voice on listeners, an effect we have forgotten to look for.

Notes

I would like to thank the Leverhulme Trust, who made possible the research for this chapter.

1. John N. King, 'William Baldwin' in *ODNB*, www.oxforddnb.com.libproxy.ncl.ac.uk/view/article/1171?docPos=1, accessed 8 July 2015. Scott C. Lucas says he died in September 1563 of the plague. See *A Mirror for Magistrates and the Politics of the English Reformation* (Amherst: University of Massachusetts Press, 2009), p.41. The source for this claim is John Stow, Brit Lib. MS Harley 367, fol.3, printed by Charles L. Kingsford, *A Survey of London by John Stow* (Oxford University Press, 1908), 1, xlviii–xlix.
2. Stow, *Survey*, xlviii–xlix.
3. Alex Ryrie, 'Edward Whitchurch', *ODNB*, www.oxforddnb.com/view/article/29233?docPos=1, last accessed 21 June 2015. For the claim that Baldwin worked as a 'corrector', see King, 'William Baldwin'.
4. Lucas, *Mirror*, p.18.
5. William Baldwin, *A Myrroure for Magistrates* (London, 1559), sig. A1^r; Giovanni Boccaccio, *The Fall of Prynces* (London, 1554), verso of title page.
6. Lucas, *Mirror*, p.8.
7. Baldwin, *Myrroure*, sig. ¶2^r.
8. Lucas, *Mirror*, pp.8–11.
9. Baldwin, *Myrroure*, sig. A1^v.
10. Lucas, *Mirror*, p.18.
11. Lucas, *Mirror*, p.50.
12. King, 'William Baldwin'.
13. The *Myrrour*'s first modern editor, privileged the first preface. See Lily B. Campbell, ed., *The Mirror for Magistrates* (Cambridge University Press, 1938).
14. Lucas, *Mirror*, pp.181–9.
15. Lucas, *Mirror*, pp.23–35.
16. William Baldwin, *Beware the Cat*, ed. William A. Ringler, Jr and Michael Flachmann (San Marino, CA: Huntington Library, 1988), p.xvi. Their source for this information is Albert Feuillerat, *Documents Relating to the Revels at Court in the Time of King Edward VI and Queen Mary* (Louvain: Uystpruyst, 1914), pp.89–125.
17. Abraham Fraunce, *The Arcadian Rhetorike* (London, 1588), sigs I2^v–I3^r; John Brinsley, *Ludus Literarius: Or, The Grammar Schoole* (London, 1612), sigs 2E2^v–2E3^{r-v}. Henry Peacham, *The Garden of Eloquence Conteyning the Figures of Grammer and Rhetorick* (London, 1577), sig. D3^r. Richard Rainolde, *A booke called the Foundacion of Rhetorike* (London, 1563), sig. N1^{r-v}.

18 On the role of the corrector, see Adrian Johns, *The Nature of the Book: Print and Knowledge in the Making* (University of Chicago Press, 1998), pp.90–91. See also Terence N. Bowers, 'The Production and Communication of Knowledge in William Baldwin's *Beware the Cat*: Toward a Typographic Culture', *Criticism* 33 (1991), 1–29. Bowers' excellent article is attentive to Baldwin's role in Whitchurch's print shop, though his end is different to mine; he explores arguments for increased literacy and the new emphasis on silent reading and reasoning.
19 Thomas Cranmer, *The Boke of common praier and administration of the Sacramentes, and other Rytes and ceremonies of the Churche, after the use of the churche of Englande* (London, 1547), sig. A2^v.
20 Boccaccio, *Fall of Prynces*, sig. 2G^r.
21 On the way in which *prosopopoeia* complicates historical-moralising in the *Myrroure*, see Jennifer Richards, '*Transforming A Mirror for Magistrates*', in Margaret Healy and Tom Healy, eds, *Renaissance Transformations: The Making of English Writing, 1500–1650* (Edinburgh University Press, 2009); Donald Jellerson, 'The Spectral Historiopoetics of the *Mirror for Magistrates*', *JNR* 2 (2010), www.northernrenaissance.org/the-spectral-historiopoetics-of-the-mirror-for-magistrates/, last accessed 23 July 2015.
22 Heidi Brayman-Hackel, *Reading Material in Early Modern England: Print, Gender and Literacy* (Cambridge University Press, 2005), p.47.
23 William Baldwin, *A maruelous hystory intitulede, beware the cat*, (London, 1584), sigs A4^{r-v}. All citations of *Beware the Cat* are from this edition, unless otherwise stated.
24 Baldwin, *Beware the Cat*, sigs A5^v–A6^v.
25 Baldwin, *Beware the Cat*, sig. E5^r.
26 Baldwin, *Beware the Cat*, sig. D5^r.
27 Baldwin, *Beware the Cat*, sig. A3^r. See Jane Griffiths, *Diverting Authorities: Experimental Glossing Practices in Manuscript and Print* (Oxford University Press, 2014), p.125.
28 Baldwin, *Beware the Cat*, ed. Ringler and Flachmann, pp.xxix–xxx.
29 Baldwin, *A maruelous hystory*, sig. A3^v.
30 Rachel Stenner, 'The Act of Penning in William Baldwin's *Beware the Cat*', *RS* (advance access, 2015), p.344.
31 John N. King, *English Reformation Literature: The Tudor Origins of the Protestant Tradition* (Princeton University Press, 1982), pp.397–8. See also Stephen Gresham, 'William Baldwin: Literary Voice of the Reign of Edward VI', *HLQ* 44 (1981), 101–16; Bowers, 'Production and Communication of Knowledge'.
32 Thomas Betteridge, *Literature and Politics in the English Reformation* (Manchester University Press, 2004), p.115.
33 Stenner, 'The Act of Penning', p.000.
34 Griffiths, *Diverting Authorities*, pp.128–9, 133.
35 Peter Elbow, 'What Do We Mean When We Talk about Voice in Texts?', in Kathleen Blake Yancey, ed., *Voices on Voice: Definitions, Perspectives, Inquiry*

(Urbana, IL: National Council of Teachers of English, 1994), pp.1–35, at pp.4–5.
36 Baldwin, *A Maruelous Hystory*, sig. A3^r.
37 Baldwin, *A Maruelous Hystory*, sig. C1^v.
38 Baldwin, *A Maruelous Hystory*, sigs C2^r–C3^r.
39 Baldwin, *A Maruelous Hystory*, sigs C8^{r-v}.
40 Baldwin, *A Maruelous Hystory*, sig. C6^v.
41 Baldwin, *A Maruelous Hystory*, sig. C4^v.
42 Baldwin, *A Maruelous Hystory*, sig. C6^v.
43 Baldwin, *A Maruelous Hystory*, sig. C7^v.
44 Baldwin, *A Maruelous Hystory*, sig. C4^v.
45 C. M. Woolgar, *The Senses in Late Medieval England* (New Haven: Yale University Press, 2006), p.84.
46 Richard Hooker, *Of the Lawes of Ecclesiasticall Politie Eyght Bookes*, (London, 1593), sig. F2^r.
47 Gavin Alexander, 'Prosopopoeia: The Speaking Figure', in Sylvia Adamson, Gavin Alexander, and Katrin Ettenhuber, eds, *Renaissance Figures of Speech* (Cambridge University Press, 2007), pp.97–112, at p.105.
48 Alexander, 'Prosopopoeia', p.109.
49 Alexander, 'Prosopopoeia', pp.109–10.
50 Baldwin, *A Maruelous Hystory*, sig. E4^r.
51 Baldwin, *A Maruelous Hystory*, sig. E2^r.
52 Baldwin, *A Maruelous Hystory*, sigs E2^v–E3^r.
53 Baldwin, *A Maruelous Hystory*, sig. E3^v.
54 Baldwin, *A Maruelous Hystory*, sig. E3^{r-v}.
55 For this substitution, see Baldwin, *Beware the Cat*, ed. Ringler and Flachmann, p.23.
56 Richard Mulcaster, *The First Part of the Elementarie Which Entreateth Chefelie of the right writing of our English tung* (London, 1582), sig. O4^r.
57 I. R Burrow, '"The peryod of my blisse": Commas, Ends and Utterance in *Solyman and Perseda*', *TC* 8 (2013), 95–120.
58 Baldwin, *Myrroure*, sig. E3^r.
59 Lucas, *Mirror*, p.2.
60 Baldwin, *Myrroure*, sigs ¶2^r–3^r.
61 This is Bodleian Library Wood 328.
62 Baldwin, *Myrroure*, sig. A1^v.
63 This preface has been commented upon as a means of drawing attention to the use of the frame in the *Mirror* to stage 'a conversation *about* power'. See Jessica Winston, '*A Mirror for Magistrates* and Public Political Discourse in Elizabethan England', *SP* 101 (2004), 381–400; Sherri Geller, 'Editing Under the Influence of the Standard Textual Hierarchy: Misrepresenting *A Mirror for Magistrates* in the Nineteenth- and Twentieth-Century Editions', *TC* 2 (2007), 43–77.
64 Neil Rhodes, *Shakespeare and the Origins of English* (Oxford University Press, 2004), pp.85–7; Rainolde, *Foundacion of Rhetorike*, sigs N1^{r-v}.

65 Baldwin, *Myrroure*, sig. E3^r.
66 Baldwin, *Myrroure*, sigs E2^v–F1^r.
67 Lucas, *Mirror*, pp.195–201.
68 Baldwin, *Myrroure*, sig. E2^r.
69 Baldwin, *Myrroure*, sig. E4^r.
70 Baldwin, *Myrroure*, sig. E4^v.

CHAPTER 5

Bibliophily in Baldwin's Mirror

Angus Vine

In his epistle to the reader, which prefaces the first completed edition of the *Mirror for Magistrates* (1559), William Baldwin sets out the volume's complex collaborative authorship and explains its convoluted literary history. He also lays the ground for the integral importance of its framing narrative: the prose passages that E. M. W. Tillyard oddly and unaccountably dismissed as 'worth more to us than to the readers at whom they were aimed'.[1] By setting out the activities of the authors, and reporting for the first time on their discussions about history, the epistle is itself the first section in that framing narrative. In this way, it also establishes from the outset the larger interpretative context – one characterised by engaged reading of history and robust historiographical debate – that connects the individual tragedies. This epistle is also the place in which Baldwin makes clear the work's literary models and origins. It is here that he expounds John Wayland's project to 'printe Lidgates booke of the fall of Princes' and notes the counsel given to him 'to procure to haue the storye contynewed from where as Bochas lefte, vnto this presente time'. It is also here that we learn about his initially reluctant involvement in the project and his refusal to 'vndertake' the commission 'excepte [he] might haue the helpe of suche, as in wyt were apte, in learning allowed, and in iudgemente and estymacion able to wield and furnysh so weighty an enterpryse'. And it is from this epistle, too, that we discover that Wayland did manage to put such a team together – that he 'procured Athlas to set vnder his shoulder' – and that, once he had done this, Baldwin did consent to join the now collaborative project.[2]

It is unsurprising, therefore, that scholars have repeatedly turned to this epistle for the light that it sheds on the *Mirror*'s complex authorship and for the clues that it gives to its Latin and English sources. Indeed, modern accounts of the work almost invariably begin with a rehearsal of what Baldwin explains here. But if scholars have long recognised the importance of the epistle, they have paid surprisingly little attention to its style and lexicon. Its striking bookishness has gone largely unnoticed, as has its very particular attention to the material form of books. And yet both are central to its rhetoric and to the way in which it sets the tone for the rest of the *Mirror*. The epistle is emphatically not just concerned with books as sources; it is also interested in their physical form and in books as objects. Having described Wayland's project, Baldwin moves from the origins of the *Mirror* to the first of the series of staged readings and historical debates that constitute the rest of the frame narrative, and here he foregrounds the books themselves: the principal topics of conversation in the frame, and what in reality served as the chief sources for him and his fellow authors. As he notes, recalling his first meeting with his collaborators, 'whan certayne of theym to the numbre of seuen, were throughe a generall assent at an apoynted time and place gathered together to deuyse thereupon, I resorted vnto them, bering with me the booke of Bochas, translated by Dan Lidgate, for the better obseruacion of his order'. Shortly afterwards, turning from Boccaccio to their English authorities, he also notes that 'we opened such bookes of Cronicles as we had there present'.[3] The epistle in this way draws attention not only to Baldwin's sources, but also to their physical form and their material presence. It portrays here the 'booke of Bochas' as something to be carried as well as read, something that has to borne as well as perused: thus emphasising for its readers that the importance of books lies in their form as well as their content and, in this reverence for material culture, also anticipating one of the *Mirror*'s central arguments and concerns.[4] Furthermore, this bookish lexicon is not just limited to the epistle's discussion of sources: it also extends to its portrayal of authorship itself. Towards the end of the epistle, Baldwin reports a remark supposedly made by George Ferrers, one of his collaborators, and a comment that is similarly attentive to material culture: 'And forasmuche frende *Baldwin*, as it shalbe your charge to note, and pen orderly the whole process, I wyll so far as my memorie and iudgment serueth, sumwhat further you in the truth of the story'.[5] Authorship here is not just presented as an intellectual process or a question of composition; it is also depicted as a material and mechanical practice – something that requires pen and paper.

There are a number of reasons why Baldwin and his fellow authors might have wanted to emphasise the material form of books in this way. First and foremost, there is the framing narrative itself. The authors, in the frame at least, come together to read and write histories. As they thumb through the pages of their 'bookes of Cronicles', primarily Hall and Fabyan, they select those lives that lend themselves best to their stated *de casibus* theme.[6] Having done this, they then reanimate those lives in the tragedies that follow in the kind of resurrective act that is so familiar in Renaissance historiography. The frame narrative is itself, of course, a form of representation and no less a fiction than any other Renaissance framing device. But both its credibility and its efficacy as a vehicle to make readers reflect on the lessons and nature of history, in the way that the authors ostensibly do, depend on the illusion of the actual presence of the books. They depend, that is to say, on readers of the *Mirror* being able to imagine Baldwin and his collaborators also as real-time readers. The references to the material form of books and to the mechanics of reading, present not only in the prefatory epistle but throughout the prose frame of the 1559 edition, go much of the way to maintaining that illusion. Without it, and without the authentication that it brings, the *Mirror*'s ability to explore what it means to read and write history would have been seriously diminished.

But there are other reasons, too, why the *Mirror* authors paid such attention to books as objects. The *Mirror* is a work not only interested in what it means to read, or even write, history. It is also interested, more fundamentally, in what history itself constitutes and, in relation to this, in what authenticates historical knowledge. This, in turn, reflects a penetrating (and perhaps surprising) recognition of the openness of history to interpretation, an awareness of the contestation of the historical record, and an understanding of the uncertainty of historical evidence and testimony. To know the past, the *Mirror* suggests, is not always a straightforward matter: a recognition that has implications for the exemplary didactic purpose so boldly stated in its full title. History in the *Mirror*, therefore, is not only something that can be debated, but something that has to be debated – as individual tragedies, but also the prose frame itself, make clear. And this is not only a narrowly historiographical matter: in the *Mirror*, those debates are also framed by its speakers as broader contests over authority and the written word, reminding us in turn of the crucial Reformation context for the work. Given this, and in light also of the *Mirror*'s underlying admonitory purpose, the question of what truly probative testimony might constitute becomes all the more acute, and the presence of such testimony, or at least its potential presence, all the more significant. Bibliophily in the *Mirror*, therefore, is neither the kind of amateur connoisseurship nor the feverish acquisitiveness that the word most commonly connotes today. Instead, it is something more vital and also more rhetorically charged: an attentiveness to material form that is less about wonder and possession, and more about historical persuasiveness. But even here there is not absolute certainty: if some of the tragedies privilege the testimonial status of the material book, others are much less confident about this. As Lord Tiptoft wryly observes in the fifteenth tragedy, and the one most explicitly concerned with historiography, 'divers writers diversly declare'.[7]

The privileging of material books, and the importance duly afforded to written testimony, is apparent from the very first *Mirror* tragedy, Ferrers' 'The fall of Robert Tresilian chiefe Iustice of Englande'. Ferrers begins the tragedy with Tresilian beseeching Baldwin to write him into a very particular kind of historical record:

> In the ruthful Register of mischief and mishap,
> Baldwin we beseche thee with our names to begin,
> Whom vnfrendly Fortune did trayne vnto a trap,
> When we thought our state most stable to haue bin,
> So lightly leese they all which all do ween to wyn:
> Learn by vs ye Lawyers and Iudges of the lande
> Vncorrupt and vpright in doome alway to stande.[8]

Tresilian here wishes that his own misspent life be registered: echoing the didactic purpose of the *Mirror* as a whole, but also its historiographical underpinnings, he directly connects the exemplary potential of his misdeeds with the question of their fixity in an authoritative historical record. Registers at the time were volumes in which information of a particular kind was regularly and accurately recorded: they ranged from specific official records such as the Register of Writs (*Registrum omnium brevium tam originalium quam iudicialium*), first published in 1531 by William Rastell, to church records of baptisms, marriages, and burials, to written records, ledgers, and accounts much more broadly and extendedly.[9] Ferrers' term, therefore, invokes a sense not only of textuality and inscription, but also of accuracy and authority. As the tragedy goes on, it is apparent that he is likewise concerned with preservation. In the very next stanza Tresilian implores Baldwin to 'print' his account 'for a president to remayne for euer': a striking anachronism in the context of his own life and times, but a powerful articulation of the *Mirror* authors' desire to secure the historical record and safeguard knowledge of the past. Slightly later, in similar fashion, Tresilian orders Baldwin to '[e]nroll and recorde' his life 'in tables made of brasse' and to '[e]ngraue it in marble that may be razed neuer': a pair of commands that both echo the prefatory epistle's attentiveness to material culture and transform an old Horatian saw about the monumental power of poetry.[10] Where Horace contrasts the durability of poetic fame with the deceptiveness of bronze and marble, Tresilian marries this faith in the written word with an understanding of, and an optimism about, a new technology and a renewed sense of the testimonial importance of historical records and archives. Ferrers does not, therefore, reject the Horatian idea: he simply refigures it, first to take account of the expectations and norms of sixteenth-century historiography, and then in light of the *Mirror*'s larger interest in the materiality of writing.

Rhetorically speaking, this manoeuvre enhances the exemplary potential of Tresilian's life. Just as his eagerness to reveal his 'mischief and mishap' underscores the moral lessons to be learned from them, so his keenness for those misdeeds to be set in stone emphasises the enduring applicability and importance of those lessons. Few readers could have missed the significance of the kind of testimony being offered here: probative, because the onetime advocate speaks from direct (and bitterly learned) experience, and historically authoritative because of his desire for that evidence to be registered and enrolled. In fact, the tragedy as a whole suggests a clear and sequential relationship between oral testimony, printed record, and exemplary potential. From its reflexive opening, it moves first to the testimony itself, delivered orally within the fictional framework of the text, but in reality, of course, by dint of its inclusion in the *Mirror*, being that printed 'president' and having the fixity that Tresilian seeks, and then in the final stanza to a rehearsal of its moral lesson. 'If sum in latter dayes, had called vnto mynde| The fatall fall of vs for wresting of the ryght,' Tresilian reflects, 'The statutes of this lande they should not haue defynde| So wylfully and wyttingly agaynst the sentence quyte'.[11] Ferrers leaves little doubt here about how Tresilian's testimony should be read. The moral lesson and the exemplary potential for contemporary Tudor readers are similarly clear: as the final couplet, 'Let them that cum hereafter both that and this compare,| And waying well the ende, they wyll I trust beware', illustrates. With that final couplet, too, the tragedy comes full circle: where it begins with writing, record-keeping, and inscription, it ends with reading, judgment, and reflection.

It is entirely fitting that Tresilian's tragedy contains the *Mirror*'s most prominent exploration of testimony and evidence. Tresilian was himself chief justice of the King's Bench under Richard II, and he falls, in the *Mirror* narrative, because of his corruptness and perversion of the law. His tragedy is, in effect, therefore an extended disquisition on the wickedness of false testimony. Indeed, early on he condemns himself for precisely this kind of calumny and deceit: 'for halfe a ryall,| We coulde by very arte haue made the blacke seme white'.[12] Slightly later he then develops this admission into a more specific condemnation of his legal judgments and corrupt interpretation of the law:

> The lawes we interpreted and statutes of the lande,
> Not trulye by the texte, but nuly by a glose:
> And words that wer most plaine whan thei by vs wer skande
> We turned by construction lyke a welchmans hose,
> Wherby many one both lyfe and lande dyd lose.[13]

Ferrers here signals a profound anxiety about textual authority and glossing, emphasised by his narrator's candidness, by the familiar pun on gloss and gloze, and also by his striking vestimentary analogy. Welshmen's hose was proverbial at the time for its poor fit and pliability and renowned for its ability to be stretched. Ferrers' analogy underscores the similar elasticity of language and warns the *Mirror*'s readers of the worrying ease with which a glossator, legal or otherwise, could stretch the meaning of a text to suit his or her purpose. There is a revealing parallel here with John Skelton's satirical poem 'Collyn Clout' (1521–2), which draws the same analogy between specious glossing and a Welshman's stockings. In Skelton's case, he uses the comparison to condemn what he sees as the increasingly prolific false interpretations of authoritative ecclesiastical texts: the 'thousande thousande' words that 'blaber, barke, and blother,| And make a Welchmans hose| Of the texte and the glose'.[14] Ferrers employs the analogy in a slightly different context, but the underlying point about the exercise of authority and the interpretation of texts is the same.

If the circumstances of Tresilian's own life made Ferrers' attention to interpretation and testimony inevitable, that focus did nonetheless also reflect other, more contemporary influences. As Annabel Patterson and Scott C. Lucas have suggested, the poem had a profound topical relevance as well, with its castigation of a corrupt justice and his deliberate misinterpretation of statute law offering recognisable historical parallels with the abuses of the judges and prosecutors in the treason trial of Sir Nicholas Throckmorton just five years earlier in 1554. Tresilian's tragedy, in Patterson's words, 'was all too easily applicable to the events of [that year]'.[15] Tresilian himself signals this topicality in the tragedy's final stanza: his deploring allusion there to the conduct of 'sum in latter dayes' makes it clear that the poem offers not only an abstract philosophical principle, but also a coruscating denunciation of more recent times. While Ferrers is careful to avoid mentioning any contemporary jurists by name, the end of the tragedy leaves his readers in little doubt that his purview was more than just historical. Furthermore, as Lucas has also argued, in noting the existence of this corruption, but attributing it only to the confoundedly inexact 'sum in latter dayes', he invites those readers to make the very identification that he so studiously avoids, and to ponder who he actually meant by this.[16]

At a more fundamental level, the tragedy's interest in the nature of testimony itself was also topical. One of the major preoccupations of early modern legal thought concerned the use and judgment of testimony: the very issues that the poem's axiomatic final couplet underscores. Developments in courtroom practice may also have been influential here: by the time of the *Mirror*, the expert witness had become a fundamental part of the legal process.[17] The implications for the *Mirror* – and, in particular, for its narrative form, its multiple testimonies, and its overall exemplary purpose – are obvious. While the context is a historiographical rather than a legal or advocatory one, the *Mirror*'s speakers, too, are presented as expert witnesses. The first-person narration, so integral to the poem's persuasiveness and rhetoric, has precisely this effect. Explanations for this strong legal influence on the *Mirror* are not hard to find. Aside from the vital importance of probative testimony to both its exemplarity and its topicality, the most compelling one lies with the identities of the authors themselves. Of the four known, named authors of the 1559 *Mirror*, two had telling connections with the law: Ferrers himself had been a member of Lincoln's Inn since November 1534, and his literary interests prior to the *Mirror* were predominantly legal and antiquarian, while Thomas Phaer, responsible for Owen Glendower's tragedy, also published legal works, including the popular handbooks *Natura brevium* (1530?) and *A Newe Book of Presidentes* (1543).[18]

In its interest in testimony and the material book, Tresilian's tragedy is programmatic of the *Mirror* as a whole. Successive narrators thus follow Tresilian's lead and present their tragedies explicitly as evidence or proof. Sir Roger Mortimer's opening gambit, 'All folke be frayle, theyr blisses brittle bee:| For proofe whereof although none other wer,| Suffyse may I, syr Roger Mortimer', and Thomas of Woodstock's command, 'In proofe whereof, O Baldwin, take payne| To hearken awhyle to Thomas of Wudstocke', are cases in point.[19] In both instances, their narrators offer their lives not only as exempla, but also as probative illustrations of a general principle: the slipperiness of fortune and the fragility of earthly fame. The same goes for Thomas Mowbray in his tragedy: he, too, instructs Baldwin and his fellow authors to '[b]eholde' in him 'due proofe of euerye parte'.[20]

Some of the *Mirror* narrators, moreover, also share Tresilian's awareness of his own place in the historical record and of his own status as text and history. Lord Clifford, for example, the murderer of Richard, Duke of York, and his son, knows that his 'faultes' have been widely bruited: indeed, he acknowledges that they have been 'published so brode in every place'. Nonetheless, he still commands Baldwin to commit his life to paper: 'therfore Baldwin write my wretched fall,| The brief wherof I briefly vtter shall'.[21] The bookish and reflexive lexicon of the prefatory epistle and Tresilian's tragedy thus extends to this one too. But here it is given not only a literary, but also an explicitly legal, dimension in the punning repetition of 'brief' and 'briefly'. A brief in the sixteenth century was something abridged: an abstract, an epitome, a summary. This is Hamlet's meaning, for example, when he speaks to Polonius of the 'abstract and brief chronicles of the time', and it is also the sense on which King Philip draws in *King John* when he likens Prince Arthur in an extended metaphor first to '[t]his little abstract' and then to 'this brief'.[22] Clifford's tragedy is certainly abridged and brief: at just seventy lines, it is the second shortest in the whole of the 1559 *Mirror*.[23] But, in early modern English, a brief could also be a legal document, a letter of authority, or a writ, and it is hard not to hear this sense at play as well.[24] Clifford's life, then, becomes a kind of self-authorised record: a gesture that directs the readers once again to the *Mirror*'s larger exploration of what constitutes reliable evidence or testimony.

This interest in books, records, and testimony did not, of course, originate with Baldwin, Ferrers, or any of the other *Mirror* authors. A similar lexical vein runs through the prefatory material to John Lydgate's translation of Laurent de Premierfait's French version of Boccaccio's *De casibus virorum illustrium*: the text that served as their principal literary model, and which Wayland printed five years earlier in 1554. Indeed, if anything, Lydgate's prologue is even more bookish than Baldwin's prefatory epistle. Lydgate spends much of this prologue explaining Boccaccio's writing about mutability and fortune. Allusions to the 'boke of Bochas' are, therefore, inevitable and abundant. So, too, are references to the books of Humphrey, Duke of Gloucester, Lydgate's bibliophilic patron, and the man who commissioned him to produce the translation in the first place: from admiration for his never-ending appetite for study ('His courage neuer dothe appall| To study in bokes of antiquitie') to praise for his virtuous reading and scholarship ('And to do pleasaunce to our Lorde Iesu,| He studieth euer to haue intelligence.| Readyng of bokes, bringeth in vertue').[25] But there is an important distinction here and a contrast that emphasises the different meanings of the word 'book' itself. The opening stanza of Lydgate's prologue and his first allusion to the 'boke of Bochas' make this clear:

> He that sumtime did his dilige[n]ce,
> The boke of Bochas, in Fre[n]ch to tra[n]slate,
> Out of latin, he called was Laure[n]ce:
> The tyme remembred truly and the date
> Is whe[n] kyng Iohn through his mortal fate
> Was prisoner brought vnto this region,
> Than he began first on this translation.[26]

Lydgate's concern here is with the date and transmission of his source; his interest is solely in its contents and not in '[t]he boke of Bochas' as an object. The same goes for his final allusion to it: near the end of the prologue he cites his patron's great esteem for '[t]he noble boke of this Iohn Bochas' and his belief of its great importance 'vnto princes … To geue exa[m]ple how this worlde doth vary'.[27] The distinction, then, is between two different and opposed understandings of the word: between book as a literary composition without regard to its material form, and book as that material form without regard to its contents.[28] Lydgate's 'boke of Bochas' refers to the former; Baldwin's 'booke of Bochas' describes both. For Baldwin and his collaborators, the material form really does matter.

The clearest illustration of this, perhaps unsurprisingly, comes from the prose frame, as the authors repeatedly reflect there on their reading, authorship, and literary method. In the passage at the end of the second tragedy, for example, Ferrers instructs Baldwin to 'take' the chronicles 'and marke them as they cum', observing that 'there are many wurthy to be noted, though not to be treated of', while in the interlude at the end of Jack Cade's tragedy Baldwin again portrays himself in the act of reading, this time in a more somnolent fashion ('Whyle he was deuisyng thereon, and every man seking farder notes, I looked on the Cronicles, and fynding styl fyelde vpon fyelde, & manye noble men slayne, I purposed to haue ouerpassed all, for I was so wearye that I waxed drowsye, and began in dede to slumber').[29] This second example is given added potency as a representation of reading by the presence of a printed manicule in the margin alongside: one of the symbols customarily used by early modern readers to mark up passages of particular note.[30] The prose frame also portrays Baldwin's fellow authors in the act of reading. In the interlude between the first and second tragedies, for instance, Baldwin depicts the intervention of an unnamed collaborator, who 'had stayed vpon syr Roger Mortimer': the first in the series of staged readings and interventions, in which the *Mirror* authors purportedly flick through the pages of the 'Cronicles ... there present' in search of suitable exemplary material and then present this to their fellows, and which act as bridging passages to bring the work as a whole together.[31] Here Baldwin negotiates between two chronologically discontinuous, but topically similar, tragedies: exemplary reading and the material book provide him with twin means to do this.

If these examples focus on the methods and mechanics of reading, the frame also represents writing and authorship in a similar material way. The last prose passage, at the end of the nineteenth and final tragedy, is a case in point: 'Whan this was sayde, every man tooke his leave of other and departed: And I the better to acquyte my charge, recorded and noted all such matters as they had wylled me'.[32] Baldwin here returns to where he began, echoing the content of his prefatory epistle in this final articulation of both the *Mirror*'s complex collaborative authorship and his own crucial secretarial role in this, and its attentiveness to the importance of the material book. Just as the fictional frame begins with an extended reflection on the *Mirror*'s own authorship and history, so it ends, in the 1559 edition at least, with this purported (and apparently conclusive) final act of inscription.

The roots of the *Mirror*'s interest in testimony and the material book are historiographical. As Baldwin makes clear at various points in the prose frame, the *Mirror* authors discover in the course of their reading and research that history is sometimes contested, and that the historical record is often discordant and even contradictory. In particular, they learn that sources do not always agree, a discovery that suggests an awareness of the collational methods of humanist history and textual criticism, and which complicates the widespread modern perception of the *Mirror*'s 'carelessness with sources'.[33] Hall and Fabyan, their two principal sources, cannot always be reconciled into a single coherent narrative: as the prose comment that follows the tragedy of Lord Mowbray unequivocally illustrates. The frame here both reveals the sources' different accounts of the origins of the dispute between Mowbray and Henry Bolingbroke and draws attention to the discrepancies between them:

> This tragicall example was of all the cumpany well liked, how be it a doubte was founde therin, and that by meanes of the diuersity of the Chronicles: for where as maister Hall whom in this storye we chiefely folowed, maketh Mowbray accuser, and Boleynbroke appellant, mayster Fabian reporteth the matter quite contrary, & that by the reporte of good authours, makyng Boleynbroke the accuser, & Mowbray the

appellant. Which matter sith it is more harde to desise, than nedefull to our purpose, whiche minde onely to diswade from vices and exalte virtue, we referre to the determinacion of the Haroldes, or such as may cum by the recordes and registers of these doings, contented in the mean while with the best allowed iudgement, and which maketh most for our forshewed purpose.³⁴

Baldwin here emphasises the indeterminacy of the matter by defending the authenticity of Fabyan's version and the reliability of his sources at the very moment at which he confirms that, for Mowbray's life, the *Mirror* authors took Hall instead as their principal authority. He therefore neither hides from the doubtfulness of the chronicle tradition nor attempts to reconcile the conflicting accounts. Instead, he leaves the resolution of the matter up to others: either to the heralds, those arbiters of early modern genealogical and historical disputes, or to those who have access to 'recordes' and 'registers', books that, as we have seen, by virtue of their specific material forms had a particular historical authority.³⁵

Given the first-person narration of the *Mirror* tragedies, there is no narratorial imperative for Baldwin to admit the discrepancy between his two sources here. The explanation for his comment lies, instead, in the *Mirror's* interest in the production and consumption of history – in the testimony needed to write it and the judgment requisite for reading it. This passage follows Tresilian's programmatic opening and makes it clear that the best historical evidence, and the most probative historical testimony, is something recorded, enrolled, and written down. Indeed, the frame at this moment picks up on the very material term ('Register') foregrounded in the opening line of the whole work. This does not mean that Baldwin and his fellow authors reject oral testimony entirely: the *Mirror* is, after all, an extended exercise in *prosopopoeia*, a rhetorical figure that, as Richard Serjeantson has pointed out, was particularly associated with testimony.³⁶ Furthermore, *prosopopoeia* was considered at the time to be especially effective at persuading the mind to the emulation of virtue – the very task that the *Mirror* sets out to do. Nonetheless, as a whole, and also in individual passages such as this one, the *Mirror* makes it clear that historical authority does ultimately lie in written testimony. '[R]ecordes', with their connotation of something taken down as evidence of a legal matter, and 'registers', with their implication of both documenting particulars and documenting accurately, regularly, and consistently, have an authority that oral narratives, however effective they may be in exemplary terms, can never possess.

But Baldwin's concern in this part of the frame is not just with the writing of historical narrative. It is also with the interpretation and reading of it. In this respect, it is notable that his discussion of the conflicting sources ends with 'the best allowed iudgement'. This is a quality, the *Mirror* suggests, needed not only by incipient magistrates, the purported audience for the work, but also by readers of history more broadly. The *Mirror*'s purpose is, in large part, to cultivate that judgment. As an imaginative work, a work that is not itself chronicle history, and that can therefore legitimately duck the question of the precise identities of the appellant and defendant, the *Mirror* is ideally suited to this. A historically conflicted matter, such as the legal dispute between Mowbray and Bolingbroke, is also perfect exemplary material, for it is the very uncertainty in the historical authorities, highlighted by Baldwin in the frame, that enables the *Mirror* to weigh up and assess the kinds of testimony, oral and written, that constitute chronicle history. And it is this process of reflection that, in turn, inculcates the importance of judgment, historical as well as moral.

A related moment occurs later in the work in the aftermath of Owen Glendower's tragedy. Here, Baldwin again stages a historical debate between the authors and raises a 'dout' over the narrative that has just been delivered. This time, ironically given Glendower's disavowal of genealogy and pedigree in his plaint, it concerns a title of honour: 'Howbeit one found a dout wurth the mouing, & that concerning this title, erle of March: for as it appereth, there were.iii. men of.iii diuers nacions together in one time entitled by that honour'.[37] Where this example differs from the previous one is that this time Baldwin does provide a resolution to the 'dout'. It 'was aunswered,' he notes, 'that euery countrey hath Marches belonging vnto them, and those so large, that they were Earledomes, & the lordes therof intituled therby'.[38] Nonetheless, the mere presence of this discussion serves to underline the model of reading advanced by the *Mirror*: one characterised by reflexive evaluation and critical debate, and one distinguished by close engagement with both the materials of history and its various forms.

If this interest in books and attention to probative testimony therefore reveal an unexpectedly active engagement with historiography, they also remind us that the *Mirror* is fundamentally a Reformation text. Its bibliophily reflects and responds to a range of broader Renaissance anxieties about the status of writing, discourse, and books: concerns about textual authority and the stability of meaning that were given added resonance in the wake of the Reformation. Tresilian's quibble on gloss and gloze, to cite just one example, was as familiar in an ecclesiastical context and religious polemic as in his own legal one. Furthermore, debates over the status of the oral and the written were also, as Brian Cummings has recently noted, at the heart of Reformation arguments about authority.[39] The 1559 *Mirror* leaves its readers in little doubt about which side of those debates it comes down on: in keeping, of course, with Baldwin's other writings and also with the raft of topical allusions that recent scholars have so assiduously documented.[40] As such, it is perhaps tempting to suggest a parallel with another reflexive, collaborative Protestant historical project, another book defined by textual instability and multiple editions, and another work concerned fundamentally with printed testimony and the written word: John Foxe's *Acts and Monuments* (1563).[41]

But that parallel only goes so far. There is the very obvious objection that the *Mirror* is not a martyrology. Its tragedies are not testimonies of faith, but in the main testimonies of bad faith. Moreover, for all its favouring of the written word, and its interest in the material form of books, the *Mirror* admits of a certain amount of doubt here. Tresilian may speak with the confidence of an avowed print revolutionary, but other narrators are palpably less certain about the power of written history or the press to fix meaning and secure knowledge of the past. Nowhere is this more apparent than in Lord Tiptoft's narrative. His tragedy traces his turbulent career from his privileged position as a loyal administrator and holder of high office under Edward IV to his arrest, trial, and execution for treason on Henry VI's readeption in October 1470. But, just as importantly, it also tackles his widespread portrayal in historiography – the perception of him as 'Butcher to, as common rumor sayes'.[42] Here, in particular, Tiptoft castigates Hall and Fabyan, and berates them for their neglect of 'causes' – for their failure to explain the reasons why he acted in the way that he did:

> Unfruytfull Fabyan folowed the face
> Of time and dedes, but let the causes slip:
> Whych Hall hath added, but with double grace,
> For feare I thinke least trouble might him trip:
> For this or that (sayth he) he felt the whip.
> Thus story writers leave the causes out,
> Or so rehears them, as they wer in dout.[43]

Tiptoft's tragedy is therefore an attempt to set the historical record straight, but it is also an extended reflection on historiography more generally, as the aphoristic final couplet of the stanza above illustrates. Moreover, as he reflects on this, he entertains a striking scepticism about history writing itself. 'But still it fares as alway it did fare,' he observes, 'Affection, feare, or doubtes that dayly brue,| Do cause that stories never can be true'.[44] By 'stories' he means histories – the two words were synonymous at the time – and by histories he means written histories.

There is, therefore, a tension at play in the *Mirror*'s bibliophily and its bookish lexicon. That tension is between a confidence in the historical authority of the written and printed word and a nagging sense, which runs through the edition as a whole, that histories are themselves subject to the same quirks, unreliability, and doubtfulness as oral testimony. Nonetheless, this does not mean that the *Mirror* resists history, as one recent critic has suggested in an otherwise useful essay on the work's structural inconsistencies.[45] Even Tiptoft does not go that far. (In fact, he shares the didactic Ciceronian vision of the other speakers, and of the *Mirror* as a whole, as introductory remarks in his tragedy make abundantly clear: 'The truth wherof yet playnly shew I shall,| That thou mayst write, and other therby rede| What thinges I did, wherof they should take hede'.[46]) Instead, this tension is a further manifestation of the polyphony that scholars have noticed elsewhere in the text and that is so characteristic of Renaissance history writing: the dialogism that Richard Niccols first identified in his edition of 1610.[47] Niccols' editorial labours have not always been admired by subsequent scholars, but in his characterisation of Baldwin and Ferrers' method as 'by way of dialogue or interlocution' he got things absolutely right.[48]

It is this dialogism, too, that ultimately explains the *Mirror*'s bibliophily. For just as this method calls previous chronicles and written histories into question, so it makes the demand for testimony that is truly probative all the more urgent. There is, in the end, little doubt about where Baldwin and his collaborators considered such testimony chiefly to lie. Printed precedents, enrolled records, and engraved tables: these are what the ghost of Tresilian seeks. But they are also what, for all its qualifications and inconsistencies, the *Mirror* as a whole advocates. This bibliophilic text really did put its historiographical faith in the material book, in the book as an object. And despite, but also because of, its interlocutory method – the disputes and exchanges of its bookish preface and prose frame – it urges its readers to do exactly the same.

Notes

1 E. M. W. Tillyard, '*A Mirror for Magistrates* Revisited', in *Elizabethan and Jacobean Studies Presented to Frank Percy Wilson in Honour of his Seventieth Birthday* (Oxford: Clarendon Press, 1959), pp.1–16, at p.14.
2 'William Baldwin to the Reader', in *A Myrrovre For Magistrates. Wherein may be seen by example of other, with howe greuous plages vices are punished: and howe frayle and vnstable worldly prosperitie is founde even of those, whom Fortune seemeth most highly to fauour* (London: Thomas Marshe, 1559), sig. A1^{r-v}.

3 Baldwin, *Myrrovre*, sig. A1ʳ. I am using 'authorities' here in the sense glossed in OED I.I: 'A book, passage, etc., accepted as a reliable source of information.'
4 The *Mirror*'s bibliophily is therefore very different to the bibliophilic vein that runs through another sixteenth-century text: Christopher Marlowe's *Doctor Faustus* (1588–9?). As Paul Budra has noted, '*Doctor Faustus* is as much about books – the physical objects – as knowledge and art'. But where the *Mirror* finds persuasiveness and meaning in material culture, Marlowe's play, he argues, portrays bibliophily as dangerous and as what distracts Faustus from proper attention to the word: see Paul Budra, '*Doctor Faustus*: Death of a Bibliophile', *Connotations* 1 (1991), 1–11. See also Paul Yachnin, '*Doctor Faustus* and the Literary System: A Supplementary Response to Paul Budra', *Connotations* 1 (1991), 74–7.
5 Baldwin, *Myrrovre*, sig. A2ʳ.
6 The extent to which the authors actually stick to this theme and remain within the *de casibus* tradition in the tragedies themselves has become a matter of critical debate: for conflicting arguments, see Paul Budra, *A Mirror for Magistrates and the de casibus Tradition* (University of Toronto Press, 2000), ch. 2 especially; and Jessica Winston, '*A Mirror for Magistrates* and Public Political Discourse in Elizabethan England', *SP* 101 (2004), 381–400.
7 *Myrrovre for Magistrates* (1559), sig. B2ᵛ.
8 *Myrrovre*, sig. A3ʳ.
9 *OED*, *s.v.* 'register', *n.* 1. 1(a) and (b), 4, and 5(a).
10 *Myrrovre*, sig. A3ʳ; and Horace, *Odes*, trans. Niall Rudd, Loeb Classical Library (Cambridge: Harvard University Press, 1990), III. xxx. 1–5: 'Exegi monumentum aere perennius| regalique situ pyramidum altius,| quod non imber edax, non Aquilo impotens| possit diruere aut innumerabilis| annorum series, et fuga temporum'.
11 *Myrrovre*, sig. B1ᵛ.
12 *Myrrovre*, sig. A3ᵛ.
13 *Myrrovre*, sig. A4ʳ.
14 John Skelton, 'Collyn Clout', in *The Complete English Poems*, ed. John Scattergood (Harmondsworth: Penguin, 1983), ll. 776–9. The phrase recurs, to a slightly different effect, in the *Garlande of Laurell* (ll. 1239–40), reinforcing its proverbiality: 'And after conveyauns as the world goos,| It is no foly to use the Walshemannys hoos'. For a further discussion of the two passages and of Skelton's use of the analogy, see Elizabeth Fowler, *Literary Character: The Human Figure in Early English Writing* (Ithaca: Cornell University Press, 2003), pp.173–5.
15 Annabel Patterson, *Reading Holinshed's Chronicles* (University of Chicago Press, 1994), pp.160–61; and Scott C. Lucas, 'The Consolation of Tragedy: *A Mirror for Magistrates* and the Fall of the "Good Duke" of Somerset', *SP* 100 (2003), 44–70, at p.45. For a compelling illustration of the need to read the *Mirror* more broadly in this kind of topically engaged way, see Andrew Hadfield, *Literature, Politics, and National Identity: Reformation and Renaissance* (Cambridge University Press, 1994), pp.81–107.
16 Scott C. Lucas, A Mirror for Magistrates *and the Politics of the English Reformation* (Amherst: University of Massachusetts Press, 2009), p.14.

17 See Barbara J. Shapiro, *Probability and Certainty in Seventeenth-Century England: A Study of the Relationships Between Natural Science, Religion, History, Law, and Literature* (Princeton University Press, 1983), pp.175–86; and Carol A. G. Jones, *Expert Witnesses: Science, Medicine, and the Practice of Law* (Oxford: Clarendon Press, 1994), pp.17–56 especially. For the implications of these developments for early modern intellectual culture more broadly, especially for natural philosophy, see R. W. Serjeantson, 'Testimony and Proof in Early-Modern England', *Studies in the History and Philosophy of Science* 30 (1999), 195–236.

18 Ferrers' publications include *The Great Boke of Statutes*, which he edited, and which first appeared in 1533, and then again in an extended edition in 1548, and a translation of Magna Carta and other statutes, first published in 1534. Phaer was revealed to be one of the *Mirror* authors in the revised prelude to Owen Glendower's tragedy in the 1578 edition: see *The Last part of the Mirour for Magistrates, wherein may be seene by examples passed in this Realme, with how greeuous plagues, vyces are punished in great Princes & Magistrats, and how frayle and vnstable worldly prosperity is founde, where Fortune seemeth most highly to Fauour* (London: Thomas Marshe, 1578), sig. D1^r.

19 *Myrrovre*, sigs B2^v and C2^r.

20 *Myrrovre*, sig. D3^r.

21 *Myrrovre*, sig. A4^v.

22 William Shakespeare, *Hamlet*, ed. Neil Taylor and Ann Thompson (London: Arden Shakespeare, 2006), 2. 2. 462; and William Shakespeare, *King John*, ed. E. A. J. Honigmann (London: Arden Shakespeare, 2007; first published 1954), 2. 1. 101–3.

23 Only Richard, Earl of Cambridge's tragedy, at fifty-six lines, is shorter.

24 See John Cowell, *The Interpreter: Or Booke Containing the Signification of Words* (Cambridge: John Legate, 1607), sig. L1^r: '*Brief (breve)* commeth from the French (*bref ou brief*. i. *brevis*) and in our common lawe, signifieth a writ, whereby a man is summoned to answer to any action: or (more largely) any precept of the king in writing; issuing out of any court, whereby he commaundeth any thing to be done, for the furtherance of iustice or good order'. The notion of counsel's brief current today – that is, the summary facts of a case and the principal points of law – was a later coinage: the earliest citation in the *OED* for this sense is not until 1631, and the first printed citation is not until the beginning of the eighteenth century.

25 *The Tragedies, gathered by Ihon Bochas, of all such Princes as fell from theyr estates through the mutability of Fortune since the creacion of Adam, vntil his time: wherein may be seen what vices bring menne to destruccion, wyth notable warnings howe the like may be auoyded. Translated into Englysh by Iohn Lidgate, Monke of Burye* (London: John Wayland, [1554]), sig. A3^r.

26 Boccaccio, *Tragedies*, sig. A1^r.

27 Boccaccio, *Tragedies*, sig. A3^r.

28 For this distinction, see further *OED*, *s.v.* 'book', *n.* 1(a) and (b).
29 *Myrrovre for Magistrates* (1559), sigs C1^r and N1^{r-v}.
30 For a history of manicules, see William H. Sherman, *Used Books: Marking Readers in Early Modern England* (Philadelphia: University of Pennsylvania Press, 2007), pp.25–53.
31 *Myrrovre*, sigs B1^v–B2^r.
32 *Myrrovre*, sig. G3^r.
33 See, for example, F. J. Levy, *Tudor Historical Thought* (University of Toronto Press, 2004; first published 1967), p.217. The fact that Baldwin foregrounds this discovery suggests that if the *Mirror* authors were careless with their sources – and they do, certainly, play fast and loose with events and chronology – they were knowingly careless about this.
34 *Myrrovre*, sigs E1^v–E2^r.
35 On the historical researches of the heralds, see Anthony Richard Wagner, *Heralds of England: A History of the Office and College of Arms* (London: HMSO, 1967).
36 R. W. Serjeantson, 'Testimony: The Artless Proof', in Sylvia Adamson, Gavin Alexander, and Katrin Ettenhuber, eds, *Renaissance Figures of Speech* (Cambridge University Press, 2007), pp.181–94, at pp.187–8.
37 *Myrrovre*, sig. G1^v.
38 *Myrrovre*, sig. G2^r.
39 Brian Cummings, '"The Oral Versus The Written", The Debates over Scripture in More and Tyndale', *Moreana* 45 (2008), 15–50. For the significance of the material book more broadly in the Judaeo-Christian tradition, see Brian Cummings, 'The Book as Symbol', in Michael F. Suarez, S.J., and H. R. Woudhuysen, eds, *The Oxford Companion to the Book*, 2 vols (Oxford University Press, 2010), I, pp.63–5; and Ernst Robert Curtius, *European Literature and the Latin Middle Ages*, trans. Willard R. Trask (London: Routledge & Kegan Paul, 1953), pp.302–47.
40 See most extensively Lucas, A Mirror for Magistrates *and the Politics of the English Reformation*.
41 On the importance of printed testimony to Foxe's project, see John N. King, '"The Light of Printing": William Tyndale, John Foxe, John Day, and Early Modern Print Culture', *RQ* 54 (2001), 52–85; and John N. King, *Foxe's Book of Martyrs and Early Modern Print Culture* (Cambridge University Press, 2006), p.8. For the reflexiveness of Foxe's text and its attention to its own collective production, see Mark Breitenberg, 'The Flesh Made Word: Foxe's *Acts and Monuments*', *Renaissance and Reformation* 25 (1989), 381–407.
42 *Myrrovre*, sig. B3^r.
43 *Myrrovre*, sig. B3^r.
44 *Myrrovre*, sig. B2^v.
45 Donald Jellerson, 'The Spectral Historiopoetics of the *Mirror for Magistrates*', *JNR* 2 (2010), para. 6. http://northernrenaissance.org, last consulted 15 May 2015.
46 *Myrrovre*, sig. B3^r.

47 For more on the *Mirror*'s polyphony and dialogism, see Budra, A Mirror for Magistrates *and the* de casibus *Tradition*, pp.73–6.
48 See *A Mirovr For Magistrates: Being a Trve Chronicle Historie of the Vntimely falles of such vnfortunate Princes and men of note, as haue happened since the first entrance of Brute into this Iland, vntill this our latter Age* (London: Felix Kyngston, 1610), sig. S7^r.

PART II

Later additions (1574–1616)

CHAPTER 6

'Hoysted high vpon the rolling wheele'
Elianor Cobham's Lament

Cathy Shrank

'As it happeneth, I haue here ready penned.ii. notable tragedies,' 'quoth Master Ferrers' in the 1578 *Mirror for Magistrates*: 'the one of Humfrey Duke of Glocester, the other of the Duches Elienor his wife'.[1] Well might Ferrers have had these complaints readily to hand: material about the Duke and Duchess seems to have been prepared by the time of the 1559 edition, where the table of contents lists the complaint of 'Good duke Humfrey murdered, and Elianor Cobham his wife banished', although no such item appeared.[2] The Gloucesters next appear in the 1571 table of contents, this time as separate complaints, positioned – precariously it transpired – as the final two poems: 'The unworthy death of the worthy Duke Humfrey of Glocester, protectour of England, contriued by false practises' and 'The penance & exile of the Lady Elyanor Cobham Duches of Glocester, for witchcraft and sorcery'.[3] Once again no corresponding items appeared in the text itself. It was not until 1578 that their tragedies reached print, in the original position intended in the 1559 table of contents, between James I and William de la Pole. Even then, Elianor was almost excluded. Her tragedy is not indexed, and her complaint was only inserted during the printing process, on an unfoliated gathering substituted for a cancelled leaf.

This chapter resituates Elianor's belated and seemingly liminal tragedy within the context of the other contributions that its author, George Ferrers, made to the *Mirror*, and of the *Mirror* tradition more generally. Perhaps due to its uncertain position within the *Mirror* and its delayed appearance, Elianor's complaint has received scant critical attention.[4] Even within its own time, it tended to be overlooked by the writers of 'female-voiced' complaint, who self-consciously place themselves within the literary tradition by name-checking precursors: Samuel Daniel's Rosamund cites Thomas Churchyard's Mistress Shore as a precedent for her complaint; Michael Drayton's Matilda compares herself to Rosamund, Shore, as well as Shakespeare's Lucrece and Thomas Lodge's Elstred.[5]

109

Neither of these well-read heroines think to reference Ferrers' Elianor. As Paul Budra notes:

> Shores's tale, not Cobham's, became the narrative paradigm into which all subsequent portrayals of women were made to fit in this tradition, or to be defined as being in opposition to. [Shore] set the pattern: a beautiful woman is tempted by sin (invariably lust), and incidentally power, and either succumbs, then dies, or resists then dies.[6]

To date, one of the few substantive treatments of Ferrers' poem thus remains Lily Campbell's 1934 article on 'Humphrey Duke of Gloucester and Eleanor Cobham His Wife', in which she declares 'that to consider the two tragedies as complementary is to misunderstand them altogether'; rather, 'they make statements of fact which are diametrically opposed' (p.124).

Campbell here overstates the incompatibility of the versions of events that the two laments present. The mainstay of her argument hinges around, first, the degree to which Humfrey's bastard uncle, Cardinal Beaufort, is blamed for the Duke and Duchess' falls; and second, the seeming mismatch between the Duchess' disavowal that she meddled in black magic and her husband's apparent belief that she did. As Campbell observes, 'the tragedy of Duke Humphrey does not stress to any such extent as does the tragedy of Eleanor Cobham the enmity of the chancellor [Beaufort]' (pp.139–40). Admittedly, a much greater proportion of Elianor's complaint is devoted to exposing and castigating Beaufort, but that is in part because her lament – like her appearances in the historical record – is focused on just one event: namely, her fall, in which Beaufort is presented as playing a crucial and malign role. Humfrey's complaint in contrast is much more diffuse, beginning with an account of the fatal squabbles conducted by previous generations of Plantagenets. Nevertheless, he still fingers the Cardinal as a prime mover against him; and, like Elianor, he recurrently draws attention to the Cardinal's dangerous pride, and claims – like her – that Beaufort acquired his Cardinal hat, not through merit, but through bribery. According to Elianor, Beaufort, 'for his gold & Summes that were not small| Payd to the pope, was made a Cardinall' (p.438); Humfrey reiterates the same claims:

> Not Gods Aungels, but Angels of old Gold,
> Lyft him aloft in whom no cause there was
> By iust desert, so high to be extold,
> (Ryches except) where by this Golden asse,
> At home and abraode al matters brought to passe,

> Namely at Rome, hauing no mean but that
> To purchase there his crimzin Cardinal hat. (p.450)

Far from being a substantial difference between them, that is, the treatment of Beaufort is a point of accord, even down to the way in which they frame themselves as Christ-figures and the Cardinal as their nemesis, figured as Caiaphas in Elianor's case (p.436), 'Herode and Pylate' in Humfrey's (p.457).

The handling of Elianor's culpability is also less troublingly inconsistent than Campbell suggests, particularly as the verse is less clear on this point than Campbell acknowledges. Humfrey admits (as does Elianor) that she commissioned horoscopes, although, tellingly, he does not commit to categorising that as 'sorcery', a definition he defers to others ('some'):

> Elianor my wife, my Dutches only deare,
> I know not how but as the nature is
> Of women al, aye curious to enquiere
> Of things to come (though I confesse in this
> Her fault not small) and that she did amisse,
> By wytches skill, which sorcery some call,
> Would know of things which after should befall. (p.453)

The crucial stanza follows shortly after:

> Yet besides this there was a greater thing,
> How she in waxe by counsel of the witch,
> An Image made, crowned like a king,
> With sword in hand, in shape and likenesse syche
> As was the kinge, which dayly they did pytch
> Against a fyre, that as the waxe did melt,
> So should his lyfe consume away vnfelt. (p.454)

Campbell makes these lines key to her argument that Humfrey's tragedy 'specifically says that Elianor did go further than trying to ascertain the future … that she did contrive against the king's life' (p.126). However, the syntax of that stanza is not entirely transparent: 'how' could introduce either a statement of fact or an accusation, and the next stanza begins by inclining towards the latter, as the Duchess is described as being 'accused' – rather than guilty – 'of this cryme' (p.454). Notice of her final conviction comes, just over ten lines later, couched in strikingly ambiguous terms: she is 'conuinced … as guiltie', the conjunction 'as' encompassing the sceptical meaning 'as if' (p.454). Certainly, there is nothing as conclusive as William Shakespeare's later depiction of the Duchess in

Henry VI Part 2 (1591) where we witness Eleanor and her confederates, on stage, conjuring a spirit (Act 1, scene 4).

That Campbell overstates the incompatibility of the Duke's and Duchess' tragedies results from her insistence that the *Mirror* needs to be read topically. She thus argues that the two Gloucester complaints were written at different times 'to mirror different current events', and 'history was therefore modified and interpreted to meet the different didactic purposes of the two tragedies' (p.155), a theory with which Scott C. Lucas concurs, suggesting that – whilst Humphrey's complaint 'offers sharp, indirect criticism of Queen Mary for her role in Edward Seymour's downfall', criticism that may well have made it the poem which resulted in the censorship of the 1554 volume (then entitled *A Memorial of Such Princes*) – Eleanor's 'appears to be Elizabethan in origin and to have no topical purpose', being instead a reworking of the fifteenth-century ballad *The Lament of the Duchess of Gloucester*.[7] This bias towards topical readings of the *Mirror* is further reflected in Lucas's subordination of Elianor's apparently untopical tragedy to a footnote, where Humfrey's is dealt with, at greater length, in the main text.

Nonetheless, despite the diverse purposes which Campbell and Lucas see motivating the two Gloucester tragedies, it is perhaps inevitable that the two complaints are read with, and against, each other: that is, after all, the way in which they were conceived. Even before they appeared in print, the tragedies of the Duke and Duchess were interrelated, as seen by their pairing – as either a single or double item – in the tables of contents in 1559 and 1571; and it is as a pair that their first print readers would have encountered them. Further to that, whatever their originary topicality, the text of the two complaints in 1578 may not be identical to the tragedy (or tragedies) as initially planned (seemingly one poem in 1559, two in 1571). Certainly, the fact that Elianor's complaint, along with its introductory and concluding prose links, fits exactly into one gathering (replacing a cancelled leaf) suggests that it was carefully adapted for the 1578 edition, being inserted during the printing process (as discussed above). At 455 lines, Humfrey's complaint in its 1578 manifestation is also substantially longer than both Ferrers' other contributions to the 1559 *Mirror* and the other complaints that the earlier volume contains.[8] The length of the Humfrey tragedy in 1578 would thus seem to be in line with the tendency for the *Mirror* poets to produce longer offerings in the post-1559 volumes, both in terms of their new compositions and through adding stanzas to extant material.[9]

It is highly likely, then, that Ferrers actively revised the Gloucester material before its eventual publication. Moreover, whilst the *Mirror* undoubtedly uses topical refiguring to comment on contemporary politics (as Lucas's monograph has shown most recently), this is not the sole 'purpose' of the work. The *Mirror* volumes also recurrently strive to interrogate the construction of historical narrative and of posthumous reputation by exposing the partiality of the written record (and here 'partial' is meant in the sense of both 'incomplete' and 'partisan'). This 'partiality' is raised from the outset of the project, by none other than 'maister Ferrers', when in the preamble to the work he reflects on Boccaccio's omission from *De casibus virorum illustrium* of such 'myserable Princes' 'as wer of our nacion' (p.69): 'he beynge an *Italien*, mynded most of the *Roman* and *Italike* story', 'Ferrers' suggests, 'or els perhaps he wanted [lacked] our country chronicles' (p.70). This interest in the lacunae and the predilections of historical narrative continues through the volume, found, for example, in the prose link following Mowbray's tragedy (where 'a doubte was found therin, and that by means of the diuersity of the Chronicles', p.110) or in the attention that is drawn to the dearth of information about Richard of Cambridge (who is 'litle fauoured of wryters, for our Cronicles speake very little of him', p.142). The book thus highlights the subjectivity of history and its own incompleteness, showing us the contributors skipping pages in their source material (when stories seem repetitive) or failing to provide the promised tragedies through forgetfulness or lack of skill, time, or industry. In the 1559 volume, for example, one of the (unnamed) contributors draws attention to 'a duke of Excester found dead in the sea between Dover and Calys, but what he was, or by what adventure he died, master Fabian hath not shewed, and master Hall hath overskipped him: so that excepte we bee friendlier vnto him, he is like to be double drowned, both in the sea, and in the gulfe of forgetfulness' (p.219). One of the contributors 'tooke vppon him seeke out that story', but that promise is unfulfilled: the Duke's story remains a gap in the *Mirror* just as it is in the historical record, 'overskipped' by Fabian, Hall, and now by this company of poets.

The second, 1563 volume draws still more sustained attention to its incompleteness. 'Ferrers' arrives with 'but a few' tragedies, 'becaus no more are redye' (p.243). Later, the tragedy of the princes in the Tower (Edward V and Richard, Duke of York) remains unwritten. 'Haue you theyr tragedy?' asks one of the contributors. 'No surely (quoth I ["Baldwin"]) The Lord Vaulx vndertooke to penne it, but what he hath done herein I am not certayne' (p.297). In summoning up the poet Collingborne, the 1563 volume also reminds readers of the fissures inflicted on the historical record by political censorship, both by the authorities (as happens to

Collingbourne), and by self-silencing (which is what Collingbourne now recommends): 'Ceas ... Baldwyn, ceas I thee exhort,| Withdrawe thy pen', his ghost advises (p.349). At the end of the volume, though, the act of censorship is done on aesthetic, not political, grounds: 'I haue certain rabets here but they are not worthe the readinge', comments 'Baldwin' in the closing lines (p.421), 'rabets' (rabbits) being a metaphor used at the beginning of the volume to indicate quickly produced but 'feble' work (p.244). As the subjects of these suppressed tragedies pass unnamed, we do not even know whose stories we are missing.

The dual perspective provided through the two Gloucester tragedies is thus compatible with the way in which the *Mirror* destabilises the authority of the historical record, with the source material for Elianor's story showing the very 'diuersity' that the *Mirror* poets comment on in the wake of Mowbray's lament. As the wife of Duke Humphrey, Henry VI's uncle, Eleanor Cobham was (next to Henry's wife, Margaret), the most powerful woman in England, particularly since Henry's lack of issue meant that Humphrey stood next in line to the throne. In 1441, Cobham was accused of witchcraft, including casting horoscopes to discover the date of Henry VI's death, and (more seriously) of ordering her accomplices to hasten the king's demise by 'devising an image of waxe lyke vnto the kynge, the whiche ymage they delte soo with, that by theyr deuylysshe incantacyons and sorcery, they entended to brynge out of lyfe lytell and lytell the kynges person, as they lytell and lytell consumed the ymage'.[10] The sensational nature of these crimes, the Duchess' high profile, her apparent unpopularity prior to her fall, and the very public nature of her humiliation – walking barefoot through the city in penance on three separate market days, when the city would be more crowded than usual – served to make her a *cause célèbre*. Her story consequently features in all the major chronicles printed prior to the *Mirror* (John Hardyng's, Robert Fabyan's, Edward Hall's), as well as at least one fifteenth-century chronicle in manuscript (entitled *An English Chronicle* by its nineteenth-century editor).[11] As Elianor herself laments in the *Mirror*, she was also made a topic for balladeers, an act which she features as a deliberate piece of propaganda, engineered by her enemies: 'And then to bring my name in more disgrace| A song was made in manner of a laye,| Which old wyues sing of me vnto this day' (p.437). Certainly a ballad about her, *The Lament of the Duchess of Gloucester*, survives in two known manuscript witnesses: Cambridge University Library Hh.4.12 (a collection of middle English verse) and

Balliol 354 ('Richard Hill's Commonplace book').[12] That Ferrers knew this poem is suggested by numerous linguistic echoes between it and 'Elianor Cobham', not least of which are the uses of Lucifer as a symbol for pride (*Lament*, l.15; 'Elianor Cobham', p.438), the reference to the 'cloth of gold' that epitomises her lost wealth and position (*Lament*, l.71; 'Elianor Cobham', p.440), and the 'farewell' to Greenwich, which intrudes oddly into Elianor's complaint at p.441, disrupting her expressions of grief at her separation from her husband.

The most unsympathetic of the prose accounts is the manuscript *English Chronicle*, the hostility of which is epitomised by its assertion that 'pride, fals couetise and lechery were the cause of her confusion', a judgement quickly followed up with an effective use of *paralipsis* (passing over a point to highlight it) in order to condemn her further: 'Othir thyngis myghte be writen of this dame Alienore, the whiche atte reuerence of nature and of wommanhood shul not be rehersed' (p.60). Yet even this chronicler leaves room for readers to doubt the veracity of the full litany of charges laid against her; she is called 'to answere to certayn articlez of nygromancie, of wicche craft or sorcery, of heresy and of tresoun', 'whereof some she denyed and some she grauntid' (p.59). Moreover, as the chronicle records, the key witness against her is one of her alleged accomplices, Master Roger Bolingbroke, principal of St Andrew's Hall, Oxford, who 'confessid' to the crime after his arrest, and who – instead of using his scaffold speech to articulate his repentance – instead asserted that he 'was nevir gilty of eny treson ayens the kyngis persone', two facts which raise questions as to whether his initial confession was made under pressure (pp.59, 60).

The potentially dubious grounds for Cobham's conviction are reflected in Fabyan's *Newe Cronycles of England and Fraunce* (printed 1516) and Hall's *Vnion of the Two Noble and Illustre Families of Lancaster and York* (1548). In both, Cobham's disgrace is juxtaposed with information about the feud between her husband and his close relatives in such a way as to suggest a connection between the two events. As Fabyan writes:

> The.xix. yere began murmure & grudge to breke at large ... atwene persones nere about the kyng, and his vncle the famous Humfrey duke of Gloceter and protectour of the lande. Agayne whome dyuers coniectures were attempted a farre whiche after were sette nere to hym, so that they lefte not tyll they had broughte hym vnto his confusion.
> And fyrste this yere dame Eleanoure Cobham, whom he was familier with or she were to hym maryed, was arrested of certayne poyntes of treason ... (sig. 2H6ʳ)

The introduction of Cobham frames her as a means by which Gloucester's enemies 'broughte hym vnto his confusion'. Hall strikes a similar note. 'Venyme will once breake oute, and inwarde grudge will sone appeare', he writes (echoing Fabyan):

> For first this yere, dame Elyanour Cobham, wife to the sayd duke, was accused of treason, for that she, by sorcery and enchauntment, entended to destroy the kynge was this yere to all men apparaunt: for diuers secrete attemptes were aduaunced forward this season, against the noble duke Humfrey of Glocester, a farre of, which in conclusion came so nere, that thei bereft him bothy lyfe and lande, as you shall hereafter. (sig. 2A4^r)

John Hardyng's *Chronicle* (printed in 1543) goes further still, stating that Cobham was 'foriudged' (sig. E7^v), a term – meaning 'judge[d ...] beforehand or without fair trial' – which casts doubt on the legality of her committal.[13]

The chronicles also hint at a religious motivation behind Cobham's conviction: Hardyng's verses note that the accusations include 'enchaunmentes, that she was in working| Agayne the churche' (sig. E7^v); the *English Chronicle* defines her crimes as 'heresy', a charge that sixteenth-century religious reformers recurrently read as evidence of proto-Protestantism and a means by which the Church suppressed dissenting views. It is therefore unsurprising that the propagandist John Foxe should cast Cobham as a martyr in the 1563 *Actes and Monuments*: 'for suspicion of heresie, that is to say, for the loue and desire of the truth she was by the papists banished into the ile of man as Hardinge and Fabian do write' (p.423). This brief comment became a point of controversy between Foxe and Nicholas Harpsfield (writing under the pseudonym Alan Cope). The 1570 edition of *Actes and Monuments* consequently includes a much-expanded section on Cobham in which Foxe makes a detailed case (comprising ten reasons or 'conjectures') as to why her conviction was unsound, the blame for which is placed firmly at Beaufort's door.

Cobham, in other words, provides a rich topic for writers who (like the *Mirror* poets) were interested in contested – and contestable – parts of history; and here the innovative decision within the *Mirror* to use *prosopopoeia* ('a rhetorical device by which an imaginary, absent, or dead person is represented as speaking') plays a crucial role in the way in which the work explores the construction of posthumous memory.[14] These stories are not told from an objective viewpoint, but from the perspective of the person who is striving to rehabilitate their reputation. As readers, we need to pay attention not simply to what the speakers are made to say by the *Mirror* poets who ventriloquise them, but how are they made to say it. Campbell might overemphasise the difference between the Duke's and Duchess' accounts when she deems them 'diametrically opposed' in points of fact, but Ferrers' treatment of them is markedly different in terms of their self-representation and how they acknowledge the part that they themselves had in the events that led to their downfall. Humfrey tends to talk in figurative language which repeatedly fashions him as a victim of circumstance, as can be seen through the list of similes that accumulate in his opening stanza:

> *As highest hills* with tempests bene most touched
> *And tops of trees*, most subiect vnto wynde,
> *And as great towers* with stone strongly cowched,
> Haue heauy falls when they be vnderminde,
> Euen so by proofe in worldy things we fynde,
> That such as clime the top of high degree
> From peril of falling neuer can be free. (p.445, emphases added)

Humfrey thus portrays his fall from power as inevitable (he talks of 'when' towers are undermined, not 'if'), and gives it precedent through a series of proverbial commonplaces which put the deliberate destruction of fortifications on the same terms as the stronger winds which naturally assail hilltops and treetops. This same passivity in regard to his fate is also evident when he uses a simile to describe the grudge that grew between himself and his brother John of Bedford (regent in Henry VI's French kingdoms):

> … like as a match doth lye and smolder,
> Long time before it commeth to the trayne.
> But yet when fyre hath caught in the poulder,
> No arte is able, the flames to restrayne. (p.451)

It is as if Humfrey has no agency in either averting or helping to fuel the 'flame' that 'burst foorth' (p.451), to the detriment of both Plantagenet kingdoms. Indeed, such internecine conflict is even attributed to the deathbed 'Prophecy' of his ancestor, Henry II:

> This kinge (some wryte) in his sicknesse last
> Sayde, as it were by way of Prophecy
> How that the Deuill, a Darnell[15] grayne had cast
> Amonge his Kin to encrease enmity,
> Which should remayne in their Posterity,
> Till mischief, and murder had spent them all
> Not leauinge one to pisse agaynst the wall. (p.448)

This stanza does not just represent Humfrey as a man of a superstitious bent: it compounds the impression of Humfrey as a man who sees himself as unable to intervene and shape his own destiny. He recurrently talks of his downfall in the passive voice: he is 'Led by the eares with false flatteries chyrme [chatter]', a feature of court life which is, moreover, presented as something that those in authority are powerless to avert: 'which neuer Prince could banishe from his gate' (p.446). Humfrey consequently finds that he 'was trapt into a snare' (p.446), whilst the internal qualities that should have 'beene stayers to Fortuners variaunce' – namely, his 'wisedome, learning, ... worldly pollicye' – are externalised, as if separate from him and out of his control, and 'al did fayle [him]' (p.446).

This same sense of helplessness is reflected in the way that Humfrey twice perceives himself as a boat (pp.447, 453), a metaphor which was frequently used in both ancient and early modern political discourse to describe good governance, where the ship is a polity, the safe passage of which through the stormy seas depends on the wisdom of its captain and the cooperation of his dutiful crew. Humphrey's deployment of this metaphor is noticeably passive; rather than steering the ship, we find him wrecked by an accident of birth: 'So neere of Kin that I was to the Crowne,| That was the Rocke that made my Ship to drowne' (p.447). Humfrey's curious distance from the events that he relates even sees him peculiarly absent from his own death, which is again described in the passive voice, in a repetition of the image of the snare (p.446):

> Thou lookest now, that of my secret murther,
> I should at large the maner how declare,
> I pray thee Baldwin, aske of me no further,
> For speaking playne, it came so at vnware,
> As I my selfe, which caught was in the snare,
> Scarcely am able the circumstaunce to shew,
> Which was kept close, and knowen but vnto few. (pp.458–9)

The gap that Humfrey's account opens up (through his inability to recount what happened) is, on one level, Ferrer's response to the opacity of the historical record and the actual mystery that surrounds Gloucester's death, but it also accords with the consistent portrayal within the complaint of Humfrey's lack of engagement with, and apparent inability to influence, the chain of events that bring about his demise.

In contrast to her husband, Ferrers' Elianor is portrayed as being very much in control of her own narrative. In the fifteenth-century *Lament*, the Duchess is eavesdropped on by an anonymous 'I' (rather like the deserted woman in William Shakespeare's *A Lover's Complaint*, whose story is accidentally overheard by its narrator): 'Throughout a palace as I can pass,| I heard a lady make great moan| And ever she sighed and said "Alas!"' (ll. 1–3). In Ferrers' version, in contrast, she deliberately sets out to recover her posthumous reputation. Witness the difference between her opening stanza and Humfrey's: where he begins with commonplace similes, which mean that his fall is initially introduced in the abstract rather than as something which happened to him, Elianor's is a textbook lesson in how someone at a disadvantage might ingratiate themselves with their audience, by 'win[ning] fauour with muche circumstaunce', as Thomas Wilson's *Arte of Rhetorique* puts it in 1553 (sig. O3ʳ). Elianor, in Wilson's terms, 'insinua[tes]' herself into the present company: 'If a poore lady damned in exile,| Amongst princes may bee allowed place,' she pleads, 'Then gentle Baldwin stay thy pen awhyle' (p.432).

Within Ferrers' poem, that is, Elianor reclaims an agency denied her in the historical record, where she habitually features in passive constructions: 'Eleanoure Cobham ... was arested'; 'Elyanor Cobham ... was accused'.[16] In her concern to recuperate her name, Ferrers' Elianor has much in common with the *Mirror*'s Mistress Shore, although they take rather different approaches. Shore is characteristically self-justifying, recurrently blaming others – the world (p.373), her beauty (p.376), her friends (p.377), the 'puissan[ce]' of a 'kynges desyre' (p.376) – and lauding the popular benefits of her influence over her royal lover, Edward IV: 'My power was prest to ryght the poore mans wrong,| My handes were free to geve where need requyred' (p.380). Like Ferrers' Humfrey, Shore also attempts to deflect any agency she has by repeatedly using metaphors to frame what happens as a natural phenomenon: 'But who can stop the streame that runnes full swyft?| Or quenche the fyer that crept is in the strawe' (p.374).[17] In contrast, Elianor claims responsibility for her moral failings, admitting her 'pryde of harte' (p.434). This admission of culpability does not, however, render her passive, as Mary Steible posits.[18] Rather, there is a strategy behind this confession, and in the limits that she places on this acknowledgement of guilt.

This control is apparent in the moment at which Elianor comes closest to resorting to the weapon of the powerless and dispossessed: namely cursing. 'The spiteful Preest would needes make me a Witch,' she declares:

> As would to god I had bene for his sake,
> I would haue clawd him where he did not itche,
> I woulde haue played the Lady of the Lake

> And as Merlin was, cloasde him in a Brake,
> Ye a Meridian, to Lul him by daylight
> And night mare to ryde on him by night. (p.439)

This initiates a further four stanzas in which she imagines inflicting the most appalling infernal punishments upon the Cardinal. Those stanzas not only vent her hatred: even here, we see her wresting back control of her own reputation, since phrasing the curse in the conditional mood – what she 'would' have done – implicitly differentiates her from the 'Witch' that Beaufort would make her. For all their vitriol, these lines also display Elianor's self-restraint. Unlike Churchyard's Mistress Shore cursing Richard III and whatever and whoever nurtured him (p.384), Elianor does not succumb to the temptation to curse, an activity of dubious legal standing after the 1563 act 'agaynst conjuracions, inchauntments and witchecraftes' (5 Eliz. I c. 16). Rather, the hypothetical 'would' allows Ferrers' Elianor to vent her spleen without committing to an act which risks depicting her as a witch, a technique that is also deployed by Michael Drayton in his portrayal of Cobham in the 1603 edition of *Englands Heroicall Epistles*. Drayton's 'Elnor' does curse 'That Prelate Bedford': 'a foule ill befall him,| … My curse pursue him where so ere he goe'.[19] However, her more extended (thirty-four-line) vituperation of Queen Margaret (Henry VI's wife) is – like that of her *Mirror* counterpart – carefully placed in the conditional: 'O that I were a Witch but for her sake,| I fayth her Queeneship little rest should take,' Elnor begins, 'I would scratch that face that may not feele the ayre,| And knit whole ropes of witch-knots in her hayre' (sig. H3^v).

Elianor's is an accomplished and carefully constructed rhetorical performance. In the prose frame immediately after her complaint, one of the company expresses surprise at the knowledge of classical literature that she displays: 'I meruayle much where she learned al this Poetry,' he observes, 'for in her days, learning was not common, but a rare thing, namely in women' (p.444). What is not commented on, but is perhaps equally striking, is Elianor's apparent grasp of the law, as much a male preserve as literary scholarship, if not more so. Elianor consistently portrays her trial as a violation of justice. She achieves this through use of emotive analogy, depicting Beaufort as Caiaphas (p.436), the chief priest who, along with the elders and the council, 'sought false witness against Jesus, to put him to death' (Matthew 26:59), but also by wielding precise legal terms. The 'processe' by which Elianor is summoned to answer charges is, in her view, 'peremptory' (p. 436), that is, brooking no challenge or debate; her 'answer dilatory' – a plea to postpone a legal action (for example, to allow time to prepare a defence) – is disallowed (p.436); and she is refused legal counsel ('ne Doctor or Proctor to allege the lawes', p.436).

Elianor here does more than simply question the legal process by which she has been convicted: she also turns the tables on her opponents, casting them as the villains as they disregard justice, one of the four cardinal virtues which – along with temperance, fortitude, and prudence – are 'requisite in him that should be in authoritie' (as John Higgins notes in the preface to his *Mirror* spin-off).[20] Elianor castigates the lawyers who, acting for the Cardinal, prosecute her 'without ruth or reason' (p.436) and pervert the law, 'deuys[ing]| By Statute law, in most vnlawful wise' (p.436), the *polyptoton* of 'lawe' 'vnlawful' further highlighting the abuse. The contravening of justice continues with her banishment, when she is stripped of 'such right of dower, as widowes haue by law' (p.437). By exposing the way in which Beaufort 'color[s]' justice, Elianor positions herself as adhering to, and upholding, Higgins' 'cardinal virtues'. In quite a rhetorical coup, she even manages to claim the virtue of fortitude:

> Then the best salue for my recureless sore
> Was to dispayre of cure for euermore,
> And as I could, my careful hart to cure,
> With pacience, most painful to indure. (p.438)

As she endorses the virtues of civic governance, she thus seizes back control of her narrative ideologically as well as linguistically.

Elianor's command over her material is duly recognised by 'one of the companye', who observes that, not only has she 'don much to moue the hearers to pitye her', she has also 'very wel knyt vp the ende of her tragedy according to the beginning' (p.444). This circularity is more than aesthetically pleasing, however. In the first stanza, Elianor set up her tale as an exemplary one, proving 'The prouerbe true, that pryde wil hauve a fall' (p.432); that sentiment also provides the closing line and the moral of her complaint (p.443). In the process, Eleanor rewrites the fifteenth-century *Lament*, the 'laye| Which old wyues sing … vnto this day' (p.437) and which she feels has brought her 'name in more disgrace' (p.437). The *Mirror* tragedy moves beyond the exclusively female audience addressed in the *Lament*, whose refrain, 'All women may be ware by me', genders the sin of pride predominantly female, something to which women are particularly susceptible and which is expressed through the Duchess' regret for her lost riches ('Farewell, damask and clothes of gold;| Farewell, velvet and clothes in grain;| Farewell, robes in many a fold').[21] Ferrers' *Mirror* tragedy extends the notion of pride beyond female vanity, linking it more firmly to the political vice of ambition: his Elianor 'longed sore to beare the name of Queene| Aspyring stil vnto a higher seate' (p.434). Further to that, by the end of the poem, the burden of the example has shifted from Elianor herself. In the *Lament*, the Duchess notes that 'As Lucifer fell down for pride,| I fell from all felicity' (ll. 28–9). Ferrers' Elianor recycles this idea, applying it instead to her enemy, Cardinal Beaufort:

> Proude Lucifer, which from the heauens on hye
> Downe to the pit of Hel below was cast,
> ...
> More hault of hart was not before his fal
> Then was this proud and pompos Cardinal. (p.438)

Beaufort, not Elianor, thus becomes the preeminent exemplar of pride, and her evocation of the proverb, not done in remorse, but in vengeful hope. Elianor even encourages Baldwin to 'paint out' the life of 'this Baal & Belligod most blinde' (p.438); Beaufort himself becomes a fitting subject for a fall of princes, to be summoned onto the page, like Ferrers' Tresilian, to recount his crimes and comeuppance.

Despite its belatedness and seeming liminality, Elianor's tragedy is thus a fitting addition to Ferrers' *Mirror* corpus. Discussions of this lament customarily refer back to Campbell's argument that Ferrers used the Cobham story to shadow the experience of Elizabeth during her sister Mary's reign, when she was accused of commissioning John Dee to cast her horoscope, along with that of Mary and her husband, Philip of Spain, an event in which Ferrers may have been directly involved: a 'George Ferys' is one of the witnesses against Dee (although Lucas points out that 'there was at least one other' person of that name, of gentry status, in Marian England).[22] Whether or not Ferrers had first-hand knowledge of this real-life drama (and Lucas is more sceptical than Campbell or Budra), Elianor's tragedy addresses two concerns that run through Ferrers' other contributions to the *Mirror*: namely, one, a concern with internecine strife, as found in the complaints of Thomas of Woodstock, Duke Humfrey, and Edmund Duke of Somerset (added in the 1563 *Mirror*); and, two, a keen interest in the proper functioning of the law. Ferrers was a member of Lincoln's Inn from 1534, a Justice of the Peace (1547–54), and the probable editor and translator of the 1533 *Great Boke of Statutes* and 1541 *Magna Carta*, the latter task undertaken as 'a good helpe for the vnlerned', that they might have knowledge of the laws that 'bynde the kyngs subiectes vnto this day'; records of his time as Master of the Revels in 1551–3 also point to his legal interests, manifested in the recurrent staging of entertainments that featured imprisonment and execution.[23]

The proper functioning of the judicial system (critiqued by Elianor in relation to her own trial) is the focus of both of Ferrers' complaints in the 1559 volume: Tresilian's tragedy, which opens the *Mirror*, and in which Richard II's Lord Chief Justice confesses that he 'wittyngly and wretchedly did wrest the sence of lawe' (p.73), and the lament of Thomas of Woodstock (the third of the *Mirror* tragedies), which depicts a country in which legal processes are continually overturned. The title informs us that 'Wudstocke' was 'vnlawfully murdred' (p.91); later, we hear that he was condemned 'without proces or doome of [his] peeres' (p.98), only posthumously charged with 'Articles nyne of ryght haynous treason' (p.98): 'But doome after death is sure out of season,' he observes, 'For who euer sawe so straunge a presydent,| As execucuion doen before iudgement[?]' (p.98). Yet Wudstocke himself is not free from blame on this part: he too abuses legal procedures, calling parliament by force, 'With swurdes and no wurdes we tryed our appeale,| In stede of Reason declaryng our Zeale' (p.96), the wordplay further highlighting the inversion of proper order. At this so-called parliament, 'Sum with shorte process were banysht the lande,| Sum executed with capytall payne' (p.96), summary sentencing which we are surely meant to perceive as 'vniust', an epithet with which he later labels Richard II (p.98). The seemingly unrepentant and un-self-reflective Wudstocke even concludes his narrative endorsing the concept of revenge, a code that is at odds with ideas of legal justice: 'For blood axeth blood as guerdon dewe,| And vengeaunce for vengeaunce is iust rewarde' (p.99).

The account that Wudstocke gives of the 1387 uprising of the Lords Appellant also contrasts starkly with the one that features in Tresilian's tragedy, where the impromptu parliament is described – not as a place of coercion, as it is in 'Wudstocke' – but as an ideal discursive space, 'Francke and free for all men without checke to debate| As well for weale publyke, as for the princes state' (p.78). For Lucas, such disparities are 'a direct result of the two different topical purposes to which Ferrers puts these poems'.[24] Yet it is equally possible to read this as symptomatic of Ferrers' fascination with conflicting or disputed versions of history: an interest which lies at the core of Elianor's complaint, its pairing with that of her husband, and with the *Mirror* project as a whole, an undertaking in which 'Ferrers' – as the interlocutor who initiates the critique of 'Bochas' – takes a leading part.

Notes

Note on names: Elianor and Humfrey are used to denote characters in the *Mirror for Magistrates*; Cobham and Humphrey/Gloucester are used of their historical counterparts. 'Baldwin' and 'Ferrers' appear within quotation marks when these names refer to their in-text personae.

1. Lily B. Campbell, ed., *The Mirror for Magistrates* (Cambridge University Press, 1938; reprinted New York: Barnes & Noble), p.431. Owing to the complex publishing history of this text, all quotations will be from this edition, with abbreviations silently expanded.
2. *A Myrrovre for Magistrates* (1559), sig. G4ᵛ.
3. *A Myrrovr for Magistrates* (1571), sig. *4ᵛ.
4. A keyword search in the MLA bibliography on 'Cobham + Mirror' produces two results: Lily Campbell, 'Humphrey Duke of Gloucester and Elianor Cobham His Wife in the *Mirror for Magistrates*', *HLB* 5 (1934), 119–55; and Jamie C. Fumo, 'Books of the Duchess: Eleanor Cobham, Henryson's *Cresseid*, and the Politics of Complaint', *Viator* 37 (2006), 447–77, an article which is in fact about the relationship between Henryson's *Cresseid* and the fifteenth-century *Lament of the Duchess of Gloucester*, rather than Ferrers' poem *per se* (search conducted 19 June 2015). Her complaint is not reproduced in the only anthology of 'female complaint', John Kerrigan, ed., *Motives of Woe* (Oxford University Press, 1991), and she makes few appearances in the two most recent book-length studies: Scott C. Lucas, A Mirror for Magistrates *and the Politics of the English Reformation* (Amherst: University of Massachusetts Press, 2009), pp.21, 91, 99, 241n; and Paul Budra, A Mirror for Magistrates and the *de casibus* Tradition (University of Toronto Press, 2000), pp.11, 63, 65–6, 70.
5. Samuel Daniel, *Complaint of Rosamund*, in *Poems and a Defence of Rhyme*, ed. A. C. Sprague (University of Chicago Press, 1965), l. 25; Michael Drayton, *Matilda* (London: James Roberts for for Nichola Ling and John Busby, 1594), sigs B1ᵛ–B2ʳ.
6. Paul Budra, *Mirror*, p.66.
7. Lucas, *Mirror*, pp.241, 241n9.
8. Ferrers' 'Robert Tresilian' is 147 lines; 'Thomas of Woodstock', 203 lines; average for the 1559 volume, 168 lines.
9. Average length for additions to 1563 volume: 492 lines.
10. Robert Fabyan, *The Newe Cronycles of England and Fraunce* (printed 1516), sig. 2H6ʳ.
11. *The chronicle of Ihon Hardyng in metre* (printed 1543); Fabyan, *Newe Cronycles*; Edward Hall, *The vnion of the two noble and illustre fameilies of Lancastre & Yorke* (1543); *An English chronicle of the reigns of Richard II, Henry IV, Henry V and Henry VI, written before the year 1471*, ed. John Silvester Davies, *Camden Society* 64 (1856).
12. *The Lament of the Duchess of Gloucester*, in R. H. Robbins, ed., *Historical Poems of the XIVth and XVth Centuries* (Columbia University Press, 1959).
13. 'forejudge, *v.*', sense 1, www.oed.com (accessed 19 June 2015).

14 www.oed.com, sense 1 (accessed 19 June 2015).
15 A weed, often growing among corn, which is particularly liable to ergot ('darnel, *n*.', sense 1a), www.oed.com (accessed 19 June 2015).
16 Fabyan, *Newe Cronycles*, sig. 2H6^r; Hall, *Vnion*, sig. 2A4^r.
17 Other such metaphors appear at ll. 85–90, 114–17, 122, 126–8, 139–42.
18 Mary Steible, 'Jane Shore and the Politics of Cursing', *SEL* 43:1 (2003), 1–17, at p.7.
19 Michael Drayton, *The Barrons Wars in the Raigne of Edward the Second. With Englands Heroicall Epistles* (1603), sig. H4^v.
20 John Higgins, *The Firste Parte of the Mirour for Magistrates* (1574), sig. *4^r.
21 *Lament*, ll. 80–82.
22 Campbell, 'Humphrey Duke of Gloucester and Elianor Cobham His Wife', pp.141–55; Lucas, *Mirror*, p.45n; see also Budra, *Mirror*, p.11.
23 H. R. Woudhuysen, 'Ferrers, George (*c*.1510–1579)', *ODNB*, www.oxforddnb.com/view/article/9360 (accessed 26 June 2015); 'To the reder', *The great Charter called in Latyn Magna Carta* (1541), sig. +2^v.
24 Lucas, *Mirror*, p.112.

CHAPTER 7

Romans in the mirror

Paulina Kewes

The conformist clergyman John Higgins (1544-c.1602) was something of a trailblazer in the transmission history of the *Mirror for Magistrates*. In 1574, he added a collection of complaints by ancient Britons to William Baldwin and others' medieval corpus, and in 1587, aside from supplying several new or revised British and medieval complaints, introduced twelve ancient Romans into a new bumper edition. Those included eleven despots (Julius Caesar, Tiberius, Caligula, Claudius, Nero, Galba, Otho, Vitellius, Severus, Geta, and Caracalla) and the treacherous soldier Laelius Hamo.

Even though Higgins' Roman complaints constitute the first poetic treatment of Roman history in Elizabeth's reign, his reasons for including them have been neglected. This neglect is all the more surprising given the fact that Higgins' concentration on the falls of corrupt emperors flies in the face of the common assumption that late Elizabethan literature was fixated on the end of the Roman republic, in contrast to the early Stuart preoccupation with imperial tyranny.

Why did Higgins import such unsavoury Romans into his omnibus edition? More generally, how do their complaints fit the broader themes of the 1587 *Mirour*, which would strongly influence later writers, among them Shakespeare and Spenser? To make Higgins' decision intelligible, this chapter first relates it to competing contemporary claims for cultural authority drawn from native and classical history, and then traces Higgins' evolving engagement with ancient Britain and Rome in his works published between 1574 and 1587. This approach emphasises that Higgins' previously unnoticed strategic transformation of Geoffrey of Monmouth's *Historia Regum Britanniae* (c.1137) provides vital clues to his political vision.

My main argument, however, is that, contrary to what we might suppose, the Roman rogues' gallery in the 1587 *Mirour* was not primarily designed to address the politics of imperial expansion epitomised by the

Romano-British conflict. Although the tragedy of Julius Caesar did dwell at length on Caesar's conquest of Britain, Higgins otherwise chose not to pursue the subject: his tragedy of Claudius, for instance, makes no allusion to the emperor's British campaign. Rather, Higgins' agenda, I suggest, is twofold. By stigmatising the ignoble complicity of seditious Britons in Caesar's victorious invasion, he speaks to anxieties about treason and foreign invasion rekindled by the discovery of the Babington Plot in late summer 1586. At the same time, by depicting a series of violent regime changes and playing up the Christian subtext – his Jove and Jehovah are virtually indistinguishable and his Tiberius becomes the unlikely champion of Christianity – Higgins warns aspirants to princely dignity that pride, tyranny, and dissimulation inevitably receive divine punishment. The sequence's relentless emphasis on the making and unmaking of imperial tyrants hints at mounting anxieties about the succession as Elizabeth grew older, the international situation worsened, and the daunting topic remained off limits. Yet, however despicable his Romans might be, Higgins wisely steers clear of the clichéd analogy with evil Roman Catholicism. His Roman collection provides a complex imaginative precedent for later treatments of Roman history in poetry and drama and wider public polemic.

'The fame of auncient **Romayne** *facts'*

The original *Mirror for Magistrates* (1559) bucked the dominant humanistic trend locating exemplarity in the Graeco-Roman tradition and Scripture.[1] Instead, the *Mirror* set up England's medieval history as a moralising political paradigm for the Elizabethan governing caste. In the dedication to 'To the nobilitye and all other in office', William Baldwin, the volume's editor-in-chief, defended the use of precedents drawn from the shared national past. 'I nede not go eyther to the Romans or Grekes', claimed Baldwin, 'neyther yet to the Iewes, or other nations', for 'Our owne countrey stories (if we reade & marke them) will shewe vs examples ynow'.[2] Major offshoots of Baldwin's collection also concentrated on national history. Higgins' *The First parte of the Mirour for Magistrates* (1574, 1575) went back in time to recount stories 'From the comming of Brute to the incarnation of our sauiour and redemer Iesu Christe' and Thomas Blenerhasset's *Second Part of the Mirror for Magistrates* (1578) added yet more legendary Britons.[3]

So did Higgins' interpolation of a raft of Roman complaints into the 1587 *Mirour* mark a regression from the nationalistic focus of the preceding three decades to the earlier humanist paradigm discarded by Baldwin et al.? Or did it nevertheless mark a new departure? While driven by several interlocking concerns, Higgins' Roman turn, I want to suggest, begins an important new phase in the English reception of Roman history. To appreciate his novelty and distinctiveness, we must look closely at how he presents the Roman conquest in the *First parte*, on which the 1587 text expands, and more broadly compare Higgins' depiction of the Romans with other contemporary accounts.

Higgins' bid to versify '*the falles of the first infortunate Princes of this lande*' was strikingly original. Aside from the Senecan tragedy *Gorboduc* (1561/2) by Thomas Norton and Thomas Sackville, no previous Elizabethan poem or play had made ancient Britain its theme. In tackling his country's remote past, moreover, Higgins invited comparisons with Graeco-Roman antiquity. His dedication to the *First parte* aggressively displays classical authorities (Plotinus, Quintus Curtius, Plutarch, Livy, Polybius, Aristotle, and Cicero) and cites ancient, mostly Roman personages (Caesar, Pompey, Sulla, Marius, Carbo, Cinna, Catiline versus Alexander of Macedon, the Persian Cyrus, and the Carthaginian Hannibal). These worthies thus form a frame of reference for the following stories of the Trojan Britons. While Baldwin's prose frame discussed the competing versions of England's medieval history, Higgins' preface remarks by contrast on the paucity and poor quality of sources for his chosen distant era.

In particular, Higgins criticises recent chroniclers for peddling irrelevant foreign tales instead of judiciously reconstructing Britain's prehistory: 'they are faine in steede of other stuffe to talke of the *Romaines, Greekes, Persians, &c.* and to fill our Historyes with their facts & fables'.[4] Higgins might seem to have a point. After all, he was writing before the publication of both Holinshed's *Chronicles* (1577, 1587) and Camden's *Britannia* (1586), which scoured Caesar, Tacitus, Josephus, and other classical authors for any scrap of information about ancient British politics and society, while unable completely to abandon the increasingly discredited Galfridian history. Then again, Higgins himself deliberately ignored even familiar classical works germane to his theme, for instance Caesar's *Commentaries*. Instead, he exploits the supposed historiographical lacuna to justify his 'owne simple invention' (sig. *6r) in embroidering upon Geoffrey's heroic narrative, a scribal copy of which he claims to have lost.

How Higgins frames the British complaints has significant implications for his presentation of the Roman ones thirteen years later. *The First parte* deletes the colloquy on the national chronicles which framed the editions of the *Mirror*. Instead, the 'Britaynes' appear to the author in a dream vision conjured up by Somnus, personifying sleep, aided by his sidekick Morpheus, after Higgins has been rereading the Baldwin *Mirror* (fol. 2ᵛ). Harking back to Chaucer's and Lydgate's dream visions, this frame survives intact in 1587, making the procession of the Roman figures part of the dream. Yet, rather than merely demoting the author to amanuensis, the device effectively makes the dreamer a stand-in for the reader, who is thus pushed towards an appropriate response to the unfolding vision of Britain's past. Meanwhile, the virtual absence of authorial envoys in the Roman sequence encourages active reading and critical judgment to figure out its meaning.

The preface to the *First parte* insists that foreign matter merits inclusion in a national history only 'wher th' affayres of both countries by warre, peace, truce, marriage, trafique or some necessary cause or other is intermixed' (sig. *5ᵛ). Higgins thus slyly advertises his own accomplishment in melding the histories – really pseudo-histories – of Britain and Rome in this work, notably in the final complaint of Nennius, the British hero instrumental in rebuffing Julius Caesar's initial invasion. While Nennius naturally emphasises his own exploits, protesting that they have been unfairly forgotten, he also provides an effective backcloth to the Roman failure. We learn how Britain before the Roman attack was well governed by its elected king Cassibelane, brother to the previous king, Lud, and to Nennius himself, and witness Caesar's insatiable appetite for conquest. Nennius's complaint, no less than the author's envoy, in which he wishes to join the pursuit of the fleeing Romans, thus fulfils Higgins' first criterion of relevance for commingling native and foreign matter: war.

But how far does the 1587 *Mirour* live up to Higgins' thematic criteria in its sequence of Roman complaints? Tellingly, the prefatory passage outlining those criteria in the *First parte* has been excised. No one glancing at a copy would expect to find any Roman lives. The title page highlights 'examples passed in this *Realme*', while 'the addition of divers Tragedies' advertised in smaller print does not mention Romans. Nor do the revamped dedication and preface. Only the table of contents, a list beginning with Brutus's son Albanact and ending with Cardinal Wolsey at seventy-four, numbered continuously across the Higgins and Baldwin sections, includes Roman names, but interspersed with complaints by the Briton Guiderius and the Picts or Scythians Londricus and Fulgentius. The framing device of the dream vision promises only 'The *Britayne* Peeres', and in due course when Julius Caesar enters, he feels obliged to clear the dreamer's – and the reader's – likely bafflement as to 'Why I a *Romayne* Prince, no *Britayne*, here | Amongst these *Britayne* Princes now appeere'. Needless to say, Caesar claims robust justification: 'By conquest sith I wanne this Ile before I fell'.[5]

Are there any other structural or thematic connections between the British and the Roman complaints? One could argue that the stage is prepared for the appearance of Julius Caesar — and Higgins explicitly invokes the theatrical metaphor — by the preceding complaints of the Britons Nennius and Irenglas (the latter added in the 1575 edition) as well as the authorial envoy. Besides, Caesar addresses Higgins directly. Although the remaining classical complaints do not include envoys and only the last Roman, Caracalla, again speaks to Higgins, some half-heartedly gesture towards connections between the fates of the two peoples. The Roman soldier Hamo confesses to masquerading as a Briton to kill King Guiderius, who then gives his differing account of the event. The sequence comprising Severus, Fulgentius, and Severus's sons Geta and Caracalla also establishes some superficial links: Severus, for example, allies with the Britons against the Picts, then slays Fulgentius at York before dying there. Elsewhere Higgins offers no justification for the inclusion of Otho or Vitellius. Overall, the level of integration in the Nennius–Irenglas–Julius Caesar sequence is absent. So we require a different rationale or, in Higgins' phrase, 'necessary cause'.

What I think justifies both sets of complaints is their potential topical application. However, the intense immediacy of the complaints where Roman and British history intersect fundamentally differs from the more abstract quality of those where they do not. To appreciate this difference and tease out its implications, we must revisit the question of the politics of Higgins' *Mirror* volumes and ask how they deal with the Romano-British wars and Rome's imperial history.

'For, things forepast are presidents to us …'

Modern critics differ in their assessment of Higgins as poet but agree that his interventions politically de-fanged the *Mirror* tradition. For Andrew Hadfield, the 1587 collection marks a 'decline', the formal complexity and oppositional potential of the Baldwin corpus 'giv[ing] way to an unproblematic, more crudely ideological series of narratives'.[6] Paul Budra ignores the Roman lives, but especially deprecates Higgins' deployment of Galfridian history, assuming it could not possibly have been relevant to contemporary concerns. 'The text', Budra argues, 'metamorphosed from an ideologically aware poetic history into a sentimental historical poem'.[7] Philip Schwyzer, less critical of Higgins' verse, still concedes that he 'diluted the politics of the anthology'.[8] Meredith Skura, arguing that Higgins' complaints evince an emergent psychological awareness, sums up the critical consensus: 'Baldwin's political edge was dulled in Higgins' 1574 addition to the *Mirror*, and further blunted with each new version'.[9]

None of these claims quite holds true. As we shall see, Higgins' political aspirations have been overlooked or misunderstood because students of his work have not considered its immediate context, nor recognised his telltale departures from the sources, above all Geoffrey of Monmouth. This is not to say that a coherent, unified political message can be extracted from Higgins' volumes. *The Mirror* in Higgins' hands remained, as always – *pace* his modern critics – a complex, multivalent text. But, I will show, his strategic selection, arrangement, and presentation of material did implicitly address some of the most controversial current problems.

We can pinpoint the contemporary application of Higgins' Romans with some precision by comparing the 1587 omnibus *Mirour* with the 1574 and 1575 editions of Higgins' *First parte*, and reading his Britons and Romans alongside his other important interpolation, the medieval English complaint of Nicolas Burdet,[10] which he wrote at the suggestion of Raphael Holinshed. There is no scope here for a comprehensive analysis, but I want to explore how Higgins' presentation of the Romano-British conflict evolved through linked complaints by Nennius, Irenglas, and Julius Caesar first printed in 1574, 1575, and 1587 respectively, with special reference to his redaction of Geoffrey's history.

Far from sentimentalising the corpus, Higgins' use of Geoffrey indicates knowing involvement with a fiercely disputed text. Ever since the Reformation, Galfridian history had been an ideological battleground, and became even more so after Elizabeth's accession. Recent scholarship has illuminated the ideological advantage Geoffrey's account of Britain's conversion to Christianity offered to those anxious to prove England's independence from Rome.[11] As a clergyman, Higgins would have been familiar with this polemic, but avoided entering the fray through, for example, the life of 'Lucius, the first Christian King of Britain', a figure claimed by Protestant and Catholic controversialists alike. Instead, Higgins deployed Geoffrey for more narrowly political purposes.

The 1574 edition, spanning the arrival of Brutus and foundation of New Troy to Caesar's unsuccessful invasion, appeared within five years of the Northern Rebellion, within four years of the papal bull of excommunication, and within three years of the Ridolfi Plot to replace Elizabeth with the Catholic Mary, Queen of Scots, to be married to England's premier peer the Duke of Norfolk. Amid the fallout from these crises, which led to

Norfolk's execution and Mary's stricter confinement, Parliament had prohibited public discussion of the succession and made it treason to question Elizabeth's title to the crown.[12] In 1574, the first Catholic missionaries began arriving from Douai, fuelling fears of popish infiltration and sedition; meanwhile, militant Protestants led by the Earl of Leicester urged Elizabeth to assist the Dutch provinces in their struggle against Philip II of Spain. The concomitant explosion of officially sponsored print, countered in turn by Catholic publications smuggled in from the Continent, polarised political discourse and rendered the Trojan myth, no less than the Roman conquest of Britain, acutely topical.[13]

Drawing on classical epic, notably Virgil's *Aeneid*, both Protestant and Catholic pamphleteers likened contemporary England to Troy, and Elizabeth to Priam, while denouncing their confessional opponents as the treacherous Greeks. For the committed Protestant Thomas Norton, who published several highly charged pamphlets in 1569–70, the papal bull challenging England's sovereignty recalled the Trojan horse, and the popish faction a dangerous fifth column resembling Sinon the Greek.[14] Conversely, the toxic Catholic libel *Treatise of Treasons* (1572) contrasted the Machiavellian atheism of the 'Partie Protestant', exhibiting 'the suttletie, falsehood, and lewed propertie of the Greekish Nation', with 'The modestie and conscience of the Catholike partie', hailed as 'the olde Troians'. Sir William Cecil and Sir Nicholas Bacon, the pillars of the Protestant regime, were scathingly reviled as 'those two Machiauellians: who (not all vnlike to Ulysses & Synon the Greekes) to make themselues & their faction lordes of your new Troy, haue forged a new faction, fraught as full of mischieuous meanings to your Priame now, as euer was the bulke of their woodden horse, to the Troianes than'.[15]

With these contextual developments in mind, we can read anew Higgins' earliest British complaints, particularly the lament of Nennius concluding the 1574 edition, and that of Irenglas, which follows it in 1575. Typically seen as a generic expression of Elizabethan patriotism, Nennius's heroic struggle against Caesar and Rome directly addressed the plotted Hispano-papal invasion on behalf of Mary Stewart, now mercifully averted. Indeed the complaint's descriptive title, the longest in the volume, advertises this contemporary resonance: 'he nowe encourageth all good subjects to defende their country from the power of forraine and usurping enemies'.[16] One almost detects echoes of Norton's anti-sedition pamphlets, collectively republished in 1570, minus their overt anti-Catholicism – perhaps because Higgins thought it would be jarring in a poem. (Even the evangelical Baldwin had eschewed explicit anti-popery.)

The 1570 Nortoniana included his and Sackville's ancient British *Tragedie of Ferrex and Porrex*, better known as *Gorboduc*;[17] suggestively, Higgins' complaints of Forrex and Porrex in his *First parte* traverse much the same ground.

If the 1574 *First parte* concluded with a gung-ho celebration of old British valour – even awarding a native hero a Latin tag, '*Vivit post funera virtus*' (fol. 74ᵛ), the addition in 1575 of the complaint of Irenglas, nephew of King Cassibelane, wholly altered the book's tenor.[18] Triumphalism surrendered to despondency and anxiety, unity to discord. The poem aptly dramatises this sudden revolution, telling how a joyful occasion – a joust honouring the recent victory over the Roman invaders – descends into catastrophe. Irenglas, who wins the joust, is rashly murdered by Elenine, cousin of Cassibelane's nephew Androgeus Earl of London. Fissures within the British body politic are exposed: the king no longer commands the allegiance of his subjects. The malcontents, Higgins strongly implied, may well court allies abroad, which is precisely what is happening when Higgins picks up the narrative in his complaint of Julius Caesar for the 1587 *Mirour*.

A mere glance at Geoffrey's *History* demonstrates the purposefulness of Higgins' adjustments, especially when compared with his slavish recycling of Herodian in the lives of Severus, Geta, and Caracalla. Take the characters of Cassibelane and Julius Caesar in Nennius's complaint. In Geoffrey, the indignant Cassivelanus rejects Caesar's haughty demand for tribute without taking anyone's advice.[19] By contrast, Higgins' Cassibelane summons his nobles for consultation and speaks eloquently about the country's ancient freedoms, to be protected at all cost (though it could be argued that this gave opportunity for the king's oratory, where Geoffrey did not); the council unanimously resolves to defy Caesar.[20] The scene melds baronial conciliarism with Collinson's monarchical republicanism familiar from Sir Thomas Smith's *De republica Anglorum* or Norton's pamphlets,[21] though it is anyone's guess whether Higgins intended to compliment or advise the queen or both. The image could be interpreted either way. Again, while Geoffrey's Caesar, a tough but worthy opponent, acknowledges the Romans' and Britons' common Trojan ancestry, Higgins makes him not just grasping and proud but devious and duplicitous. Higgins' Caesar stoops low enough to anoint his sword with poison (fol. 72ᵛ): this kills Nennius, not Caesar's superior martial strength, a possible reminder of the Machiavellian diplomacy of that latter-day Caesar, Philip II. The association of Julius Caesar with King Philip would come to the fore in Higgins' tragedy of Caesar.

As with counsel and magisterial integrity, so with succession: in Geoffrey, the just and widely admired Cassivelanus is generous towards the sons of his elder brother King Lud, who do not feel wronged by their uncle's accession; conversely, in Higgins, Elenine tauntingly denounces Cassibelane's title, asserting that the crown rightfully belongs to Lud's son Androgeus: 'As for the king we doubte if he be heyre,| The kingdome is the Earle of *Londons* right'.[22] Androgeus is not Mary, Queen of Scots in drag. Rather, Irenglas's tragedy subtly alludes to the papal bull's aspersions on Elizabeth's title, and ventilates the apprehension, intensified by the unmasking of the Ridolfi Plot, that some Englishmen would betray the queen. Crucially, at that very moment the government was developing its self-serving distinction between persecuting Catholics for their religion, which it denied, and vigorous prosecution of Catholics for their alleged treason. Within a few years Cecil's pamphlet *The Execution of Justice in England* (1583), translated into Latin and Continental vernaculars for an international audience, would stoutly defend this distinction.

Higgins' oration of Julius Caesar, which in the 1587 omnibus *Mirour* follows the revised orations of Nennius and Irenglas, again manipulated Geoffrey in reprising Caesar's British campaigns.[23] His key change was to blacken the character of Androgeus, Earl of London. In Geoffrey's *History*, the hot-headed Androgeus allies himself with the Romans, but after Cassivelanus's defeat he makes peace between Caesar and his uncle-king, with whom he also reconciles.[24] Not so his counterpart in Higgins, who epitomises the ugly traits of rebels and traitors. He rises against Cassibelane and connives in Caesar's enslavement of his countrymen; a useful tool of the Romans, 'in *Britayne* [Androgeus] beare[s] for aye a shrowding sheete of shame'. Meanwhile Cassibelane's extreme distress at his subjects' disloyalty – which again has no equivalent in Geoffrey – renders him almost feminine, a delicate pointer to the tide of loyalist pamphlets and sermons which dwelled extensively on the bond of love between the female monarch and her people: 'His losse perdy in war not greude him halfe so sore,| As for to see his people liege erst subiects euermore,| To fight agaynst the royall king, which lou'd them so before' (fol. 81ʳ).

These alterations sharpen the polemical edge of Caesar's monologue, and there is no great mystery as to why. Higgins signed the revised dedicatory epistle on 7 December 1586, three days after the public proclamation of Mary, Queen of Scots' death sentence. Mary had been condemned for participating in the Babington Plot on 25 October, and the following months saw a mounting clamour for her execution until she went to the block on 8 February. Higgins' book went through the press at the same time as the second edition of Holinshed's *Chronicles*, which recounted the gory executions of the Babington plotters, as well as furnishing a thoroughly revamped description of Britain and the various Roman conquests.[25]

Even more so than its predecessors, the 1587 *Mirour* explicitly encouraged readers to apply its stories to the present. A commendatory poem by Thomas Newton, prolific editor, translator, and, like Higgins, a clergyman, urged the reader to 'Confer the times, perpend the history' and then seek out 'the drift whereto it tendes'. For, Newton explained, 'things forepast are presidents to us,| Whereby wee may things present now discusse' (sig. C2ᵛ). It was surely not coincidental that, rather than echoing the commonplace that the past serves as a guide to the present, Newton instead stressed that historical precedents facilitate *discussion* of current affairs – perhaps suggesting that such discussion is obliquely carried out by the complaints themselves. With the weightiest problem of all, the succession, under strict embargo, these lines invited readers to look for possible subtextual references.

Culminating in Britain's painful surrender to Rome, the now complete sequence from Nennius to Irenglas to Julius Caesar spoke volumes to a nation lately rocked by the Babington Plot, and the previous Throckmorton conspiracy, and facing imminent Spanish invasion. The shocking defections on 21 January 1587 of Rowland York, who surrendered Zutphen to the Spanish, and William Stanley, who betrayed Deventer, intensified fears of treason.

We have become so inured to the ubiquitous condemnations of dissension and corresponding calls for unity in Elizabethan literature that we often miss seminal instances of the trope. Higgins' treatment of the Roman invasion is an example. Caesar, his mouthpiece, bluntly admits that the free, fearless, and warlike Britons would have been invincible had they stood together: 'I haue no cause of *Britayne* conquest for to boast'. Only 'civill discorde', the bane of commonwealths and inevitable precursor to rebellion and 'treason', brought them under the Roman yoke.[26] Higgins' cautionary lesson, and its mode of expression, would be quickly echoed by other literary works, above all the history plays of the Armada years. Think of the following lines spoken by the French Dauphin, his plan to subdue England dashed, in *The Troublesome Reign of John, King of England* (1589–90) attributed to George Peele: 'it boots not me| Nor any prince nor power of Christendom| To seek to win this island Albion| Unless he have a party in the realm,| By treason, for to help him in his wars'.[27] Or the Bastard of Faulconbridge's memorable finale to Shakespeare's *King John*

(1596): 'This England neuer did, nor neuer shall| Lye at the proud foote of a Conqueror,| But when it first did helpe to wound it selfe'.[28] Behind such lines lurks the ghost of Higgins' Caesar. Except that the success of Caesar's enterprise gave the point greater weight.

'To take the empires sway'

If the meaning of Higgins' Roman conquest narrative is fairly transparent, what should we take from the rest of the Roman lives? After all, even Caesar's oration continues for another 124 lines after he quits Britain, and ten more despots follow.

Perhaps the first thing to notice about Higgins' poetic Roman venture is its novelty. While many types of polemical and didactic writing were steeped in ancient Roman lore, no Elizabethan prior to Higgins' 1587 *Mirour* had poetised Roman history just as no Elizabethan prior to Higgins' 1574 *First parte* had poetised British history.[29] It is difficult to overestimate how original Higgins' Roman complaints appeared. Discounting descriptions of Britain's Roman past in Elizabethan chronicles and antiquarian writing, before 1587 we find virtually no home-born retellings of Roman history even in prose, with the exception of William Barker's pedestrian continuation of Appian (1578). Of the few Roman plays, only the interlude, *Apius and Virginia* (c.1564; pub. 1575), is extant; the vogue for Roman tragedies lay in the future. So we are left with translations, most notably Arthur Golding's Caesar (1565) and Thomas North's Plutarch from the French of Amyot (1579), and a pseudo-Senecan tragedy *Octavia* about Neronian tyranny rendered into English by Thomas Nuce (1566, 1581).[30]

Intriguingly, Higgins nowhere alludes to Rome's glorious republican past, for contemporary moral and political writing the model of civic virtue, liberty, and martial valour.[31] Although Higgins only discusses Rome at the moment of the republic's demise, his narrative of that defining moment could have easily juxtaposed the heyday of the republic with the degeneracy of empire, but he dwells exclusively on the latter, except for a cursory vignette of the 'good raigne' of Augustus, when 'was borne the Lord of light', tucked into the complaint of Tiberius.[32] Why?

When Higgins published his poetic roll call of Roman tyrants, the uses of imperial history were becoming exceptionally topical. Though the Catilinarian conspiracy had previously featured in Tudor political discourse, sustained comparisons to imperial despots had not; the Old Testament provided a more fruitful supply of admonitory examples. Not even the Marian evangelicals had moved beyond mere name-calling, as in John Hales's promiscuous lineup of 'ancient and famous tyrants and cruell murderers, Pharao, Herode, Caligula, Nero, Domitian, Maximine, Diocletian, Decius'.[33]

By the mid-1580s, however, Catholic polemicists were drawing ever more elaborate – and ever more insulting – parallels between Elizabethan England and imperial Rome. The corrosive libel *Leicesters Commonwealth* (1584) maliciously insinuated that the Earl of Leicester was plotting to advance the Yorkist claim of his brother-in-law the Earl of Huntingdon.[34] Feigning concern for the too trusting queen, the anonymous libeler – perhaps the Jesuit Robert Persons – warned that the seemingly loyal Huntingdon would soon play Brutus to Elizabeth's Julius Caesar. He even ventriloquised Caesar's regrettable incredulity on receiving intelligence of Brutus's designs – 'I am sure (quoth he) that my Brutus will never attempt anything for the Empire while Caesar liveth, and after my death let him shift for the same among others as he can' – before spelling out the subversive political moral. Elsewhere the piece likened Leicester to Sejanus, the grasping favourite of the wily and corrupt Emperor Tiberius, on account of the earl's illicitly gained riches, 'for that he layeth up whatsoever he getteth and his expenses he casteth upon the purse of his Princess'.[35] The logic of the comparison, while superficially sympathetic to Elizabeth, implied that she was another Tiberius.

What renders these passages so distinctive is that they draw extended parallels between the circumstances allegedly obtaining then and now, not simply abuse or praise some contemporary by analogy with a particular Roman. Besides, while *Leicesters Commonwealth* wallows in all manner of history, 'both sacred and profane, foreign and domestical', it repeatedly circles back to the Roman empire for its examples of ambitious aspirers to the crown: 'This did all these in the Roman Empire who rose from subjects to be great princes and to put down emperors' (p.65).

I am not suggesting, of course, that Higgins was echoing *Leicesters Commonwealth* or other Catholic libels. If anything, he probably read his fellow-divine Thomas Bilson's 1585 tract *The True Difference betweene Christian Subjection and Unchristian Rebellion*, which by contrast identified Cardinal Como as Cicero to William Parry's Brutus, and Elizabeth's Caesar – Parry had been executed for conspiring to kill the queen in 1585: 'Cicero neuer sayd so much in the praise of Brutus and Cassius that slew Caesar in the Senate house: as Como doth to incite this Traitour to murder the Queene of England'.[36] The attraction of tendentious Roman parallels was growing stronger in both the Protestant and the Catholic camp.

The succession was on everyone's mind. Indeed, the regime's near-hysterical dread of a successful regicide provoked in October 1584 the so-called Bond of Association, which bound subscribers to kill not only anyone involved in assassination attempts but also any pretender benefiting from such an attempt, whether assenting to it or not, as well as their heir, whether guilty or not.[37] Such publicly sanctioned violence, really lynch law, against the Scottish queen and her son James, was utterly unprecedented. While the Bond was never implemented, its very existence, coupled with the endemic fear of treason and subversion, made bloody regime changes such as those recounted by Higgins' Romans devastatingly apposite.

Higgins' choice of emperors for presentation reflects his preoccupation with the succession. For instance, the run of obscure short-lived emperors from the year 69 (Galba, Otho, Vitellius) might seem more understandable in the light of the fact that their brief reigns constituted what was in effect an extended succession crisis (this might have been made clearer had Higgins had access to Tacitus's *Histories*, which devotes a lot of space to it, especially under Galba, who named a successor and made a disastrous choice). As it is, Higgins had clearly lost interest by the time he got to Vitellius, and does not offer a single concrete fact about him, even though he clearly used Suetonius, who provides a lot of lurid detail. His account of Septimius Severus and his sons has plenty about the succession to Septimius, and then about Caracalla's securing his position by murdering his brother. (It seems a little strange that Geta is included at all, given that Higgins follows Herodian in presenting him as basically a pleasant chap, and also that what is said about him is then mostly repeated in the account of Caracalla.) The succession issue might also explain two otherwise unexpected omissions, namely Domitian and Commodus – both got very unfavourable coverage from the sources Higgins used, Suetonius for the one and Herodian for the other, so he certainly was not short of information about them, and on the face of it is seems surprising that they were not included in the *Mirour*'s sequence of tyrants. But both succeeded to the imperial office without difficulty, Domitian on the death of his brother and Commodus on that of his father. Their inclusion might have weakened Higgins' underlying theme, that bad emperors were also ones who seized the throne, usually by murdering their predecessors or rivals.

Given the dangers of the succession question, Higgins understandably eschewed one-to-one correspondences in the Roman tragedies, the method of mischievous popish pamphleteers. Rather, their force derives from the accumulating references to the proprieties of regnal transitions, which have no counterpart in the Baldwin *Mirror*. Granted, Baldwin's Duke of Gloucester hankers after the crown, but there are many other concerns in the related constellation of complaints; while the series pertaining to Richard II revolves round royal misgovernment and magisterial misconduct rather than succession. Higgins' British lives broach the topic more consistently, but again mixed with other themes.

By contrast, Higgins' Roman tyrants obsess about how they had gained the throne – through adoption, descent, election by soldiers, usurpation, rebellion, civil war, regicide, conspiracy, murder, or combinations of these; how brutal, devious, and corrupt their reigns had been; and how they were overthrown, each gory fall perpetuating the cycle of violence. The titles repeatedly underscore their untimely ends – Caesar 'slayne in the Senate house', Tiberius 'poysoned by Caius Caligula', Caligula 'slayne by Cherea and others', Claudius 'poysoned by his wife Agrippina', Nero 'miserably slewe himselfe', Galba 'slayne by the souldiers'.[38] Higgins' Roman monsters have no favourites, counsellors, allies, servants, or spouses to gloss their doings – we hear from them alone. This, and the lack of envoys, further underscores their fixation on competition for the throne, the means of seizing and retaining power, and the various grim ends of emperors killed by their disgruntled subjects, spouses, or rivals, or else forced to kill themselves. Each in turn acknowledges the justice of his comeuppance, deferring to Jove, Jehovah, or both.

Higgins' achingly topical treatment of imperial successions is thrown into sharp relief when compared to John Foxe's seemingly similar but in fact vastly different approach to the same material in his *Actes and Monuments*, the ultimate expression of Elizabethan Protestantism. Starting with the second edition of the *Actes* in 1570, Foxe portrays 'heathen persecutyng Emperours … from Tiberius to Licynius' as 'scourges to the Senate and people of Rome' for rejecting Christ.[39] Although a tool in God's hands, the tyrants themselves, he stresses, did not escape punishment. And he gives a cheery list of all the nasty ways they died: 'Examples of the iust plage of God vpon the Romaine Emperours persecuting & resisting Christ, tyll the time of Constantine' (p.63). But, unlike Higgins, he is mostly uninterested in how the tyrants obtained the throne, and makes no distinction between usurpers and legitimate successors. What matters to Foxe is that they persecuted early Christians and duly suffered for it.

The only complaint in Higgins' Roman *Mirour* which comes close to adopting a Foxean perspective is that of Tiberius. Like Foxe, Higgins relates the apocryphal story of the emperor supposedly urging the senate to accept Christ as God, and retaliating with characteristic vindictiveness when they refused. Higgins even reproduces Pontius Pilate's alleged letter to Tiberius, while casting doubt on its authenticity in a marginal note.[40] But elsewhere in the Roman sequence there is no mention of Christian martyrdom; besides, the Roman people and senate, rather than being guilty of idolatry, emerge as innocent victims of their evil rulers.

Higgins' is no reformist manifesto à la Foxe but a more narrowly political reflection. True, Higgins is deeply committed to the ideal of providential justice. But in the Roman *Mirour* providentialism serves to stigmatise immorality and imperial misrule, not to lambast anyone who refuses to embrace Christianity. In fact, Higgins' indiscriminate use of Jove and Jehovah underlines the basic identity of the moral code embraced by ancient Romans and contemporary Protestants alike. This, in turn, has suggestive implications for how we should view the Romans' attempts to oppose imperial despotism.

The original Baldwin *Mirror* purveyed advice, which, admittedly, could be astringent – but in this differed little from, say, *Gorboduc* or other 1560s tragedies such as *Cambises* or *Horestes*. As for the book's insistence on the legitimacy of resistance, that too could easily be found in contemporary polemic, historiography, imaginative writing, and religious works. Higgins' Roman complaints if anything intensified the emphasis on the right to rise up against tyranny. Consider the violent removal of the depraved Caligula, self-confessed perpetrator of untold atrocities:

> For which the *Romaynes* did my life detest ...
> Wherefore to rid mee *Cheria* thought it best,
> Some others eke t'accomplishe it were bolde,
> In thirty steedes they stabde me through the brest
> My life was naught, and thus at last I dyde,
> My life procurde both Gods and men my foes. (fol. 87ʳ)

There is absolutely no sense here that the tyrannicides acted wrongly; on the contrary, Caligula is the only guilty party. Similarly, Nero concedes 'The *Senate* all, and people did mee hate, |And sought which way they might my death procure ... They mee proclaymde a foe to publique weale' (fol. 91ᵛ). It is instructive that Higgins does not differentiate between the lawful actions of the Senate and Cherea's conspiracy. Both appear justified.

Higgins' omnibus *Mirour* was both timely and influential. As copies reached the booksellers' stalls, Peter Wentworth, recalcitrant Puritan MP, composed a substantial tract aiming to persuade the queen that she should finally resolve the long-festering succession crisis by naming an heir.[41] Wentworth marshalled pertinent examples, or 'mirrour[s]', from scripture and history, stressing 'the miserable state of this land after King Lucius, and after the death of King Gorbodug and his two sonnes, Ferrex, and Porrex', and commending the practice of adoption followed by 'the Romane Emperours': 'Thus Julius Cæsar adopted Octavius Augustus, and hee Tiberius Cæsar. Nerva, Trajan. Adrian, Antoninus Pius: and hee againe Antoninus Philosophus'.[42] Three years later, in 1590, an enterprising publisher capitalised on the success of the bumper *Mirour* by reprinting in one volume an updated version of Lydgate's *Serpent of Division* (c.1422), a prose life of Caesar showing the dangers of civil discord – rejigged here to glorify ancient Britons à la Higgins, and the Norton–Sackville 'British' succession tragedy *Gorboduc*. This book too admonished 'the wise Governours' to 'make this example a mirrour to their minds, of this manly man Julius'.[43] In 1591, Henry Savile published his historical sketch *Ende of Nero and Beginning of Galba* together with his translation of Tacitus's *Historiae* (covering the period from Nero to Vespasian) and *Agricola* (the biography of the one-time governor of Britain and Tacitus's father-in-law).

Savile's Tacitus was a sophisticated intervention in the debate about international politics as well as a cannily oblique commentary on the succession.[44] Signed 'A. B.', the preface, sometimes credited to the Earl of Essex, enjoined the reader to ponder the implications of Tacitus's *Histories* in a manner presupposing the mirror metaphor: 'In these fower bookes of the storie thou shalt see all the miseries of a torne and declining state'. The preface then outlined the *Histories*' ostensible contemporary application, worth quoting in full since it would work equally well for Higgins' Romans: 'If thou mislike their warres be thankfull for thine owne peace; if thou doest abhorre their tyrannies, love and reverence thine owne wise, just, and excellent Prince. If thou doest detest their Anarchie, acknowledge your owne hapie governement, and thanke god for her, under whom England enjoyes as manie benefites, as ever Rome did suffer miseries under the greatest Tyrant'.[45]

It might seem sacrilegious to mention Higgins' Roman complaints in the same breath as Savile's Tacitus, the era's most acclaimed treatment of Roman history. But the two should be considered together. When they are, we see that, for all his stylistic infelicities, Galfridian excursions, and historical distortions, Higgins had pioneered a new approach, at once imaginative and political, to writing about imperial Rome.

His Romans illustrate a quickening of interest in Roman history in the 1580s amongst both intellectuals and middlebrow readers. This perhaps reflects wider European problems, which explain why, about then, Tacitus – whom Higgins did not use – began to attract serious attention on the Continent.[46] France experienced an even more serious succession crisis, triggered in 1584 by the death of the heir to the crown, the Duke of Anjou, and the revival of the Catholic League; and of course William of Orange, leader of the Dutch in their struggle against Spanish rule, was assassinated that year. One might argue that this phenomenon entailed anxieties not just about succession in various realms but about the fundamental 'state' of each polity and of Europe generally, threatened by a new universal monarchy or prolonged internal chaos. In short, sophisticated contemporaries might have seen the English succession crisis as woven into a larger European crisis of political authority, since events in France, the Netherlands, and Scotland significantly shaped the trajectory of English politics. Roman history could illuminate these concerns not only in elite publications such as Savile's Tacitus but also more popular ones such as Higgins' *Mirour*, which deliberately invited the reader to make cross-period, cross-national comparisons between ancient Britain and Rome, medieval and early Tudor England, and the Elizabethan present.

No lesser a figure than the Earl of Essex apparently 'much commend[ed]' a literary work inspired by Higgins' *First parte* – though inferior to it, William Warner's *Albions England. Or Historicall Map of the same Island*.[47] This was a breathless narrative in doggerel verse – and some bits of humdrum prose – from Noah to James I, which went through seven ever-expanding editions from 1586 to 1612. The *Mirour* too must have attracted some socially exalted, or at least educated, readers alive to its topical flavour. Indeed, with Leicester's Netherlands mission under way, how difficult could it have been to grasp the subtext of Caesar's recollection 'that in my warres in *Fraunce* | Some *Britaynes* thether came amongst the *Galles* to fight'? Like contemporary English, their mythic ancestors evince solidarity with 'the Nations whilome free' (fol. 79^r), whom the rapacious despot seeks to enslave.

Overlooked by historians of historiography and political culture, Higgins' work has been pooh-poohed by Shakespeare scholars. Yet one wonders how far the self-reflexive monologues of Higgins' wicked Romans might have fed into Tarquin's guilty ruminations in *Lucrece* (1594).[48] Or whether Higgins' reliance on Herodian in his lives of Severus, Geta, and Caracalla might not prefigure Peele and Shakespeare's use of the same historian in *Titus Andronicus* (c.1594), a play which highlights the troubling ramifications of cross-cultural, cross-confessional warfare and the danger of treason and defection, when Goth troops are suborned to intervene in Rome's domestic politics securing the elevation of Emperor Lucius.[49] And can we really be certain that, as a recent editor of *Julius Caesar* said of Higgins' complaint of Caesar, 'Shakespeare, like most modern readers would take nothing from it'.[50]

Notes

This chapter was written in the marvellously congenial setting of the Huntington Library, and I owe warm thanks to the Huntington's staff. I have greatly benefited from the conversation and advice of Helen Cooper, Susan Doran, Noel O'Sullivan, Glyn Parry, Richard Proudfoot, Malcolm Smuts, and Henry Summerson. The anonymous reader supplied a useful suggestion.

1. On contemporary conceptions of magisterial virtue, see Norman Jones, *Governing by Virtue: Lord Burghley and the Management of Elizabethan England* (Oxford University Press, 2015), ch. 1.
2. *A Myrroure For Magistrates* (London, 1559), sig. ¶2ᵛ.
3. For a state-of-the-art account of the *Mirror*'s transmission, see Harriet Archer, 'The Mirror for Magistrates, 1559–1610: Transmission, Appropriation and the Poetics of Historiography', unpublished DPhil thesis (University of Oxford, 2012).
4. *The First parte of the Mirour for Magistrates* (London, 1574), sig. *5ᵛ.
5. *Mirour*, sig. C4ʳ; fol. 77ᵛ.
6. *Literature, Politics and National Identity: Reformation to Renaissance* (Cambridge University Press, 1994), p.102; see also pp.99–100.
7. A Mirror for Magistrates *and the* de casibus *Tradition* (University of Toronto Press, 2000), pp.34–5.
8. *ODNB* article on Higgins; see also Schwyzer, *Literature, Nationalism, and Memory in Early Modern England and Wales* (Cambridge University Press, 2004), pp.111ff.
9. 'A Mirror for Magistrates and the Beginnings of English Autobiography', *ELR* 36 (2006), 26–59, at pp.37–8.
10. For an illuminating analysis of Burdet's complaint, see L. D. Green, 'Modes of Perception in the *Mirror for Magistrates*, *Huntington Library Quarterly* 44 (1981), 117–33, at pp.122–4.
11. John E. Curran, *Roman Invasions: The British History, Protestant Anti-Romanism, and the Historical Imagination in England, 1530–1660* (Newark: University of Delaware Press, 2002); Felicity Heal, 'What Can King Lucius Do for You? The Reformation and the Early British Church', *English Historical Review* 120 (2005), 593–614.
12. Susan Doran and Paulina Kewes, 'The Earlier Elizabethan Succession Question Revisited', in Susan Doran and Paulina Kewes, eds., *Doubtful and Dangerous: The Question of Succession in Late Elizabethan England* (Manchester University Press, 2014), pp.20–44, esp. 27–30.
13. Peter Lake, *Bad Queen Bess? Libels, Secret Histories, and the Politics of Publicity in the Reign of Queen Elizabeth I* (Oxford University Press, 2016), chs 1–3.
14. *An addition declaratorie to the bulles, with a searching of the maze* (London, 1570). See also his *A warning agaynst the dangerous practises of Papistes, and*

specially the parteners of the late Rebellion (London, [1569]), which likens the Northern rebels to Sinon.

15 *A Treatise of Treasons against Q. Elizabeth, and the Croune of England* (n.p. [Louvain], 1572), sig. b6ʳ, fol. 85ʳ. John Leslie's *A defence of the honour of the right highe, mightye and noble Princesse Marie Quene of Scotlande* (1569) adapted Virgil's Book VII to portray Mary as Lavinia. On these exchanges, see Tricia A. McElroy, 'Executing Mary Queen of Scots: Strategies of Representation in Early Modern Scotland', unpublished D.Phil. thesis (University of Oxford, 2005), and Lake, *Bad Queen Bess*, chs 1–3.

16 *First parte*, sig. *2ᵛ.

17 *All such treatises as have been lately published by Thomas Norton* (London, 1570).

18 Fol. 74ᵛ. The same tag concludes Burdet's complaint in Higgins' *The Mirour for Magistrates … newly imprinted, and with the addition of diuers tragedies enlarged* (London, 1587), fol. 252ᵛ, which further underscores the connection between his ancient Britons and medieval Englishmen.

19 Geoffrey of Monmouth, *The History of the Kings of Britain*, trans. Lewis Thorpe (London: Penguin, 1966), pp.77–8.

20 *First parte*, fols 70ᵛ–71ʳ.

21 Patrick Collinson, 'The Monarchical Republic of Queen Elizabeth I', *Bulletin of the John Rylands Library of Manchester* 69 (1986–1987), 394–424.

22 Geoffrey, *History*, pp.106, 113; Higgins, *The First Parte of the Mirour for Magistrates* (London, 1575), fol. 80ʳ.

23 For Caesar's Roman career, Higgins relied on Suetonius and Richard Grafton, gleaning a few details from Plutarch and the Chronicle of St Albans. See Douglas Bush, 'Classical Lives in the *Mirror for Magistrates*', *Studies in Philology* 22 (1925), 256–66, at pp.256–7, 266. Bush does not mention Geoffrey.

24 *History*, pp.113–15, 118.

25 Paulina Kewes, 'History Plays and the Royal Succession', in Paulina Kewes, Ian W. Archer, and Felicity Heal, eds, *The Oxford Handbook of Holinshed's Chronicles* (Oxford University Press, 2013), pp.493–509, at pp.495–8.

26 *Mirour*, fols 79r, 80r, 80v. See below for discussion of a modernised and revised edition of Lydgate's *Serpent of Division* (1422), which attributes Britain's fall to 'debate and discorde' between 'the over rash king *Cassibelan* & Androgenes', but says nothing about treason: 'whiles unity and love stood … undevided in the boundes of *Brutaine*, the mightye *Julus* was quite unable to vanquishe the least parte of them'. *The Serpent of Devision … Whereunto is annexed the Tragedye of Gorboduc* (London, 1590), p.7; cf. the original *The Serpent of Division*, ed. H. N. MacCracken (London: Oxford University Press, 1911), pp.50–1, which does not mention discord.

27 George Peele, *The Troublesome Reign of John, King of England*, ed. Charles R. Forker (Manchester University Press, 2011), Pt. II, Sc. 9, ll. 25–9.

28 *King John*, in *William Shakespeare, The Complete Works: Original-Spelling Edition*, gen. eds Stanley Wells and Gary Taylor (Oxford University Press, 1986), Sc. 16, ll. 2567–9.

29 There are various medieval and early Renaissance complaints by classical figures, but mostly of women, and mostly Ovidian – Chaucer's Cleopatra and various Lucreces would be the nearest to history. There were also verse versions of *Titus and Vespasian* and the *Siege of Jerusalem*. See *The Siege of Jerusalem*, ed. Ralph Hanna and David Lawton, Early English Text Society, o.s. 320 (2003): this one is alliterative; and *Titus & Vespasian: or The Destruction of Jerusalem in Rhymed Couplets*, ed. J. A. Herbert (London: Roxburghe Club, 1905). (There is also a prose version that forms part of a longer still-unedited text that is itself a translation from French.)

30 For an account of the circulation of works about Roman history, see Paulina Kewes, 'Henry Savile's Tacitus and the Politics of Roman History in Late Elizabethan England', *Huntington Library Quarterly* 74 (2011), 515–51, at pp. 517–25, and Kewes, 'Roman History, Essex, and Late Elizabethan Political Culture', in R. Malcolm Smuts, ed., *The Oxford Handbook of the Age of Shakespeare* (Oxford University Press, 2016), pp.250–68.

31 See Freyja Cox Jensen, *Reading the Roman Republic in Early Modern England* (Leiden: Brill, 2012).

32 *Mirour*, fol. 84^r.

33 Delivered to Queen Elizabeth in winter 1558–9, the *Oration* was first printed in John Foxe's *Actes and Monuments* (London, 1576), p.2032 at www.hrionline.ac.uk.

34 On *Leicester's Commonwealth*, see Peter Lake, 'From *Leicester his Commonwealth* to *Sejanus his fall*: Ben Jonson and the Politics of Roman (Catholic) Virtue', in Ethan H. Shagan, ed., *Catholics and the 'Protestant nation': Religious Politics and Identity in Early Modern England* (Manchester University Press, 2005), pp.128–61, and Lake, *Bad Queen Bess*, ch. 5.

35 *Leicester's Commonwealth: A Copy of a Letter Written by a Master of Cambridge (1584) and Related Documents*, ed. Dwight C. Peck (Athens, OH and London: Ohio University Press, 1985, repr. 2006), pp.118, 74.

36 Thomas Bilson, *The True Difference betweene Christian Subjection and Unchristian Rebellion* (Oxford: Joseph Barnes, 1585), p.504.

37 See 'Lincolnes Inne "Association for the defence of Queen Elizabeth"', printed in *The Egerton Papers*, ed. J. P. Collier, Camden Society, 12 (840), pp.108–11. For discussion, see Susan Doran and Paulina Kewes, 'Associations and Enterprises: The Scottish Context of the Bond of Association' (forthcoming).

38 *Mirour*, sig. B4^r.

39 John Foxe, *Actes and Monuments* (London, 1570), pp.14, 63 at www.hrionline.ac.uk.

40 *Mirour*, fol. 85^r. Higgins' source was the *Flores Historiarum*, a medieval Latin chronicle of English history from the creation of the world until the early fourteenth century, first printed by Matthew Parker in 1567.

41 Paulina Kewes, 'The Puritan, the Jesuit, and the Jacobean Succession', in Doran and Kewes, eds, *Doubtful and Dangerous*, pp.47–70.

42 *A Pithie Exhortation to her Maiestie for establishing Her Successor to the Crowne* ([Edinburgh], 1598)], pp.15, 30, 23.

43 *Serpent*, p.23. Maura B. Nolan, 'The Art of History Writing: Lydgate's *Serpent of Division*', *Speculum* 78 (2003), 99–127.
44 Kewes, 'Henry Savile's Tacitus'.
45 *The ende of Nero and beginning of Galba: Four bookes of the Histories of Cornelius Tacitus*, trans. Henry Savile (Oxford: Joseph Barnes and R. Robinson for Richard Wright, 1591), sig. ¶3^{r-v}.
46 R. Malcolm Smuts, 'Varieties of Tacitism', in Paulina Kewes, ed., *Ancient Rome and Early Modern England: History, Literature, and Political Imagination* (forthcoming).
47 C. G. Moore Smith, *Gabriel Harvey's Marginalia* (Stratford-upon-Avon: Shakespeare Head Press, 1913), p.232.
48 When any influence is acknowledged, it is that of the *Mirror*'s complaint form rather than Higgins' Rome; see Heather Dubrow, '"A Mirror for Complaints": Shakespeare's *Lucrece* and Generic Tradition', in Barbara Kiefer Lewalski, ed., *Renaissance Genres: Essays on Theory, History, and Interpretation* (Cambridge, MA: Harvard University Press, 1986), pp.399–417.
49 Naomi Conn Liebler, 'Getting It All Right: *Titus Andronicus* and Roman History', *Shakespeare Quarterly* 45 (1994), 263–78.
50 *Julius Caesar*, Arden 3, ed. David Daniel (Walton-on-Thames: Nelson and Sons Ltd, 1998), p.94.

CHAPTER 8

'Those chronicles whiche other men had'
Paralipsis *and Blenerhasset's* Seconde Part of the Mirror for Magistrates *(1578)*

Harriet Archer

Used to denote the Old Testament Books of Chronicles, but associated in the metrical preface to *The Chronicle of John Hardyng* (1543) with histories of all kinds,[1] the classificatory term 'paralipomena' refers to that which is supplementary, or that which has been left out.[2] The story of Thomas Blenerhasset's *Seconde Part of the Mirror for Magistrates*, printed in 1578 by the otherwise unknown printer Richard Webster, is at all levels one of lacunae and supplements, omissions and interpolations. Largely excluded from the *Mirror* canon in critical discourse, the *Seconde Part*, despite its partial reprinting in Richard Niccols' 1610 edition, has occupied a liminal position in relation to the rest of the corpus.[3] But whether we see a place for Blenerhasset's *Mirror* text alongside those of William Baldwin, John Higgins, and Niccols, or categorise the work as a piece of opportunistic 'fan fiction', it has much to tell us about how historical poetry was being read, written, and theorised in Elizabethan England. This chapter suggests that Blenerhasset's repeated insistence on loss, absence, and isolation, when read as a calculated deployment of the rhetorical trope *paralipsis*, productively illuminates his metapoetic aims within and beyond the *Mirror* tradition.

Blenerhasset's *Seconde Part* acts as a prequel to the 1563 *Mirror*, and a sequel to Higgins' *First Parte* (1574), texts framed collectively by his mendacious printer's account as 'a booke alredy in print, Entituled *The first and third part of the Mirrour for Magistrates*'.[4] It comprises a fictive prose frame which narrates the collection's composition, and twelve complaints in the voices of loosely historical figures, hitherto 'excluded out of the *English* Mirrour of Magistrates', and doomed to remain 'couered and hidden with those mistie cloudes of fylthy forgetfulnes' (fol. 1ʳ) without Blenerhasset's help. These begin where Higgins' *First Parte* left off, with the legendary British king Guidericus, the son – according to Geoffrey of Monmouth – of Kymbelinus.[5] The work concludes with an exchange between Harold and William I, giving an account of failed diplomatic negotiation culminating in the Norman Conquest. The series of laments includes autobiographical narratives spoken by, among others, Uther Pendragon, King Alfred, and Constantine's mother, Queen Helena – an encomiastic allegory of Elizabeth I.

It has been suggested that Blenerhasset's *Seconde Part* is a tedious, puritanical reiteration of the standard *de casibus* model.[6] What's more, Blenerhasset gets his historical facts wrong. Unlike the collections by Baldwin and Higgins, the *Seconde Part* was not printed by Thomas Marshe, and Blenerhasset himself was unconnected with the original circle of contributors. Crucially, in 'The Authours Epistle', Blenerhasset stresses that the work was composed not within a supportive, metropolitan literary milieu, but without help, whilst in transit on active service:

> Souldiers ... be not alwayes lusking in our Forte or Castle, but be as tyme and occasion wyll permyt, here to day, wee knowe least our selues, where to morrowe ... [T]he most part of these my Princes dyd pleade their causes vnto me, euen in the Sea, a place in fayth, not meete to penne Tragedies. (sig. *iii^v)

Altogether, there is a case to be made that the text ought to be excised from the *Mirror* canon, to exist on the periphery like George Cavendish's *Metrical Visions* (1550s, MS), Richard Robinson's *Reward of Wickedness* (1574), or the later *Mirrors for Magistrates* by Anthony Munday and George Whetstone.[7] Kathleen Tillotson's assertion that 'Blenerhasset is, so to speak, an unsuccessful applicant for admission to the *Mirror*' remains unchallenged, despite Lily B. Campbell's inclusion of the *Seconde Part* in her 1946 edition of *Parts Added to the* Mirror for Magistrates.[8] If Blenerhasset is mentioned at all, it is often in conjunction with Higgins, perhaps thanks to Campbell's edition, which reproduces their works in tandem, but this pairing is in no way representative of the two authors' divergent appropriations of Baldwin's original *Mirror* work.

Blenerhasset's complaints do tend to follow the *de casibus* trajectory of their predecessors. However, the *Seconde Part* also deviates dramatically from its models, in three particularly important ways. Firstly, Blenerhasset's authorial narrative of composition is contained in the 'Epistle', rather than a preface or frame, because Blenerhasset's *Mirror* was ostensibly written as a private exercise for a friend. Secondly, a printer's note claims that the text was printed without Blenerhasset's knowledge. The author is stationed 'beyond the Seas', serving on the island of Guernsey; he 'wyl marueile at his returne', Webster says, 'to find [his book] imprinted' (sig. *2ʳ). Thirdly, in the main body of the text, Blenerhasset's complaints are framed, not by a dream vision or pseudo-non-fictional narrative, but by a digressive dialogue between the personifications 'Memory' and 'Inquisition', a wholly new intervention in the evolution of the *Mirror* corpus.

These figures anticipate Spenser's Eumnestes and Anamnestes, in that they mirror the duality of Aristotelian memory.[9] Unlike Spenser's characters, however, their roles become muddled, and their approach to recounting British history is based on an associative and contingent process of historical recollection, as the following exchange demonstrates:

> O *Memory* (*quoth Inquisition*) what dyd become of *Edmunde Ironsyde*, of whom you made mention …? That vertuous valiaunt Prince (quoth *Memory*) was miserably made away by an Earle. By an Earle? (quoth *Inquisition*) I haue here an Earle called *Edricus*, who murthered a Kynge, it maye bee, that chaunce hath yeelded vntoo vs the factour vnlooked for. (fol. 58ᵛ)

The work can appear excessively alliterative, bizarrely ahistorical, and unforgivably pompous and prudish if we assume, as criticism to date has, that it was meant with a straight face. However, Mike Pincombe has shown in this volume that to regard Baldwin's *Mirror* as a work of high tragic seriousness is to miss its sophisticated manipulation of genre and form. Clues abound that the same goes for Blenerhasset's *Seconde Part*.

Here, I want to focus on one of these: Blenerhasset's deployment of variations on the trope *paralipsis*. Sometimes referred to as *occupatio* or occupation,[10] and otherwise known as *occultatio*,[11] *paralipsis* is the rhetorical method of drawing attention to something by appearing to ignore or pass over it. Mark Antony's claim 'I come to bury Caesar, not to praise him', and his speeches that follow, is perhaps the most familiar – and devastating – early modern instance of paraliptic oratory.[12] But the satirical force of Baldwin's *Mirror* complaints, too, depends on a related sleight of hand, by which readers' support is elicited for the very actions professed to have condemned the historical figure in question. Thomas Elyot's *Dictionary* (1538) illustrates the concept with a legal example: *paralipsis* is 'a colour in rhetorike, where the playntyfe in preuentynge the wordes of the defendaunt, rehercheth that whiche he will laye for excuse, and disproueth it'.[13] This is one of the more respectable delineations to be found in sixteenth-century reference works, however; the trope is frequently associated with deception or underhand dealing, and even sexual dissembling.[14] In Richard

Sherry's *Treatise of Schemes and Tropes* (1550), this dissembling speech works to expose an interlocutor's greater dishonesty:

> *Occupatia* ... is, when we make as though we do not knowe, or wyl not know of ye thyng y^t wee speke of most of al, in this wyse: I wyl not say that y^u tokest money of our felowes, I wyl not stand much in thys that y^u robbedst kingdoms, cityes, and al mens houses: I passe ouer thy theftes.[15]

Sherry's superlative is important: *paralipsis* points to the thing we speak of 'most of al'. George Puttenham's discussion of 'Paralepsis, or the Passager' shares this emphasis:

> It is ... as if we set but light of the matter, and that therefore we do passe it ouer slightly when in deede we do then intend most effectually and despightfully if it be inuectiue to remember it: it is also when we will not seeme to know a thing, and yet we know it well enough.[16]

These definitions convey the interplay of apparent nonchalance with strong, decisive rhetorical intent which, I argue, characterises the *Seconde Part*'s casual, even flippant approach to national history.

Attention to the use of *paralipsis* throughout the *Seconde Part*, as well as the operation of a more nebulous paraliptic mode, provides one way to unlock what Blenerhasset wanted his text to do, why it is far more than an iterative extension of the series of ancient histories it purports to complete, and how Blenerhasset conceptualised his own place in the *Mirror* tradition. The paraliptic mode works in a variety of ways in the *Seconde Part*, but all revolve around the rhetorical dismissal of contexts and resources, considerations or motivations, to which the work actively draws our attention. This chapter posits a double helix model for interpreting Blenerhasset's use of *paralipsis* – on the one hand it emphasises his originality and independence, while at the same time it foregrounds his influences and aspirations. When these two facets of his literary practice are held in tension, Blenerhasset's radical engagement with the late Elizabethan negotiation of poetic authority begins to emerge.

There are four occasions in the *Seconde Part* when Blenerhasset draws attention to a group of writers, and then asks that the reader dismiss them, one way or another. In his 'Epistle', Blenerhasset enacts a feat of practical *paralipsis*, claiming not to have access to certain essential historical texts:

> I had not those Chronicles whiche other men had: my Memorie and Inuention were vnto me in stead of *Grafton, Polidore, Cooper*, and suche like, who dyd greatly ayde other men. (sig. *4^r)

His use of the dismissive phrase 'and suche like' at once evokes the homogeneity of the sprawling Elizabethan chronicle literature, and Blenerhasset's disregard for it, although his paraliptic reference to these particular chroniclers provides insight into his actual reading of history. He probably means Richard Grafton's *Chronicle at Large* (1569), or one of its abridgements; Polydore Vergil's *English History*, first printed in Basel as *Polydori Vergilii urbinatis Anglicae historiae libri XXVI* (1534); and *Cooper's Chronicle* (1560), in which Thomas Cooper extended the chronicle history of Thomas Lanquet (1521–45) up to the present day.

Although he played fast and loose with the details, it has been established that these were precisely the chronicles which Blenerhasset did consult.[17] In addition, he is shown to have been indebted to Fabyan, and to share occasional similarities with John Hardyng, Geoffrey of Monmouth, John Stow and Matthew of Westminster.[18] It is clear, then, that Blenerhasset did have chronicle histories available, either in hard copy or, less plausibly, from memory. By denying this influence, though, both paratextually and through his silent deviation from their narratives, and claiming that he must rely instead on his 'Diligence and Memory' (sig. *iiii^v) or 'Memory and Inuention' (sig. *iiii^r), he demands that his readers face up to the contingency of historical truth. Blenerhasset foregrounds the central historiographical anxiety of the day, and one with which Baldwin's and Higgins' *Mirror*s also explicitly grapple: the unreliability or absence of ancient British historical records.[19]

While bereft of historical resources, though, Blenerhasset has managed, he tells us, to convey four texts to his isolated garrison. But these volumes are of no practical use:

> as for bookes, I was altogether destitute: for … I could not beare about with me a librarie but for cariage sake, contented myself with … the thirde *Decade* of *Titus Liuye*, with *Boswelles Concordes of Armorie*, with *Monsignor de Lange*, that notable Warriour, & with the vnperfect *Mirrour for Magistrates*: whiche bookes made nothing to this purpose. (sig. *iiii^r)

This extract delivers another shade of *paralipsis*: Blenerhasset claims that he did have these books to hand, but that he did not use them.

It is true that these texts could have offered Blenerhasset scant assistance when researching the *Seconde Part*'s histories. Livy's third decade treats the Second Punic, or so-called Hannibalic, War (218–201 BC),[20] led by the generals Hannibal and Scipio Africanus, while Bossewell purports to set out the central tenets of heraldry. 'De Lange' probably refers to

Raymond de Rouer's *Instructions sur le Faict de la Guerre* (1548), attributed to Guillaume du Bellay, seigneur de Langey.[21] There is little of relevance here for a sequence chronicling British regnal history 'from the conquest of Caesar, vnto the commyng of Duke William the Conquerour'. As for Baldwin's *Mirror*, Higgins had written a physical copy of the book into his fictive process of composition, recounting how he had read it carefully before falling asleep to be visited by Morpheus and the series of lamenting Britons.[22] But Blenerhasset takes a pragmatic view of the *Mirror*'s redundancy when composing a prequel, diverting attention away from considerations of style, genre, or mood, by focusing pedantically on content.

However, Livy's emphasis on the causation of historical events, of which the Elizabethan historiographical theorist Thomas Blundeville was also a vehement advocate, was finding favour in contemporary intellectual culture.[23] The 'connection between morality and outcome … more clearly apparent than the mechanism by which that connection is formed', which D. S. Levene argues characterises the third decade, resonates with the broader context of the *Mirror* tradition.[24] Blenerhasset's reference highlights the *Mirror*'s comparable use of these techniques, and repositions the form as a fashionable mode of history writing, while Livy's acknowledgement that Rome's foundational narrative is 'more beautified and set out with Poets fables, than grounded vpon pure and faithfull records' anticipates the *Seconde Part*'s historiographical scepticism.[25] Hannibal does in fact feature in Blenerhasset's complaint of Guidericus, but as an example of 'Roming *Rumor*': that Hannibal might 'once agayn assayle| The *Roman* state' is a 'truthlesse tale', but the fear it instils in his Roman adversaries aids Guidericus as he advances across Italy (fol. 5ʳ). Additionally, Livy's Hannibal's final speech, 'an elaboration of the theme of "the fickleness of fortune" in the Polybian fashion', perhaps lent itself to Blenerhasset's subject matter, while Blenerhasset's kings Harold and William provide a bathetic counterpoint to the classical parallel lives tradition which Livy's Hannibal and Scipio encapsulate.[26] Bossewell's *Concorde of Armourie* outlines the moral qualities required to be considered gentle or noble; in particular the text's delineation of the four cardinal virtues, Prudence, Justice, Fortitude, and Temperance, and their necessity in those of noble rank based on Cicero's *De Officiis*, forges links with earlier *Mirror* prefaces.[27] But it is Bossewell's dedication to William Cecil, simultaneously arguing that the dearth of books on his chosen subject will consign its details to oblivion and demonstrating his debt to a heavily imitated hypotext, which most powerfully prefigures the *Seconde Part*. The collection of books seems orchestrated to emphasise Blenerhasset's military credentials, and command of languages, rather than his qualifications as a historian of Britain or a poet. This bias, though, also belies the formative pertinence of his travelling library to his historiopoetic practices. His reference to the *Mirror* itself gestures towards Blenerhasset's debt to, and his Oedipal emulation of, his text's generic predecessor. In professing to imitate and surpass one of the most popular and influential poetic collections of his age, Blenerhasset would be making a bold statement, but not a new one. By dismissing the *Mirror*'s usefulness altogether, he signals a more thoroughly internalised inheritance of Baldwin's metatextual playfulness, as well as the desire to strike out into new territory.

Blenerhasset also betrays this desire when he recounts the trouble that he has had composing the complaints, and demands that when his reader has time to peruse the work, he 'ceasse then to thinke on the *L. Buchurst*, or *Sackuyll*, let *Gascon* and *Churchyarde* be forgotten' (sig. *iii[v]). Would the inscribed friend have been especially likely to think of this particular trio, Thomas Sackville, George Gascoigne, and Thomas Churchyard, before Blenerhasset mentioned them? The workings of *paralipsis* suggest that he certainly would have after they were cited in this way. All three poets have connections to the *Mirror* canon, albeit to widely differing degrees, but it is possible to argue that what really inspires Blenerhasset's off-kilter choice is their greater significance for contemporary literary innovation.

Sackville and Churchyard both contributed complaints to the 1563 *Mirror*, so it is logical that Blenerhasset should wish to surpass or supersede their examples within the *de casibus* genre, while Gascoigne, a 'soldier-poet' like Blenerhasset and Churchyard,[28] arguably follows the *Mirror*'s example in his posthumous autobiographical narrative 'Dan Bartholmew of Bathe'. No mention is made, however, of Higgins or Baldwin, whose chronological schema Blenerhasset co-opts. Are Sackville, Churchyard, and perhaps even Gascoigne, the authors more closely associated, by 1577, with *de casibus* verse complaints? Or is Blenerhasset drawing particular attention to them among the *Mirror* collaborators? They are certainly the more frequently named within the seam of burgeoning critical discourse which was, by the final decades of the century, beginning to shape the canon: William Webbe, probably following E. K.'s gloss in the *Shepheardes Calender*, calls Gascoigne 'the very cheefe of our late rymers'.[29] Sackville, of course, wrote the 1563 *Mirror*'s fêted Induction and the complaint of Henry Duke of Buckingham, and Churchyard the much-imitated complaint of Jane Shore. Sackville's Induction anticipates Blenerhasset's *Seconde Part* in some respects, including his use of personifications, and an overtly fictive, rather than 'pseudo non-fictional', frame.

Looking beyond the *Mirror*, though, these authors' resonances with Blenerhasset's interests are amplified. Churchyard's other work lends itself to Blenerhasset's evident interest in the risks and opportunities of unstable textual transmission and interpretation. In *The Contention bettwyxte Churchyard and Camell* (1560), 'Churchyard … counters Camell's charges of offensive intent by insisting that *Davy Dycars Dreame* be read as a work of fiction, a monologue spoken in character rather than as a direct authorial address'.[30] Churchyard achieves a degree of protection by generating hermeneutic uncertainty around authorial intent. In asking readers to 'forget' Churchyard, the *Seconde Part* hints at potential poetic heredity by deploying a related form of interpretative misdirection. If Churchyard sought to deflect critical opprobrium by highlighting multiple possible interpretations, Gascoigne did so, after his *Hundreth Sundrie Flowres* (1573) scandalised its earliest readers, by diffusing blame among multiple carefully constructed *personae*.[31] Through its evocation of these three figures, Blenerhasset's paratext is resituated among authors not primarily known for their moral or historiographical writings, but for poetic innovation and the construction of authorial fictions, signalling a new context for Blenerhasset's appropriation of the *Mirror* form. Although Gascoigne didn't contribute to the *Mirror*, his *Glasse of Government* (1575) and *Steele Glas* (1576) suggest an affinity with the metaphor. However, as Gillian Austen argues, the 'thoroughly medieval' *Steele Glas* 'has its revolutionary aspect as the earliest original, nondramatic experiment in English blank verse'.[32] As we will see, therefore, Blenerhasset's reference to Gascoigne draws on the reputation of a popular contemporary to bolster several of his own poetic interests. Sackville, too, offers a precedent for Blenerhasset's experiments with unrhymed verse, as an early proponent, alongside Thomas Norton, of blank verse in the Inns of Court tragedy *Gorboduc* (1565).

The Induction which follows Blenerhasset's unrhymed hexameter complaint of Cadwallader is probably the most famous section of the *Seconde Part*, as it discusses the use of iambic English verse to imitate Latin poetry.[33] Memory asks Inquisition, 'wyll you penne this mans meterlesse Tragedy as he hath pronounst it?', and Inquisition replies that,

> it agreeth very wel with the *Roman* verse called *Iambus*, which consisteth on sixe feete, euery foote on two syllables, one short and an other long, so proper for the Englishe toung, that it is greate maruaile that these ripewitted Gentlemen of *England* haue not left their Gotish kinde of ryming. (fols 40^{r-v})

From the 1540s in England, the quantitative verse movement pitted metres 'based on the time value of syllables' against accentual verse, based on rhythm or rhyme.[34] Here Blenerhasset throws his hat into the ring alongside more famous literary theorists. Like the printed correspondence between Spenser and Gabriel Harvey, *Three Proper, and Wittie, Familiar Letters* (1580), Blenerhasset's Memory and Inquisition address this debate in an ostensibly private yet ultimately publicised exchange, foregrounding Blenerhasset's engagement with contemporary poetics. The prose link draws out the significance of this debate to the contrast between the 'rude *Gothes*', symbolic of an uncivilised 'dark age' in European history, and the cultural and moral perfection brought about in Elizabethan England.[35] It closely echoes, for example, the description of 'our rude and beggerly ryming, [which was] brought first into Italie by *Gothes* and *Hunnes*, whan all good verses and good learning to, were destroyed by them' in Roger Ascham's *The Scholemaster* (1570).[36]

Memory and Inquisition cite the failure of a series of contemporary poets in the prose link to support this digression; once again, though, sensitivity to Blenerhasset's use of the paraliptic mode suggests that the dismissal of these authors emphasises their importance to Blenerhasset's nascent poetics. Following his disquisition on inferior rhyming poetry, the narrator laments,

> O what braue beames and goodly tymber might be found amongst *Churchyardes Chippes*, if he had not affected the ryming order of his predecessors? Which Meeter made not onely hym inferiour vnto *Horace*, but it also made a great inequalitie to be betwixt *Buchurst* and *Homer:* betwixt *Phaer* and *Virgill:* betwixte *Turberuile* and *Tibullus*: betwixt *Golding* and *Ouid:* betwixt *George Gascon* and *Seneca*. (fol. 40ᵛ)

There is rather more of significance hidden amongst this list than the rhetorical bluster lets on. *Churchyardes Chippes* appears to serve simply as an example of sixteenth-century rhyming verse, and as such seems like a curiously specific choice, until we explore its contents in more detail. Among a selection of anecdotes, fables and historical accounts, the anthology includes the *de casibus* tragedy of Sir Simon Burley, executed for treason under Richard II in 1388.[37] In Churchyard's complaint, which not only appropriates the 1550s *Mirror* form but also treats fitting late medieval subject matter, Burley takes personal issue with William Baldwin over his exclusion from the 1559–63 collection. Is he so insignificant or base that Baldwin has forgotten his name, Burley asks.[38] Blenerhasset's reference to the *Chippes*, then, points the reader not primarily to an example of unsuccessful poetry, but to another character 'excluded out of the English *Mirrour of Magistrates*' (fol. 1ᵛ), hinting that his reading of this poem – the first *de casibus* complaint whose speaker is substantially concerned with their omission from the *Mirror* – set up the *Seconde Part*'s oblique relationship to the central *Mirror* corpus, and inspired the restoration of more 'forgotten' historical accounts.

As for the rest of the passage, the links between Churchyard and Horace, Sackville (Lord Buckhurst) and Homer are less clear. Thomas Phaer's translation of the *Seven First Bookes of the Aeneid* (1558) obviously invites the comparison with Virgil, while the pairing allows another erstwhile *Mirror* contributor to be included in the *Seconde Part*'s catalogue,[39] and Blenerhasset follows Ascham in citing Phaer as an example of a successful author let down by his recourse to poetic 'custome'. The rationale behind the citation of George Turbervile, and his choice of classical counterpart is also uncertain. Turbervile was, like Blenerhasset, a translator of Ovid, and of Dominicus Mancinus's *Plaine Path to Perfect Vertue* (1568), but his relation to Tibullus in Blenerhasset's prose frame probably derives from his *Epitaphes, Epigrams, Songs and Sonets* (1567), which Turbervile hopes will 'be a Glasse and Myrror' for his readers,[40] and in which Turbervile, like the Roman elegiac poet Tibullus, addresses amorous poems to a series of pseudonymous or anonymous lovers, frequently in hexameter and heptameter couplets.[41] Despite Memory and Inquisition's claims, though, Turbervile does use blank verse, in six of the *Heroycall Epistles* (1567–70).[42] In fact, his collection closes with 'The Translator to the captious sort of Sycophants', in which he describes how effectively he has made a Roman poet speak English.[43] Like his bid to dismiss Sackville, Gascoigne, and Churchyard in the paratext, Blenerhasset's disparaging reference to Turbervile here seems to belie their common interests.

As to Inquisition's other references, Arthur Golding's popular translation of Ovid's *Metamorphoses* first appeared in 1565, and was printed a further two times by 1575. Golding 'enjoyed the patronage of the Earl of Leicester', as Blenerhasset may have aspired to do, and his *Metamorphoses* have a sympathetic confessional tenor, hinting, like the *Seconde Part*'s complaint of Cadwallader and its framing passages, at contemporary disputes over church adornment and apparel.[44] Golding translated the Latin text in hexameter couplets, considered a sufficiently close approximation of Latin poetry '[a]s that he may in English verse as in his owne bée soong'.[45] Inquisition's equation of George Gascoigne with Seneca could derive from his translation with Francis Kinwelmersh and Christopher Yelverton, of *Jocasta* (1566, not printed until 1572/3) as part of the revival of interest in Senecan tragedy at the Inns of Court during the 1560s,[46] although *Jocasta* is of course actually 'a translation of an Italian play, itself a version of a Latin rendering of Euripides', and written in blank verse.[47] As Winston and others have demonstrated, the *Mirror* emerged from Inns of Court culture, while also encouraging the development of dramatic tragedy in the 1560s. Austen notes that the 'tacit connection' between *Jocasta* and *Gorboduc* 'is confirmed by [Gabriel] Harvey, who notes both 'The Myrrour of Magistrates' and 'The Tragoedy of King Gorboduc' on the (cropped) title page in his copy of [Gascoigne's] *Posies*',[48] while as Winston observes in this volume, *Jocasta* was itself identified as a 'Mirror for Magistrates' in a printed marginal note.[49] Blenerhasset's series of references serves to embed his own *Mirror* within this framework of textual aims and affiliations through his paraliptic assertions.

In addition to Gascoigne's translation of *Jocasta*, Lämmerhirt suggests his 'Certayne notes of Instruction concerning the making of verse or ryme in English' as another connection with Blenerhasset's preoccupations.[50] Significantly, the text makes up part of the epistolary frame of the *Posies* (1575), and is presented as a letter to Edouardo Donati, an Italian gentleman of whose existence there is no evidence.[51] Austen suggests that Gascoigne's choice of medium allows him to 'understate the significance of what he would have known was a new kind of writing in English' and, while ostensibly written for manuscript circulation, Gascoigne may have intended to have it printed from the outset.[52] This scenario correlates closely to the *Seconde Part*'s paratextual set-up: like Gascoigne, Blenerhasset too may be seen to slip 'behind a ludic mask which is neither certainly fictional nor certainly fact'.[53] Like his exhortation to forget Sackville, Gascoigne, and Churchyard, or his claim not to have had access to Grafton, Polydore Vergil, and Cooper, this critical passage provides us with insight into what Blenerhasset was reading, and creates another intratextual community in which to situate our reading of his work.

Further enriching the proliferating stock of referents just out of the inscribed Blenerhasset's reach, Memory and Inquisition frequently raise the usefulness of certain legendary biographies, only to exclude them from the *Seconde Part*'s historical pageant. This paraliptic approach to chronicling draws attention to notable British and English rulers whose stories are left out of Blenerhasset's collection, while our awareness of the contingency of historiographical recording is reinforced. Inquisition notes that eagerness to hear Cadwallader 'hath made vs to ouerpasse king *Arthur* and *Cariticus*' and, according to Memory, 'so haue we forgot two or three other'. The West Saxons are 'worthy the speaking of … But we wyl not spende our time in hearing these deuout men' (fol. 41ʳ). The hapless historians also recount a number of near misses. Inquisition grudgingly accepts Egelrede's complaint, although he claims to have 'no minde to heare him speake' (fol. 54ᵛ); Edricus is warned that he must 'be briefe: for wee haue no tyme too bestowe in hearing the complayntes of those miserable Princes' (fol. 59ʳ); Memory responds to Cadwallader's appearance with surprise: 'in good fayth I had almost forgotten the man' (fol. 35ᵛ).

But does the paraliptic strategy of the paratextual and framing narratives extend to the voices of the complaints themselves? For the most part, the informality and disorder of the prose frame contrasts starkly with the tragic hyperbole of the verse. However, in common with the mismatched moral lessons Jennifer Richards observes in Baldwin's *Mirror* (p.84), several of Blenerhasset's laments adopt this narratological disjunction. Guidericus's complaint, for example, is packaged as a warning against excessive ambition, but describes his resistance to 'forrayne tyranny', refusal to pay tribute, and the civil unrest threatened by the loyalty of his brother to Rome, in terms likely to win an Elizabethan reader's approval in the defiant 1570s (fol. 4ʳ). Cadwallader's fall takes the form of a decline in status, as he renounces his kingship in Britain to become a priest in Rome, and he concludes by suggesting a generic lesson about the mutability of fortune and the 'miserable end' of great men including Caesar, Socrates, Aristotle, and Solon. But Blenerhasset depicts Cadwallader's comfort *increasing* as a member of the clergy, who 'turne a leafe or two', 'sometime sing a Psalme', and do 'nought but play and pray': the real focus of Cadwallader's story inheres not in the fact of his fall, but in the satirical portrayal of ecclesiastical life which follows (fol. 40ᵛ). By putting forward speakers who dismiss the substance of their own histories in favour of a pat, but incompatible, moral conclusion, Blenerhasset's *Mirror*, too, steps beyond the educative remit of the *de casibus* form to generate a more unstable, yet topically engaged, moral vision.

In the following two instances, furthermore, the pervasive paraliptic mode bleeds into the discourse of a historical speaker, drawing attention to something which they claim to omit or deny. Queen Helena addresses her 'louing Lords, and you my subiects' to quell their anxieties over her decision to marry a Roman, with elegant rhetorical strategies of persuasion. Is Blenerhasset scripting Elizabeth I's justification for a putative French marriage? Helena heads off concerns that she has been overcome by superficial admiration, and argues instead that she has the nation's wellbeing at heart:

> Perhaps you think I loue, because I see
> His comely corps, and seemely sanguine face.

> You be deceaude, no outward brauery,
> No personage, no gallant courtly grace.
> What though hee bee by birth of royall race?
> I recke it not, but this I do regarde,
> My common weale by him may bee preserude. (fol. 20ᵛ)

Taken alone, this stanza reads as a standard rhetorical deployment of *paralipsis*, listing qualities Helena ostensibly does not value, only to reinforce her auditors' appreciation of these qualities in her choice of suitor. However, two stanzas above, Helena had listed these qualities – 'His comely corps, his friendly promise plight,| His famous actes, his Noble royall race', in addition to a coy inference of 'Some other thinges which here I could recite' – as precisely the features which 'The *Romans* hart within my brest dyd place'. This example of *paralipsis* used within the complaint itself, then, carries a highly destabilising weight, rendering Helena a duplicitous witness, compromising our trust in her testimony, and throwing the whole premise of first-hand historical accounts into doubt.

Vortiger, sometime king of the Britons, follows Helena, and her eagerness to have her history retold is diametrically reversed in his reluctance to speak. Having revealed with unusual brevity how he usurped the throne and was burned to death, he asks Memory, 'What may I more of my misfortune say?| I sigh to see, I silent ceasse to tell| What me destroide' (fol. 25ʳ), a dissenter from the *Seconde Part*'s confessional format. Desperate to omit his own account, he begs his listeners, 'Let that suffice, and let me nowe departe', before an imperious Memory demands that he finish the tale (fol. 25ᵛ). Vortiger objects that 'For me to shew how I aloft was stayde,| Were to erect a schoole of Trechery' (fol. 25ʳ). His reasoning lays bare part of Baldwin's satirical strategy, since Baldwin and his co-authors sometimes did exactly this, retelling the falls of rebels ostensibly as negative *exempla*, when in fact they approved, to some degree, of their behaviour. Just as Richards shows Baldwin exploring the educative and affective force of immoral speech in her chapter in this volume, Vortiger equates the negative impact of his story specifically with speaking aloud when he claims that 'Silence is best, let no man learne by me', placing emphasis on the oral repetition of his tale in addition to their 'reading' of his wicked deeds. He also explodes the educative premise of the *Mirror* and its recensions, when he claims that the use to which his history is put fully depends on the character of its readers: 'As good men can by wicked workes beware,| So wicked men by wicked workes be wise' (fol. 25ʳ). Here, again, Blenerhasset's employment of the paraliptic mode reveals at once a deep-seated scepticism regarding the *Mirror*'s purported aims, and a pervasive affinity with Baldwin's metapoetic tendencies.

As we have seen, Blenerhasset's paraliptic references served to construct a scaffolding of Protestant intellectual culture and reformist thought, which drew together contributors to the early *Mirror* collections with the Leicester circle of which Blenerhasset aspired to be a part, and contemporary poetic innovators. Blenerhasset's use of the *Mirror* as a vehicle for the construction of this network demonstrates the work's enduring popularity, and its malleability. Blenerhasset's Memory suggests in the prose frame that, seeing the efforts of the translators cited, the legendary critics '*Zoilus* and *Momus*, will crie out, O vayne glorious heade, whiche now for a singularitie dooth indeuour to erect a new kinde of Poetrie in England'. Tantamount to a mission statement, this calls for a new reading which locates Blenerhasset's work between that of Gascoigne's recognised new style, and Spenser, whose *Shepheardes Calender* also inaugurated a new poetry the following year.[54] Blenerhasset supports this new kind of poetry with a paraliptic foundation of successful contemporary authors, making a tentative and coded, but fully referenced, foray into literary innovation: as Spenser's *Shepheardes Calender* was soon to demonstrate, even a 'New Poete' must validate their invention with a firm grounding in the work of reputable predecessors.[55] It is this framework of references within which, I have argued, we should situate Blenerhasset's text the better to understand its relationship to the *Mirror for Magistrates* of Baldwin and Ferrers, and its place within the ongoing tradition. Furthermore, the historical complaints' adoption of paraliptic strategies occur at moments of historiographical tension, which complicate the existing scholarly narratives that attempt to explain Blenerhasset's poetic practice. This account suggests that later readers and imitators of Baldwin are indeed alert to his texts' playfulness and irreverence, in ways we are only beginning to identify and understand.

Notes

This chapter is adapted from part of my DPhil thesis, 'The *Mirror for Magistrates*, 1559–1610: Transmission, Appropriation and the Poetics of Historiography' (University of Oxford, 2012). I would like to thank my supervisor, Paulina Kewes, and my examiners, Jane Griffiths and Mike Pincombe, for their advice in writing and revising my work on Blenerhasset, as well as Andrew Hadfield for his comments on this chapter.

1 John Hardyng, *The Chronicle of John Hardyng*, 'Preface' by Richard Grafton? (London: Richard Grafton, 1543), sig. *vi^r–^{v}.

2 "Paralipomenon, n.", *OED Online*. Oxford University Press, June 2015. Web. Accessed 25 May 2015. 2. 'Material omitted from the body of a text, and appended as a supplement'.
3 Richard Niccols, ed., *A Mirour for Magistrates* (London: Felix Kyngston, 1610).
4 Thomas Blenerhasset, *The Seconde Part of the Mirrour for Magistrates, containing the falles of the infortunate Princes of this Lande* (London: Robert Webster, 1578), 'The Printer to the friendly Reader', sig. *2ʳ. All further references to this text will be given in parentheses.
5 Geoffrey's legend is followed by Holinshed and Shakespeare; the historical Cunobelinus's sons were named Adminius, Togodumnus, and Caratacus.
6 See, for example, E. M. W. Tillyard, '*A Mirror for Magistrates* Revisited', in Herbert Davis and Helen Gardner, eds, *Elizabethan and Jacobean Studies* (Oxford: Clarendon Press, 1959), pp.1–16, at p.10; Paul Budra, A Mirror for Magistrates *and the* de casibus *Tradition* (University of Toronto Press, 2000), pp.27–8; Scott C. Lucas, 'Hall's Chronicle and the *Mirror for Magistrates*: History and the Tragic Pattern', in Mike Pincombe and Cathy Shrank, eds, *The Oxford Handbook of Tudor Literature, 1485–1603* (Oxford University Press, 2009), pp.356–71, at p.370.
7 Anthony Munday, *The Mirrour of Mutabilitie* (London: John Allde for Richard Ballard, 1579); George Whetstone, *A Mirour for Magestrates of Cyties* (London: Richard Jones, 1584).
8 Kathleen Tillotson, review, '*The Mirror for Magistrates*. Edited from the Original Texts in the Huntington Library by Lily B. Campbell', *MLR* 34:4 (1939), 585–7, at p.586.
9 See Jerry Leath Mills, 'A Source for Spenser's Anamnestes', *PQ* 47:1 (Jan. 1968), 137–9; Aristotle, 'On Memory and Recollection', in Jeffrey Henderson, ed., *On the Soul, Parva Naturalia, On Breath: Aristotle VIII* (Cambridge, MA and London: Harvard University Press, 1957), pp.285–313.
10 See H. A. Kelly, '*Occupatio* as Negative Narration: A Mistake for *Occultatio/Praeteritio*', *MP* 74:3 (1977), 311–15 for the history of the term '*occupatio*'s' usage.
11 Richard A. Lanham, *A Handlist of Rhetorical Terms* (Berkeley: University of California Press, 1991), p.104.
12 William Shakespeare, *The Tragedie of Julius Caesar*, in *Mr William Shakespeares Comedies, Histories, & Tragedies* (London: I. Iaggard and E. Blount, 1623), pp.121–2.
13 Thomas Elyot, *The Dictionary of Syr Thomas Eliot Knyght* (London: Thomas Berthelet, 1538), sig. Pivʳ.
14 George Puttenham, *The Arte of English Poesie, Contriued into Three Bookes: the First of Poets and Poesie, the Second of Proportion, the Third of Ornament* (London: Richard Field, 1589), Book III, p.194.
15 Richard Sherry, *A Treatise of Schemes and Tropes, Very Profytable for the Better Vnderstanding of Good Authors, gathered out of the best grammarians and oratours* (London: John Day, 1550), sig. Dviʳ.
16 Puttenham, *The Arte of English Poesie*, p.194.

17 Rudolf Lämmerhirt, *Thomas Blenerhassets "Second Part of the Mirror for Magistrates": Eine Quellenstudie* (Weimar: Uschmann, 1909).
18 Lämmerhirt, *Quellenstudie*.
19 See Philip Schwyzer, *Literature, Nationalism and Memory in Early Modern England and Wales* (Cambridge University Press, 2004), ch. 4, 'Ghosts of a Nation: *A Mirror for Magistrates* and the Poetry of Spectral Complaint', pp.97–126; Donald Jellerson, 'The Spectral Historiopoetics of the *Mirror for Magistrates*', *JNR* 2:1 (2010), 54–71.
20 The so-called third decade of Livy's *Ab Urbe Condita*, or Books 21–30, was printed in numerous volumes across continental Europe in the sixteenth century. The most recently printed in 1577 was *Decas Tertia* (Lyon: Sébastien Gryphe, 1554). In 1561, Thomas Marshe printed Anthony Cope's *History of Two the Moste Noble Capytaynes of the Worlde, Anniball and Scipio* (previously printed in 1544 and 1548 by Thomas Berthelet), 'gathered and translated into English oute of Titus Liuius, and other authoures', which treated the same period as the third decade.
21 By Michel de Vascosan for Galliot du Pré in Paris.
22 John Higgins, 'The Authours Induction', *The First Parte of the Mirour For Magistrates* (London: Thomas Marshe, 1574), fol. 1[r].
23 Thomas Blundeville, *Of Wryting and Reading Hystories* (London: William Seres, 1574), sig. C4[r].
24 D. S. Levene, *Livy on the Hannibalic War* (Oxford University Press, 2010), pp.344–5.
25 Livy, *The Romane Historie*, trans. Philemon Holland (London: Adam Islip, 1600), p.2; see S. Clark Hulse, *Metamorphic Verse: The Elizabethan Minor Epic* (Princeton University Press, 1981), p.215.
26 Andreola Rossi, 'Parallel Lives: Hannibal and Scipio in Livy's Third Decade', *TAPA* 134:2 (2004), 359–81, at p.360.
27 See John Bossewell, *Workes of Armourie* (London: Richard Tottell, 1572), fol. 4[v].
28 See Adam McKeown, *English Mercuries: Soldier Poets in the Age of Shakespeare* (Nashville: Vanderbilt University Press, 2009).
29 William Webbe, *A Discourse of English Poetrie* (London: John Charlewood for Robert Walley, 1586), sig. Ciii[v]; Edmund Spenser, *The Shepheardes Calender* (London: Hugh Singleton, 1579), fol. 48[r].
30 Scott C. Lucas, 'Diggon Davie and Davy Dicar: Edmund Spenser, Thomas Churchyard, and the Poetics of Public Protest', *SS* 16 (2002), 151–66, at p.156.
31 See Cyndia Clegg, *Elizabethan Censorship*, pp.103–4; Gillian Austen, *George Gascoigne* (Cambridge: D. S. Brewer, 2008), p.18.
32 Austen, *Gascoigne*, p.164.
33 See Derek Attridge, *Well-Weighed Syllables: Elizabethan Verse in Classical Metres* (Cambridge University Press, 1974), p.111; and Robert Cummings, 'Abraham Fleming's *Eclogues*', *TL* 19 (2010), 147–69, at p.166.
34 Cf. Kelly A. Quinn, 'Samuel Daniel's Defense of Medievalism', in Clare A. Simmons, ed., *Medievalism and the Quest for the 'Real' Middle Ages* (London and Portland, OR: Frank Cass, 2001), pp.29–44, at pp.30–2.

35 Quinn, 'Samuel Daniel's Defense of Medievalism', p.31.
36 Roger Ascham, *The Scholemaster* (London: John Day, 1570), fol. 60^r.
37 Thomas Churchyard, *The Firste Parte of Churchyardes Chippes, contayning twelue seuerall labours* (London: Thomas Marshe, 1574), fols 46^v–56^v.
38 Churchyard, *Churchyardes Chippes*, fol. 46^v.
39 The complaint of Owain Glyn Dŵr is attributed to Thomas Phaer in the *Last Part of the Mirour for Magistrates* (1578).
40 George Turbervile, *Epitaphes, Epigrams, Songs and Sonets with a Discourse of the Friendly Affections of Tymetes to Pyndara His Ladie. Newly Corrected with Additions* (London: Henry Denham, 1567), 'To the Reader'.
41 Turbervile claims that his love poems 'are written in honour of Anne Russell, daughter of the second earl of Bedford, under the name of Pandora or Pyndara' (Raphael Lyne, 'Turbervile, George (*b.* 1543/4, *d.* in or after 1597)', *ODNB*), while Tibullus addresses Delia, actually Plania. Tibullus's elegies were not printed in England until Charles Hopkins's translation of 1694, but were regularly reproduced in Latin across continental Europe throughout the sixteenth century, usually alongside those of Catullus and Propertius, and became a byword for bawdy, pagan love poetry.
42 Ovid, *The Heroycall Epistles of the Learned Poet Publius Ouidius Naso*, trans. George Turbervile (London: Henry Denham, 1567), Epistle XI: Canace to Machareus; XII: Medea to Iason; XIII: Laodameia to Protesilaus; XIV: Hypermnestra to Lynceus; XX: Acontius to Cydippe; and XXI: Cydippe to Acontius.
43 Ovid, *The Heroycall Epistles*, 'The Translator to the captious sort of Sycophants', sig. X2^{r-v}.
44 Raphael Lyne, 'Golding's Englished *Metamorphoses*', *TL* 5:2 (1996), 183–200, at pp.191–2.
45 Ovid, *Metamorphosis* (London: William Seres, 1567), trans. Arthur Golding, Preface, sig. A3^{r-v}.
46 See Chapter 11 in this volume.
47 Austen, *Gascoigne*, p.54. The Italian play was Lodovico Dolce's *Giocasta* (1549), derived from R. Winter's Latin version of *Phoenissae* (Basel, 1541).
48 Austen, *Gascoigne*, pp.54–5.
49 George Gascoigne, *The Posies* (London: Richard Smith, 1575), sig. D2^v.
50 Lämmerhirt, *Quellenstudie*, p.63, n.3. See also Austen, *Gascoigne*, p.101.
51 Austen, *Gascoigne*, p.102.
52 Austen, *Gascoigne*, p.102.
53 Austen, *Gascoigne*, p.103.
54 Spenser, *Shepheardes Calender*, E. K.'s dedication to Gabriel Harvey.
55 Spenser, *Shepheardes Calender*; See Harriet Archer, ' "New Matter Framed Upon the Old": Chaucer, Spenser, and Luke Shepherd's "New Poet" ', in Tamsin Badcoe, Gareth Griffiths, and Rachel Stenner, eds, *Chaucer and Spenser* (Manchester University Press, forthcoming).

CHAPTER 9

Richard Niccols and Tudor nostalgia
Andrew Hadfield

Like many of the most popular literary texts of the sixteenth and seventeenth centuries – the *Arcadia, Amadis de Gaul*, The Psalms – *A Mirror for Magistrates* might best be seen as a work in continual evolution.[1] Once the idea of *A Mirror* had been established with its combination of English/British history and political comment/analysis, a series of variations were not only possible but good enough ideas to be carried out by future writers. Lévi-Strauss once famously (notoriously?) remarked that animals were 'good to think', and the same might be said of historical poetry in the English Renaissance.[2] While Baldwin's project concentrated on the use of English history to instruct magistrates how to govern through the representation of positive and negative examples, later writers broadened the nature of the *Mirror*. John Higgins saw the need for a prequel and obligingly wrote a series of histories of important figures from the island's ancient past – Forrex, Porrex, Nennius, Cordelia, Humber et al. Writing on Guernsey the soldier-poet Thomas Blenerhasset (c.1550–1624) followed suit and delved into the ancient history of the British Isles to produce a series of tragedies of Britons who were interesting and often great rather than ones whose stories would obviously teach readers how they might act as magistrates: Vortigern, Uther Pendragon, King Harold. The historical nature of the poetry seemed to have pushed its original didactic purpose to one side. But perhaps this is an unfair way of approaching the issue and we should just accept that good ideas which hold two notions in tension – which we can call historical poetry and didactic literature – will move in different directions throughout their time together. It is best not to prejudge and we should wonder whether *A Mirror* actually changes for the better or just becomes a related but different beast. The 1587 edition printed by Henry Marshe includes elements of the Baldwin edition along with material from those of Higgins and Blenerhasset, omitting some tragedies and including some new Roman complaints as well as those of Cardinal Wolsey and James IV of Scotland – who over-reached himself at

Flodden Field, and, like the Cardinal, felt the wrath of Henry VIII – in order to establish a reliable canon.

Do these changes chart a loss of focus from the original design of William Baldwin's project, which mined history with a clear didactic focus, using the past to tell a series of stories useful for any magistrate eager to perform their tasks well or simply avoid a grisly fate? Or should they be read more generously as new departures, imaginative uses of a nuanced genre that could be manipulated in a variety of ways? Should we accept that things change over time or lament a process of ideological reduction as a once critical genre grew staid, familiar, and conservative?[3]

Perhaps the most maligned of all *Mirror* authors is Richard Niccols (1583/4–1616), who oversaw the 1610 edition as the popularity of the genre was coming to an end.[4] Certainly the few critics who have commented on Niccols' work and edition have not been favourably impressed. Paul Budra has argued that the rot set in from the start with the introductory verse dedicated to Lord Charles Howard, Earl of Nottingham, 'that was a banal and sycophantic plea for patronage' and in which 'instead of displaying a critical mirror to a flawed magistrate, Niccols begs his favour.'[5] Niccols' life records are not abundant, and much information is contained in his writing. He was educated at Magdalen Hall, Oxford, having earlier taken part in the Earl of Essex's raid on Cadiz. He graduated in 1606 and began a precarious life as a poet dependent on the support of a number of patrons: Howard, Sir Thomas Wroth, and James Hay, Earl of Carlisle, and their families. Niccols clearly wrote fluently and he produced a number of substantial poems in the fourteen years that he was active. His choice of subjects shows that he responded to current events and the needs of his possible patrons as one might expect from a writer in his position who had to secure support in order to survive. His first published poem, *Expicedium: a funeral oration, upon the death of the late deceased princesse of famous memorye, Elizabeth* (1603), which appeared while he was still at Oxford, is clearly an attempt to attract attention, but it also reveals Niccols' reading and his immersion in contemporary poetic culture, as it contains significant reference to the relatively recent death of Edmund Spenser through a lament for the death of Colin Clout. Perhaps Niccols was close enough to Spenser to have been one of the poets described by William Camden who threw pens and poems into his grave during the funeral service in Westminster Abbey.[6] Niccols later imitated Spenser's *Mother Hubberd's Tale* in his *The Beggar's Ape*, probably unwisely given the offence that Spenser's poem caused the Cecil family through the representation of the crafty fox supporting his crooked cubs, a clear allusion to William Cecil, Lord Burghley and his son, Sir Robert, who was often mocked for his deformity.[7] Niccols' poem was eventually posthumously published in 1627, long after Sir Robert Cecil's death in 1612. Niccols was also strongly influenced by Michael Drayton, Spenser's heir apparent, which places him within the tradition of shepherd poets at odds with mainstream Stuart political culture outlined by Michelle O'Callaghan.[8]

We do not know why Niccols decided to work on a new edition of the *Mirror*, but he produced a revised version of John Higgins' more complex and diverse edition of 1587 in 1610–11, and it is easy to see why the work might have interested him. By this time he had established himself as a skilful poet working within a tradition of oppositional poetry which looked back to the reign of Elizabeth for inspiration, a significant component of early Jacobean literary culture, often fiercely critical of the corruption of the Jacobean court and keen on the military values inspired by Prince Henry, which celebrated the heroic Protestant struggle against decadent Catholic Europe.[9]

Niccols was a writer who found the present tawdry and corrupt, as *The Beggar's Ape* and the last work published in his lifetime, *Sir Thomas Overburies Vision* (1616), demonstrate. The second poem, in which a ghost laments his fate, is closely related to the poems in the *Mirror* and was based on the notorious murder of Sir Thomas Overbury who was poisoned in the Tower of London on the orders of Frances Howard, Lady Somerset, because of Overbury's opposition to her marriage to the King's favourite, Robert Carr.[10] Overbury laments his own sinful life but also points the finger at Lady Somerset, as Niccols attacks the vices of the present using a literary mode from the past to suggest that society was losing its way and needed to remember its core values. In many ways Niccols was a deeply nostalgic writer – clearly one thing that drew him to a *Mirror* – casting the reign of Elizabeth as a golden age of daring, panache, and proper values. He is also the only poet to celebrate the artillery barracks in London, which he did in a longish chorographical poem published in 1616, *London's Artillery*, a work that owes much to the chorographic writing of Michael Drayton and William Vallans.[11] Written after Prince Charles inspected the volunteers in the artillery grounds, Niccols makes use of Camden, Stow, and Holinshed to chart the significance of the military features of the capital in verse with a series of prose illustrations of the matter represented very much in the style of *Poly-Olbion*, the first edition of which had been published in 1612. There is no record of Niccols in the army apart from his experience in Essex's Cadiz expedition of 1596–7, but one of the constant features of Niccols' poetry is his obsessive need to contrast the soft, effeminate life of the court with the hard, manly life inspired by military values, so perhaps his experience with Essex helped define his subsequent values.[12]

Niccols approves of war as a means of testing the nation's mettle and expunging the indolence and self-interest which corrode England's hierarchy and established order. In a long section early on in *London's Artillery*, Niccols laments the neglect of arms (signalled in the margin) and provides his solution to the nation's ills:

> But soft, I seeme too bitter gainst the times,
> And some perhaps, who patronise such crimes [i.e., corruption, laziness]
> Will taxe my plaints, as vttered in despight,
> Out of a warre-thirst gainst the sweet delight
> Of blessed peace, which heau'n doth still bestow
> Vpon our state, but let such fondlings know,
> I to my countrie, wish no wounds of steele,
> Onely it grieues my soule to see th'increase
> And fruite of plenty, which our happie peace,
> So long enioyd, could carefully prouide,
> Deuour'd and gate up by their wanton pride,
> Who, like a treacherous Peere, that bearing sway
> In state affaires, makes euery one giue way
> To his designes, sights for foes at home,
> That so our selues, our selues may ouercome.
> Tis that (alas) that with selfe-spoyling hand
> Exhasts the golden treasures of our land,
> Wastes townes and cities, makes our people bare,
> Turnes rich men poore, brings poore men to despaire
> It is that *Omphale*, that by her charmes,
> Makes our *Herculean* youth, neglecting armes,
> Put on the habit, looks, lockes, pace and face,
> Of tender women, to their beards disgrace:
> It is the Harlot ...
> That is the cause of martiall mens decay;
> For since their swords do purchase peace from farre,
> Wise peace should keepe them still to keepe out warre:
> Those lazie *Lozels*, that on soft downe beds,
> Till no one day laying their phantasticke heads
> Vnto the pillow, study and deuize
> On some quaint English, French, or Tuscan guise,
> Who to maintaine strange fashions and new cuts,
> Do wring their poore racke-rented tenants guts;
> Who kindling lust at euery female eye,
> Fell forests, woods, make lands and lordships flie[.][13]

Niccols has managed to hoard together a cluster of good and bad things on either side of a division he has assumed. On the one hand we have masculine vigour, rigorous vigilance, training, and planning, allied to old English values whereby the aristocracy cared for the peasants who lived with relative independence; on the other we have the effeminate luxury of lazy courtiers who exploit everyone, have virtually no connection with England, preferring foreign products and styles, and who chop down forests for their own pleasure partly in order to impress women who they want to seduce. Niccols follows Drayton in recognising the significant ecological changes that were taking place throughout England as ancient forests were chopped down to foster more intensive agriculture, a development that both poets thought was of dubious value.[14] Men with means have become addicted to changes in fashion and have started to follow what their counterparts in Tuscany and France wear, clothing tastes that have infected native practices and made Englishmen effeminate so that they prefer lying in soft beds to preparing for war. Omphale was the queen of Lydia who bought Hercules when he was sold into slavery and forced him to wear women's clothes (he later served her as a military champion and she bore him a son). The legend informs Spenser's representation of Artegall's imprisonment and effeminisation at the hands of the Amazon, Radigund, in *The Faerie Queene*, Book V, yet more evidence that Niccols was particularly interested in this section of Spenser's poem.[15] The clear message is that gender traffic should be the other way: women when in positions of authority should be fostering martial values, not using their power to make men more like them. And the attack on military figures who fail to perform their duties properly is a familiar one that goes as far back as *The Iliad* and Achilles' sulking in his tent with Patroclus, prolonging the Trojan War when he had the power to end it.[16]

The dedicatory poem addressed to the captains of the musters describes them as 'worshipfull favourers of artes and followers of armes', joining together the military and poetry, a common combination in early modern England.[17] The passage makes clear that what is required is a 'warre thirst', the desire for battle that will offset the 'sweet delight' of peace because those times of plenty and ease have now turned sour. Niccols believes that peace is laying towns waste as military men search for ever more intense pleasures exhausting the 'golden treasures' of the land, a judgement that shows how ignorant he was of the extraordinary costs of war in Elizabeth's final years, when the protracted war with Spain cost an estimated £4,500,000.[18] Prince Henry and Elizabeth serve as pointed contrasts to James and his effeminate court with its alien values, because even in times of long-term peace the people should be vigilant and prepared for the outbreak of war. The passage contrasts decent English old-fashioned values from a vanishing age when everyone knew their place and society was coherent and consistent to those fostered by James who had an unpopular Danish queen; who had made peace with Spain; and whose court had been notoriously licentious and entertained a major scandal involving poison, a foreign woman's mode of killing, and which Niccols later described in great detail in *Overburys Vision*.[19]

The design, purpose, and many of the individual poems in Niccols' *Mirror* are very much in line with the sentiments and ideals of *London's Artillery*. Niccols made the work strictly English in focus, removing the Roman tragedies and pointedly expunging all Scottish elements, a move that enables him to conflate English and British identity at the expense of a wider understanding of the different nations and identities contained in Britain.[20] The tragedies were arranged in chronological order, with a collection of eleven new additional poems (mainly of English monarchs, ten tragedies, and a poem celebrating Elizabeth) at the end, but there were no interlinking prefaces explaining the context of each poem. Niccols clearly thought that the historical verse could stand on its own as he was prepared to make explanatory additions and marginal annotations to direct the reader when necessary, as the notes to *London's Artillery* indicate.

Niccols then added his own section of more reflective and significant tragedies omitted from the existing main section of the *Mirror* entitled *A Winter Night's Vision*, using his favourite technique of the dream vision as a linking device, a further sign of his knowledge of medieval English literature and his commitment to an older style of vernacular poetry. In the letter to the reader he is candid about his poetic process, as he is elsewhere, telling us that he did not have time to revise the whole text, as had been his original plan, but he has been able to add ten tragedies in a new section. In the induction he finds the *Mirror* on a bleak winter's day and Lady Memory kindly dictates the stories of the missing tragedies to him, a record of the deeds of dead heroes, which in itself shows how far we have come from Baldwin's original design. The new tragedies include King Arthur, Edmund Ironside, Harold Godwin, King John, Edward II, the princes murdered in the tower, and Richard III, a mixture of the familiar and expected, and some new departures which testify to the extent of Niccols' assiduous reading of Holinshed and Stow. In line with his conception of *A Mirror* as a verse record of key moments in English history, Niccols seems to have seen his most important role as editor as that of updating the text to include the most significant work of recent historians unavailable to the earlier editors and writers. Niccols' *Mirror* concludes with *England's Eliza*, a patriotic survey of the reign of Elizabeth, recording the key events, especially of the later years. English history is narrated to celebrate the nation's military achievements and to produce a story of its prowess and success in defending itself from invasion and foreign exploitation.

Niccols' *Mirror* stamps the authority and vision of its editor on the texts that he uses, pulling the stories together into a coherent whole: the very opposite of Annabel Patterson's understanding of Holinshed's *Chronicles* as a pluralist and liberal enterprise with diverse and diverging voices.[21] Niccols can be an enterprising and insightful reader of the literature and history he incorporated into his projects, but it is important to wonder how aware he was of what he was doing and how much control he had over each part. Was he an astute writer who knew exactly how he wanted to use the sources and authorities at his disposal, or was he really a magpie selecting useful bits and pieces that attracted him and which he could then recycle? The tragedy of *Richard III* is a good case in point. It is among the most eloquent and carefully crafted tragedies in Niccols' work, obviously modelled on the history by Thomas More.[22] A case can be made, however, that Niccols was also strongly influenced by Shakespeare's play, which he could have read in the quarto first published in 1597, as it was republished four times (1598, 1602, 1605, 1612) before Niccols' *Mirror* and was still performed regularly in the early seventeenth century, all signs of the play's popularity as well as the significant appeal of the advent of the Tudors in the seventeenth century, especially to those at odds with the Jacobean regime.[23] Niccols omitted the original version from the 1563 edition of the *Mirror* in his 1610 edition, substituting his own, obviously believing he could do a better job for readers eager to have the most up-to-date historical writing, having seen Shakespeare's play, and so being informed by more recent historical work than his predecessor. Shakespeare added the ghosts tormenting Richard the night before the Battle of Bosworth, which Niccols duly incorporates into his version:

> I thought that all those murthered ghosts, whom I
> By death had sent to their vntimely graue,
> With balefull noise about my tent did crie,
> And of the heau'ns with sad complaint did craue,
> That they on guiltie wretch might vengeance haue:
> To whom I thought the Judge of hean'n gaue eare,
> And gainst me gaue a iudgement full of feare.

> For loe eftsoones, a thousand hellish hags
> Leauing th'abode of their infernall cell,
> Seasing on me, my hatefull bodie drags
> From forth my bed into a place like hell,
> Where freends did naught but bellow, howle and yell,
> Who in a sterne strife good gainst each other bent,
> Who should my hatefull bodie most torment.[24]

Niccols' lines are decent enough as poetry, but rather limited. There is nothing of Richard's awful night of torment in the 1563 edition, which describes Richard's eagerness for battle with an enemy for whom he feels particular malice; his lack of good fortune on Bosworth field; and his ignominious end as his body is 'hurreyed and tugged like a Dogge,| On horseback all naked and bare as I was borne.| My head, hands, & feete, downe hanging like a Hogge'.[25] More importantly, there is nothing of the complexity of Richard's speech in Shakespeare's play in which the doomed king imagines that he is already on the battlefield calling for another horse, becoming separated from himself in his agonised panic, realisation of his guilt and impotence in the face of an overwhelming threat with justice on its side:

> O, no. Alas, I rather hate myself,
> For hateful deeds committed by myself.
> I am a villain. Yet I lie; I am not.
> Fool, of thyself speak well. Fool, do not flatter.
> My conscience hath a thousand several tongues,
> And every tongue brings in a several tale,
> And every tale condemns me for a villain.
> Perjury, perjury, in the direst degree;
> All several sins, all used in each degree,
> Throng to the bar, crying all, 'Guilty, guilty!'
> I shall despair. There is no creature loves me,
> And if I die, no soul will pity me.[26]

Shakespeare depicts a soul already suffering the torments of damnation as his language, once his most trusted weapon, fails him as the syntax breaks down and his disconnected words express his lack of control. Niccols represents the pains of hell and the hopeless suffering of Richard but in a much more conventional manner, having Richard's ghost describe the fiends who will drag him down to hell after his death the next day. Niccols' lines might appear to be a clever combination of Shakespeare, Marlowe's *Doctor Faustus*, and the earlier editions of the *Mirror*. The style is very clearly *Mirror*esque in tone, with the dead returning to warn the living to avoid their fate, and further supports an argument that what

Niccols was doing was revising the original – here, literally enough, in replacing one tragedy of Richard with another – in line with better history and, of course, better poetry of a familiar old-fashioned mode.

In other parts of his edition Niccols appears to be drawing on his experience of seeing English history plays on the stage, again, focussing attention on the *Mirror* as a project rooted in the Tudor past, especially if, as is possible, Niccols was making use of plays he saw in the 1590s. The tragedy of King John casts the king as wronged and abused by papists, having to fight the rebel barons and perishing through the use of poison. This would surely have reminded readers of the representation of John's death on the stage in the two plays dealing with his reign performed in the 1590s which showed that his demise took place at the hands of the evil monks of Swineford Abbey, who poison him because he dares to stand up to the church and the papacy, a familiar Protestant explanation of the King's end.[27] Niccols could have seen either Shakespeare's play or *The Troublesome Reign* – now attributed to George Peele – in London, especially if he was the son of the Richard Niccols, lawyer of the Inner Temple, who wrote the pious *A Day Starre for Darke Wandring Soules: Shewing the Light by a Christian Controversie*, published posthumously in 1613.[28] The concluding moral of Niccols' poem is very much in the tradition of *Mirror* epitaphs:

> Behold the effects of Henries curse
> On his last sonne, for his rebellious prise:
> Let Princes learne, that wheare debate, the nurse
> Of discord, doth the Prince and Peeres diuide,
> Nothing but destruction can that State betide:
> Of which let that sad time of my short reigne,
> A Mirrour unto future time remaine.[29]

Is there a covert allusion to Mary Stuart, described by Elizabeth as the 'daughter of debate', in her poem 'The Doubt of Future Foes', which had been circulating in miscellanies since the 1570s?[30] There is a marked contrast between a powerful central authority based on austere military values and weak rule which leads to disaster. John is caught between two worlds but is not quite enough of a military man to establish his authority when threatened by determined enemies, which is how he is represented in both plays. Elizabeth, by way of contrast, frequently depicted as a military ruler eager to guard her nation and her people from invasion, was astute enough to identify the threat to her rule, and to eliminate her enemies.[31] The dying John can explain to his son, the future Henry III, later to become one of England's most successful military rulers, that he must not tolerate division between the crown and the nobles, a lesson that applies in 1610 as it did in 1216. Elizabeth was a notably popular ruler, especially when viewed retrospectively. In contrast James, who had started to fall out with many of his English nobles, was viewed sceptically by many others, partly because he always seemed to be changing favourites and no one could be certain where they stood in the pecking order, and partly because the royal finances were in a terrible state and he was dependent on the good will of courtiers he had to tax heavily and reward sparsely.[32]

The same can be said about Niccols' representation of Edward II, like John, a wronged king who comes to a bad end because he allows the evil fop Piers Gaveston to dominate his court and stamp his minion's character upon it. As a result Edward presides over an effeminate group of selfish and incompetent nobles who have no interest in the welfare of the nation, only their own pleasure and profit. The military backbone of Edward I's stern and powerful rule dissipates as the royal coffers are emptied on frivolous pursuits which provide nothing of substance for the people of England. Edward is taken in by Gaveston's flattery and this leads to exactly the same sort of discord between ruler and advisers that took place in John's reign and which Niccols was concerned had started to dominate the character of that of James:

> My Gaveston in maiesties great armes
> Being safely hug'd, no change of fortune feares;
> He wantons with the King, soothes his harmes,
> He plays the Buffons part, he flouts and ieers
> The courtly actions of the honour'd Peers:
> The great in counsell and the noble bourne,
> Are made the subiect of his hatefull scorne.[33]

History, for Niccols, consists of a series of recognisable patterns that are repeated if no one intervenes to stop them, a reading and use of the past that is in keeping with the spirit of the first edition of the *Mirror*.[34] Edward is not a wise enough king to recognise that his fate is likely to be that of John – or even worse – one hundred years earlier. After the expansive years that England enjoyed under the rule of Edward I, 'the hammer of the Scots', the son betrays the father's legacy, not realising that armed peace has to follow conflict. Those who are able to offer wise counsel are silenced and what we have is a form of tyranny in which the lusts of the monarch and his inner circle are satisfied at the expense of everyone else.[35] If only the monarch had listened to advice and read his history properly, he could have avoided the rebellion that inevitably followed, his deposition, and the ignominious death that cemented his posthumous reputation.[36]

Nearly three hundred years on, James is making the same mistakes – by 1610 he was already known to be enraptured by Robert Carr, raising him above his station and so causing discontent and discord at court.[37] Niccols surely expects his readers to make the parallels and worry that James may be going the way of Edward, and might even suffer something approaching the same awful end. The event had been represented on stage in Christopher Marlowe's play performed in the early 1590s and revived on a number of occasions in various theatres in the early 1600s, making this another play that Niccols could well have seen on stage as well as read, using its powerful message to enhance his use of historical poetry.[38]

The final part of Niccols' *Mirror*, *England's Eliza*, represents Elizabeth as she is often seen today in popular imagery, as the queen who was able to rule because she adopted masculine values, a choice that led to a golden age of peace and plenty supported by the military daring of her heroes.[39] Unlike John and Edward II, the queen is immune to the deceitful arts of the court, and does not allow her advisers to be emasculated.[40] Instead, her reign is dominated by military values and the endless struggle with Catholic rebels and traitors, against which she and her loyal chief subjects successfully struggle with united, patriotic purpose. Niccols cunningly – or, perhaps with a degree of ignorance – adapts Edmund Spenser's representation of Elizabeth, so that Elizabeth becomes Fidessa, a symbol of the true faith.[41] In *The Faerie Queene* Duessa disguises herself as Fidessa to fool the Red-Cross Knight, and whereas Astrea, the Goddess of Justice, flees the earth in disgust at mankind's behaviour, in *England's Eliza* she returns to support the embattled queen.[42] Niccols adapts Spenser so that the Gods of war work together to support the Queen of England. Jove looks down 'from his celesiall throne| With eies of pitie on poore Englands woes', and, sorry for England's current plight, provides the country with a mighty sovereign:

> No sooner did this Empires royall crowne
> Begirt the temples of her princelie hed;
> But that *Ioue*-born *Astrea* straight came downe
> From highest heauen againe, to which in dread
> Of earths impietie before shee fled:
> Well did shee know, *Elizaes* happie reigne
> Would then renew the golden age againe.

> The heau'ns did smile on her with sweet delight,
> And thundering *Ioue* did laugh her foes to scorne,
> The god of warre did cease from bloodie fight,
> And fruitfull Plentie did her land adorne
> With richest gifts, powr'd from her plenteous horne,
> The happie feeds, which th'hands of peace did sow
> In euerie place with goodlie fruit did grow.[43]

Niccols is either adapting his source with a clear understanding of how his text works or, more likely, simply bulldozing his way through literary history and forcing more complicated works to dance to his tune. The verses cited balance images of peace and war. We are reminded of Jove's part in defeating her enemies militarily but, with his protection, Elizabeth is able to produce the cornucopia, the horn of plenty, as the land is blessed with the abundant fruits of peacetime.[44] Elizabeth's peace stands in marked contrast to the idle and luxurious peace of the reigns of John and Edward II (and, by implication, James). Jove laughs at her enemies, a warning that they are only temporarily vanquished, and will surely return to threaten England's golden age and time of abundance. Elizabeth is ruling peacefully because she understands the need to be prepared for battle, protecting her subjects and enabling them to flourish in a well-ordered society. The God of War has ceased 'from bloodie fight', but he has not forgotten his military arts, and he makes sure that England's enemies know whose side he is on. His vigilance is vital because the main threat to Elizabeth will come from within:

> Yet, if your English Romanized hearts,
> Gainst natures custome swell with foule defame,
> Brandish your stings, and cast your vtmost darts
> Against the greatnesse of her glorious name,
> Yet shall it liue to your eternall shame;
> Yea, though Rome, Spaine, and hell it selfe repine,
> Her fame on earth with sun-bright light shall shine.[45]

Elizabeth's glory was such that no combination of hostile powers was able to threaten her throne. Her example needs to be copied by future generations of monarchs if they wish to shine brightly against the massed forces of darkness assembled by Rome, Spain, and their Catholic cohorts. Perhaps Niccols was reminding readers not only of the Catholic forces that had threatened James in 1605, but the origin of the *Mirror*, its publication aborted because of a sudden regime change and the accession of Mary, depriving potential readers of its powerful insights into English history and politics.

It is not easy to see Niccols as a subtle or sophisticated poet. His work relies on a straightforward distinction between vigilant militarism and effete decadence which dissipates the gains that war brings, and he is not a nuanced and elegant writer. But what he achieved deserves rather more praise than he often receives, critics usually dismissing him as an incompetent editor whose intervention marked the end of the influence of the *Mirror*.[46] Niccols was updating and adapting the *Mirror* so that it could have an influence on contemporary political thinking and action. He was widely read in recent English literature and had a clear understanding of how he wanted to make use of the literature that he liked: Spenser, Drayton, the *Mirror*, and the history plays of the 1590s. Where he positioned his writing and the influences he identified suggest, on the one hand, that he looked backwards to Tudor literature for inspiration. However, on the other, he looked backwards in order to move forwards, and his aim was to update and recast the *Mirror* for his generation of readers. Niccols' *Mirror*, very much like the original project of Baldwin, provided a useful and compendious guide to – predominantly – English history, pointing out lessons for anyone planning to take up public office, however humble. Niccols saw it as his duty to remind readers that peace was a fragile achievement and that one could not believe that James, the self-styled 'rex pacificus', could preserve peace if he did not do a better job of preparing for the possibility of war.[47] Favourites had to be put back in their places and corruption at court had to stop, proper order be restored and sound, decent government reinstated. What Niccols recommends is in line with the criticism of the Jacobean court and its morals made by many contemporaries.[48] If Niccols was not much of an original thinker or poet, he deserves at least some credit for his ability to synthesise ideas from the past and so create something new. And, in doing so, he was not the writer who killed off a project, but someone who prolonged the life of one of the most significant and multi-faceted works of sixteenth-century English literature.

Notes

1 See Andy Kesson and Emma Smith, eds, *The Elizabethan Top Ten: Defining Print Popularity in Early Modern England* (Farnham: Ashgate, 2013).
2 Claude Lévi-Strauss, *Totemism*, trans. Rodney Needham (London: Merlin, 1964), p.89.
3 Elizabeth M. A. Human, 'House of Mirrors: Textual Variation and the *Mirror for Magistrates*', *Literature Compass* 5:4 (2008), 772–90.
4 For details of Niccols' life, see the *ODNB* entry.

5 Paul Budra, A Mirror for Magistrates *and the* de casibus *Tradition* (University of Toronto Press, 2000), pp.32–3.
6 Andrew Hadfield, *Edmund Spenser: A Life* (Oxford University Press, 2012), pp.395–6.
7 Richard Peterson, 'Laurel Crown and Ape's Tail: New Light on Spenser's Career from Sir Thomas Tresham', *Spenser Studies* 12 (1989), 1–36.
8 Andrew Hadfield, 'Michael Drayton's Brilliant Career', *Proceedings of the British Academy* 125 (2004), 119–47; Michelle O'Callaghan, *The 'Shepheardes Nation': Jacobean Spenserians and early Stuart political culture, 1612–1625* (Oxford: Clarendon Press, 2000); William B. Hunter, Jr, ed., *The English Spenserians: The Poetry of Giles Fletcher, George Wither, Michael Drayton, Phineas Fletcher and Henry More* (Salt Lake City: University of Utah Press, 1977); James Doelman, ed., *Early Stuart Pastoral* (Toronto: Centre for Reformation and Renaissance Studies, 1999).
9 Curtis Perry, *The Making of Jacobean Culture* (Cambridge University Press, 1997); Roy Strong, *Henry, Prince of Wales and England's Lost Renaissance* (London: Thames and Hudson, 1986).
10 Alastair Bellany, *The Politics of Court Scandal In Early Modern England: News Culture and the Overbury Affair, 1603–1660* (Cambridge University Press, 2002).
11 William Vallans, *A Tale of Two Swannes: Wherein is comprehended the original and increase of the River Lee* (London, 1590). On the influence of Vallans on later chorographic poetry, especially Spenser and Drayton, see Andrew McRae, *Literature and Domestic Travel in Early Modern England* (Cambridge University Press, 2009), pp.33–5; on the historical scholarship in the edition, see Jean R. Brink, *Michael Drayton Revisited* (Boston: Twayne, 1990), pp.81–96; Anne Lake Prescott, 'Marginal Discourse: Drayton's Muse and Selden's "Story"', *SP* 88 (1991), 307–28.
12 It is also likely that Niccols was influenced by his reading of *The Faerie Queene*, Book V, especially canto 9, which includes a pointed contrast between the soft life of Elizabeth's courtiers and the hard life of the military: see Andrew Hadfield, 'Spenser and the Stuart Succession', *Literature and History* 13:1 (Spring 2004), 9–24.
13 Richard Niccols, *London's Artillery, briefly containing the noble practise of that wothie societie: with the moderne and ancient martiall exercises, natures of armes, vertue of magistrates, antiquitie, glorie and chronography of this honourable cittie* (London, 1616), pp.7–8.
14 Sara Trevisan, '"The Murmuring Woods Euen Shuddred As With Feare": Deforestation in Michael Drayton's *Poly-Olbion*', *The Seventeenth Century* 26 (2011), 240–63.
15 Jane Aptekar, *Icons of Justice: Iconography and Thematic Imagery in Book V of The Faerie Queene* (New York: Columbia University Press, 1969), pp.183–6; Clare Carroll, *Circe's Cup: Cultural Transformations in Early Modern Ireland* (Cork University Press, 2001), pp.28–48.
16 Homer, *Iliad*, trans. Stanley Lombardo (Indianapolis: Hackett, 1997), Book 11.

17 Niccols, *London's Artillery*, sig. A3ʳ; D. J. B. Trim, 'The Art of War: Martial Poetics From Henry Howard to Philip Sidney', in Mike Pincombe and Cathy Shrank, eds, *The Oxford Handbook of Tudor Literature, 1485–1603* (Oxford University Press, 2009), pp.587–605. It is possible that Niccols knew his contemporary, Ralph Birkenshaw, who was a muster master in Ireland and a published poet: Andrew Hadfield, 'War Poetry and Counsel in Early Modern Ireland', in Brendan Kane and Valerie McGowan-Doyle, eds, *Elizabeth I and Ireland* (Cambridge University Press, 2014), pp.239–60.
18 Wallace T. MacCaffrey, *Elizabeth I War and Politics 1588–1603* (Princeton University Press, 1992), p.64.
19 See the two hostile accounts: Anthony Weldon, *The Court and Character of King James* (London, 1650); Arthur Wilson, *The History of Great Britain, being the Life and Reign of King James I* (London, 1653).
20 Jenny Wormald, 'James VI and I: Two Kings Or One?', *History* 68 (1983), 187–209; Jenny Wormald, 'The Union of 1603', in Roger A. Mason, ed., *Scots and Britons: Scottish Political Thought And The Union of 1603* (Cambridge University Press, 1994), pp.17–40.
21 Annabel Patterson, *Reading Holinshed's Chronicles* (Chicago University Press, 1994). See also Annabel Patterson, *Early Modern Liberalism* (Cambridge University Press, 1997), pp.100–9, *et passim*. For a critique of Patterson's arguments, see John Watts, 'Monarchy', in Paulina Kewes, Ian W. Archer, and Felicity Heal, eds, *The Oxford Handbook of Holinshed's Chronicles* (Oxford University Press, 2013), pp.375–88.
22 O'Callaghan, *'Shepheardes Nation'*, p.71; Philip Schwyzer, *Shakespeare and the Remains of Richard III* (Oxford University Press, 2013), p.209.
23 Andrew Gurr, *The Shakespearian Playing Companies* (Oxford: Clarendon Press, 1996), p.389.
24 Richard Niccols, *A Mirour For Magistrates* (London, 1616), p.764.
25 *The Mirror for Magistrates*, ed. Lily B. Campbell (Cambridge University Press, 1938), p.370 (ll. 281–3). The description of Richard's death shows that he is now to be seen in terms of the rhyme of the poet Collingborne, whom Richard had executed for his 'foolish rhyme', 'The Cat, the Rat, and Lovel our Dog, |Do rule al England under a Hog' in the previous tragedy (p.349, ll. 69–70).
26 William Shakespeare, *King Richard III*, ed. James R. Siemon (London: Methuen, 2009), 5.3.189–201.
27 George Peele, *The Troublesome Reign of John, King of England*, ed. Charles R. Forker (Manchester University Press, 2011), pt. scene 8, ll. 51–148 (pp.297–303); William Shakespeare, *King John*, ed. E. A. J. Honigmann (London: Nelson, 1998, rpt. of 1954), 5.7.28–64.
28 *ODNB* entry.
29 Niccols, *Mirour*, p.701.
30 Elizabeth I, *Collected Works*, ed. Leah S. Marcus, Janel Mueller and Mary Beth Rose (University of Chicago Press, 2000), p.133.

31 Perry, *Jacobean Culture*, pp.157–72; Alexandra Walsham, '"A Very Deborah"? The Myth of Elizabeth I as a Providential Monarch', in Susan Doran and Thomas S. Freeman, eds, *The Myth of Elizabeth* (Basingstoke: Palgrave, 2003), pp.143–68.
32 Roger Lockyer, *The Early Stuarts: A Political History of England, 1603–1642* (London; Longman, 1989), ch. 4.
33 Niccols, *Mirour*, p.708.
34 Andrew Hadfield, *Literature, Politics and National Identity: Reformation to Renaissance* (Cambridge University Press, 1994), ch. 3; Scott C. Lucas, A Mirror for Magistrates *and the Politics of the English Reformation* (Amherst: University of Massachusetts Press, 2009).
35 On tyranny, see Rebecca Bushnell, *Tragedies of Tyrants: Political Thought and Theater in the English Renaissance* (Ithaca, NY: Cornell University Press, 1990).
36 On the significance of counsel in early modern political thought, see John Guy, 'The Rhetoric of Counsel in Early Modern England', in Dale Hoak, ed., *Tudor Political Culture* (Cambridge University Press, 1995), pp.292–310. On history, see D. R. Woolf, *Reading History in Early Modern England* (Cambridge University Press, 2000).
37 David Harris Willson, *King James VI & I* (London: Cape, 1956), pp.334–44; Alan Stewart, *The Cradle King: A Life of James VI & I* (London: Chatto and Windus, 2003), pp.257–78.
38 Gurr, *Shakespearian Playing Companies*, pp.323, 327, 441. On Edward's death, see Andrew Hadfield, 'Marlowe's Representation of the Death of Edward II', *NQ* 56:1 (March 2009), 40–1.
39 The literature on the ways in which Elizabeth has been represented as a powerful, military leader and Amazon is vast: see, for example, Carole Levin, *The Heart and Stomach of a King: Elizabeth I and the Politics of Sex and Power* (Philadelphia: University of Pennsylvania Press, 1994); Tom Betteridge, 'A Queen for All Seasons: Elizabeth I on Film', in Doran and Freeman, eds, *Myth of Elizabeth*, pp.242–59; Michael Dobson and Nicola J. Watson, *England's Elizabeth: An Afterlife in Fame and Fantasy* (Oxford University Press, 2002).
40 This was, in fact, exactly what courtiers had complained of at the time, but history was quickly rewritten after Elizabeth's death: see John Guy, 'Introduction: The 1590s: The Second Reign of Elizabeth I?', in John Guy, ed., *The Reign of Elizabeth I: Court and Culture in the Last Decade* (Cambridge University Press, 1995), pp.1–19.
41 It is possible that Copley was reacting to Anthony Copley's Catholic response to *The Faerie Queene*, which cast Elizabeth as a true member of the faith misled by her evil and duplicitous Protestant counsellors: Anthony Copley, *A Fig for Fortune* (London, 1596). For comment, see Frederick Morgan Padelford, 'Anthony Copley's *A Fig for Fortune*: A Roman Catholic Legend of Holiness', *MLQ* 3 (1942), 525–33; Matthew Dimmock and Andrew Hadfield, 'Two Sussex Authors: Thomas Drant and Anthony Copley', in Matthew Dimmock, Andrew Hadfield, and Paulo Quinn, eds, *Art, Literature and Religion in Early Modern Sussex* (Farnham: Ashgate, 2014), pp.41–60, at pp.55–9.

42 See Margarita C. Stocker, 'Astraea' and Anthea Hume, 'Duessa', in A. C. Hamilton, ed., *The Spenser Encyclopedia* (University of Toronto Press, 1991), pp.72, 229–30.
43 Niccols, *Mirour*, p.784.
44 Michael Drayton's first edition of *Poly-Olbion* (1612) showed a figure of Britannia holding a cornucopia, suggesting that it was the unification of Britain under James that had created a golden age.
45 Niccols, *Mirour*, p.787.
46 See the damning judgement in *Parts Added to the* Mirror for Magistrates, ed. Lily B. Campbell (Cambridge University Press, 1946), introduction, pp.10–11.
47 On James as 'rex pacificus', see Anthony Miller, *Roman Triumphs and Early Modern English Culture* (Basingstoke: Palgrave, 2001), pp.107–19.
48 Perry, *Jacobean Culture*, ch. 5.

CHAPTER 10

A mirror for magistrates
Richard Niccols' Sir Thomas Overburies Vision *(1616)*

Michelle O'Callaghan

Richard Niccols' 1610 edition of *A Mirror for Magistrates* is credited with bringing the tradition to a close. For Paul Budra, his edition epitomises the exhaustion of this genre of historical writing; once fashioned as a book of counsel directed at the political elite, in Niccols' hands, the language of counsel has been reified into moral platitudes and popularised for an urban citizenry.[1] Yet, from its early history, the *Mirror for Magistrates* was not a mirror confined only to magistrates; rather the English histories it offered imagined a body of citizens among its readership. Critics have pointed to the significance of 'Shore's Wife', in particular, first published in the 1563 *Mirror*, in opening the subject matter of the *Mirror* to other histories alongside those of the ruling classes. 'Shore's Wife' was a highly influential text, initiating a vogue for female complaint in the 1590s and shaping the new sub-genre of domestic tragedy.[2] It provides an example of how the *Mirror* not only generated expanded new editions, but also offshoots, and sub-genres. For Richard Helgerson and Wendy Wall, one of the key innovations of 'Shore's Wife' was to produce a type of citizen history, 'what might be thought of as the first "anti-political history," a commoner's history to set against the royal history of Richard III'.[3]

Niccols' most striking innovation on the *Mirror* format comes not in his 1610 edition, but rather his ghost complaint, *Sir Thomas Overburies Vision* (1616), published at the height of the Overbury scandal. Cast as a continuation of his edition of the *Mirror*, one of its most arresting features is the use of the ghost complaint not to give voice to the historical dead, but to the very recently deceased. Tragic history is domesticated in *Overburies Vision* to speak to the interests of an urban citizenry. The ghosts of the condemned who are given voice in the text belong to the classes of individuals immediately below that of the political elite, and most directly in their service. Through their complaints, *Overburies Vision* imagines an alternative historical and political space identified with these figures for the governed. The type of citizen this text interpellates, however, does not simply reflect and give voice to popular public opinion. Instead, the popular public voice imagined in the text is held up to critique, and what is offered in its place is a critical public. Through *Mirror*-inspired ghost testimonials, *Overburies Vision* offers an admonitory mirror that educates an urban citizenry in modes of 'true' historical apprehension.

The publishing history of the Niccols edition of the *Mirror* extends beyond its first appearance in 1610, and raises questions about the cultural forces that shaped the market for historical literature in this period. The impetus for a new edition of the *Mirror* in 1610 probably came from its printer, Felix Kingston, and his perception of the potential market for this kind of book. No new edition of the *Mirror* had appeared for over twenty years. Between 1559 and 1587, the *Mirror* had gone through at least seven editions, all printed and sold by Thomas Marshe, with a rival collection, *The Seconde Part of the Mirrour for Magistrates*, printed by Thomas Dawson for Richard Webster. Kingston had owned the copy of the *Mirror* since the late 1590s, alongside much of Marshe's other copy and printing materials.[4] It was probably Kingston who commissioned Niccols to work on the new edition, given that he printed Niccols' *The Cuckow* in 1607, the same year he entered the new edition of the *Mirror* in the Stationers' Register. Since Kingston had also printed Michael Drayton's *Legend of Great Cromwell* in 1607, it is perhaps surprising that Drayton did not take on this task, given his *Mirror*-inspired historical poetry. Yet, Drayton was occupied in these years with his own major project, *Poly-Olbion*; the first part was published in 1612. The new edition of the *Mirror* was a substantial undertaking both for the new editor and for the printer. Given the printing outlay, Kingston must have envisioned a market for such a work in 1610. This was the year that King James's heir, Henry, was installed as Prince of Wales. Anticipation of the establishment of his new court had encouraged major publishing ventures: George Chapman dedicated the second part of his translation of Homer's *Iliad* (1609, 1611) to Henry; and Drayton addressed his *Poly-Olbion* to the prince on the premise that he had 'a naturall interest in my Worke; as the hopefull Heyre of the kingdoms of this Great Britaine: whose Delicacies, Chorographicall Description, and Historie, be my subiect' (sig. ¶ii^r). Niccols also dedicated his new addition to the *Mirror*, *A Winter Nights Vision*, to the prince, offering his volume as a rival for Henry's attention:

> Yet while your English *Homer* silent seekes
> To consummate his great Mœonian song,
> Our Britan Princes, greater then the Greekes,
> To shew their deeds vnto your Grace do throng.

Intriguingly, this dedication to Henry was replaced by a dedication to Charles Howard, Earl of Nottingham, at some stage after the volume's publication.[5]

By the end of 1612, Henry was dead. A common theme in the elegies written for the prince was that his death had prompted a crisis in public epideictic poetry. Prince Henry had consciously fashioned himself during his brief life in exemplary terms. Writers often cast his death as a literary problem whose consequence was the 'foreclosure' of genres of exemplary poetry, and 'of the kind of texts poets had always aspired to write'.[6] That said, Niccols' 1610 edition of the *Mirror for Magistrates* does not seem to have found much of a market before Henry's death, since evidence suggests it did not sell well – the cancelled dedication to the prince may also indicate that the book failed to find favour at Henry's court. From 1619 to 1621, a decade after it first appeared, Kingston repackaged copies of the 1610 edition that had gone unsold, giving it a new title page that returned to the title of Lydgate's translation of Boccaccio's *The Fall of Princes – The Falls of Unfortunate Princes*. There were at least four separate issues across these years, sold concurrently by two booksellers, Thomas Adams and William Apsley, suggesting that, this time, it did find a readership. This burst of activity suggests something more than a desire to shift old stock; it suggests that Kingston had identified a new market for the book in these years. A clue to this readership is in the militaristic, neo-Elizabethan subtitle given to the volume: *Whereunto is added the famous life and death of Queene Elizabeth, with a declaration of all the warres, battels and sea-fights, during her raigne: wherein at large is described the battell of 88 with the particular seruice of all such ships, and men of note in that action*. The repackaging of Niccols' *Mirror* coincides with the start of the Thirty Years' War, and a groundswell of popular opinion advocating military intervention in support of Frederick and Elizabeth. It also coincides with the revival of the ghostly complaint in the form of the prose news pamphlet. Thomas Gainsford's 'Vox Spiritus, or Sir Walter Rawleighes Ghost', circulated widely in manuscript in early 1620 alongside Thomas Scott's *Vox Populi, or Newes from Spain* (1620). Scott would go on to publish his own ghost news pamphlets from the Low Countries – *Robert Earle of Essex his Ghost, sent from Elizian* (1624) and *Sir Walter Rawleigh's Ghost or, Englands Forewarner* (1626).

The reworking of the *Mirror*-tradition of ghost testimonies in the 1620s was politically purposeful. These ghosts of Protestant heroes provided rhetorical figures for imagining history 'unfolding and dilating' in the present and for formulating a sphere of active public opinion.[7]

One of the links in this story of the ghostly afterlife of the *Mirror* is Niccols' *Sir Thomas Overburies Vision* (1616), which anticipates the ghost news pamphlets of the 1620s. Unlike the ghosts of the *Mirror* and earlier offshoot ghost complaints, such as Drayton's *Matilda* and *Legend of Great Cromwell*, the ghosts that Niccols makes speak in *Sir Thomas Overburies Vision* are the very recent dead. In the case of the ghosts of Richard Weston, Anne Turner, Sir Gervase Elwes, and James Franklin, executed for complicity in Overbury's murder, they were still warm in their graves. Published in 1616, soon after the trials and executions that had been held from late October to early December 1615, Niccols' ghost complaint is embedded in the popular news culture that drew its energy from the court scandal unfolding over these years. News of the scandal was communicated across all media, through talk, in manuscript channels, through newsletters and verse libels, and through print, from broadside ballads and engraved portraits of Overbury to quarto pamphlets, like Niccols' *Sir Thomas Overburies Ghost*.[8]

The news culture that flourished in these years was, in part, dependent on a particular set of political circumstances arising out the factional skirmishes at court. From around 1613, a loose alliance of peers, including William Herbert, Earl of Pembroke, and Sir Ralph Winwood, worked to undermine the influence wielded by the royal favourite, Robert Carr, Earl of Somerset. Rumours that Overbury's death in the Tower resulted from poisoning were investigated by Winwood, who obtained a confession from Elwes that implicated Weston, Turner, and Sir Thomas Monson; a trail of complicity that quickly led to the Earl and Countess of Somerset, who were arrested in October 1615.[9] The talk, libels, ballads, and pamphlets occasioned by the scandal, as well as the crowds that attended the trials and executions, were not, however, simply the offshoot of factional intrigue at court. Instead, they testify to widespread popular public interest in state affairs that provides evidence for 'an active public opinion' shaped by both political and commercial interests.[10] In terms of printed material, entrepreneurial stationers capitalised on popular interest in the scandal, which had begun with the divorce and remarriage of Lady Francis Howard to the royal favourite, Robert Carr, in 1613.

The activity of the bookseller, Laurence Lisle, across these years is indicative of both the market for scandalous material and commercial interests in exploiting contentious events. Lisle entered *Sir Thomas Overbury, His Wife, Now a Widow* in the Stationers' Register just two weeks before the Somerset marriage on 26 December 1613. It was an immediate bestseller, going into five impressions in 1614. To manage the demand, Lisle employed three printers – Thomas Creede, Edward Griffin, and George Eld – which meant that at least two presses were at work simultaneously. The appeal of the *Wife* derived from its associations with Overbury, who had died in the Tower in September 1613, his former friend, Carr, and his new 'Wife', Lady Frances. 'On the "paper stage", which emerged in the late sixteenth century', as Paul Hammer argues, 'what mattered was not historical accuracy but the uses to which historical ideas and characters could be convincingly redeployed and sold'.[11] In 1616, Lisle published a seventh impression, now given a highly topical title that advertised its connection with the murder trials: *Sir Thomas Overbury his Wife with new elegies upon his (now known) untimely death: whereunto are annexed, new news and characters written by himself and other learned gentlemen* (*STC* 18909). Lisle repackaged the collection, which now included a set of 'Elegies of severall Authors, on the untimely death of Sir Thomas Overburie poysoned in the Tower'. Two further impressions of *Sir Thomas Overbury his Wife* appeared in 1616: the eighth added two new elegies and a commemorative engraving of Overbury; while the ninth impression included a further set of five elegies and epitaphs on Overbury. These additional elegies were either commissioned by Lisle or offered by those wanting to join this print community. The interests of politics and commerce coincide in this print event orchestrated by Lisle. The publication of strategically variant editions in quick succession can be seen as a type of serial publication in which the printed book took on a dynamic form.

In the long term, this level of public interest was not sustained and the stream of Overbury publications petered out soon after the Somersets were pardoned by the King in July 1616. This pattern of activity, in which intense public discussion flares at particular moments and then subsides, is consistent with Peter Lake and Steven Pincus' account of the episodic nature of the pre-Civil War public sphere.[12] A model of public opinion is central to arguments for the formation of early modern publics because it constitutes the link between the state and a wider civil society. Public opinion is, however, a highly unstable conceptual category and historical phenomenon. In the case of the Overbury scandal, public opinion was by no means uniform or uniformly oppositional. Responses to the executions ranged from the triumphalist to sympathetic, particularly in the case of Elwes and Turner. Moreover, the way Niccols imagines this news culture in *Overburies Vision* would suggest that the 'active public opinion' it embodied was often viewed with suspicion, even by those participating in this publication event. The sphere of public discussion was not only plural, but internally dissonant.

The induction to *Sir Thomas Overburies Vision* is a vivid imagining of this new world of news. The ghost testimonies in this pamphlet are framed by a scene of speaking, reading, and writing that distantly recalls the earlier prose frames to Baldwin's *Mirror*, in which authors come together to read, write, and discuss historical narratives, and to reflect on issues of testimony and judgement. The topical opening acclamation to Niccols' pamphlet – 'When poyson (O that poyson and foule wrong,| Should euer be the subiect of my song!)| Had set loud Fame vpon a loftie wing' (A3ʳ) – registers the jarring shift of the *Mirror* tradition into the present. The primary generic function ascribed to the *Mirror* in this opening passage is conventional – 'loud Fame [set] vpon a loftie wing', or *fama*, the remembrance of the exemplary dead. But the coupling of fame with poison discloses the other perjorative meaning of '*fama*' as rumour, which spreads 'Throughout our streetes with horrid voice to sing| Those vncouth tidings, in each itching eare' (p.1). The mode of public poetry exemplified by the *Mirror*, with its political and ethical admonitory function, has been compromised, tainted by 'vncouth tidings' which have forced it onto the 'streetes' and into 'each itching eare' (p.1). In this arena, testimony and judgement, which should underpin admonition, are either silenced or rendered suspect.

When ghost testimonies are merged with the dream vision in the *Mirror* histories, such as 'The Lamentation of King James the Fourth', first printed in Higgins' 1587 edition, the scene of speaking is typically an ill-defined chamber and or some other abstract place of sleep. Abstraction locates the history in the distant past, but, since the ghost talks to the author in the present, a typological relationship is established between past and present. By contrast, *Sir Thomas Overburies Vision* employs a mode of *topographia* that shifts the world of the *Mirror* from the abstract distant past into the present. The opening scene is vividly realised, investing the form of the ghost complaint with an insistent topicality. The action the poem imagines is unfolding in living memory, it is 'news', but a 'news' that is recorded within the ritualised and authorised forms of memory-writing represented by the *Mirror*. The landscape the speaker inhabits is not just recognisably London; instead, time and place coincide to locate the poem in the immediate present, at the very recent scenes of the trials and executions of the ghosts who haunt the poem. The speaker, along with 'th'inconstant vulgar' (p.1), who

> Frequent the *Forum*, where in thickest throng,
> I among the rest did passe along to
> To heare the iudgement of the wise, and know
> That late blacke deede, the cause of mickle woe[.] (sig. A3ʳ)

A marginal note glosses the '*Forum*' as the Guildhall, the scene of a number of the trials of the accused in 1615: Weston on the 19 and 23 October, and Elwes on 16 November; both attempts to bring Sir Thomas Monson to trial on 30 November and 4 December were aborted because the size of the crowds meant the judges could not enter.[13] So too, the speaker is prevented from hearing the judges because of the press of the crowds at Guildhall.

The equation that *Sir Thomas Overburies Vision* establishes between the classical forum and the Guildhall sets in place a *topos* that condenses issues to do with oratory and public opinion. The term 'forum', in the period, denoted a place of public assembly, oratory, and the law. It was available for use by contemporaries to pose questions about who is authorised to speak and to put in place distinctions between the select judgement of the few and the vulgar opinion of the many. The preacher, Henry Cross, when inveighing against 'idle pernicious bookes [that] poyson' the young, in his *Vertues Commonwealth* (1603), used the example of the classical forum and its representative orators – Demosthenes and Cicero – to amplify his argument about the dangers of certain types of books that dissociate ethics from rhetoric. Cross cites Demosthenes' declamation against 'the rude multitude', who expected him to speak *ex tempore*, 'for it is an impudent boldnesse for a man to take vpon him to teach others that which he hath not bene taught', and then Cicero's complaint that the few 'noble Orators are put out of the way', by the many who possess 'a boldnesse' divorced from skill.[14] The unstable *locus* both of elite civic oratory and of popular public opinion – the 'rude multitude' – the forum is used by Cross not only to distinguish between these modes of public discourse but to set them at odds.

The forum in *Sir Thomas Overburies Vision* similarly functions negatively to compare authorised testimony, 'the iudgement of the wise', with that caricature of public opinion, the 'beast of many heads' (p.1). The speaker cannot 'heare' the judges' testimony at the trial, and so 'know' the deed, because of the crowds and their talk. Instead, he is forced to 'obserue how euerie common drudge,| Assum'd the person of an awefull Iudge' (pp.1–2). Authorised testimony, in which the arts of logic and rhetoric coincide to move men to proper judgement, has been short-circuited in Niccols' pamphlet by a debased version of *vox populi*. What follows, as the marginal note advertises, is 'A description of the vulgar' that is remarkable for its embodied, performative, and parodic depiction of persuasive speech:

> Here in the hall amidst the throng one stands
> Nodding his head, and acting with his hands,

> Discoursing how the poysons swift or slow
> Did worke, as if their nature he did knowe:
> An other here, presuming to outstrippe
> The rest in sounder iudgement, on his lippe
> His finger layes, and winketh with one eye,
> As if some deeper plot he could descrie[.] (p.2)

The aspect of rhetoric Niccols uses to characterise public opinion is *actio* or delivery, the combination of voice, countenance, and gesture required to move the audience. Delivery was crucial to the arts of oratory, Cicero argued, because the orator can only stir the passions of the audience through his own performance.[15] What Niccols provides, however, is a parody of *actio* in his 'Description of the vulgar', which characterises the persuasive powers of popular orators through gestures that are comically stylised, paying lip service to forms of logic and rational argument, including proof and evidence. The scene sketched in the *Vision* imagines private individuals coming together in the forum-Guildhall and fashioning themselves as citizens who claim the right to discourse on affairs of state. However, since the mode of representation is low and comic, this collective civic subjectivity is derided as vulgar and irrational, and identified generically with *fama* as rumour, the poisonous error figured in the Induction.

Libels play a key role in Niccols' imagining of this popular sphere of public political discussion. The speaker contemplates a scene composed of

> Th'ignoble vulgar cruell, mad in minde:
> The muddie spawne of euery fruitlesse braine,
> Daub'd out in ignominious lines, did staine
> Papers in each mans hand, with rayling rimes
> Gainst the foule Actors of these wel-knowne crimes:
> Base wittes, like barking curres, to bite at them
> Whom iustice vnto death shall once condem. (p.3)

Verse libels are often viewed as the defining genre of early modern public opinion, as a form of news and mode of political debate that enabled early modern individuals to turn themselves into citizens by engaging in discussion of affairs of state.[16] Court scandals and factional skirmishes were publicised through verse libels – Lady Frances Howard and Robert Carr were the subject of a series of interconnected libelling campaigns that ran from Howard's divorce to their conviction for complicity in Overbury's murder. The executions of Weston, Elwes, Turner, and Franklin are cited and celebrated – 'vengeance cropt' them – in a number of surviving verse libels, including the ballad, 'There was an old lad rode an old pad', 'From

Roberts coach to Robins carr', and the pair of answer poems that stage a debate between mercy and justice over whether Frances Howard should be executed or pardoned.[17]

For Niccols, verse libels, 'rayling rimes', are both a popular form of public political discourse, associated with the urban citizenry, and polluting, poisonous. Alastair Bellany has written incisively of the paradoxical embarrassment of libels. Verse libels were a ubiquitous part of early modern political culture, and yet, as he points out, 'Virtually no one had a good word for the practice: stylistically, socially, legally, politically and morally, libelling was seen as disreputable, dangerous, damned'.[18] *Overburies Vision* represents libels as the corrupted product of a disordered, irrational popular subjectivity, the 'mad in minde', and as a corrupting mode of persuasive writing. Associated with Juvenalian satire, which turns 'wittes' into 'barking curres', 'rayling rimes' incite passions in their audience that are destructive and 'cruell' (p.3). What finally prompts the speaker to 'leaue the *Forum*' is the recognition 'how whispering rumour fed| The hungrie eares of euery vulgar head| With her ambiguous voyce' (p.3). In his observations on the popular discoursing of the times, represented through the various forms of the news, the speaker stands in for an alternative critical public, capable of assessing the reliability of the judgements expressed by the vulgar. It is a public implicitly composed of the few, who respond to certain modes of public opinion, such as verse libels, those dishonourable and discreditable 'ignominious lines' (p.3), with scepticism, refusing to give them credit as vehicles for the discovery of truth.[19] These forms of news are not only represented as 'ambiguous' (p.3), doubtful, and disturbingly open to various interpretations, but also as eliciting emotional responses from their audiences that are irrational and vicious.

The speaker returns home, to the solitary bedchamber, the conventional *locus* for *Mirror* dream visions. Here, *Overburies Vision* enters a new generic terrain that is distinguished topographically from the discursive world of the forum. Niccols had imitated the dream vision of 'Sackville's Induction' in his *Winter Nights Vision*, the induction to his additions to the *Mirror*. With *Sir Thomas Overburies Vision*, he returns to this framework. Niccols takes care not only to advertise himself to the reader as the editor of the *Mirror*, but to assimilate his pamphlet to its histories, identifying *Overburies Vision* as a further instalment. The prose frame to 'Sackville's Induction' is selective about the intended audience, pointing out that the *Mirror* 'is written for the learned (for such all Magistrates are or should be)'.[20] And the ghost of Sir Thomas Overbury is similarly selective about who he talks to, appearing to Niccols, and craving 'Thy pens assistance' because he is the author of 'that true (*Mirrour for our Magistrates*)' (p.17), and, as such, possesses the requisite ethical authority to speak for the dead and to the unfolding events. A critical public and its representative author promoted in *Overburies Vision* are defined through their independence from the forum, which in turn is imagined as a debased sphere of popular opinion. The model of admonition that it offers is identified with a select public that stands in a critical relationship to an unregulated popular public.

One of Niccols' innovations in the *Mirror* format is the combination of *topographia* with *prosopopoeia*. In his induction in Baldwin's *Mirror*, 'Sackville' is taken by Sorrow on a tour of the underworld, led through various allegorical and mythological figures until he encounters the ghosts of English history – 'Then first came Henry duke of Buckingham'.[21] Like the forum-Guildhall which opens the poem, the topography of Niccols' dream vision is localised in London. Overbury's ghost takes the speaker on a tour of London, beginning with the Tower, the scene of his imprisonment and poisoning. Place triggers historical memory and, by extension, a typological relationship between past and present. When the speaker contemplates the Tower gate, he calls to mind the murder of the two princes in the Tower, the executions of Robert Devereux, Earl of Essex, Lady Jane Grey, Anne Boleyn, and Margaret Pole, Countess of Salisbury (p.6). Later, Overbury's ghost also provides a history of place, beginning with the Tower's foundation in 1066 by William the Conqueror, who 'Did stoope our neckes to *Norman* rule' (p.13), and running through the murders committed within its walls by Richard III. Overbury's murder is incorporated within a long line of acts of treason and tyranny. The historical memory encoded within the Tower walls establishes a typology between past and present that transforms Overbury into a historical exemplum, but one who is located in the immediate present, rather than distant past. The story Overbury tells is 'news', and he narrates a tale of court scandal. And yet, told through the ghostly figure of *prosopopoeia* it produces a mode of testimony, of bearing witness to the truth, which is made credible by association with the *Mirror* tradition.[22] This is not the type of 'news' and false testimony that Niccols wants to locate in the popular forum.

Niccols' quasi-historical narrative, by imagining Overbury's reaction to his own murder, and to the ghosts of those executed for this crime, aims to teach readers how to respond to and comprehend the scandal that has engulfed the Jacobean court. This *Mirror* for the present reinstates the role of tragedy, alongside *fama*, as the appropriate generic frame for comprehending current events. Tragedy, not satire or 'rayling rimes', is necessitated by the times, since the latter incite emotions that are negative and destructive – a false mode of admonition that is cruel and vicious rather than compassionate and just. Ghost complaint poetry accords with Sir Philip Sidney's description of tragedy, that by 'stirring the affects of admiration and commiseration, teacheth the uncertainty of this world'.[23] The rhetorical means by which it stirs these emotions of admiration and pity is *prosopopoeia*. The ghosts are like Cicero's orator-actors who offer a doleful performance intended to move the audience to compassion and inflame 'the mind to the emulation of virtue'.[24] Histories in the *Mirror*, such as that of the poet Collingbourne, are similarly prefaced by directions for a mode of reading or apprehension in which sympathetic visualisation and judgement go hand-in-hand.

> For the better perceyuing whereof, you must ymagin that you se him a meruaylous wel fauoured man, holdinge in his hand, his owne hart, newely ripped out of his brest, and smoaking forth the lively spirit: and with his other hand, beckening to and for, as it were to warne vs to auoyde: and with his faynte tounge and voyce, sayeing as coragiously as he may, these words that folowe.[25]

Perception is an activity of the mind, of judgement, and the senses. It is no coincidence that this lively textual image of Collingbourne is associated explicitly with the figure of the poet, thus underlining the centrality of fiction-making, feigning to the persuasive powers of rhetoric.

The other innovation Niccols introduced to his edition of the *Mirror* is closely related to the rhetorical figure of *prosopopoeia*. The new histories in *A Winter Nights Vision* are headed by portrait-woodcuts of their subjects, from King Arthur to Richard III, while Elizabeth I graces the separate title page for *England's Eliza*.[26] These portrait-woodcuts are based on the style of the classical medallion, depicting their subjects in profile and in armour with the symbols of office, typically the sword or sceptre and orb – Richard III, the usurping tyrant, is portrayed holding a dagger in a posture that denotes treachery.[27] These visual images supplement and reinforce the mode of lively apprehension advocated in the tragedy of the poet Collingbourne. More specifically, with their classical and militaristic design, these woodcuts codify the status of these figures as historical exempla. *Sir Thomas Overburies Vision* similarly incorporates woodcuts of the ghost of Overbury and of those executed for his murder – Weston, Turner, Elwes, and Franklin. While the engraving of Overbury's ghost is full-length, holding a torch, the other figures emerge out of the waters of the Thames framed by the arch through which the condemned enter the Tower. The aim of these woodcuts is to direct apprehension to different ends than the portrait-woodcuts of Niccols' *Mirror*. Both sets work together with the rhetorical mode of *prosopopoeia* in bodying forth, bringing the dead back to textual life to speak to the present. However, in the case of the woodcuts in *Overburies Vision*, this visual and textual re-animation is codified through a different set of prompts.

Prosopopoeia is a rhetorical tool for 'person-making', the creation of a character and performance of an accompanying ethos.[28] In the case of the ghosts of those executed, all apart from Franklin are portrayed both in the woodcuts and in the texts as penitents. They are depicted holding their hands aloft in supplication, with the hangman's rope around their necks. The ghost of Franklin departs from this type: he tugs at his rope, figuring his resistance to the narrative of penitence in which he is placed; a representation that is commensurate with his scaffold performance, when he refused to make public confession of his guilt.[29] Yet, while Franklin is 'a man agast' who 'would haue shrunke away' from Overbury's ghost (p.47), nonetheless, Niccols scripts a ghost testimony for Franklin in which he finally acknowledges his guilt. The woodcuts that accompany the text are intended both to move and, in doing so, to educate the emotional response of the readers. The lively ghost complaints of *Overburies Vision* work to evoke pity for those executed, even while relating the horrors of their crime. This complex mode of compassionate admonition invites the reader to temper blame with pity. Unlike Overbury, who is a more conventional figure of pathos, undeserving of his tragic misfortune, these ghosts deserve their fate and duly acknowledge the justice of their execution. Nonetheless, the audience is prompted to feel sympathy for their fall.

Sir Gervase Elwes and Anne Turner, the two figures who receive the most sympathetic portrayal in *Overburies Vision*, were credited with exemplary scaffold performances. Turner convinced the crowd at Tyburn of her repentance through her modest dress, penitent demeanour, and words. Those assembled, it was reported, viewed her 'with tears of pity and admiration'. Elwes similarly delivered an exemplary last speech that, as Bellany notes, 'was a particularly satisfying mixture of vice punished and virtue renewed'.[30] Versions of his speech circulated in a pamphlet, which went into at least three editions, and in the form of ballads, only one of which survives; Turner's scaffold performance was similarly the subject of both pamphlets and ballads. The one extant ballad, *Mistris Turners Farewell to all Women*, was put together using recycled woodcuts, purporting to show Turner's transformation from whore to virtuous penitent: the picture of a matron dressed in sober garb, subscribed

'Mistris Turner', is placed beside that of a bare-breasted court lady holding a feather fan, subscribed 'Lady Pride'.

Overburies Vision incorporates the genre of the scaffold speech into the *Mirror*. All of the condemned, apart from Franklin, provide convincing performances of repentance. However, it is the figure of Anne Turner who is depicted as particularly piteous. So moved is he by her performance, her 'teares of penitence', that Overbury's ghost 'did seeme with teares| To chide her fate', and the speaker imagines Turner going straight 'to heauen' (pp.37–8). To an extent, this is in keeping with popular responses to her scaffold performance. Even so, while Niccols' Turner shares characteristics with her other instantiations in contemporary ballads and pamphlets, she has been transposed within a different generic framework. Cast as a tragic figure of fallen beauty, Anne Turner borrows some of the affective power of the *Mirror*'s Jane Shore. For Richard Helgerson, 'Shore's Wife' is a 'hybrid form' that couples 'passion with history', and suggests 'that tragic emotion may not be the exclusive province of the great'.[31] Turner, like Shore, is an 'eroticised penitent', her combination of beauty and feminine frailty turns her into an emblem of ethical memory that is particularly appealing and designed to inflame the moral sense of the reader.[32] The woodcut of Turner in *Overburies Vision* depicts a young, beautiful woman, with flowing hair, holding one hand aloft in supplication, while clasping the other to her breast. Her appearance in the text is framed by the response of Overbury's ghost: 'in a moments space, another stood| In the same place; but such a one whose sight| With more compassion moou'd the poysoned Knight' (pp.25–6). The sight of the hangman's rope around her neck prompts the speaker to express the mix of compassion and judgement stirred by this figure: 'O how the cruell cord did mis-become| Her comely necke, and yet by Lawes iust doome| Had been her death' (p.26). Through the figure of Turner, mediated via 'Shore's Wife' and the *Mirror*-tradition, ethical judgement is represented as properly directed, in part, by the passions. *Sir Thomas Overburies Vision*, alongside many of the ballads and pamphlets that purported to give a truthful relation of the scaffold speeches, provides a model of public opinion which advocates mercy and pity as an appropriate collective, shared emotional public response, thus making a place for sympathy and compassion within models of public debate.

Scaffold testimonies and ghost complaints elicit confessions from their subjects that encourage a certain voyeurism. The way that Turner in *Overburies Vision* is laid open to the male gaze eroticises pity, and has the further effect of implying that what is revealed is illicit, secret. Turner, along with her fellow, male penitents, lays open for apprehension the workings of the conscience normally kept from public view. Of course, all made public testimony of their crimes at their trials. However, the form of the ghost testimony writes their stories as a type of 'secret' history of the court, discovering a political world that is normally hidden from public view, and here only made visible through the extraordinary, supernatural agency of the ghost.[33] What the ghosts have in common are stories of victimisation by great men and women at court, in which they have faced and failed to negotiate ethical dilemmas, largely because their moral character has been fatally compromised by the position in which they were placed by the powerful. Weston, for example, is consumed by shame, and tells a story of the dangers of clientage in which great men require their servants to act against their conscience. Elwes tells a similar story, his 'weake conscience' (p.41) failed him when faced with an ethical dilemma – the poisoning of Overbury – demanded by the terms of his service to great men. The court is portrayed as systemically corrupt, to the extent that men can only rise through bribery. Turner tells a feminised version of this narrative of court corruption. Her two feminine faults, pride and vanity, leave her open to manipulation: she is drawn into Overbury's murder not by malice or greed, 'but loue, deare loue to those| That were my friends, and thy too deadly foes' (p.27). In the revelation of their crimes, Weston, Turner, and Elwes are all depicted with the capacity for virtue, and all are corrupted and fall through their contact with the court. The narratives of victimisation that they relate locate the origins of their moral failure in those at court in a position to wield favour and oblige service. With the system of clientage so fatally compromised, the ghosts represent the consequences of a fundamental breakdown in the structures that should bind the governors and the governed, great men and women and those who serve them. The affective mode of tragedy, which stirs 'commiseration', insists that the reader engage with the wider sociopolitical structures that led to their downfall.

As historical exempla, the ghosts of *Sir Thomas Overburies Vision* figure the tragic consequences of a corrupt court and morally degenerate nobility, the terrible results of which are not only the murder of an innocent man, Overbury, but the downfall of comparatively ordinary men and women who act in the service of the powerful. *Overburies Vision* does close with an official form of commemoration. Overbury's grateful ghost gives voice to a paean to King James that echoes John of Gaunt's famous speech in Shakespeare's *Richard II*, although silently replacing the faults of Richard II with the successes of James against the forces of popery and in bringing the guilty to justice. Yet, its vision of a 'thrise happie land' (p.55) sits uneasily alongside the other stories that the ghosts tell of court scandal, of clandestine murder plots fuelled by sexual intrigue, power, and money. In doing so, the pamphlet looks forward to an alternative mode of narrating political history that structures the ghost news pamphlets of the 1620s, with their secret histories of Spanish plots, and the later secret histories of the late seventeenth and eighteenth centuries. *Sir Thomas Overburies Vision* testifies to the continuing utility of the *Mirror* format and to the complex, nuanced, and flexible model of public political poetry it made available.

Notes

1 Paul Budra, 'The *Mirror for Magistrates* and the Politics of Readership', *SEL* 32 (1992), 1–13; see also Lily B. Campbell, 'Introduction', *The Mirror for Magistrates* (New York: Barnes and Noble, 1938), p.20.
2 See, for example, Wendy Wall, 'Forgetting and Keeping: Jane Shore and the English Domestication of History', *RD* 27 (1996), 123–56; and Richard Helgerson, 'Weeping for Jane Shore', *SAQ* 98 (1999), 450–76.
3 Helgerson, 'Weeping for Jane Shore', p.455.
4 Thomas Marshe's copy passed to his son, Henry, then to the printer, Thomas Orwin, in 1591. Orwin's widow, Joan, took over his business at his death, and when she died around 1597, her copy passed to her son from a previous marriage, Felix Kingston, who printed all subsequent editions of the *Mirror*; see *STC*, III, pp.99–100, 114–15, 130, and *A Transcript of the Records of the Stationers Company*, ed. Edward Arber (London, 1875–77, 1894), II, pp.586, 709.
5 'Note on Sales', *TLS*, 22.ix.21; for the dedicatory verse to Henry, see Bodleian Arch. A. e. 116/2, O04r.
6 Michael Ullyot, 'The Life Abridged: Exemplarity, Biography, and the Problem of Metonymy', *JNR* 3 (2011), paras. 5–7.
7 Michelle O'Callaghan, 'Dreaming the Dead: Ghosts and History in the Early Seventeenth Century', *Reading the Early Modern Dream: Terrors of the Night*, ed. Katharine Hodgkin et al. (London and New York: Routledge, 2008), pp.81–96.
8 See Alastair Bellany, *The Politics of Court Scandal in Early Modern England: News Culture and the Overbury Affair, 1603–1660* (Cambridge University Press, 2002).
9 Bellany, *Court Scandal*, pp.65–73.
10 Pauline Croft, 'The Reputation of Robert Cecil: Libels, Political Opinion and Popular Awareness in the early Seventeenth Century', *TRHS* 1 (1991), 68–9.
11 Paul Hammer, 'The Smiling Crocodile: The Earl of Essex and Late Elizabethan "Popularity"', in Peter Lake and Steven Pincus, eds, *The Politics of the Public Sphere in Early Modern England* (Manchester University Press, 2007), pp.95–115, at p.108.

12 Peter Lake and Steven Pincus, 'Rethinking the Public Sphere in Early Modern England', in Lake and Pincus, eds, *Politics of the Public Sphere*, pp.1–30.
13 Bellany, *Court Scandal*, pp.76–7.
14 Henry Cross, *Vertues Commonwealth: or the High-way to Honour* (1603), sigs O2ᵛ–3ʳ.
15 Cicero, *De Oratore*, III.lvi.213–14.
16 See Thomas Cogswell, 'Underground Verse and the Transformation of Early Stuart Political Culture', in Susan Amussen and Mark Kishlansky, eds, *Political Culture and Cultural Politics in Early Modern England* (Manchester University Press, 1995), pp.277–300; David Colclough, *Freedom of Speech in Early Stuart England* (Cambridge University Press, 2005), pp.9, 196–250.
17 Alastair Bellany and Andrew McRae, eds, *Early Stuart Libels*, www.earlystuartlibels.net, H1, H3, H20, K1iv, accessed 1 June 2015.
18 Alastair Bellany, 'The Embarrassment of Libels: Perceptions and Representations of Verse Libelling in Early Stuart England', *Politics of the Public Sphere*, p.145.
19 See Brendan Dooley, 'News and Doubt in Early Modern Culture: Or Are We Having a Public Sphere Yet?', in Brendan Dooley and Sabrina Baron, eds, *The Politics of Information in Early Modern Europe* (London and New York: Routledge, 2001), pp.276–8.
20 *Mirror*, p.297.
21 *Mirror*, p.317.
22 R. W. Serjeantson, 'Testimony: Artless Proof', in Sylvia Adamson et al., eds, *Renaissance Figures of Speech* (Cambridge University Press, 2007), p.187.
23 Sir Philip Sidney, *Defence of Poetry*, ll. 21–7.
24 Serjeantson, 'Testimony', p.188.
25 *Mirror*, p.346.
26 The subjects of other portrait-woodcuts are: King Edmund; Prince Alfred; Godwin, Earl of Kent; Robert, Duke of Normandy; Richard I; King John; Edward II; and the princes in the Tower.
27 Felix Kingston had taken over Thomas Marshe's printing stock, including a set of woodcuts of medallions of the Roman emperors, which he used to illustrate *The Historie of the Romane Emperors* (1604). Given that these woodcuts had first been used by Marshe in 1571, Kingston had to commission new engravings to replace those lost or damaged and may have employed the same engraver for the *Mirror* woodcuts. See A. R. Braunmuller, 'Thomas Marsh, Henry Marsh, and the Roman Emperors', *The Library*, n.s. 6 (1984), 32–5.
28 Gavin Alexander, 'Prosopopoeia: The Speaking Figure', *Renaissance Figures of Speech*, pp.98–103.
29 Bellany, *Court Scandal*, pp.227–8.
30 Bellany, *Court Scandal*, p.222.
31 Helgerson, 'Weeping for Jane Shore', pp.457, 455.
32 Wall, 'Forgetting and Keeping', pp.129–30.
33 On secret histories, see Rebecca Bullard, *The Politics of Disclosure, 1674–1725: Secret History Narratives* (London: Pickering & Chatto, 2009), pp.1–10.

PART III

Reading the Mirror
Poetry and drama

CHAPTER 11

Rethinking absolutism
English de casibus *tragedy in the 1560s*

Jessica Winston

Near the end of the *Mirror for Magistrates* (1559 edition), the authors page through the chronicles as they discuss whose story to tell next. The research is laborious, and William Baldwin, despite serving as project leader, falls asleep. As he explains it, while 'every man [was] seeking farder notes, I looked on the Chronicles, and fynding styl fyelde upon fyelde, & manye noble men slayne, I purposed to have overpassed all, for I was so wearye that I waxed drowsye, and began in dede to slumber'. Even in sleep, he is unable to let go of his tasks, and with his 'imagination styll prosecuting this tragical matter', the next complaint appears to him in a dream vision, spoken by the headless ghost of Richard, third Duke of York (1411–60), holding the hand of his dead son, the Earl of Rutland. The vision is grisly: the duke's 'brest was so wounded that his hearte might be seen' and 'all his body embrued with his own bloud'. The author, afraid, tries to turn away, but is called to attention by 'a shrekyng voice out of the weasande pipe of the headless bodye' (p.181).[1] The monotonously dull transmogrifies into the strangely grotesque, but newly compelling.

In some sense, Baldwin's experience may be common: who hasn't nodded off in study, only to find himself still contemplating his research in dreams? Yet here the author's changed relation to his sources serves as an emblem for two traditions of reading the earliest editions of the *Mirror for Magistrates* – as tediously repetitive or unexpectedly intriguing. In one view, the *Mirror* is 'the greatest composite monument' of the mid-Tudor 'drab age' – a commendable effort in English historical verse, significant as an encapsulation of Tudor political ideas and as a source for later English history plays.[2] In the other, the *Mirror* is a politically charged, radical collection, fascinating for its comment on mid-Tudor politics and governance.[3] In sum, the *Mirror* is a work 'that everyone thinks is dull, but which is about as radical and subversive as anything produced in the period'.[4]

The *Mirror* is based on John Lydgate's *Fall of Princes* (c.1431–9), itself a version of Boccaccio's *De casibus virorum illustrium* (c.1358), and this chapter broadens treatments of radicalism in the *Mirror* by exploring its transformation of the *de casibus* genre. In its reworking of *de casibus* tragedy, the *Mirror* offers an alternative to the absolutist model of governance assumed in the *de casibus* tradition and it provided an example for others of the time to query absolutism too. This influence emerges in the English neoclassical tragedies of the early 1560s, particularly Jasper Heywood's translation of Seneca's *Troas* (pub. 1559), Thomas Sackville and Thomas Norton's *Gorboduc* (perf. 1561/2), Alexander Neville's translation of Seneca's *Oedipus* (pub. 1563), and George Gascoigne and Francis Kinwelmersh's *Jocasta* (c.1566), an expansive translation of Euripides' *Phoenissae* ('Phoenician Women') by way of Lodovico Dolce's *Giocasta* (1541).[5] To develop these points, this chapter first explores the *de casibus* genre and the *Mirror*'s key innovations, with an emphasis on their political implications. The chapter then turns to the neoclassical plays, focusing on their allusions to the *Mirror*, since these capture each play's endorsement or departure from the absolutist model of governance at the heart of *de casibus* tragedy.

Generic and political conventions of *de casibus*

According to William Baldwin, the *Mirror* began as a continuation of John Lydgate's *Fall of Princes*, an amplification and translation of Boccaccio's *De casibus virorum illustrium* via Laurent de Premierfait's *Des cas des nobles hommes et femmes* (c.1409), showing 'chiefly of suche as Fortune had dalyed with here in this ylande' (p.68). The *Mirror* is not simply an extension, however: it both imitates and diverges from some prime features of medieval exemplars of the *de casibus* genre, particularly the acceptance of absolutism in this tradition, thus opening up the possibility of representing alternatives to absolutism in literature, which were further developed in mid-Tudor neoclassical plays.

While many readers will be familiar with the general shape of *de casibus* poetry, a quick overview is useful to isolate those central features altered in the *Mirror*. *De casibus* poetry is a story, usually derived from ancient history or mythology, and told in prose or verse on the falls of high-born men and women. Such tales demonstrate the vicissitudes of fortune and, in this way, help listeners to appreciate their prosperity. As Chaucer's Monk urges in his *de casibus*, he speaks so that 'no man truste on blynd prosperitee;| Be war by thise ensamples trewe and olde'.[6] The Monk of the *Canterbury Tales* addresses a cross-section of society ('no man'), but, more traditionally, *de casibus* concentrates on an elite audience, a point that is explicit in Lydgate's *Fall of Princes*. Referring back to Boccaccio, Lydgate says that the genre shows the 'fall of nobles with every circumstance':

> Therein to shewe Fortune's variaunce,
> That other might as in a myrour se,
> In wordly worship may no surety be.⁷ (sig. A1ʳ)

In other words, *de casibus* concerns the 'fall of nobles' so that 'other' – other nobles – might see that 'worldly worship' (i.e. rank or power) is insecure.

This audience is important, since so much *de casibus* poetry concerns the relationship between nobles and their others, and how they should rule. The point emerges clearly in the *Fall*, since his audience was very elite: he composed the *Fall* at the request of his patron, Humphrey, Duke of Gloucester (1390–1447), the lord protector of England, and Lydgate emphasises the relevance of the book to the princes' way of ruling, an orientation that emerges in the 'envoys', freely composed verses that draw out the moral of select tragedies. At the end of the first tragedy, describing the fall of Adam and Eve, Lydgate's envoy admonishes rulers to rule their people with 'right wyseness', unless they must 'forwardly destroy them or oppresse'. He further counsels:

> So ayenwarde [oppose] their corages well dresse
> Lowly to obeye to your magnificence,
> Or disobey by inobedience. (sig. B1ʳ)

Building on a gendered hierarchy, Adam over Eve, the envoy urges princes to keep their subjects in obedience, yet it also exposes the rigidly hierarchical governing structure underlying the poem. For Lydgate, *de casibus* is for princes, written to assist princes to rule wisely, well, and absolutely over their subjects. While ideally princes govern in 'right wyseness', they should act 'forwardly' – that is, proactively – to suppress opposing ideas, forcing, if necessary, the people into obedience, a keyword repeated three times, in 'obeye', 'disobey', and 'inobedience'.

This absolutist ideal continues through the end of the *Fall*. In the second to last envoy, Lydgate advances another version of it:

> Noble princes with your bright eyen clere
> Aduertise in your discretion
> That no flaterer come in your court so nere,
> By no fraude of false disception. (sig. Gg1ᵛ)

Lydgate warns princes to use their wisdom, their 'bright eyen clere', to avoid sycophants, especially anyone who is not of noble birth, who 'came up of nought'. This is likely sage advice, but implicit in it is an absolutist model of governance, governing is about one clear-eyed ruler who governs with discretion. This implicit acceptance of absolutism is further apparent in a recurring theme – the difference between a 'noble prince' and a tyrant. For instance, in one envoy, Lydgate details how a 'noble prince' should act, by avoiding 'riotous watchyng', 'fleshly lustes and vicious companye'. He should also 'oppresse no man, do no tyranny', and 'sucour the nedy, pore folke do releue', so that 'men report the prudent policye| Of your last age when it draweth to eve' (sig. Ff1r). For Lydgate, a benevolent ruler – in contrast to a tyrant – abstains from excess: riotousness, lust, and despotism; he seeks instead to help the needy. While Lydgate speaks generally, he may address 'your last age' to Gloucester, since, as David Lawton observes, in Book Nine, Lydgate 'shafts home the entire moral of the *Fall of Princes* to Gloucester himself', indicating that he will become old and die, and 'these facts alone dictate prudence and the pursuit of virtues'.[8] In sum, these and similar passages underscore the model of governance at the heart of the *Fall* – one all-seeing (bright-eyed) ruler, who attentively and kindly, but nevertheless absolutely, governs his subjects.

Genre and politics in the *Mirror*

In the *Mirror*, Baldwin and his co-authors build on and alter several formal and political conventions of *de casibus* poetry. As in the *de casibus* tradition, the *Mirror*'s authors write in verse, and they deal primarily with illustrious, well-born men in high places, such as Tresilian, Chief Justice to the Richard II, and King Edward IV. The 1559 edition includes only one commoner, the rebel Jack Cade, a pretender to power who thinks he should be king. Moreover, like the *Fall*, the authors of the *Mirror* develop a central theme about fortune. As early as the second complaint, the speaker refers to Fortune as the 'subtyll quean', calling on ideas that echo the *Fall of Princes*: 'Fortune lulde me in her lap,| And gaue me gyftes mo than I dyd require' (p.87).

Even as the *Mirror* follows the *Fall*, the authors innovate in terms of audience, authorship, and politics. First, in terms of audience, as we saw in Lydgate, *de casibus* poetry addresses illustrious men and aims to improve rulers. The *Mirror* widens its imagined readership beyond a single prince or political elites to speak to magistrates generally, defined in Baldwin's dedication as 'nobles and all other in office' (p.63).[9] In Elizabethan England, 'magistrate' referred to a range of office holders, any person involved in the administration of the law or any member of the national or local government: the prince, a member of the privy council, the lord mayor, the city aldermen, a Justice of the Peace (JP), a town recorder, a rural landowner, a judge, or a lawyer.[10] As a mirror for magistrates, the *Mirror* advises this relatively large group. Thus, in the first tragedy concerning Robert Tresilian, the co-author George Ferrers, himself a former magistrate (as a member of Parliament and JP for Hertfordshire), warns magistrates to protect the law, and not to use it merely to protect the powerful.[11] As Ferrers states, he wants 'to warn all of his authorytie and profession, to take heed of wrong Iudgementes, mysconstruyng of lawes, or wrestyng the same to serue the princes turnes' (p.71). In speaking to magistrates, Ferrers assumes a model of governance that differs from the *Fall*. While there is still a prince in this structure, between the prince and the people is a large group of office holders, who keep the people, but also the prince, in line.

Even as it widens the audience, the *Mirror* also expands the sense of who was authorised to offer *de casibus* advice. In earlier *de casibus* poetry, the author has credentials by virtue of his vocation (like Chaucer's Monk) or by virtue of his patron, who like Lydgate was asked to compose *de casibus* verse. Moreover, Mike Pincombe points out that usually *de casibus* poetry involves a dream vision.[12] In a sense, a dream vision authorises the author as a special, even providentially chosen, person to present the narrative. Yet, in the *Mirror*, poetry emerges at the request of a printer and through the labour of poets. Indeed, Baldwin and his colleagues draw attention to their own hard work. In the opening, Baldwin proclaims that the *Mirror* is too difficult to compose alone; he falls asleep while poring over the chronicles; at the end of the 1559 edition he 'recorded and noted all such matters as they [his coauthors] had wylled me' (p.240). The prose frame, a feature that has no precedent in Lydgate, highlights that the complaints are products of intentional labour – not divine or supernatural inspiration, nor derived from the force of a patron's power. In a sense, Baldwin's grotesque dream vision emphasises that the majority of the *Mirror* is *de casibus* without reverie – complaints composed by educated, but non-noble men to advise a broad group of national and local civic office holders.[13]

These innovations have political implications, suggesting a view of the polity that differs from earlier *de casibus* exemplars, especially the *Fall of Princes*. While the *Fall* imagines a political system that is elite and absolutist, something involving only illustrious individuals – princes and nobles – the *Mirror* imagines governance anew as more inclusive, comprised of a range of local, regional, and national office holders together ruling the commonweal. This emphasis emerges in the *Mirror*'s opening lines, which call attention to the importance of officers in this maxim: 'Well is that realme governed, in which the ambicious desyer not to beare office', since 'there is nothing more necessary in a common weale, than that the officers be diligent and trusty in their charges' (p.63). The realm depends on officers, numerous officers, to maintain peace and order in the state, and, as Lydgate does for princes in the *Fall*, the authors of the *Mirror* sagely advise officers to do their jobs well: do not put personal gain above the good of the commonweal, uphold the law and do not interpret it for the benefit of the powerful. Baldwin summarises the point; offices are not 'gaynful spoyles for the gredy to hunt for, but paynefull toyles for the heedy to be charged with' (p.63). In this way, as imagined in the *Mirror*, the political nation consists of a diverse and sizeable group. This is not to say that governance in the *Mirror* is popular or populist, but it nevertheless involves large numbers of magistrates at the local, regional, and national level, who together administer law and justice in the land, and who need advice about the appropriate dispositions and virtues of officers. Moreover, in advancing this alternative, the *Mirror* deliberately imagines limitations on the powers of the monarch, presenting the prince as only one among the many who rule the realm.[14]

While the *Mirror* advances a broader idea of the polity than the *Fall*, this idea was consistent with other works of the time, most notably William Bavand's *Good Ordering of the Commonweal* (1559), a translation of the Lutheran-influenced German author Johannes Ferrarius Montanus's *De republica bene instituenda*, first published in Basel in 1556. Deeply influenced by the ideas in Cicero, including *De officiis* ('on duties') and *De legibus* ('on laws'), the treatise presents magistrates as the backbone of an orderly society, and it aims, like the *Mirror*, to help magistrates to 'be put in remembrance of their duties'.[15] In articulating a broad model of governance, the *Mirror*'s authors also wrote along the same lines as John Aylmer, who, in a treatise written for 'faithful and trewe subjectes', imagines England as something other than an absolute monarchy: 'The regiment of Englande is not a mere Monarchie, as some for lacke of consideration thinke, nor a mere Oligarchie nor Democracie, but a rule mixte of all these, wherein ech one of these haue or should haue like authoritie'.[16] On the whole, then, the authors of the *Mirror* reimagined Lydgate and other *de casibus* precursors in order to cultivate a magisterial class along the lines of other authors at the time, and were thinking about new models of governance. In this context, the authors of the *Mirror* opened new ways for others to develop this thinking, especially the tragic playwrights of the 1560s.

From noble princes to magistrates and back again: Jasper Heywood's *Troas*

The earliest allusions to the *Mirror* occur in translations of classical, especially Senecan and neo-Senecan, drama. Before discussing specific texts, it is worth pausing to note that the association of the *Mirror* with neoclassical drama was logical, but not inevitable. According to Chaucer's Monk, *de casibus* tragedies, including the *Mirror*, are usually in prose or verse, not drama, and tragedy in general was more a matter of style than genre.[17] In addition, Senecan drama differs in emphasis from the *Mirror*, since the *Mirror*, as we have seen, concerns the role of magistrates, while Senecan tragedy traditionally directs its commentary toward princes and rulers. In Seneca's *Agamemnon*, for instance, the Chorus comments: 'O Fortune, beguiler by means of the great blessings of thrones, you set the exalted in a sheer, unstable place. Never do sceptres attain calm peace or a day that is certain of itself'.[18] In its focus on the instability of princes, those 'sceptres' that never attain 'calm peace', Senecan tragedy aligns more directly with traditional medieval *de casibus* tragedies, such as the *Fall*.

In his translation of Seneca's *Troas* (1559), Jasper Heywood established a firm association between *de casibus* and Senecan tragedy. He did so by amplifying the inherently Senecan theme of princely instability, while incorporating 'mirror' language. In this way, Heywood offered up a strong reading of Seneca as a version of *de casibus* poetry – that is, as a form of *speculum principis*, as advice to an absolutist prince. Yet, by linking Seneca strongly with the *de casibus* tradition, and by doing so through 'mirror' language, Heywood set the stage for later authors to link these traditions in their plays, but to a different end – to imagine a model of governance that is more like the *Mirror*'s, and even in some cases to criticise absolutism.

Heywood's *Troas* is the first translation of a Senecan tragedy into English, and it tells the story of the women of Troy in the aftermath of the Trojan War, presenting Queen Hecuba's sorrow, the sacrifice of her daughter, Polyxena, and the assassination of her grandson, Astyanax. As written by Seneca, the play already contains a pronounced *de casibus*-type theme concerning the natural insecurity of those in high positions. From the opening lines of the play, Hecuba presents herself as a victim of fortune: 'Never did Fortune give greater proofs of how unstable the place is where the proud stand' (ll. 4–6). Or, as she says in Heywood's translation: 'For never gave she plainer proof than this ye present see:| How frail and brittle is th'estate of pride and high degree'.[19]

Yet, as Heywood worked, he adapted the text to amplify this *de casibus* theme already present in the play.[20] In just these lines, he expands 'fragili' to 'frail and brittle', and translates 'superbi' as 'pride' and then adds 'and high degree', thus playing up the misfortunes of those in high place and position. The word 'estate' also enhances the relevance to an English context. Moreover, nudging the tale toward *de casibus* tragedy stresses the direct resonance of the episode to the audience in the new phrase 'than this ye present see'. Ostensibly directed within the play by Hecuba toward the women of Troy, the line is also an invitation to the reader, perhaps Heywood's dedicatee, Queen Elizabeth, to think on Hecuba's misfortunes.[21]

More drastically, Heywood altered several of the choral odes, composing new lines to enhance the *de casibus* theme. At the end of Act 1, Heywood adds a chorus on kingly misfortune, where the main idea is that kings 'are but dust' (1.Cho.52). To bring out this point, he incorporates passages from elsewhere in Seneca's dramatic oeuvre, namely parts of odes in *Thyestes* and the *Medea*. Halfway through the new chorus, he incorporates lines about Fortune from *Thyestes*:

> No one should trust too much in success,
> no one despair of misfortune improving.
> Clotho mixes the two, forbidding Fortune
> to rest, and spins each destiny around. (ll. 615–18)

Heywood renders the lines:

> In slipper joy, let no man put his trust;
> Let none despair that heavy haps hath past.
> The sweet with sour, she [i.e. Fortune] mingleth as she lust.
> (1.Cho.37–9)

In this way, Heywood turns to other Senecan plays to play up a particularly Senecan theme concerning the falls of princes, while aligning the play closely with *de casibus* verse.

In addition to these Senecan passages, Heywood aligns the play with *de casibus* tradition by adding 'mirror' language to his translation.[22] At the end of this first chorus, Heywood writes that Hecuba is an example of kingly misfortune:

> And Hecuba that waileth now in care,
> That was so late of high estate a queen,

A mirror is to teach you what you are:
Your wavering wealth, O princes, here is seen. (ll. 53–6)

The lines on 'wavering wealth, O princes,' recollect *de casibus* verse, and they may allude here directly to the *Mirror*, especially those passages where speakers tell Baldwin numerous times to 'Warn all princes' or versions of this phrase (ll. 88, 153, 190, 160, 169).

Although Heywood employs 'mirror' language, his text is more *de casibus* than *Mirror*. As we have seen, in the *Mirror*, despite the incidental admonition to princes and peers, the speakers usually advise a broader population of 'magistrates'. While some speakers warn 'princes', others advise Baldwin to 'warn men' (p.177), 'warn all men' (p.130), and 'warn all states' (p.139). If tragedies in the *Mirror* help magistrates to appreciate their duties, in *Troas* the story is aimed, more like the *Fall*, to assist the prince, perhaps especially the 'prince' to whom Heywood dedicated the work – Queen Elizabeth. *Troas* is less a mirror for *magistrates*, than a fall of *Princes*.

Heywood reinforces this princely audience in another addition, in Act 2. Here, the ghost of Achilles requires the sacrifice of Polyxena. Achilles' son, Pyrrhus, wants to carry out the demand, but the Greek general Agamemnon resists, since he says he dislikes taking this kind of arrogant action; he has been chastened by the fall of Troy and of King Priam, in particular. In the original, Agamemnon says: 'But that arrogance was broken by the very cause that could have produced it in others, Fortune's favour. You make me proud, Priam, you make me fearful' (ll. 268–70). Heywood translates: 'Thou Priam perfect proof present'st, thou art to me eftsoons| A cause of pride, a glass of fear, a mirror for the nones' (2.3.73–4). Heywood makes the statement ominous, since he leaves out Agamemnon's assertion that Fortune once supported him. He also adds the 'glass' and 'mirror' language, as well as the phrase 'for the nones', to highlight Priam's fall and his role as *de casibus* exemplar, especially relevant to the present moment. Overall, the lines illustrate what the preceding chorus urged, that princes must learn from the falls of Hecuba and Priam, which is what Agamemnon has done (or at least says he has done) here.[23]

One of Heywood's major innovations in *Troas* is to bring together Senecan tragedy with *de casibus* verse. In *Troas*, Heywood illustrates the precarious nature of princely power. At the same time, in speaking to princes, he implicitly endorses (or at least in no way questions or offers an alternative to) the model of governance that lies behind both Seneca and *de casibus* literary forms – absolutism. At the same time, in his use of 'mirror' language, Heywood set the stage for the later playwrights to frame classical tragedy as *de casibus* tragedy, but with an alternative political valence. Later playwrights use Heywood's hybrid form to advance the *Mirror*'s alternative to the absolutist state, and this aim is especially evident in moments that invoke 'mirror language'.

More *Mirrors for Magistrates*: Gorboduc, Oedipus, Jocasta

This alternative is most fully developed in Thomas Sackville and Thomas Norton's *Gorboduc*. Both authors certainly knew the *Mirror* (Sackville's poetry appeared in the edition of 1563) and both must have been aware of Heywood's translations of *Troas* and *Thyestes*, since, by the early winter of 1562, Heywood's *Troas* had appeared twice in print (with a third edition on the way), and his *Thyestes* had appeared in 1560, with a preface that explicitly praises the *Mirror* alongside the poetry of Sackville and Norton.[24]

Like the *Mirror*, *Gorboduc* looks back to the chronicles to develop its theme, but it does so in a dramatic form modelled on Seneca, with lengthy speeches, quick verbal exchanges, and a choral ode between each act. Like *Troas*, *Gorboduc* takes up Senecan themes, anatomising the fall of a king, the obliteration of a familial line, and the collapse of a civilisation. In this play, the ancient British King Gorboduc divides his realm between his sons, with disastrous consequences, leading ultimately to the death of both sons, the murder of the king and queen by a mob, and the outbreak of civil war.

At least initially, it seems as though the play works like *Troas*: the play invokes 'mirror' language and it seems to do so to emphasise a more traditional *de casibus* theme, its corresponding audience and, implied, absolutist ideal for governance. For instance, at the end of Act 1, the Chorus comments on the king's action:

> And this great king that doth divide his land,
> And change the course of his descending crown,
> And yields the reign into his children's hand,
> From blissful state of joy and great renown,
> A mirror shall become to princes all
> To learn to shun the cause of such a fall.[25]

Seeming to follow Heywood, Sackville and Norton align their neo-Senecan drama with *de casibus* tragedy. Gorboduc is a 'great king', who as the result of a bad decision, moves from 'blissful state of joy and great renown' to an exemplar of kingly tragedy. The play is a *de casibus* tale about the fall of a prince directed toward 'princes all'. With this warning, the play – even as it shows the decline of an absolute monarch – seems to support the idea and ideal of absolutism, since it assumes that Gorboduc's story is something that 'princes all' (perhaps even princes exclusively) need to know.

Yet rest of the play moves away from this address to princes, using the *de casibus* theme to show the limits of the model of governance implied in the *de casibus* tradition. King Gorboduc is an absolute king, and, in the face of conflicting advice, he disastrously abdicates the throne. In the play, there is a strong sense that, while the individual king, Gorboduc, is flawed, the larger issue is the very model of rule on which his kingship depends – the king and counsel alone cannot ensure a stable state, since this model allows the king, however well intentioned he may be, to make poor decisions when his counsellors do not agree, and often events outrun the ability of the king or his counsellors to keep up with the changing times.[26] Indeed, the play continually poses alternative models of governance, concluding with the suggestion of Eubulus, whose name means 'good counsel', that the best model involves the king-in-parliament. Referring to what *should* have occurred to avert the current crisis, he observes that, before the crisis started, 'parliament should have been holden,| And certain heirs appointed to the crown' (5.2.264–5). In these lines, the play widens the imagined polity beyond the king, or the king-in-council, to the king-in-parliament, a widening that is in keeping with the *Mirror*'s expanded notion of the polity, as well as John Aylmer's view of the mixed polity.[27]

Gorboduc widens its view of the polity in another way – its performance context. Sackville and Norton composed the play for performance during the Christmas revels at the Inner Temple in January 1561/2. In the period, many young men came to the Inns of Court in order to gain some legal knowledge and to make contact with social and political circles at court and in London. Many aimed themselves to become magistrates, and would, like Sackville and Norton, become members of parliament and counsellors and administrators in Elizabeth's government, or they would take on other roles as JPs, judges, lawyers, town recorders, local magnates, or civic officials. In other words, even as the Chorus details the falls of princes and explicitly addresses 'all princes' in its opening act, in its performance context the play orients this 'mirror' to a collective of future magistrates. In this way, the play, like the *Mirror for Magistrates*, advises a broader class of men on the arts of the rule. In this sense, Sackville and

Norton follow *Troas*, employing a Senecan framework to develop a *de casibus* theme, but they depart from *Troas* and, in vein of the *Mirror*, envision a broader polity, even examining the limitations of an absolutist form of rule: even a well-intentioned, well-counselled king can make a catastrophic decision.

Neville's *Oedipus* and Gascoigne and Kinwelmersh's *Jocasta* function similarly to *Gorboduc*. Both deal with Oedipus and do so in order to advance a *de casibus* theme, but they address this theme to a broad audience of present and potential magistrates, and in this way also implicitly imagine an alternative to an absolutist political order.

For instance, in *Oedipus*, Neville replaces Seneca's third chorus with a freely composed ode that explicitly raises a *de casibus* theme, the precarious state of kings. The ode begins 'See, see the miserable estate of princes' careful life', and concludes:

> Let Oedipus Example be of this unto you all,
> A Mirrour meete. A Patern playne, of Princes careful thrall.
> Who late in perfect Joy as seemed, and everlastyng blys,
> Tryumphantly his lyfe out ledde, a Miser now outright he is.[28]

Even as the Chorus advances a *de casibus* tale about the fall of Oedipus, it departs from the *de casibus* tradition. Whereas in the *Fall*, these examples are addressed to princes, in Neville they are presented to a broader audience, 'you all', which here must mean an audience of educated men, many of whom would become magistrates. In his preface to *Oedipus*, Neville explains that he wrote for some 'familiar friends' (sig. A3ᵛ), probably while he was a student at Cambridge. His play was then published in London by Thomas Colwell, who had his shop in Fleet Street, near the Conduit. With this circulation, the play's readership would have included men at the nearby Inns of Court, where Neville himself was admitted in 1562, the year before the play's publication. In this sense, Neville's 'you all' turns *Oedipus* itself into a version of the *Mirror*, directing the lesson about the fall of a high-born man toward a more general audience of present and future magistrates. The play serves to warn friends and readers about the precarious nature of power – princes are subject to terrible fates, but so is anyone in an administrative or legal position. More important, underlying the presentation of *Oedipus* as a 'Mirror' is a subtle, alternative vision of the polity – one where a variety of men, not just princes, need to meditate on the arts of rule. In this way, *Oedipus*, like *Gorboduc*, builds on the example of the *Mirror* to advance an alternative to the absolutist model of governance in the *de casibus* tradition.

Gascoigne and Kinwelmersh's *Jocasta* works in a similar way. Written by two members of the Inns of Court, the authors composed *Jocasta* for performance at Gray's Inn for the Christmas revels of 1566. This time, the source is not Seneca, but a translation of Lodovico Dolce's *Giocasta* (an expansive translation of Euripides). In the final chorus, Gascoigne and Kinwelmersh reinforce the main lesson:

> Example here, lo take by Oedipus,
> You kings and princes in prosperitie,
> And every one that is desirous
> To sway the seate of worldly dignitie
> How fickle 'tis to trust in fortunes wheel:
> For him whom now she hoyseth up on hye,
> If so he chaunce on any side to reele.
> She hurles him down in twinkling of an eye.[29]

Unlike the choral odes from Heywood and Neville, this chorus is not an addition; it is present in the source, although expanded here.[30] Even so, Gascoigne and Kinwelmersh continue in the tradition of using neoclassical tragedy as a mirror for magistrates. Here, they present Oedipus as an example of 'kings and princes in prosperity', suggesting that the story is traditional *de casibus*. Yet they immediately generalise the advice to 'every one that is desirous| To sway the seat of worldly dignity', a phrase that would appeal to most of their audience, which was similar to the audience of *Gorboduc* at the Inner Temple – those current and potential magistrates in the audience at Gray's Inn. As in the earlier plays, the appeal to a wider audience of magistrates suggests a model of governance more in line with the *Mirror* than the *de casibus* tradition, since it implies that governance might involve a broad group of magistrates, not just a single ruler. It is notable in this regard that *Jocasta* was read as a version of the *Mirror*. When the play was reprinted in the *Posies* (1575), a marginal note added next to a speech by Oedipus states, 'A Mirror for Magistrates', and Gabriel Harvey wrote on the title page in his copy of the play, 'A Mirror for Magistrates'.[31]

As these examples show, in the first few years after the *Mirror* appeared in print, playwrights recognised immediate parallels between medieval *de casibus* and Senecan tragedy, and they looked to the *Mirror* for the language to moralise and make explicit the lessons that could be learned from the falls of princes. Yet the early neoclassical playwrights also used the Senecan tradition to query the model of governance at the heart of the *de casibus* tradition, a line of questioning first initiated and made possible by the *Mirror*. In this way, the early English tragedies responded to the *Mirror*'s representation of governance, either invoking it to advance a traditional *de casibus* model (as Heywood did in *Troas*), or alluding to it to reimagine and even to criticise an absolutist model along the lines of the *Mirror* itself (as did *Gorboduc*, *Oedipus*, and *Jocasta*).

In this way, this chapter revises two important arguments about the anti-monarchic criticism in mid-Tudor neoclassical drama and in the *Mirror*. First, Linda Woodbridge has argued that the mid-Tudor translations of Seneca should be read alongside resistance theory, as expressed in John Ponet's *A Short Treatise of Politic Power* (1556) and Christopher Goodman's *How Superior Powers Ought to be Obeyed of their Subjects* (1558). The translations of Seneca are 'dissident plays', 'seething with tyranny, power, abuse, and resistance'; they are 'contemporary with much resistance writing, and did similar cultural work'.[32] Woodbridge's argument is persuasive, but this chapter also qualifies it in demonstrating that not all of the Senecan or neoclassical tragedies were equally critical of absolutism, let alone tyranny. *Troas*, even as it shows the falls of princes, nevertheless implicitly evokes and endorses absolutist rule, while *Gorboduc*, *Oedipus*, and *Jocasta* speak to a broader polity. Second, relative to the *Mirror*, Scott C. Lucas has argued that the *Mirror* is also in dialogue with resistance theory. This chapter links Lucas and Woodbridge, suggesting that the radicalism of the Senecan translations, and other neoclassical plays of the time, may stem less from their classical sources than from what happened when the translators shaped their works into dramatic versions of *de casibus* verse, following the reinvention of that genre in the *Mirror*.[33] The authors of *Gorboduc*, *Oedipus*, and *Jocasta* drew upon the model of the *Mirror for Magistrates* to cultivate a new, more populated and involved model for the governance of England. While the plays do not seek to overhaul or eliminate the monarchic model, they also do not endorse a traditional, narrowly absolutist model of political authority. In this sense they were as politically imaginative and, at least potentially, as radical and subversive as the *Mirror*, and this is true partly because the *Mirror* shaped their political worldview.

In a classic treatise on reception studies, Charles Martindale contends that reception shapes our interpretations: '[O]ur current interpretations of ... texts, whether or not we are aware of it, are, in complex ways, constructed by the chain of receptions through which their continued readability has been affected'.[34] Martindale's point is not universal, however, as in the case of the *Mirror* and its neoclassical reception. Clearly, early interpreters of the *Mirror* built upon, even intensified, the *Mirror*'s political themes.

Yet, strikingly, these early interpretations did not impact now established traditions of understanding the *Mirror*. One reason may be that, through the twentieth century, the early English classical tragedies were also viewed as lesser monuments of England's 'drab' literary age.[35] While the neoclassical plays are fascinating in their own right, they can be viewed, too, as all too quiet versions of the shrieking voice in Baldwin's dream vision, calling us to attend still further to the *Mirror*'s compelling political legacy.

Notes

1 *The Mirror for Magistrates*, ed. Lily B. Campbell (1938; rpt. New York: Barnes and Noble, 1960). Further references will be to page numbers in this edition.
2 C. S. Lewis, *English Literature in the Sixteenth Century, Excluding Drama* (Oxford: Clarendon Press, 1954), p.240. Lily Campbell sees the work as a source for 'Orthodox Tudor doctrine' (*Mirror*, p.52).
3 Scott C. Lucas offers an extensive overview of the *Mirror*'s political valences in *'A Mirror for Magistrates' and the Politics of English Reformation* (Amherst: University of Massachusetts, 2009).
4 Andrew Hadfield, 'Graymalkin and Other Shakespearean Celts', Shakespeare's Birthday Lecture, 8 April 2013, Folger Library, podcast, http://folgerpedia.folger.edu/Shakespeare%27s_Birthday_Lecture.
5 On *Jocasta*'s date, see George Gascoigne, *A Hundreth Sundrie Flowres*, ed. G. W. Pigman (Oxford: Clarendon Press, 2000), pp.513–14.
6 Geoffrey Chaucer, 'The Monk's Prologue and Tale', in *The Riverside Chaucer*, 3rd ed., ed. Larry D. Benson (Boston: Houghton Mifflin, 1987), pp.240–52, ll. 1995–8; see also ll. 1973–81, and M. C. Seymour, 'Chaucer's Early Poem *De casibus virorum illustrium*', *Chaucer Review* 24:2 (1989), 163–5.
7 John Lydgate, *The Fall of Princes* (London: John Wayland, 1554), STC 3177.5.
8 David Lawton, 'Dullness in the Fifteenth Century', *ELH* 54 (1987), 761–99, at p.768.
9 The first title of the *Mirror* addressed '*all suche princes*'; the title of the 1559 *Mirror for Magistrates* signals a shift in audience to a broader group of legal and governmental officers.
10 See definition 1a and 1b in 'magistrate, n.,' *OED Online*. Oxford University Press, June 2015. Web. Accessed 30 June 2015.
11 On George Ferrers as magistrate, see Charles Beem, 'From Lydgate to Shakespeare: George Ferrers and the Historian as Moral Compass', *Latch* 2 (2009), 101–14, at p.108.
12 Mike Pincombe, 'William Baldwin and *A Mirror for Magistrates*', *RS* 27 (2013), 183–98, at p.188.
13 Sherri Geller also points out the frame helps us readers to see that the complaints are written by people. See 'Editing under the Influence of the Standard Textual Hierarchy: Misrepresenting *A Mirror for Magistrates* in the Nineteenth- and Twentieth-Century Editions', *TC* 2 (2007), 43–77.

14 Scott C. Lucas, 'Hall's *Chronicle* and the *Mirror for Magistrates*: History and the Tragic Pattern', in Mike Pincombe and Cathy Shrank, eds, *The Oxford Handbook of Tudor Literature, 1485–1603* (Oxford University Press, 2009), pp.356–71, at p.366.
15 William Bavand, *A Woorke of Ioannes Ferrarius Montanus, Touching the Good Ordering of a Common Weale* (London: John Kingston for John Wight, 1559), *STC* 10831, preface, sig. iii^r.
16 John Aylmer, *An Harborowe for Faithful and Trewe Subiectes, against the Late Blowne Blaste, Concerning the Government of Wemen* (London: John Day, 1559), *STC* 1005, title and sigs H2^v–H3.
17 See Mike Pincombe, 'Sackville Tragicus: A Case of Poetic Identity', in A. J. Piesse, ed., *Sixteenth-Century Identities* (Manchester University Press, 2000), pp.112–32.
18 Here and throughout, I cite the Loeb translations of Senecan tragedies, *Seneca: Tragedies*, ed. and trans. John G. Fitch, 2 vols (Cambridge: Harvard University Press, 2002), II, pp.57–61.
19 *Troas*, in Jessica Winston and James Ker, eds, *Elizabethan Seneca: Three tragedies* (London: Modern Humanities Research Association, 2012), ll. 7–8.
20 The analysis of *Troas* here borrows from some points in Winston and Ker, 'A Note on Jasper Heywood's "Free" Compositions in *Troas*', *MP* 110 (2013), 564–75.
21 The points in this paragraph develop from *Elizabethan Seneca*, p.28.
22 Lydgate refers to nobles who, in reading *de casibus* poetry, might 'as in a myrour se' the insecurity of their positions (*Fall*, A1^r).
23 It is not clear that Heywood's 'mirrors' allude directly to the *Mirror*. 'Mirror' language is common in *de casibus* verse, and the *Mirror* and *Troas* appeared in print in 1559; it is not clear which one was composed first. To me, it seems likely that he was aware of the collection. In his 'Preface' to his translation of *Thyestes* (1560), written only a year later, he praises the *Mirror* by name, and he could have known the *Mirror* in its earlier form, the suppressed edition of 1554. Moreover, although he lived in Oxford, he was very aware of the London literary scene. For instance, his 'Preface' to *Thyestes* was either inspired by or modelled on Barnabe Googe's 'Preface' to the *Zodiac of Live*, both of which were in production in 1560. See, *Elizabethan Seneca*, pp.38–9.
24 See the Preface to *Thyestes* in *Elizabethan Seneca*, ll. 91–2, 95–6.
25 Thomas Sackville and Thomas Norton, *Gorboduc, or Ferrex and Porrex*, ed. Irby B. Cauthen, Jr (Lincoln: University of Nebraska Press, 1970), 1.2.388–93.
26 On events outrunning counsel, see Dermot Cavanagh, *Language and Politics in the Sixteenth-Century History Play* (Houndmills: Palgrave, 2004), pp.36–57.
27 On Gorboduc and the 'mixed polity', see Stephen Alford, *The Early Elizabethan Polity: William Cecil and the British Succession Crisis, 1558–1569* (Cambridge University Press, 1998), pp.100, 102.
28 Alexander Neville, *The Lamentable Tragedie of Oedipus* (London: Thomas Colwell, 1563), *STC* 22225, sig. D2^r.

29 Gascoigne and Kinwelmersh, *Jocasta*, in Pigman, ed., *A Hundreth Sundrie Flowres*, 5.Cho.1–8.
30 Pigman, ed., *Hundreth Sundrie Flowres*, p.547.
31 George Gascoigne, *The Posies* (London: Richard Smith, [1575]), *STC* 11637, sig. D2ᵛ; and in Pigman, ed., *Hundreth Sundrie Flowres*, p.516.
32 Linda Woodbridge, *English Revenge Drama: Money, Resistance, Equality* (Cambridge University Press, 2010), p.131.
33 Scott C. Lucas, '"Let None Such Office Take, Save He that Can for Right His prince Forsake": *A Mirror for Magistrates*, Resistance Theory and the Elizabethan Monarchical Republic', in John F. McDiarmid, ed., *The Monarchical Republic of Early Modern England* (Aldershot: Ashgate, 2007), pp.91–108.
34 Charles Martindale, *Redeeming the Text: Latin Poetry and the Hermeneutics of Reception* (Cambridge University Press, 1993), p.7.
35 This view of the period has been roundly criticised, but, as this volume indicates, critics are still working to rethink the literary and political legacy of the mid-Tudor period.

CHAPTER 12

'They do it with mirrors'
Spenser, Shakespeare, Baldwin's Mirror, and Elizabethan literature's political vanishing act

Bart van Es

The political orientation of Baldwin's original *Mirror*

In 1559, in the Preface to the first edition of the *Mirror for Magistrates*, its general editor, William Baldwin, established what he hoped would be a productively interactive relationship between his reader and the ensuing historical verse orations.

> Here as in a looking glass, you shall see (if any vice be in you) how the like hath been punished in other heretofore ... [which] ... I trust will be a good occasion to move you to the sooner amendment. (*Mirror* (1559), π3^{a-b})

Baldwin's introduction establishes the crucial self-examining dynamic of this particular form of history. Whereas his model, Lydgate, compared the writing of history to a clear mirror because it provided an image of the past and thereby saved it from oblivion, for Baldwin it had become essential for one to relate history to one's own situation. In this way, the supreme function of the historical mirror became not its capacity to reflect the past, but its power to effect self-improvement in the present.

As Paul Budra's study of the collection has demonstrated, the *Mirror*'s insistence on making the past a corrective image of the present was, to a significant degree, a new development.[1] It was also a political one. Herbert Grabes' survey of the mirror metaphor in early modern literature shows a marked increase in its corrective function in the years following Baldwin's 1559 publication.[2] The *Mirror*, through its numerous reprints, adaptations, and extensions, came to be a significant influence on the way in which early modern readers approached historical material. It was as follows, for example, that the compilers of Holinshed's *Chronicles* addressed their readers in the 'Notable Advertisement Touching the Sum of all the Foresaid History' that concluded their account of events in Britain up to the Norman Conquest:

> Whatsoever hath been mentioned before, either concerning the subversion of people, the desolation of provinces, the overthrow of nobles, the ruin of princes, and other lamentable accidents diversely happening upon sundry occasions: let us (I say) as many as will reap fruit by the reading of chronicles, imagine the matters which were so many years past to be present, and apply the profit and commodity of the same unto ourselves.[3]

Unlike in standard humanist defences of the profit of history (which stressed the politic lessons to be learned for statecraft), the entire emphasis in the 'Advertisement' was on the moral utility of 'imagining' distant disasters as 'present' to the reader.[4] It placed a twin emphasis on national Providence and personal introspection that had a strong sermonising aspect with which the reader was expected to engage. Earlier, John Stubbes, arguing against the prospect of Queen's marriage to the Duke of Alençon in *The Discovery of a Gaping Gulf*, had been even more blunt about the political aspect of this kind of self-recognition. Pressing a parallel between the present monarch and the deposed King Henry VI, he had stated explicitly that 'our English book of fallen magistrates' offered 'a pattern of imitation to our present Queen Elizabeth'.[5]

Stubbes's *Discovery of a Gaping Gulf Whereinto England is Like to be Swallowed by another French Marriage* must be ranked amongst the most incendiary publications of Elizabeth's reign: famously, its author was punished for its outspokenness through the loss of a hand. The second edition of Holinshed's *Chronicles* likewise had a controversial (albeit less violent) reception, with the Privy Council intervening to censor key sections of the history even after the book went to press.[6] Both these texts address the political concerns of what might be called a 'middle order' of English society, a group ranging from literate artisans to the lower gentry who were interested but not directly involved in the governance of the state.[7] What is worth highlighting in this context is that these works made the activity of reading for parallels in history the central objective for readerly engagement with the past.

Baldwin's *Mirror* should be recognised as a formative influence that helped to stimulate this new mode of reading. Thanks to Baldwin's injunctions, 'the mirror' in early modern England became not only a metaphor for ideal, truthful *composition* but also a metaphor for the ideal *interpretation* of texts.[8] In the wake of its composition, a large body of literature took shape that impressed upon readers the need to see themselves into long-passed historical episodes.[9] Following the success of Baldwin's original, others (stimulated by the publisher, Thomas Marshe) sought to replicate its success by producing 'prequels' under the headings of *The First* and later *The Second Volume of the Mirror for Magistrates*. Anthony Munday (using a different publisher) trumped even this strategy by subtitling his collection of verse orations based on biblical history *The Principal Part of the Mirror for Magistrates*. Other collections, under variations of that title, brought a still wider range of recent and ancient stories to the fore. The running heads of the original *Mirror for Magistrates* reiterated each oration's status as 'a mirror' to its readers, thereby enforcing a conscious effort to see oneself into the past. The mirror thus had a two-way function: it allowed one to look to the past but also reflected the present. It was this continual effort of updating that gave the endless mirror expansions and collections their long lives.

It was not merely the editorial front matter of Baldwin's *Mirror* that gave it a potentially oppositional aspect; the history of its publication further enforced its status as an anti-tyrannical work. The book, which is still to be found as an appendix in Shakespeare editions and vaguely associated with the comforting 'Tudor Myth', had begun life as a decidedly dangerous political text. It had been midway through printing in 1555 when Queen Mary's Lord Chancellor stayed the press and prevented distribution. Even under Elizabeth the work was considered suspect and its more sensitive stories were only gradually released. It was not until 1578 that what we think was the complete original run of orations had finally emerged.

Filled with discord, uncertainty over succession, and conflicts of loyalty between dynasties, it is not difficult to see why the *Mirror* might have made for uncomfortable reading for Mary or for Elizabeth at the beginning of her reign. The collection's emphasis, crucially, was on the personal conscience over and above obedience to the sovereign. Its first speaker, Robert Tresilian, Chief Justice of England under Richard II, is condemned at the opening of his oration 'for misconstruing the laws and expounding them to serve the Prince's affections'.[10] Along with 'other his fellows' Tresilian has placed the desires of his king above his own moral judgement. To criticise such obedience in a subject was clearly dangerous, especially if readers 'as in a looking glass' viewed Tresilian's case as a parallel for their own situation, which might be that of principled opposition to the new religious settlement of the English church. In a world where foreign powers backed a different religion it was all too easy to imagine that a civil war, like that depicted in Baldwin's original collection of ghostly speeches, might once more lie ahead. Richard Robinson, gaoler to Mary, Queen of Scots in 1574, could certainly see the present age in the

Mirror (composing his own dream vision on Baldwin's model featuring, amongst others, Helen of Troy). Just like John Stubbes in the *Gaping Gulf* five years later, Robinson could see that a love affair or marriage alliance with a foreign prince had brought catastrophic consequences in the past.

The *Mirror*, then, had form as a text of political opposition. What is remarkable, however, is the way that the *Mirror* altered with time. It is one thing to say that each generation could find their present political concerns reflected in past history. It is another, however, to say that better times also offered a more positive way of interpreting those dismal events. Amazingly (given that its orations chronicled nothing but civil conflict, corruption, and personal ambition), those who provided additions to the *Mirror* in the 1580s and 1590s seem to have regarded the original text as a monument of patriotism: for them it was the beginning of a national project of memorialisation, recording past struggles with an eye to the providentially insured future that lay ahead. The 1610 edition, which assembled the great body of later additions, looked back on a now glorious Elizabethan epoch and ended this collection with a celebratory composition called *England's Eliza*, thus shifting its register from lamentation to eulogy and turning the *Mirror* into something lustrous and bright.

Baldwin, who assembled the original work in a spirit of loyal opposition to Mary, could not have foreseen such a reception history. Baldwin's original ghosts stress the sanctity of the individual conscience over and above national achievement; their emphasis is entirely on the *fall* of princes, with foreign conquests seen as a distraction at best. Whether Baldwin would have continued to support such a position a few decades later is an open question: the mirror-maker cannot control what is seen by the users of the work he creates.

Spenser and the Mirror

Spenser, who described himself as a 'poet historical', had a good deal in common with William Baldwin. The two men were educated as Erasmian humanists; they were anti-Catholic polemicists; literary innovators across multiple genres (including allegory); and poets profoundly interested in the new mode of authorship made possible through print. Both had a missionary zeal to fashion the moral outlook of their readers that combined with an ambitious project to create a new vernacular literature; they were also interested in memorialising the past. Planning his own literary career in the late 1560s and early 1570s, Spenser would have had almost no models of print publication by living authors in English that he could look to. *The Mirror for Magistrates*, which in 1571 came out in its third Elizabethan edition, must have offered inspiration; if we count the Marian publication, stopped at the press in 1554, it was the first poetic miscellany in the vernacular of any kind. As Spenser wrote to Gabriel Harvey at the end of the 1570s, a sixth (still further expanded) Elizabethan edition was available from the booksellers. Even though it is the names of Sidney, Drant, and Dyer that are mentioned in the correspondence as models for the new English poetry, the concrete example of the *Mirror* must also have loomed large. Admittedly, at the literary level, Baldwin's fourteeners could have only limited appeal for an aspirant poet laureate. In its ethical and political aspects, however, the *Mirror*, along with other key works of the Marian and early Elizabethan period (from morality plays to the *Acts and Monuments*), must be considered a formative influence on *The Faerie Queene*.

Just as in Baldwin's Preface, the metaphor of the mirror is dominant in the way that Spenser introduces his great epic to the reader. Already in the Proem to Book I the poet describes the 'Mirrour of grace' that is his sovereign and in the next he glories in the hall of mirrors he has created, inviting the Queen to do likewise:

> And thou, O fayrest Princesse vnder sky,
> In this fayre mirrhour maist behold thy face
> And thine owne realmes in lond of Faery,
> And in this antique ymage thy great auncestry.[11]

The mirror occurs in each of the first instalment's Proems, and on each occasion Spenser relates it to an 'antique' image. Through a variety of historical analogies, from the pure Christian church of St George's legend to the imperial glory of Arthur's reign, the monarch is brought to reflect upon her own condition. The time of Eden, the reign of Astraea, the foundation of Troynovant, and the age of Hercules were all used by Spenser as epochs to set against the reign of this current queen. Through fairyland Spenser established a palimpsest of historical moments, and in a series of prefatory Proems to his books he attempted to engage his monarch directly in the task of connecting them with her own time. The message is certainly one of praise but it is also one of forceful political persuasion: in favour of empire, Protestantism, and more specifically in support of Spenser's patrons, including the Earl of Leicester, Sir Walter Ralegh, and the former Lord Deputy of Ireland, Lord Grey.

Spenser was profoundly self-conscious about the interactive dynamic that sustained his historical fiction, nowhere more so than in the episode in Book III that begins with the Knight of Chastity, Britomart, herself looking in a mirror. That mirror reveals her destined husband: the quasi-historical sixth-century warrior (who featured, for example, in John Hardyng's verse chronicle) Artegall. In the ensuing canto, Britomart's vision is placed in a wider historical context by the magician Merlin, whose prophecy (which, from the perspective of Spenser's readership, is really history) tells of the line of Britons ending on the reign of the present queen. After describing the triumphs of Elizabeth's reign, however, Merlin glimpses an unspeakable future that can be judged only on the basis of the prophet's awestruck expression, which is witnessed by Britomart and her companion Glauce:

> But yet the end is not. There *Merlin* stayd,
> As ouercomen of the spirites powre,
> Or other ghastly spectacle dismayd,
> That secretly he saw, net note discoure:
> Which suddein fitt, and halfe extatick stoure
> When the two fearefull wemen saw, they grew
> Greatly confused in behaueoure;
> At last the fury past, to former hew
> He turnd againe, and chearfull looks did shew.
> (*The Faerie Queene* III.iii.50)

The episode of Merlin's 'stoure', a momentary vision of danger to the succession, can be seen as Spenser's response to a number of Elizabethan political crises, perhaps the most obvious of which is the maelstrom of political prophecy surrounding Elizabeth's proposed marriage to Alençon in the years 1579–82. This was, of course, the crisis that caused John Stubbes to invoke the lessons of 'our English book of fallen magistrats' as 'a pattern of imitation to our present Queen'. In that period Spenser was already working on his epic and discussing it with Gabriel Harvey. At the same time, he was directly involved in the propaganda war against Alençon, alluding numerous times to the match in *The Shepheardes Calender*, in part by way of historical parallels.[12] The fact that Spenser's printer, Hugh Singleton, was also Stubbes's confirms the poet's connections with low-church Protestant circles in which the *Mirror for Magistrates* was important. When, some time in the 1580s, Spenser wrote his prophetic history of British monarchs (whose troubled reigns take up the majority of canto three of *The Faerie Queene*'s Legend of Chastity) its relationship to Baldwin's *Mirror* would have been difficult to ignore.

The first three books of Spenser's epic were published in 1590 and even then Merlin's 'halfe extatick stoure' and Britomart's vision in the mirror could still have contained echoes of the Alençon Crisis for his readers (especially those hot Protestants who took their political agenda from the *Gaping Gulf*). Yet in the years that followed, with new worries on the horizon (such as the succession or rebellion in Ireland), that context effectively died away. The Alençon Crisis, in any case, was never the only candidate for an historical allusion: the Queen's earlier near-fatal attack of smallpox, for example, was another possibility, and many critics have felt that the 'stoure' was an expression of concern not about the Queen's threatened marriage but rather its opposite: a criticism of her now certain childlessness.

In a 2002 article, David Wilson-Okamura shifted the interpretative context for the events in Book III's history of the fall of princes forward to the moment of the first instalment's publication: 1589–90.[13] On the basis of a comparison of commentaries on the death of Marcellus described in the *Aeneid*, Wilson-Okamura saw Merlin's forestalled prophecy primarily as a response to the execution of Mary, Queen of Scots: an event for which Spenser offers quiet, modestly conservative, commendation. It was the matter of Mary's death, he argued, that was of principal concern in 1590, not the matter of the Queen's by then nonexistent marriage prospects.

Wilson-Okamura's argument is a good one. Whatever the moment of the episode's composition, the image it would mirror in 1590 would undoubtedly be most strongly coloured by the most recent political events. Yet the juxtaposition of the Alençon Crisis (at its height between 1579 and 1580) and Mary's execution (1586/7) does point up an interesting point of difficulty in reading Spenser's politics. If a political mirror functions in relation to a particular moment, then the politics of such a mirror also become as momentary as an image in a glass.

1590 is a particularly unreflective moment in relation to Merlin's 'halfe extatick' moment of terror. It came safely after the Alençon Crisis, after the death of Mary, Queen of Scots, and after the defeat of the Armada. It also came comfortably *before* the onset of poor harvests, before the full crisis in Ireland, and before the Queen began to age so visibly that the succession again became a fully live issue. 1590, then, might indeed be the moment when Elizabeth could look in the mirror and find herself the fairest of them all – the moment at which a certain kind of oppositional Spenserian politics vanished. Crudely speaking, the early 1590s might be approached as the tranquil eye of the political storm that was Elizabeth's reign and thus also a moment where Baldwin's *Mirror for Magistrates* could exert little subversive pressure (however much its protagonists complained of monarchical corruption or the twisting of laws). Certainly it is difficult to see the fourth edition of *The Shepheardes Calender* or the first of

Mother Hubberds Tale, both published in 1591, offering much of a political reflection. These texts were the product of the Alençon crisis years during which Spenser produced one set of explicitly partisan literature, but they would not have looked especially fiery at this time. Famously *Mother Hubberds Tale* was, according to Nashe, 'rekindled' as a political text only by the rash words of Gabriel Harvey.[14] As such it is another example of the kind of changeful mirror that Elizabethan political commentary could offer to a readership on the lookout for present parallels. Like other political compositions in Spenser's *Complaints* volume (such as the 'long since dedicated' *Virgil's Gnat*), *Mother Hubberds Tale* 'long sithens completed in the raw conceipt of my youth' only revealed its politics through memories of the past. These already demonstratively old tales were dated still further by the advertised gap between their composition and publication. Their politics had 'long sithens' disappeared.

Spenser's delayed publication hides political fires, but it might also work the other way. *Colin Clouts Come Home Againe*, dated 'from my house of Kilcolman, the 27. of December. 1591' but *published* in 1595, may initially have mirrored a resplendent Cynthia as ruler of the sea. Yet, by its date of publication, with rising Irish rebellion and famine in England, it would have read very much more as a poem of exile and neglect. Its complaint about Ralegh's expulsion from court following a minor indiscretion would have shifted radically over time to include the much more serious affair of his clandestine marriage: whereas in 1591 this 'Shepherd of the Ocean' was an ideal go-between taking Spenser to his monarch, he became, just a few years later, the supreme example of a cast-off poet and thus a dangerous parallel for Colin Clout. *Colin Clouts Come Home Againe*, in 1595, was about homecoming to Ireland, not England, and thus implicitly reflected on some dark days ahead.

The examples of *Mother Hubberds Tale* and *Colin Clouts Come Home Againe* work to reveal the potential mutability of Britomart, a quasi-historical figure before a 'mirrhour plaine' who is emblemic of a kind of political reading that vanishes at the blink of the eye of its beholder. By the time of Book III's publication, whatever fears are envisaged by Merlin had receded; the prophecy might even have changed from one of warning to one of fulfilment. Equally, by the time it was reprinted for the second instalment it might again have caught the light of recent developments: a worsening situation in Ireland, the prospect of King James with his antipathy to Spenser, and some revival in political prophecy. If the episode had appeared for the first time in 1596, then it would certainly be read very differently today.

The case of Britomart's prophetic experience raises wider questions about how we read early modern politics in the light of Baldwin's injunction in his preface to the *Mirror for Magistrates*. It is generally assumed that the parts of the *Mirror* that were still dangerously political at the time of its first Elizabethan publication were reinserted only when that danger had abated. The reverse argument, however, is also tenable: instead of being a sign that the prophetic episodes were now safe, their publication may reflect a new relevance. A smart editor might reintroduce such material at the point where this old history had a fresh political application and, if questioned about motivation, could answer truthfully that this poetry had been composed under very different circumstances long in the past. Just as with Spenser's delayed publications, political agency in such choices could appear and then vanish by aligning historical mirrors in the right way. The tragedy of Duke Humphrey and Elianor Cobham, which Marshe first included in the sixth Elizabethan edition (published 1578), is a telling example. Like the mirror episode in Book III of *The Faerie Queene*, this is a story of prophecy and magic highly relevant to the Alençon Crisis, which had sparked off an obsessive public interest in prognostication.[15] It is difficult to see how Marshe's publication of a 'newly corrected and enlarged' mirror showing 'with how grievous plagues vices are punished in great princes' at this time could be entirely innocent, especially when the addition concerned secret involvement with 'witches skill' and 'sorcery' to divine the succession to the crown. According to the ghost of Duke Humphrey, the Duchess deployed 'magic and skill supernatural':

> These cunning folks she set on work to know
> The time how long the King should live and reign,
> Some by the stars and some by devils below
> Some by witchcraft sought knowledge to attain.[16]

The oration newly restored to the *Mirror* in 1578 contained extensive speculation about lines of succession and concerned the fall of a man who had 'ruled this realm years mo than twenty' (fol. 40ª), a disturbing match with the Queen's own two-decade-old reign. Gloucester, as narrator, is obsessed with historical cases of usurpation and the fall of royal favourites 'whereby the world may see as in a glass| The unsure state of them that stand most high' (fol. 47ª). Could Marshe really have been unaware of the sensitivity of this material in 1578?

These rhetorical questions about intention can also be directed at Spenser. Is the poet canny or foolhardy in the way he publishes? How far do we trust his claims to be publishing old work? With *Colin Clouts Come*

Home Againe this is certainly an open question. Do we take at face value the claim that this work was fully completed in 1591 but happened not to be released until 1595? If so, was that built-in delay itself a savvy way of both voicing a political complaint and vanishing as a political agent? Are we *reading* politics *into* Spenser's texts or are we missing politics that are visible only when we approach the text from the right angle?

One way of circumventing those stark choices is to acknowledge that Elizabethan readers do seem to have read their politics *into* texts. They were encouraged to do so by the *Mirror for Magistrates*, which, in each new edition, told its readers to update old literature by seeing themselves in past histories 'as in a looking glass'. For those who had had their interpretative strategies shaped by the reading of historical mirrors, texts might well change responsively with the times.

To the late sixteenth-century reader Spenser's poem might then have been more of a mirror than a patchwork of one-off allusions. Indeed the poet himself seems to have been willing to approach his creation in this manner. As is well known, in 1596 when he added three new books to his poem, Spenser extended the characterisation of Duessa so that she now represented not just Mary Tudor (as she had done in 1590) but also Mary, Queen of Scots.[17] The receptivity of Spenser's readership to such more recent linkage is proved by early manuscript annotations. In 1597 John Dixon was certainly quite comfortable with the idea that Duessa could be a mirror for both Catholic Queens.[18] For others it was not even required that the action move on for additional parallels to accumulate: in another copy of the poem, Arthur's request for the commission to rescue Belge is accompanied by the autograph addition of the names of Leicester and Essex alike.[19] As these annotations testify, by bringing his distant analogies closer to the present age Spenser had made them still more sensitive mirrors of current concerns. Arthur and Artegall consequently acted as mirrors to any number of English magistrates.

In a culture attuned to the function of text as mirror, the implications of connection between past and present were far-reaching, and during the years of the monarch's reign the complexity of analogy increased. The implications of the most favoured parallels (Astraea and Arthur) were productively double-edged in their politics: they could mark moments of decline or glory depending on the current state of affairs. Seeing *The Faerie Queene* as a poem begun in 1580, published in 1590, and then extended in 1596 changes the way in which we read its politics.

The Mirror for Magistrates, then, teaches us to pay particular attention to the uncertain distances between periods of composition and reception – sometimes manipulated by authors, sometimes beyond their control. For Spenser especially, whose 'moment' of writing is so very long and ill defined, separating agency from chance is a very difficult task. It is in the dark space between the *mirror* of composition and the *mirror* of interpretation that Spenser performs his political vanishing act. That 'vanishing act' depended on a dynamic relationship between reader and text: a relationship that the *Mirror for Magistrates*, through its numerous editions, had helped to create. Probably more than any other poetic composition in the vernacular, Baldwin's *Mirror* had fostered a politically allusive mind-set amongst the general reading public. The creation of such a readership is arguably the collection's most important legacy.

Coda: Shakespeare and the Mirror

In 1595, Shakespeare wrote the following exchange in *Richard II* for the scene in which the monarch is deposed by Bolingbroke:

> KING RICHARD: An if my word be sterling yet in England,
>   Let it command a mirror hither straight,
>   That it may show me what a face I have,
>   Since it is bankrupt of his majesty.
> BOLINGBROKE: Go, some of you, and fetch a looking-glass.
> NORTHUMBERLAND: Read o'er this paper while the glass doth come.
> KING RICHARD: Fiend, thou torments me ere I come to hell!
> BOLINGBROKE: Urge it no more, my Lord Northumberland.
> NORTHUMBERLAND: The commons will not then be satisfied.
> KING RICHARD: They shall be satisfied. I'll read enough,
>   When I do see the very book indeed
>   Where all my sins are writ, and that's myself.
>   *Enter one with a glass.*
>   Give me that glass, and therein will I read.[20]

The exchange and whole idea of King Richard's request for a mirror is Shakespeare's invention: it is a remarkable bit of theatre and also, I would argue, a remarkable bit of politics.

What does this exchange tell us about Shakespeare's personal loyalty to his monarch, and what can the *Mirror for Magistrates* tell us about how this position should be understood? The scene certainly proved to be highly contentious. It was cut in its entirety from the first three printed editions and first appeared (in a textually unreliable version) only under King James in 1608. The play as a whole provides the one undeniable case of a Shakespearean production that was interpreted as subversive in the dramatist's lifetime. On Saturday 7 February 1601 a group of followers of the Earl of Essex paid for the work to be performed at the Globe playhouse as a prelude for their attempted coup, which began the following day. Without doubt, then, *Richard II* and its deposition scene could be understood by Shakespeare's contemporaries as reflective of Queen Elizabeth's position. There is much less agreement, however, on the intentions of the author himself. Examining Richard II in the *Mirror for Magistrates* may provide a partial (though ultimately frustrating) answer to this riddle.

Modern commentators on *Richard II* have expressed surprise that the play could ever have been felt to provide a strong parallel to Shakespeare's monarch. Blair Worden has even gone so far as to question whether the play put on the eve of the Essex rebellion could have been Shakespeare's at all.[21] After all, *Richard II* presents the fall of the monarch as tragic. The King, in the final stages of his life, is gentle and explicitly Christ-like in his suffering. His earlier behaviour is rash and somewhat greedy, but by no means malign. Richard's faults, such as they are, bear no comparison to Elizabeth's (who was, if anything, overly cautious and parsimonious). Worden's argument that the play put on by Essex's followers could not have been Shakespeare's has won few converts; it does, however, do much to clear the author of personal involvement. If we look purely at the king's character, any subversive intention on Shakespeare's part disappears.

The scene with the mirror, however, complicates matters because it brings a very different text into play. Shakespeare's signals could hardly be clearer: 'a mirror', 'a looking-glass', 'the glass', 'the very book indeed| Where all my sins are writ', '*a glass*', 'that glass, and therein will I read' – to audiences in the last decade of the sixteenth century these were unmistakable references to a single work. Those looking for 'the very book indeed' where Richard's sins (so absent in *Richard II*) were to be found are directed to Baldwin, whose *Mirror* was by this point out in its seventh Elizabethan edition. In the fifth of its original orations, readers would find:

> A Mirror
> How King Richard the Second
> Was for his evil governance
> Deposed from his seat, and
> Miserably Murdered.[22]

In Baldwin's version, the ghost of Richard is quite explicit about the 'vicious story' of his exploitative and corrupt taxation, hopeless governance, and dependence on cronyism. Here was a mirror that Essex and his followers could certainly use.

So does Shakespeare's allusion to the *Mirror for Magistrates* make his text more subversive? On one level the answer is obviously yes. The audience are reminded of a picture of royal injustice, a king who is deposed 'for his evil governance' by means of divine providence. Baldwin's book was originally one of resistance to tyranny and one can easily imagine a crowd at the Globe in 1601 being inspired by the memory of its strongly Protestant rallying cry. Even this game of mirrors, however, remains brilliantly non-committal. Another way of reading the episode is to contrast the 'real' Richard on stage with the distortions that the rebels press upon him, such as those found in the paper that Lord Northumberland repeatedly forces into his hands. Just like Spenser's, Shakespeare's politics can vanish as quickly as they appear.

The mirror scene in *Richard II* is of little use in recovering the author's personal convictions, but it is powerful testimony to the impact of the *Mirror for Magistrates*, not only on the reading public but also on the audience that attended plays. Shakespeare was unusually careful in gathering sources for its story, combining Baldwin's *Mirror* with the chronicles of Hall, Holinshed, and Froissart as well as Samuel Daniel's verse history *The Civil Wars*. The *Mirror* may itself have encouraged the playwright's researches, given that the prose introduction to Richard's tragedy makes mention of the competing claims of the chroniclers, notably on the matter of the Mowbray–Bolingbroke quarrel (which remains powerfully ambiguous in Shakespeare's play). Baldwin's protagonists are also Shakespeare's and an awareness of the way their stories can be twisted depending on the motivation of the teller is one thing that the collection as a whole reveals. What the *Mirror for Magistrates* brought to its readers was not so much a specific political position as a readiness to discover politics in other texts.

Notes

1 Paul Budra, A Mirror for Magistrates and the *de casibus* Tradition (University of Toronto Press, 2000).
2 Herbert Grabes, *The Mutable Glass: Mirror-Imagery in Titles and Texts of the Middle Ages and the English Renaissance* (Cambridge University Press, 1982). Grabes's book was first published in German under the title *Speculum* in 1973.
3 Raphael Holinshed, *Chronicles*, 3 vols (1587), II, 202.
4 On humanist habits of reading for historical parallels, see Bart van Es, 'Chapter 19: Historiography and Biography', in Patrick Cheney and Philip Hardie, eds, *The Oxford History of Classical Reception in English Literature: 1558–1660* (Oxford University Press, 2015), pp.433–60.
5 John Stubbes, *The Discoverie of a Gaping Gulf* (1979), D2^a.

6 On the cancelled sections, see Steven Booth, *The Book Called Holinshed's Chronicles: An Account of its Inception, Purpose, Contributors, Contents, Publication, Revision and Influence on William Shakespeare* (San Francisco: Book Club of California, 1968), pp.58–64; Cyndia Susan Clegg, 'Which Holinshed? Holinshed's Chronicles at the Huntington Library', *HLQ* 55 (1992), 559–77; Keith I. Maslen, 'Three Eighteenth-Century Reprints of the Castrated Sheets in Holinshed's *Chronicles*', *The Library*, 5th Series, 8 (1958), 120–24. The censored material is reprinted in *The Castrations of the Last Edition of Holinshed's Chronicle* (London: William Mears & Co., 1723).

7 On class composition of the readership of Holinshed's *Chronicles*, see Bart van Es, 'Later Appropriations', in Paulina Kewes, Ian W. Archer, and Felicity Heal, eds, *The Oxford Handbook of Holinshed's Chronicles* (Oxford University Press, 2013), pp.575–92. On the crucial difference in intended readership between the printed *Gulf* and the Sir Philip Sidney's manuscript *Letter to Queen Elizabeth* on the same subject, see Peter Beal, 'Sir Philip Sidney's *Letter to Queen Elizabeth* and that "False Knave" Alexander Dicsone', *EMS, 1100–1700* 11 (2002), 1–15.

8 For readers of the period and the possibility of a new willingness to embrace 'cornucopian' interpretation, see also Kevin Sharpe, *Reading Revolutions: The Politics of Reading in Early Modern England* (New Haven: Yale University Press, 2000).

9 W. F. Trench, *A Mirror for Magistrates: Its Origin and Influence* (Edinburgh: Riverside Press, 1898). See also Lily B. Campbell, *Tudor Conceptions of History and Tragedy in 'A Mirror for Magistrates'* (University of California Press: Berkeley, 1936), pp.9–20, and Budra, *Mirror*, pp.3–13.

10 William Baldwin, *The Mirror for Magistrates* (London: Thomas Marshe, 1559), sig. A3[a].

11 Edmund Spenser, *The Faerie Queene*, ed. A. C. Hamilton, 2nd ed. (Harlow: Longman, 2001), II.Proem.4.6–9. Subsequent references are to this edition and appear in the text.

12 On Spenser's connections with Stubbes and his use of Queen Dido as an historical parallel to Elizabeth, see Richard McCabe, '"Little booke: thy selfe present": The Politics of Presentation in *The Shepheardes Calender*', in Howard Erskine-Hill and Richard A. McCabe, eds, *Presenting Poetry: Composition, Publication, Reception, Essays in Honour of Ian Jack* (Cambridge University Press, 1995), pp. 15–40, at pp.33–5.

13 David Wilson-Okamura, 'Spenser and the Two Queens', *ELR* 32 (2002), 64–84.

14 See Richard S. Peterson, 'Spurting Froth upon Courtiers: New Light on the Risks Spenser Took in Publishing *Mother Hubberds Tale*', *TLS*, 16 May 1997, 14–15.

15 On this context, see Bart van Es, 'Priuie to his Counsell and Secret Meaning: Spenser and Political Prophecy', *ELR* 30 (2000).

16 Baldwin, *The Last Part of the Mirror for Magistrates* (London: Thomas Marshe, 1578), f. 44[b].

17 See Richard A. McCabe, 'The Masks of Duessa: Spenser, Mary Queen of Scots, and James VI', *ELR* 17 (1987), 224–42.
18 Graham Hough, *The First Commentary on 'The Faerie Queene', Being an Analysis of the Annotations in Lord Bessborough's Copy of the First Edition of 'The Faerie Queene'* (privately published, 1964), pp.8–10.
19 See Alastair Fowler, 'Oxford and London Marginalia to *The Faerie Queene*', *NQ* 206 (1961), 416–19, at p.417, and also John Manning, 'Notes and Marginalia in Bishop Percy's Copy of Spenser's *Works* (1611)', *NQ* 229 (1984), 225–7. Another near-contemporary set of annotations (appearing in the Cambridge University Library copy of *The Faerie Queene*) blithely assign to Arthur and Artegall at the court of Mercilla the roles of '[Fr]ench and Scotch [amba]ssadors' – the author evidently being unconcerned about the fact that this reading could not possibly be sustained for any of the knights' other actions. For details, see Anon., 'MS Notes to Spenser's "Faerie Queene"', *NQ* 202 (1957), 509–15, at p.512.
20 William Shakespeare, *Richard II*, Arden 3, ed. Charles R. Forker (London: Thompson Learning, 2002), 4.1.264–76.
21 For details of the performance and the Essex rising, see Blair Worden, 'Shakespeare in Life and Art: Biography and *Richard II*', in Takashi Kozuka and J. R. Mulryne, eds, *Shakespeare, Marlowe, Jonson: New Directions in Biography* (Aldershot: Ashgate, 2006), pp.23–42.
22 Baldwin, *Mirror* (1559), f. 16^b.

CHAPTER 13

'Most out of order'
Preposterous time in the Mirror for Magistrates
and Shakespeare's histories

Philip Schwyzer

As Jack Cade's rebellion gathers strength in *Henry VI Part 2*, a follower warns the rebel leader that the king's forces 'are all in order and march towards us' (4.2.174).[1] Cade's response casts scorn on the idea of orderly progression, proposing the counter-principle of the free-for-all: 'But then are we in order when we are| Most out of order' (4.2.175–6). Cade, whose very name has been held to recall the genre of *de casibus* tragedy, might be remembering his appearance in the *Mirror for Magistrates*.[2] First appearing in the 1559 edition of the *Mirror*, his story is introduced 'in order next folowynge' that of the Duke of Suffolk; yet in the prose link following his tragedy a dispute erupts among the poets over whether Cade's tragedy has been placed in the right order after all.[3] The prose passages that frame Cade's tragedy are symptomatic of the *Mirror* poets' persistent obsession with chronological order, as well as of their chronic inability to impose it on their unruly materials. Much as they may seek to present a host of historical figures marching 'all in order' out of the past, time in the *Mirror* is multi-layered, multidirectional, and anything but orderly. As I shall argue here, one of the chief links between the *Mirror for Magistrates* and Shakespeare's history plays is their shared fascination with temporal sequence and its transgression.

From the opening pages of the 1559 edition of the *Mirror*, Baldwin and his fellow authors are preoccupied by the problem of order. The word first occurs with reference to their literary model, Lydgate's *Fall of Princes*, which Baldwin brings to the poets' gathering 'for the better obseruacion of his order' (p.69). Here the term refers to a way of proceeding, but even in the opening epistle the problem of order in the sense of sequence rears its head. Ferrers laments that Lydgate's translation of Boccaccio fails to include the famous falls of ancient Britons and of medieval Englishmen such as Richard I and King John. To include these worthies in the *Mirror* would, however, create a parallel sequence with Lydgate's, whereas 'the printers mynde is to haue vs followe where *Lidgate* left' (p.70), that is, in the latter half of the fifteenth century. No sooner has Ferrers recited the first tragedy, that of Robert Tresilian, than another poet breaks in to emphasise the importance of chronological order: 'Althoughe it be not greatly appertinent to our purpose, yet in my iudgement I thynke it woulde do wel to obserue the times of men, and as they be more aunciente, so to place theym' (p.81). The unnamed poet then proceeds to break his own rule by reciting the history of Roger Mortimer, who died 'a yere before the fall of these Iustices'. The emerging but still obviously fragile chronological protocol is reinforced by Ferrers in the following prose link: 'seyng it is best to place eche person in his ordre, *Baldwin* take you the Chronicles and marke them as they cum' (p.91).

Order, in the sense of chronological sequence, is clearly crucial to the poets' *order*, or way of proceeding. Yet the apparently simple task of placing 'eche person in his ordre' gives rise to constant disputation and frustration amongst the assembled authors. Neither in the 1559 *Mirror* nor in its various sequels and additions are the vexing problems of chronology out of view for long. The introduction to the tragedy of Richard II prompts a nervous observation that 'his personage is so sore intangled as I thinke fewe benefices be at this day' (p.110). Specifically, his biography is bound up with those of the 'maskers' who conspired to assassinate Henry IV and restore Richard to the throne, whose 'matter so runneth in this, that I doubt which ought to go before'. The masquers cannot reasonably be placed before Richard II, nor, having predeceased him by several weeks, can they be placed after. Proving unassimilable to the chronological scheme, they must be set aside, as agreed by the poets in the following prose link. A few pages later, the same fate befalls Lord Say and the Bishop of Salisbury, who died in Cade's rebellion. When one of the assembly proposes to wind back the narrative clock to a point before Cade's own death in order to include these elite victims, another insists: 'Nay rather let vs go forward, for we haue a great many behynde that maye not be omitted' (p.179).

When used with reference to time, the preposition 'behynde' commonly indicates the past, but may in early modern usage also refer to the future. The ambiguous position of time's 'behynde' is indicative of the problems with chronological orderliness that beset the *Mirror*.[4] (It can indeed be 'monstrous', as one of Cade's rebels opines in Shakespeare's play, 'to come behind folks' [*Henry IV Part 2*, 4.7.76].) When the poet says 'let vs go forward', he conjures an image of the past as a static landscape through which the historical writer progresses; yet when he speaks a moment later of the many that remain 'behynde', the image shifts to one in which the poets watch from a fixed position as an ongoing procession of historical figures passes by. Are the poets marching through history or watching history march past? Do they speak from the temporal vantage point at which their project has arrived (e.g. 1450, the year of Cade's death), or from that of the Marian or Elizabethan present? The tragic figures who lie 'behynde' Cade belong at once to the future and the past; the temporal present of the *Mirror*'s tragedies always arrives simultaneously, if not always seamlessly, from multiple directions.

As the 1559 edition proceeds, the number of historical figures omitted in order to prevent chronological inconvenience continues to mount, ultimately equalling if not exceeding the number of tragedies included. The laments of Duke Humphrey and his wife Eleanor are promised in the table of contents, yet when Ferrers suggests he requires more 'leasure' (p.161) to deliver them properly, they are dropped, apparently without reprieve. Likewise, the case of a certain Duke of Exeter drowned in the reign of Edward IV is said to require further research; Baldwin proposes the substitution of another drowned Duke, Clarence, and the unnamed Duke of Exeter is not heard of again. Baldwin is seemingly compelled to keep turning the leaves of his chronicle, moving at a steady pace in one direction only; if a ghost fails to seize its moment to emerge, the chance is gone forever.

The Seconde Parte of the Mirror for Magistrates, first published in 1563, brings Baldwin and his collaborators together for the second meeting promised at the end of the first edition, in which the project will be carried further. In this case, however, the members of the assembly are not obliged to extemporise their laments on the spot, for Baldwin and Ferrers have brought a bundle of tragedies already composed by a range of poets. The only purpose of the second gathering is to hear these tragedies and 'place them in due order' (p.244). The task which had been described in the 1559 edition as 'not greatly appertinent' has become the sole point of the meeting. For this purpose, one whom 'we made, & call the reder' is appointed to 'take the cronycles, & note theyr places … as they cum' (pp.244–5).

A prose passage later in the *Seconde Parte* provides a clue to the motives behind the poets' extraordinary emphasis on chronological sequence. In his introduction to Sackville's Induction, Baldwin recalls that the original Marian edition of the *Mirror* had been suppressed because 'some of the counsayle would not suffer the booke to be printed in suche order as we had agreed and determined' (p.297). What exactly did the Privy Council (and more precisely Bishop Stephen Gardiner, identified by Baldwin in 1559 as the chief hinderer of the original edition) find objectionable in the poem's 'order'? The term can hardly refer simply to the poets' adoption of the Boccaccio/Lydgate format, since the council did not object to Wayland's republication of the *Fall of Princes*; and Sackville, who at some point in the later 1550s planned a new version of the *Mirror* project, also planned to follow 'such order as Lydgate (folowing Bocchas) had already vsed' (p.297). More probably, the council's objections bore on the book's chronological sequence (why commence with a corrupt Chief Justice?), and the authors' evident determination to encroach upon the present, both through the forward movement of the tragedies and the parallels with contemporary figures they suggest.[5] Sackville had apparently proposed to allay any such objections through a radical resequencing of the *Mirror* materials; his collection would begin with his own tragedy of Buckingham (d.1483), followed by the poems already composed for the banned edition of the *Mirror*, and so proceeding 'backwarde euen to the time of William the Conquerour' (p.297). Although Baldwin in 1559 did not adopt Sackville's principle of chronological regression, his tireless insistence on preserving strict chronological order seems designed to prove to potential censors that there is nothing more sinister implied in the sequence of the tragedies.

Fascinatingly, the problem of order continues to appear in prose passages added to the *Mirror* in editions long postdating Baldwin's death and the threat of Marian censorship. In the 1578 edition, the long-promised tragedies of Duke Humphrey and his Duchess Eleanor finally appear. Where in previous editions Ferrers had promised to produce these tragedies at greater leisure, here (in a conversation still supposedly taking place at some point in the 1550s) he reports that he has them ready penned. Even so, issues of sequence must be resolved before the poet can proceed.

> But whether of them is fyrst to be placed in the order of our boke, I somewhat stande in doute. For albeit the sayde Dukes death happened before the deceasse of the Duches, yet was her fall first, which fynally was cause of ouerthrow to both. why shoulde you doubte then (quod the rest of the company) for seyng the cause doth alwaies go before theffect and sequel of any thing: it is good reason you should begin with her first. (p.431)

The apparently straightforward judgement of the poets that cause should precede effect opens a chronological can of worms which the company has studiously avoided in all previous editions. The problem of the Duke and Duchess of Gloucester is essentially the same as that posed by Richard II and the participants in the masquers' conspiracy (whose downfall was a consequence of the overthrow of Richard, yet who met their deaths before Richard himself). In 1559, the poets had resolved the problem by prioritising Richard's case and then consenting to omit the masquers altogether. Two decades later, they (or whoever is voicing them now) reverse the established convention and permit issues of causation to override strict chronology. The fall of the Duchess comes both before that of the Duke (as cause of his overthrow) and after (in that she survived him). By violating their strict adherence to order, the poets open up a panoply of alternative temporalities with different relations to the Elizabethan present.

The relationship between cause and effect had been central to the *Mirror* project from the beginning. Leaving aside the handful of ghosts who are content to blame their downfall on fickle fortune, the vast majority of subjects trace their destruction to a specific vice or failing. John Tiptoft, Earl of Worcester, urges Baldwin to be rigorous in linking cause to effect, for 'causes are the chiefest thinges| That should be noted of the story wryters,| That men may learne what endes al causes bringes' (p.198). Yet while the temporality of causation and the temporality of morbidity are both linear in themselves, one cannot be lain over the other without causing wrinkles and ruptures in the textual web of time. In some cases, the writers must struggle with causes that postdate their effects, or which became known only after an individual met his death (as in the case of many of Richard of Gloucester's victims, who could not know of his ambition for the throne).

As I have argued here, the *Mirror* poets' obsession with chronological sequence reflects a perceived need to regulate (and to be seen to regulate) the relationship between the historical eras of their subjects and the present (a need prompted, at least in part, by wariness of censorship). Yet this chronological regulation breaks down repeatedly and irretrievably. In addition to the permutations introduced by the problems of cause and effect, there are three main factors ensuring the disruption of linear temporality in the *Mirror*. These are:

1) the complexities of chronicle time, on which the poets perforce rely;
2) the inherent multitemporality of the ghost;
3) the uncertain temporal location of the prose links, especially in editions after 1559.

In *The First Parte*, Baldwin is instructed by Ferrers: 'take you the Chronicles and mark them as they cum' (p.91). Here we may imagine that

Baldwin is silently skimming the pages of Fabyan and Hall in search of proper names. In the *Seconde Parte*, a more rigorous procedure is adopted whereby the chronicle is read aloud by one 'whom ... we made, & call the reder' (p.245). In each case the point of the exercise is to ensure that the tragedies are sequenced in the correct order. Yet this method has some inherent dangers, for the chronicles do not in fact recount events annalistically, in a strict sequence, but are full of moments of foreshadowing and retrospection. (In terms of the sources cited by Baldwin, this is true of Fabyan, doubly true of Hall, and supremely characteristic of More.) The case of the deposed Richard II and the conspirators who plotted the assassination of Henry IV provides a case in point. The first chapter of Hall's chronicle concludes with Richard's abdication, his imprisonment, and the announcement of his imminent death: 'after his resignacion he was conueighed to the castell of Ledes in Kent, & from thence to Poumffret wher he departed out of this miserable life, as you shall heare herafter'.[6] For a reader 'marking' the chronicle in order to note the downfalls 'as they cum', this would seem the natural point at which to insert Richard's tragedy. Yet the next chapter goes on to tell of the conspiracy to restore him to the throne, into which the chronicler must insert the slightly awkward reminder that 'kyng Richard ... was yet a liue'.[7] Only after the hapless masquers have been disposed of does Hall proceed to tell of Richard's own death in prison. Later sections of the chronicle, largely derived from More's *History of Richard III*, are still more marked by temporal twists and turns. More sets the near simultaneous deaths of the arch-enemies Hastings and Rivers in ironic apposition, allowing each to foreshadow the other, so that it is impossible to say which event occurs first.[8] This complex weave may be reflected in the *Seconde Parte of the Mirror* when Baldwin tells us that he would not permit the reader to continue reading from the chronicle after the tragedy of Rivers, but proceeded immediately to insert the tragedy of Hastings.

The temporal order of the *Mirror* is undermined in no less fundamental ways by the speakers of the tragedies, who are – broadly speaking, at least – ghosts.[9] More particularly, they are revenants, the dead who return to speak. Especially in the *First Parte*, Baldwin takes some care to distinguish the speakers of the tragedies from the actual souls of the departed. They are products of the poetic imagination, and they are typically imagined speaking at a moment very shortly after their deaths (thus Richard II and Warwick are both imagined laid out in St Paul's). On the whole, an effort is made to indicate that the dead have knowledge only of their own lives and deaths, and not of what transpired after – this is crucial to the

Mirror writers' case that their tragedies do not comment directly on persons living in the present. Yet there are points at which the dead reveal an uncanny knowledge of what should be for them unknown futurity. John Tiptoft criticises the chroniclers Fabyan and Hall for insufficient attention to the true causes of events; Shore's wife claims to have listened from the grave to the slanders spoken about her; Hastings instructs Baldwin to tell 'What since [his death] ensued', but hints at some knowledge of his future reputation when he begs Baldwin to 'shyeld my torne name' (p.293). At such points, the dead (whose role is always to recount events of which the poets have learned from chronicles written after their deaths) seem to have insight into their posthumous reputations, which they may either embrace or reject.

The temporality of revenance in the *Mirror* centres its disruptive force around the preposition 'now'. The tragic speakers may use 'now' to refer to a juncture in their own histories ('My Lorde must dyne, and now midday was past', p.290). More commonly, the term indicates the moment in which the dead speaker addresses Baldwin ('marke me now I pray the Baldwin marke', p.183), or more broadly to the occasion of the *Mirror*'s composition ('Bolenbrooke| Of whom duke Mowbray tolde thee now of late', p.183). On occasion, the ghosts use 'now' to refer explicitly to the context of reception, as when Tresilian in the 1578 edition addresses himself to 'Ye iudges now liuing' (p.79) or the Blacksmith questions the wisdom of clerks 'both nowe and then' (p.405). These revenants seem to inhabit a sixteenth-century present as well as belonging to their own fourteenth- or fifteenth-century eras, a point most apparent when Tresilian employs a paradoxical doubling of the second-person plural: 'If Iudges in our dayes, would ponder well in minde,| The fatall fall of vs ...' (p.80).

When Baldwin portrays himself and his collaborators struggling hopelessly to maintain temporal decorum in the face of slippery chroniclers and unruly ghosts, we may wonder whether the depiction is entirely sincere or there is some sly joke involved. Yet one aspect of the *Mirror*'s multitemporality is genuinely out of Baldwin's control, resulting as it does from his death in 1563. The prose passages of the *Seconde Parte* include both recently composed or revised material and unrevised text from the reign of Mary. The fiction that the poets have gathered to review the tragedies on a specific day is thoroughly disrupted, as the conversation washes back and forth over a period of almost ten years (c.1554–63). Radically dislocated in time, the meeting of the poets takes place 'seuen nightes' (p.235) after their first gathering, but subsequent to the banning of the first edition and Sackville's abortive attempt at a different *Mirror* project; the poets gather under a Protestant regime which has condemned the doctrine of Purgatory (p.346), but also in the reigns of the Catholic monarchs Mary and Philip (pp.387, 420); they meet prior to the death of Lord Vaux in 1556 (p.297), but subsequent to the publication of Rastell's edition of More's *History of Richard III* in 1557.[10] Although later editions of the *Mirror* attempt some tidying of the prose links, the chronological confusion only mounts further. In the 1587 *Mirror*, the long-deceased Baldwin concludes a speech condemning rebellion against Mary and Philip by introducing the tragedy of Nicholas Burdet, newly delivered to him by Raphael Holinshed (d. 1580). Even the titles of succeeding editions of the *Mirror* are characterised by temporal confusion, as the original *Mirror* (1559) and its *Seconde Parte* (1563) are supplemented by a new *First Parte* (1574) and an entirely different *Seconde Parte* (1578), prompting the redesignation of the original *Mirror* and its *Seconde Parte* as *The Last Parte*.

'Mark how well the sequel hangs together': disordered time in Shakespeare's histories

There is a solid critical consensus that William Shakespeare knew and used the *Mirror for Magistrates* in a good many of his histories and tragedies. Yet those who have scoured the history plays for verbal echoes or nuggets of historical information from the *Mirror* have found comparatively few examples. Geoffrey Bullough's judgement with regard to *Richard II* could be applied to most of the histories: 'That Shakespeare knew the *Mirror* well is certain. Whether he took much from it for this play is less sure.'[11] Writing more than forty years after Bullough, Charles Forker concurs that 'It would be astonishing if Shakespeare had not made himself familiar with these poems in at least a cursory way [yet] it is difficult to establish specific indebtedness.'[12] In the *Mirror*, it appears, Shakespeare found few facts he could not have found elsewhere, and still less worth emulating stylistically. Although he certainly drew on the *de casibus* theme in some of his works, Shakespeare was far less influenced by the *Mirror* in this regard than were such contemporaries as Spenser, Drayton, Daniel, and Lodge. Although he may have been rather more intrigued by the work's often daring politics, direct influence is again difficult to determine.[13] Yet there is one distinctive aspect of the *Mirror* that finds a remarkable echo in Shakespeare's works, not least the history plays. This is their shared predilection, verging on a compulsion, to indulge in unconventional and preposterous temporal effects.

In all his genres and at all stages of his career, Patricia Parker has argued, Shakespeare was drawn irresistably to 'preposterous reversals of order, succession, and sequence'.[14] Preposterous or back-to-front temporal sequences are arguably especially characteristic of his history plays. Although his elite protagonists lay constant emphasis on the principles of 'fair sequence and succession' (*Richard II*, 2.1.200) and 'lineal, true-derivèd course' (*Richard III*, 3.7.190), their chronological idealism is undermined not only by the bloody and irregular successions portrayed on the stage but by the fact that the sequence of the plays is 'literally preposterous', beginning as it does with *Henry VI* and concluding with *Henry V*.[15] Richard II, in the chronology of composition, is successor to Richard III (an observation that adds point to Edward IV's lament in *Richard III*: 'the order was reversed', 2.1.87). Effects in the history plays frequently precede their causes, as acknowledged in the closing speech of *Henry V*, wherein the Chorus foresees a dire future which he knows will be familiar to the audience from their theatregoing past: 'Which oft our stage hat shown' (Epilogue, 13).[16] As Baldwin, towards the end of the *Seconde Parte*, refers both forward and back to an as-yet-unpublished *First Parte* (p.387), so Shakespeare's two tetralogies of history plays encounter each other both coming and going.

Just as the lineal succession of one monarch by another is challenged in a number of the history plays, so the orderly sequence of time is often threatened and sometimes boldly overturned. Thus the deposed Richard II complains that time itself has turned upon him: 'I wasted time, and now doth time waste me' (5.5.49). Richard's soliloquy on time occurs as he lies imprisoned in Pomfret castle, in that zone between two deaths (his deposition and his physical death), which provokes temporal anxiety in both Hall's chronicle and the *Mirror*. In this chronological no-man's-land, Shakespeare's Richard speaks of being divorced from his own 'true time' (5.5.48): 'my time| Runs posting on in Bolingbroke's proud joy,| While I stand fooling here, his jack of the clock' (5.5.58–60). The 'Jack of the clock' was the name given to the automata who struck the hours in many English churches; not quite part of the clock and often not quite in sync with it, the Jack made an apt image of doubled and disordered time. The image occurs as well in *Richard III*, when Richard rounds on Buckingham with the accusation that 'like a jack, thou keep'st the stroke| Betwixt thy begging and my meditation' (4.3.117–18).[17]

Henry IV Part 2 is a play particularly troubled by the problem of misordered time. Only one of its characters, Northumberland, features in the *Mirror*, and the influence of his poetic tragedy is not strongly apparent in the play. Yet many of the characters complain of the same temporal confusion that troubles the *Mirror* poets. The Archbishop of York (one of those named in the prose links but passed over by the poets, p.131) declares that 'The time misordered doth, in common sense,| Crowd us and crush us to this monstrous form' (4.1.259–60). It is natural enough that the rebels should see the time since the deposition of Richard II as out of joint. Yet Henry IV himself seems at risk of losing his temporal coordinates. Despairing at his subjects' endless appetite for rebellion, he imagines what he would have felt if, as a young man, he had encountered his own future in a book:

> O God, that one might read the book of fate,
> And see the revolution of the times ...
> The happiest youth, viewing his progress through,
> What perils past, what crosses to ensue,
> Would shut the book and sit him down and die. (3.1.44–52)

The book Henry imagines himself reading sounds more than a little like the *Mirror for Magistrates*. Technically, of course the *Mirror* is not 'the book of fate', but more properly a book of fates.[18] Yet its insistence on monitory exemplarity encourages the reader to experience the tragedies not only as a record of past lives, but as an account of their own potential future experience and 'crosses to ensue'. The *Mirror*'s relentless insistence on misfortune may indeed be enough to drive the reader to proleptic despair.

Future and past are mingled again in *Henry IV Part 2* when John of Lancaster admonishes the rebel Hastings for attempting to predict the time to come. 'You are too shallow, Hastings, much too shallow,| To sound the bottom of the aftertimes' (4.1.276–7). More commonly one would expect the marine depths to signify the past and the dead, as they do in *Richard III* when Clarence dreams of skeletons 'scattered in the bottom of the sea' (1.4.28), and in *The Tempest* ('Full fathom five thy father lies', 1.2.400). In *Henry V*, too, the seabed signifies the past, albeit in the future perfect tense; Canterbury urges Henry to 'make your chronicle as rich with praise| As is the ooze and bottom of the sea| With sunken wreck and sunless treasuries' (1.2.163–5). John of Lancaster's marine metaphor may indicate the future, but it cannot help connoting the past. His preposterous 'bottom', like the *Mirror*'s 'behynde', faces both ways.

Of all the histories, none is more closely engaged with both the *Mirror* and the tangled shape of time than *Richard III*.[19] That the play should be indebted to the *Mirror* is hardly surprising, since the first and second parts feature the tragedies of no fewer than six characters who appear in the play (Clarence, Edward IV, Rivers, Hastings, Buckingham, and Richard himself), as well as those of Mistress Shore (who haunts the wings) and the poet Collingbourne (who goes unmentioned, but finds a parallel in Shakespeare's Scrivener). Sackville's induction to Buckingham's tragedy has also been seen as an influence on the play, specifically in its vision of Hell, which finds an echo in Clarence's dream of damnation (1.4.43–63).[20] Yet in spite of the heavy overlap of personalities and events, points at which Shakespeare can be caught borrowing directly from Baldwin and his fellows are, as ever, relatively few and far between. The play's deeper debt to the *Mirror* lies in its extraordinarily disordered and multiple temporality.

The play opens with Richard addressing the audience much like a ghost in the *Mirror* stepping out of the past to collar Baldwin. The opening word of his soliloquy, 'Now', which wreaks such temporal havoc in the *Mirror*, has a similar and even more radical effect in the play. Even before another syllable is uttered, Richard's 'now' has at least three temporal referents, potentially referring to a moment in the late fifteenth century when the historical Richard would have spoken, to that moment in the late sixteenth century when an actor addresses the audience, and a moment relative to what has transpired before upon the stage, specifically the three parts of *Henry VI*. With Richard's next words the temporal maze becomes still more convoluted. 'Now is the winter of our discontent| Made glorious summer by this son of York' (1.1.1–2). Heard on its own, the first line draws an unavoidable equation between the present ('now') and 'the winter of our discontent' ('now *is* the winter …'). The second line repositions that winter – and, by implication, 'now' itself – in the past, preceding the summer of Yorkist rule. Like a man rocking a small boat, Richard in his first appearance causes time to slip and slide in a queasy fashion, highlighting both his chronological proximity to the audience and his uneasy relationship to any version of the present.

In the same soliloquy, Richard will suggest an uncanny foreknowledge, reminiscent of the *Mirror*, of the Tudor chronicles whereby he is 'determinèd to prove a villain' (1.1.30). His posthumous reputation, as Linda Charnes notes, 'has always already preceded him'.[21] Shakespeare reverses the sequence of *The Seconde Parte of the Mirror for Magistrates*, allowing Richard to appear in advance of the various victims whose destruction he will cause. Nonetheless, as in the *Mirror*, effects precede their causes, for Richard's own character is the effect of actions that have not yet taken place, and of narratives that, in the time of the play, have not yet been written. Later in the play, the reversal of cause and effect is made the matter of sardonic comment by the Scrivener, when he reveals how he was commanded to copy out the indictment of Hastings before his crimes had been committed or his examination taken place: 'mark how well the sequel hangs together' (3.6.4).

As if in response to Richard's elusive 'Now', the historical present eludes definite location at many points in the play. The second scene takes place at some impossible moment shortly following the death of Henry VI (1471), whilst Clarence lies imprisoned in the Tower (1478), Richard is pursuing marriage with Anne Neville (1472), and Edward IV is suffering from the illness which will soon take his life (1483). This scene flits back and forth over a period of slightly over a decade, similar to the period embraced in the *Mirror*'s prose frame, whose two successive meetings slide between the early 1550s and the early 1560s. Comparable telescoping of time is found later in the play. Following his coronation, Richard signals his intention to murder his wife, marry Clarence's daughter to a low-born man, and deal with any threat from Clarence's son (4.2.53–7); he also charges Tyrrel to kill the princes, and bring news of the deed to him before he sleeps (4.2.84). When Tyrrel returns to report the deed before supper on the same evening, he finds Richard inhabiting a moment some weeks or months in the future, when Anne's death has been accomplished, Clarence's daughter married off, and the son imprisoned (4.3.36–9). The events between Buckingham's rebellion of autumn 1483 and Henry Tudor's successful invasion of summer 1485 are collapsed still more brazenly. In the central passages of the play, where Shakespeare is mirroring More's *History* (roughly from Edward's death to Richard's coronation), he follows the course of events with near-calendrical precision; in the earlier and later sections, by contrast, he employs versions of the double-time scheme that famously characterises *Othello*, and which have an important exemplar in the prose frame of the *Mirror*.[22]

In the final act of the play, Richard and his rival Richmond are confronted with a procession of ghosts, including no fewer than five (Henry VI, Clarence, Rivers, Hastings, Buckingham) whose tragedies are recorded in the *Mirror*. Shakespeare's introduction of ghosts to the oft-told story of Richard's final night is an innovation (earlier accounts speak of nightmares or evil spirits). As in the *Mirror*, the ghosts appear in order of their demise, a point stressed by Buckingham's deliberate identification of himself as Richard's 'last' (5.5.122) victim. Not only does the scene incorporate telegraphed versions of five of the *Mirror*'s tragedies, it fills a gap in the preceding text by including the ghosts of the princes in the Tower (which Baldwin declares have been assigned to the absent Lord Vaux). If the play begins by presenting Richard as a *Mirror*-style ghost addressing an audience positioned as Baldwin, it concludes with Richard-as-Baldwin harangued by angry ghosts. Positioning him relentlessly in relation to the past ('Think how thou stabbedst me in my prime of youth', 5.5.73) and the future ('Let me sit heavy on thy soul tomorrow', 5.5.71, 85), the ghosts reassert the strict temporality of causation which Richard has evaded for so long.

Conclusion

In none of the acknowledged sources of Shakespeare's history plays are the problems of chronological order and homogenous time so relentlessly addressed or so thoroughly problematised as in the *Mirror*. Likewise, in no Elizabethan text thought to have been influenced by the *Mirror* are the problems of misordered time so persistently highlighted as in Shakespeare's histories. It is indeed tempting, in this case, to speak in terms of cause and effect, and to propose that Shakespeare was influenced by the permutations wrought upon the shape of time which he noted in the pages of the *Mirror*. Yet, when we find the temporality of causation so thoroughly interrogated and disrupted in both texts, it may be wiser to draw back. Conventional chronology tells us that the *Mirror* came before the history plays, and that Baldwin lies 'behynde' Shakespeare. Yet today, does not almost every reader come to Baldwin after Shakespeare, and read the *Mirror*'s tragedies with Shakespeare's characters behind them? Might we not then begin to ask how Baldwin (d.1563) may have been influenced by Shakespeare (b.1564)? The question is of course preposterous.

Notes

1 All references to Shakespeare's plays are to *The Norton Shakespeare*, ed. Stephen Greenblatt et al., 2nd ed. (New York: W. W. Norton, 2008).
2 On Cade and *de casibus*, see Patricia Parker, *Shakespeare from the Margins: Language, Culture, Context* (University of Chicago Press, 1996), p.37.
3 *The Mirror for Magistrates*, ed. Lily B. Campbell (Cambridge University Press, 1938), p.170. Further page references in text.
4 Shakespeare, too, occasionally uses 'behind' with reference to what lies in store, as in Macbeth's 'the greatest is behind' (1.3.115). More common in Shakespeare and elsewhere is the use of the preposition with reference to the past, as in 'My grief lies onward and my joy behind' (Sonnet 50).

5 See Scott C. Lucas, A Mirror for Magistrates *and the Politics of the English Reformation* (Amherst: University of Massachusetts Press, 2009), p.245.
6 Edward Hall, *The Union of the Two Noble and Illustre Famelies of Lancastre and Yorke* (1548), Henry IV, fol. ix^r.
7 Hall, Henry IV, fol. xii^r.
8 Moments before Hastings is himself condemned to death, More has him musing with satisfaction on the 'takyng of [the Queen's] kynred and of their puttyng to death, whiche were by hys assent before devysed to be beheaded at Pomfrete, this selfe same daye, in the whiche he was not ware that it was by other devised that he hym selfe should the same daye be beheaded at London ...' Hall, Edward V, fol. xiii^r.
9 On the extent to which the *Mirror's* tragic subjects can be identified as ghosts, see Philip Schwyzer, *Literature, Nationalism, and Memory in Early Modern England and Wales* (Cambridge University Press, 2004), pp.105–17.
10 In *The Seconde Parte*, a poet observes that 'Syr Thomas More and Hall call hym [Dorset] the Queenes sonne' (p.267); this indicates access to a text of More's *History* separate from the version included in Hall, most probably the Rastell edition.
11 Geoffrey Bullough, *Narrative and Dramatic Sources of Shakespeare, Vol. III: Earlier English History Plays* (London: Routledge & Kegan Paul, 1960), p.367.
12 William Shakespeare, *King Richard II*, ed. Charles R. Forker (London: Thomson Learning, 2002), p.139.
13 See Andrew Hadfield, *Shakespeare and Renaissance Politics* (London: Thomson Learning, 2004), esp. pp.44–52.
14 Parker, *Shakespeare from the Margins*, p.29.
15 Parker, *Shakespeare from the Margins*, p.36.
16 As Marjorie Garber notes, 'the first tetralogy predicts the second; the second also predicts the first'; see '"What's Past Is Prologue": Temporality and Prophecy in Shakespeare's History Plays', in Barbara Kiefer Lewalski, ed., *Renaissance Genres: Essays on Theory, History, and Interpretation* (Cambridge: Harvard University Press, 1986), p.323.
17 On Shakespeare's clock jacks and their significant failure to keep time, see Tiffany Stern, 'Time for Shakespeare: Hourglasses, Sundials, Clocks, and Early Modern Theatre,' *JBA* 3 (2015), 16–18. The image recurs, with apparent reference to *Richard III*, in Middleton's *The Puritan*, 3.1.
18 The more immediate echo is of Spenser's *Faerie Queene*, where Redcrosse finds himself debating, as Henry does, with Despair: 'Their times in his eternall booke of fate| Are written sure, and haue their certaine date.| Who then can striue with strong necessitie ...'
19 This discussion of *Richard III* and the *Mirror* draws on and develops passages in Philip Schwyzer, *Shakespeare and the Remains of Richard III* (Oxford University Press, 2013).
20 Bullough, *Narrative and Dramatic Sources, Vol. 3*, p.233.
21 Linda Charnes, *Notorious Identity: Materializing the Subject in Shakespeare* (Cambridge: Harvard University Press, 1993), p.28.

22 On Shakespeare's experimentation with double time in *Richard III*, see Zdeněk Stříbrný, *The Whirligig of Time: Essays on Shakespeare and Czechoslovakia* (Cranbury, NJ: Associated University Presses, 2007), pp.87–93. On double-time's 'proximation and superimposition of supposedly disparate temporal points' as a form of the preposterous, see Jonathan Gil Harris, *Untimely Matter in the Time of Shakespeare* (Philadelphia: University of Pennsylvania Press, 2009), pp.182–3.

Select bibliography

Attridge, Derek, *Well-Weighed Syllables: Elizabethan Verse in Classical Metres* (Cambridge University Press, 1974).
Austen, Gillian, *George Gascoigne* (Cambridge: D. S. Brewer, 2008).
Bellany, Alastair, *The Politics of Court Scandal in Early Modern England: News Culture and the Overbury Affair, 1603–1660* (Cambridge University Press, 2002).
Bradford, Alan T., 'Mirrors of Mutability: Winter Landscapes in Tudor Poetry', *ELR* 4 (1974), 3–39.
Brown, Richard Danson, '"A Talkatiue Wench (Whose Words a World hath Delighted in)": Mistress Shore and Elizabethan Complaint', *RES* 49 (1998), 395–415.
Budra, Paul, A Mirror for Magistrates *and the de casibus* Tradition (University of Toronto Press, 2000).
Bush, Douglas, 'Classical Lives in "The Mirror for Magistrates"', *SP* 22 (1925), 256–66.
Campbell, Lily B., 'Humphrey Duke of Gloucester and Elianor Cobham His Wife in the *Mirror for Magistrates*', *HLB* 5 (1934), 119–55.
  Shakespeare's "Histories": Mirrors of Elizabethan Policy (San Marino: Huntington Library, 1947).
Clegg, Cyndia, *Press Censorship in Elizabethan England* (Cambridge University Press, 1997).
Collinson, Patrick, *This England: Essays on the English Nation and Commonwealth in the Sixteenth Century* (Manchester University Press, 2011).
Davies, James, *A Myrroure for Magistrates. Considered with Special Reference to the Sources of Sackville's Contributions*, (University of Leipzig: Dr Seele and Co., 1906).
Eisenstein, Elizabeth L., *The Printing Press as an Agent of Change: Communications and Cultural Transformations in Early-Modern Europe*, 2 vols. (Cambridge University Press, 1980).
Ellis, Jim, 'Embodying Dislocation: *A Mirror for Magistrates* and Property Relations', *RS* 53 (2000), 1032–52.
Escobedo, Andrew, 'The Tudor Search for Arthur and the Poetics of Historical Loss', *Exemplaria* 14 (2002), 127–65.

Nationalism and Historical Loss in Renaissance England: Foxe, Dee, Spenser, Milton (Ithaca and London: Cornell University Press, 2004).

Farnham, Willard, 'John Higgins' *Mirror* and *Locrine*', *MP* 23 (1926), 307–13.

The Medieval Heritage of Elizabethan Tragedy (Oxford: Basil Blackwell, 1956).

Geller, Sherri, 'What History Really Teaches: Historical Pyrrhonism in William Baldwin's *A Mirror for Magistrates*', in Peter C. Herman, ed., *Opening the Borders: Inclusivity in Early Modern Studies* (University of Delaware Press, 1999), pp.150–84.

'Editing under the Influence of the Standard Textual Hierarchy: Misrepresenting *A Mirror for Magistrates* in the Nineteenth- and Twentieth-Century Editions', *TC* 2 (2007), 43–77.

Grabes, Herbert, *The Mutable Glass: Mirror-Imagery in Titles and Texts of the Middle Ages and English Renaissance*, trans. Gordon Collier (Cambridge University Press, 1982).

Grafton, Anthony, and Jardine, Lisa, '"Studied for Action": How Gabriel Harvey Read His Livy', *P. & P.*, 11 (1990), 30–78.

Green, Lawrence D., 'Modes of Perception in the *Mirror for Magistrates*', *HLQ* 44 (1981), 117–33.

Hadfield, Andrew, *Literature, Politics and National Identity: Reformation to Renaissance* (Cambridge University Press, 1994).

Hampton, Timothy, *Writing from History: The Rhetoric of Exemplarity in Renaissance Literature* (Ithaca and London: Cornell University Press, 1990).

Harper, Carrie Anna, *The Sources of the British Chronicle History in Spenser's Faerie Queene* (Bryn Mawr College Monographs, VII; Philadelphia, Pennsylvania: Bryn Mawr, 1910).

Hulse, S. Clark, *Metamorphic Verse: The Elizabethan Minor Epic* (Princeton University Press, 1981).

Human, Elizabeth M. A., 'House of *Mirrors*: Textual Variation and *The Mirror for Magistrates*', *LC* 5 (2008), 772–90.

Jellerson, Donald, 'The Spectral Historiopoetics of the *Mirror for Magistrates*', *JNR* 2 (2010), 54–71.

Kewes, Paulina, 'Henry Savile's Tacitus and the Politics of Roman History in Late Elizabethan England', *HLQ* 74 (2011), 515–51.

King, John N., *English Reformation Literature: The Tudor Origins of the Protestant Tradition* (Princeton University Press, 1982).

Lämmerhirt, Rudolf, *Thomas Blenerhassets 'Second Part of the Mirror for Magistrates'. Eine Quellenstudie* (Weimar: Druck von G. Uschmann, 1909).

Leath Mills, Jerry, 'A Source for Spenser's Anamnestes', *PQ* 47 (1968), 137–9.

Liebler, Naomi Conn, ed., *Early Modern Prose Fiction: The Cultural Politics of Reading* (New York and London: Routledge, 2007).

Lindley, David, *The Trials of Frances Howard: Fact and Fiction at the Court of King James* (London and New York: Routledge, 1993).

Lucas, Scott, 'Diggon Davie and Davy Dicar: Edmund Spenser, Thomas Churchyard, and the Poetics of Public Protest', *SS* 16 (2002), 151–66.

'Hall's Chronicle and the Mirror for Magistrates: History and the Tragic Pattern', in Mike Pincombe and Cathy Shrank, eds, *The Oxford Handbook of Tudor Literature, 1485–1603* (Oxford University Press, 2009), pp.356–71.

A Mirror for Magistrates and the Politics of the English Reformation (Massachusetts Studies in Early Modern Culture; Amherst: University of Massachusetts Press, 2009).

McKeown, Adam, *English Mercuries: Soldier Poets in the Age of Shakespeare* (Nashville: Vanderbilt University Press, 2009).

McRae, Andrew, *Literature, Satire, and the Early Stuart State* (Cambridge University Press, 2004).

Maslen, R. W., *Elizabethan Fictions: Espionage, Counter-Espionage, and the Duplicity of Fiction in Early Elizabethan Prose Narratives* (Oxford: Clarendon Press, 1997).

'William Baldwin and the Tudor Imagination', in Mike Pincombe and Cathy Shrank, eds, *The Oxford Handbook of Tudor Literature, 1485–1603* (Oxford University Press, 2009), pp.291–306.

Miller, Edwin, *The Professional Writer in Elizabethan England: A Study of Nondramatic Literature* (Cambridge, MA: Harvard University Press, 1959).

Norbrook, David, *Poetry and Politics in the English Renaissance* (Oxford University Press, 2002).

O'Callaghan, Michelle, *The 'Shepheards Nation': Jacobean Spenserians and Early Stuart Political Culture, 1612–1625* (Oxford: Clarendon Press, 2000).

'Dreaming the Dead: Ghosts and History in the Early Seventeenth Century', in Katharine Hodgkin, Michelle O'Callaghan, and S. J. Wiseman, eds, *Reading the Early Modern Dream: The Terrors of the Night* (New York and London: Routledge, 2008), pp.81–96.

Orgel, Stephen, 'Margins of Truth', in Andrew Murphy, ed., *The Renaissance Text: Theory, Editing, Textuality* (Manchester University Press, 2000), pp.91–107.

'Marginal Maternity: Reading Lady Anne Clifford's *A Mirror for Magistrates*', in Douglas A. Brooks, ed., *Printing and Parenting in Early Modern England* (Aldershot: Ashgate, 2005), pp.267–89.

Overell, Anne, and Scott C. Lucas, 'Whose Wonderful News? Italian Satire and William Baldwin's *Wonderfull Newes of the Death of Paule the III*', *RS* 26:2 (2010), 180–96.

Pearsall, Derek, ed., *Chaucer to Spenser: An Anthology of Writings in English, 1375–1575* (Oxford: Blackwell, 1999).

Peck, Linda Levy, *Court Patronage and Corruption in Early Stuart England* (London: Routledge, 1990).

ed., *The Mental World of the Jacobean Court* (Cambridge University Press, 1991).

Perry, Curtis, *The Making of Jacobean Culture: James I and the Renegotiation of Elizabethan Literary Practice* (Cambridge University Press, 1997).

Pincombe, Mike, 'A Place in the Shade: George Cavendish and *de casibus* Tragedy', in Mike Pincombe and Cathy Shrank, eds, *The Oxford Handbook of Tudor Literature, 1485–1603* (Oxford University Press, 2009), pp.372–88.

'William Baldwin and *A Mirror for Magistrates*', *RS* 27 (2011), 183–98.

Pincombe, Mike, and Cathy Shrank, 'Doing Away with the Drab Age: Research Opportunities in Mid-Tudor Literature (1530–1580)', *LC* 7 (2010), 160–76.

Richards, Jennifer, 'Transforming *A Mirror for Magistrates*', in Margaret Healy and Tom Healy, eds, *Renaissance Transformations: The Making of English Writing, 1500–1650* (Edinburgh University Press, 2009), pp.48–63.

Schulze, Ivan L., 'Blenerhasset's *A Revelation*, Spenser's *Shepheardes Calender*, and the Kenilworth Pageants', *ELH* 11 (1944), 85–91.

Schurink, Fred, 'Manuscript Commonplace Books, Literature, and Reading in Early Modern England', *HLQ* 73 (2010), 453–69.

Schwyzer, Philip, *Literature, Nationalism, and Memory in Early Modern England and Wales* (Cambridge University Press, 2004).

Shenk, Linda, *Learned Queen: The Image of Elizabeth I in Politics and Poetry*, ed. Carole Levin and Charles Beem (Queenship and Power; New York: Palgrave Macmillan, 2010).

Shrank, Cathy, '"These few scribbled rules": Representing Scribal Intimacy in Early Modern Print', *HLQ* 67 (2004), 295–314.

  Writing the Nation in Reformation England, 1530–1580 (Oxford University Press, 2004).

Skura, Meredith Anne, '*A Mirror for Magistrates* and the Beginnings of English Autobiography', *ELR* 36 (2006), 26–56.

  Tudor Autobiography: Listening for Inwardness (University of Chicago Press, 2008).

Smuts, Malcolm, 'Court-Centred Politics and the Uses of Roman Historians, c. 1590–1630', in Kevin Sharpe and Peter Lake, eds, *Culture and Politics in Early Stuart England* (Basingstoke: Macmillan, 1994), pp.21–44.

Summit, Jennifer, *Memory's Library: Medieval Books in Early Modern England* (University of Chicago Press, 2008).

Tillyard, E. M. W., *Shakespeare's History Plays* (London: Chatto and Windus, 1944).

  '*A Mirror for Magistrates* Revisited', in Herbert Davis and Helen Gardner, eds, *Elizabethan and Jacobean Studies* (Oxford: Clarendon Press, 1959), pp.1–16.

Trench, W. F., A Mirror for Magistrates: *Its Origin and Influence* (1898).

van Es, Bart, *Spenser's Forms of History* (Oxford University Press, 2002).

  'Michael Drayton, Literary History and Historians in Verse', *RES* 59 (2007), 255–67.

Williams, Ralph G., 'I Shall Be Spoken: Textual Boundaries, Authors, and Intent', in George Bornstein and Ralph G. Williams, eds, *Palimpsest: Editorial Theory in the Humanities* (Ann Arbor: University of Michigan Press, 1993), pp.45–66.

Winston, Jessica, '*A Mirror for Magistrates* and Public Political Discourse in Elizabethan England', *SP* 4 (2004), 281–400.

  'Seneca in Early Elizabethan England', *RQ* 59 (2006), 29–58.

Worden, Blair, 'Historians and Poets', in Paulina Kewes, ed., *The Uses of History in Early Modern England* (San Marino, CA: Huntington Library, 2006), pp.69–90.

Zimmermann, Hugo, *Quellenuntersuchungen zum ersten Teil von J. Higgins Mirror for Magistrates* (München, Neustadt a. d. Haardt: Aktien-Druckerei 1902).

Index

Absalom, 47
Achilles, 168, 207
Adams, Thomas, 183
Aesop, 73, 75
affect, 7, 10, 29, 30, 38, 39, 42, 46, 48–9, 56, 58, 61, 64, 73, 78, 84, 159, 191, 193, 194
Agamemnon, 207
Albertus Magnus, 78
   De virtutibus animalium, 77
Albion, 135
Alençon, Duke of. *See* Francis, Duke of Alençon and Anjou
Alexander the Great, 47
Alexander, Gavin, 78–9
Allde, Edward, 81
Anjou, Duke of. *See* Francis, Duke of Alençon and Anjou
Anne of Denmark, 169
annotation. *See* marginalia
Antony, Mark, 10, 149
Apius and Virginia, 136
Apollo, 23
   oracle, 23
Apsley, William, 183
Aristotle, 42, 56, 63, 128, 158
   memory, 149
   Poetics, 56
   tragedy, 42, 56, 63
Arthur, King, 220, 225
Ascham, Roger, 156
   Schoolmaster, 155
Astraea, 174, 220, 225
Augustus, 136
Austen, Gillian, 154, 157
Aylmer, John, 204, 209

Babington Plot, 127, 134, 135
Bacon, Nicholas, 132
Badius, Jodocus, 42
Baldwin, William, 17–30, 71–85
   Beware the Cat, 24, 44, 56, 73, 74–81

Canticles or Ballads of Solomon, 18, 21, 22, 23
   death, 3, 71, 234, 237, 243
   dramatist, 41
   dream, 44, 63, 65, 199, 203, 213
   Funerals of King Edward the Sixth, 25
   motto, 24
   Treatise of Moral Philosophy, 9, 21, 22–4, 25
Barker, William, 136
Barnard of Cluny, 49
Bavand, William
   Good Ordering of the Commonweal, 204
Beaufort, Cardinal Henry, 110–11, 116, 120–2
Bellany, Alastair, 189, 192
Betteridge, Thomas, 76
Bible, 21, 23, 24, 28
   Adam and Eve, fall, 201
   Book of Genesis, 22
   Book of Job, 47
   Chronicles, 147
   Gospel of Matthew, 22, 120
   Great Bible, 71
   Matthews Bible, 71
   New Testament, 22
   Old Testament, 22, 47, 136
   Psalms, 22, 164
   Song of Songs, 21
   Vulgate, 21
Bilson, Thomas
   True Difference between Christian Subjection and Unchristian Rebellion, 137
Blenerhasset, Thomas, 3, 8, 10, 11, 147, 164
   Second Part of the Mirror for Magistrates, 3, 8, 127, 147–60, 164, 182, 218, 238
Blundeville, Thomas, 152
Boccaccio, Giovanni, 2, 26, 27, 29, 39, 40, 41, 42, 49, 74, 90, 96, 201, 234
   as 'Bochas', 27, 28, 29, 33, 62, 74, 82, 89, 123, 234
   De casibus virorum illustrium, 26, 33, 39, 40, 96, 113, 183, 199, 200, 231
   'boke of Bochas', 90, 96, 97
   Decameron, 29

Index

Bodleian Library, 82, 83
Boleyn, Anne, 190
Bolingbroke, Henry. *See* Henry IV
Bolingbroke, Roger, 115
Bond of Association, 138
Book of Common Prayer, 71
Bossewell, John, 151
   Works of Armoury, 152
Bosworth Field, Battle of, 170, 171
Braham, Robert, 27
Brutus, 129
   foundation of Britain, 3, 127, 131
Brutus, Marcus Junius, 137
Buchanan, George, 5
Bullough, Geoffrey, 238
Burrant, Robert, 62

Cade, Jack, 28, 36, 232
   rebellion, 231, 232
Cadiz, 165, 166
Caesar, Julius, 3, 10, 129, 131, 133, 137, 149, 158
   conquest of Britain, 127, 132, 152
Caiaphas, 120
Caligula, 137
Cambridge
   university, 42, 210
      Cambridge University Library, 114, 230
Camden, William, 165
   Britannia, 128, 166
Campbell, Lily B., 4, 12, 110, 117, 122, 148
   Mirror for Magistrates (1938), 4
   Parts Added to the Mirror for Magistrates, 4, 148
   reading of Gloucester complaints, 110–12
Carr, Robert, 11, 166, 174, 184–5, 188
Cassibelane, 129, 133, 134
Cassius, 137
Catholic League, 142
Catilinarian conspiracy, 136
Catullus, 163
Cavendish, George
   Metrical Visions, 64, 70, 148
Cecil, Robert, 166
Cecil, William, 132, 152, 166
   The Execution of Justice in England, 134
Chaloner, Thomas, 6, 38, 58, 65, 66, 72, 83
Chapman, George
   Iliad, 182
Charles I, 166
Charnes, Linda, 241
Charon
   ferry, 67
Chastelain, Georges
   Le Temple de Bocace, 66
Chaucer, Geoffrey, 24, 25, 27, 40, 41, 49, 129, 145

Canterbury Tales, 9
   Monk's Tale, 17, 40, 200, 203, 205
Churchyard, Thomas, 6, 8, 46, 109, 120, 153–4, 155, 156, 157
Churchyard's Chips, 155
Davy Dycars Dreame, 154
'Tragedy of Sir Simon Burley', 155
Cicero, 102, 128, 137, 187, 188, 191
   De legibus, 204
   De officiis, 152, 204
Cinthio, Giraldi, 42
civil war, 38, 135, 139, 141, 158, 185, 208, 218, 219
Clemen, Wolfgang, 60
Cobham, Eleanor, 112, 114–16, 119, 122
Collinson, Patrick, 133
Colwell, Thomas, 210
Commodus, 138
Constantine, 139, 148
Cooper, Thomas, 150, 157
   Chronicle, 151
Cope, Alan. *See* Harpsfield, Nicholas
counsel, 6, 9, 83, 89, 121, 134, 139, 173, 179, 181, 209–10, 214
Cranmer, Thomas, 74
Creede, Thomas, 185
Cross, Henry, 187
   Virtue's Commonwealth, 187
Cummings, Brian, 100
Cunliffe, J. W., 17

Daniel, Samuel, 8, 238
   Civil Wars, 228
   Rosamund, 109
Dante Alighieri, 25, 66
Dawson, Thomas, 182
Day, John, 62
de casibus tragedy, 2, 8, 18, 28, 29, 39, 40, 49, 64, 90, 148, 153, 155, 156, 158, 199–213, 231, 238
De contemptu mundi, 49
Dee, John, 122
Demosthenes, 187
Devereux, Robert, 141, 142, 165, 166, 167, 183, 190, 225, 227
Dido, 229
Diocletian, 137
Dixon, John, 225
Dolce, Lodovico
   Giocasta, 200, 211
Dolman, John, 6
Domitian, 137, 138
Drant, Thomas, 220
Drayton, Michael, 8, 166, 168, 176, 238
   England's Heroical Epistles
      Elianor Cobham, 120

Drayton, Michael (*cont.*)
  Legend of Great Cromwell, 182, 184
  Matilda, 109, 184
  Mortmeriados, 1
  Poly-Olbion, 1, 2, 166, 180, 182
du Bellay, Guillaume, 152
Dudley, Robert, 132, 137, 142, 156, 220, 225
Dyer, Edward, 220

Edward I, 173
Edward II, 174, 175
Edward III, 72, 74
Edward IV, 36, 101, 119, 202, 233, 239, 242
Edward V, 113
Edward VI, 2, 9, 23, 25, 37, 41, 46, 72, 73
Eld, George, 185
Elizabeth I, 46, 122, 131, 132, 137–8, 145, 148, 166, 168, 172, 173, 174, 175, 179, 191, 206, 207, 217, 218, 220, 221, 222, 224, 227
  'The Doubt of Future Foes', 172
  marriage, 158, 217, 221
  smallpox, 222
Ellis, Jim, 7, 37, 53, 62
Elwes, Gervase, 184, 185, 187, 188, 191, 192, 194
Elyot, Thomas
  Dictionary, 149
emotion, 10, 29, 30, 37–40, 41, 44–7, 49, 50, 60–1, 73, 78, 79, 189–91, 192, 193
empire, 126–7, 136, 137, 139, 140, 174, 220
  Roman, 130, 137, 140, 141
Erasmus, Desiderius, 5, 18–23, 27, 28, 219
  Adagia, 23
  Enchiridion Militis Christiani, 23
  Erasmian paraphrase, 21
  Moriae Encomium, 72
  Novum Instrumentum, 21, 22
  'Paraclesis', 21, 22
Essex Rebellion, 227, 230
Essex, Earl of. *See* Devereux, Robert
Euripides, 67, 157, 211
  Phoenissae, 200

Fabyan, Robert, 28, 29, 90, 98, 101, 113, 114, 115, 151, 236, 237
  Chronicle, 65
Farnham, Willard, 17
Ferrers, George, 3, 6, 7, 9, 10, 38, 41, 43, 48, 54, 67, 72, 90, 96, 97, 102, 115, 160, 203, 231, 232, 233, 234
  character, *Beware the Cat*, 73, 75, 76
  complaints, 73, 92–5, 109–10, 112–14, 117, 118, 122–3, 203
  Master of the King's Pastimes, 73, 74, 75
Ficino, Marsilio, 24
  'Argumentum', 24

Flodden Field, 165
Forker, Charles, 238
Fortune, 39, 40, 41, 42, 43, 45, 51, 59, 60, 61, 92, 95, 96, 118, 152, 158, 200, 201, 202, 205, 206, 207
  apostrophe to, 60, 61
  Lady Fortune, 47
  wheel, 2, 41, 84, 211
Foxe, John, 7, 116, 139, 140
  Acts and Monuments, 7, 101, 105, 116, 139, 145, 220
Francis, Duke of Alençon and Anjou, 142, 217, 221, 222, 223, 224
Franklin, James, 184, 188, 191, 192, 193
Froben, Johann, 18–25
Froissart, Jean, 66, 228
  Chronicles, 65, 66

Gainsford, Thomas
  'Vox Spiritus, or Sir Walter Raleigh's Ghost', 183
Galfridian legend. *See* Geoffrey of Monmouth, *History of the Kings of Britain*
Gardiner, Stephen, 3, 72, 218
Gascoigne, George, 8, 153, 154, 155, 156, 157, 160
  'Certain Notes of Instruction', 157
  'Dan Bartholmew of Bathe', 153
  Edouardo Donati, 157
  Glasse of Government, 154
  Hundreth Sundrie Flowres, 154
  Posies, 157, 211
  Steele Glas, 154
Gascoigne, George, and Francis Kinwelmersh
  Jocasta, 11, 156, 157, 200, 210, 211, 212
Gaveston, Piers, 173
Geller, Sherri, 4, 44, 55
Geoffrey of Monmouth, 147
  History of the Kings of Britain, 3, 10, 126, 130, 131, 133, 134, 141, 151
George, Duke of Clarence, 57
George, Saint, 220
ghost complaint, 181, 182, 183, 184, 186, 191, 192, 193
ghosts, 50, 51, 166, 169, 170, 171, 181, 183, 184, 186, 189, 190, 191, 192, 194, 195, 207, 235, 236, 237, 241, 242–3, 244
Globe playhouse, 227, 228
Glyndŵr, Owain, 35, 58
Golding, Arthur, 136, 155, 156
Goodman, Christopher
  How Superior Powers Ought to be Obeyed of their Subjects, 212
Googe, Barnabe, 214
Gorboduc. *See* Norton, Thomas, and Thomas Sackville: *Gorboduc*

Gorboduc, king, 208, 209
Gosson, Stephen, 41
Goths, 142, 155
Gower, John, 27
Grabes, Herbert, 216
Grafton, Richard, 3, 6, 71, 150, 157
   Chronicle at Large, 151
Green, Lawrence D., 6, 17
Gregory, Philippa, 2
Grey, Lady Jane, 190
Griffin, Edward, 185
Griffiths, Jane, 76
Grimalkin, 75
Guernsey, 3, 148, 164
Guildhall, 187–8, 190
Gunpowder Plot, 175

Hale, John, 137
Hall, Edward, 6, 28, 29, 90, 98, 99, 101, 113, 114, 116, 236, 237
   Union of the Two Noble and Illustrate Families of Lancaster and York, 6, 115, 236, 239
Hammer, Paul, 185
Hannibal, 151, 152
Hardyng, John, 114
   Chronicle, 116, 147, 151, 221
Harpsfield, Nicholas, 116
Harrier, Richard, 17
Harvey, Gabriel, 155, 157, 211, 220, 221, 223
Harvey, Gabriel, and Edmund Spenser
   Three Proper, and Witty, Familiar Letters, 155
Haslewood, Joseph, 4
Hawes, Stephen, 26
   Conversion of Swearers, 26
   Pastime of Pleasure, 26
Hay, James, Earl of Carlisle, 165
Hecuba, 205, 206, 207
Helen of Troy, 219
Helgerson, Richard, 181, 193
Henry II
   deathbed prophecy, 117
Henry III, 172
Henry IV, 28, 35, 36, 43, 58, 98, 100, 232, 236
Henry V, 36, 37
Henry VI, 36, 114, 117, 120, 217, 242
   readeption, 101
Henry VII, 242
Henry VIII, 41, 165
Henry, Prince of Wales, 166, 168, 182, 183
   death, 183
Henryson, Robert
   Testament of Cresseid, 124
Herbert, William, 184
Hercules, 168, 220

Hermes Trismegistus. *See* Mercurius Trismegistus
Herodian, 133, 138, 142
Heywood, Jasper, 11, 42, 205, 211
   Thyestes, 208
   Troas, 11, 42, 200, 205–8, 210, 212
Higgins, John, 2, 3, 4, 7, 10, 39, 64, 65, 121, 126–43, 147, 148, 153, 164, 166
   First Part of the Mirror for Magistrates, 3, 10, 39, 64, 65, 121, 126, 127, 128–9, 131, 133, 136, 139, 142, 147, 151, 152, 164, 218, 238
Hill, Richard
   Commonplace Book, 115
Holinshed, Raphael, 7, 131, 161, 238
   Chronicles, 7, 128, 135, 166, 169, 170, 216, 217, 228
Homer, 155, 156
   Iliad, 168, 182
Hooker, Richard, 78
Horace, 42, 92, 155, 156
   Ars poetica, 42
Hotson, Leslie, 18
Hotspur, Henry, 61
Howard, Charles, 165, 183
Howard, Frances, 11, 166, 184, 185, 188, 189
Howard, Henry, 24–6
   'The Great Macedon', 25, 26
   'Wyatt Resteth Here', 24
humanism, 3, 5, 18–20, 22, 23, 24, 26–30, 98, 127, 128, 217, 219, 228
Humphrey, Duke of Gloucester, 96, 115, 116, 118, 201, 202

Inner Temple, 209, 211
Inns of Court, 156, 157, 209, 210, 211
   Gray's Inn, 211
   Lincoln's Inn, 95, 122
Inquisition (personification), 149, 154, 155, 156, 157, 158

James VI and I, 5, 11, 138, 142, 168, 169, 173, 174, 175, 182, 185, 194, 223, 226
Jehovah, 127, 139, 140
Jellerson, Donald, 61
John of Lancaster, Duke of Bedford, 117
John, King, 173, 174, 175, 231
Jove, 127, 139, 140, 174, 175

King, John N., 71, 76, 78
Kingston, Felix, 4, 182, 183, 195, 196

Lake, Peter, 185
Lament of the Duchess of Gloucester, 112, 114, 118, 121, 122
Lämmerhirt, Rudolph, 157
Langton, Christopher, 25
   Very Brief Treatise of Physic, 25

Lanquet, Thomas, 151
Lant, Richard, 48
Laura, 45
Laurent de Premierfait, 33, 39, 96
    Des Cas des Nobles Hommes et Femmes, 200
Lausberg, Heinrich, 60, 61
Leicester's Commonwealth, 137
Lejeune, Philippe, 61
Leland, John, 25
    Naeniae in Mortem Thomae Viati, 24, 25
Lévi-Strauss, Claude, 164
Lewis, C. S., 1, 5, 7, 8, 17
Lindsay, David, 62, 65
    Tragical Death of David Beaton, 62, 63, 65
Lisle, Laurence, 184, 185
Livy, 128, 151, 152
    Ab Urbe Condita, 151, 152
Lodge, Thomas, 41, 109, 238
    Elstred, 109
Lucian, 67
    Menippus, 67
Lud, 129, 134
Lutheranism, 48, 204
Lydgate, John, 2, 8, 18, 29, 40, 41, 42, 49, 74, 96, 97, 129, 200, 216
    Fall of Princes, 2, 3, 17, 18, 26–8, 29, 39, 40, 53, 71, 72, 74, 82, 89, 90, 96, 183, 199, 200–4, 205, 207, 210, 231, 234
        prologue, 96, 97
    Serpent of Division, 141
    Troy Book, 27

Magna Carta, 104
Manutius, Aldus, 20
Margaret of Anjou, 114, 120
marginalia, 75, 76, 80–1, 83, 84, 140, 157, 169, 187, 211, 225, 230
Marlowe, Christopher
    Doctor Faustus, 103, 171
    Edward II, 174
Marprelate, Martin, 8
Marshe, Henry, 3, 164
Marshe, Thomas, 3, 9, 148, 182, 196, 217, 224
Marsilius of Padua, 5
Martial, 22
    epigrams, 22, 25, 32
Martindale, Charles, 212
Martini, Simone, 45
Mary I, 3, 38, 46, 71, 73, 83, 112, 122, 175, 218, 219, 225, 237, 238
Mary, Queen of Scots, 11, 131, 132, 134, 138, 172, 218, 222, 225
Matthew of Westminster, 151
Medwall, Henry
    Fulgens and Lucres, 44

Memory (personification), 149, 154, 155, 156, 157, 158, 159
Lady Memory, 169
Menippus, 67, 68
Mercurius Trismegistus, 23, 24
Mercury, 22, 23
Merlin, 11, 120, 221–2, 223
Mirror for Magistrates, complaints
    Albanact, 65, 129
    Alurede, 148
    Arthur, 169
    Blacksmith, Michael an Gof, 237
    Cadwallader, 154, 156, 158
    Caligula, 126, 140
    Caracalla, 126, 130, 133, 138
    Cardinal Wolsey, 129, 164
    Claudius, 126, 127
    Clifford, 36, 63, 64, 96
    Collingbourne, 113, 114, 191, 241
    Edmund Ironside, 169
    Edmund, Duke of Somerset, 38, 122
    Edricus, 149, 158
    Edward II, 169, 173–4
    Edward IV, 36, 47, 241
    Egelrede, 158
    Elianor Cobham, 10, 109–23, 224, 234, 235
    Ferrex, 133
    Fulgentius, 129, 130
    Galba, 126, 138
    George Plantagenet, Duke of Clarence, 24, 57, 58, 233, 241, 242
    Geta, 126, 130, 133
    Guidericus, 152, 158
    Guiderius, 129, 130
    Harold and William I, 148, 152
    Harold Godwin, 169
    Hastings, 236, 237, 241, 242
    Hellina, 148, 158, 159
    Henry Bolingbroke, 29
    Henry Percy, 35, 41
    Henry VI, 29, 36, 242
    Henry, Duke of Buckingham, 29, 41, 66, 153, 190, 234, 241, 242
    Humfrey, Duke of Gloucester, 38, 73, 109–19, 122, 123, 139, 224, 234–5
    Irenglas, 64, 130, 131, 132, 133, 134
    Jack Cade, 28, 36, 40, 97, 202, 231
    James I of Scotland, 36
    James IV of Scotland, 164, 186
    Jane Shore, 8, 109, 110, 119, 120, 153, 181, 193, 237, 241
    John Tiptoft, 29, 36, 61, 92, 101–2, 235, 237
    Julius Caesar, 126, 127, 129, 130, 131, 133, 134, 135, 136, 142
    King John, 169, 173

Laelius Hamo, 126, 130
Londricus, 129
Mortimers, 56, 57, 95, 97, 232
Mowbray, 28, 29, 38, 43, 95, 98, 113, 114
Nennius, 129, 130, 131, 132, 133
Nero, 126, 140
Nicholas Burdet, 131, 238
Otho, 126, 130, 138
Owen Glendour, 24, 29, 35, 58, 60, 61, 62, 95, 100
Owen Glendour (*Memorial*), 59, 60
Porrex, 133
Princes in the Tower, 169
Richard II, 35, 38, 43, 58, 65, 66, 72, 83–4, 227, 228, 232
Richard III, 171, 241
Richard III (*Winter Night's Vision*), 169, 170–2, 191
Richard Neville, Earl of Warwick, 65
Richard Plantagenet, Duke of York, 44, 45, 63–4, 199
Richard, Earl of Cambridge, 35, 113
Rivers, 236, 241, 242
Robert Tresilian, 38, 42, 73, 92–5, 99, 100, 101, 102, 122, 123, 202, 203, 218, 232, 237
Severus, 126, 130, 133, 138
Thomas Montague, Earl of Salisbury, 35, 58, 61, 64
Thomas of Wudstocke, Duke of Gloucester, 38, 41, 95, 122–3
Tiberius, 126, 127, 136, 139
Uter Pendragon, 148
Vitellius, 126, 130, 138
Vortiger, 159
William de la Pole, Duke of Suffolk, 36, 54–5, 58, 68, 231
Mirror for Magistrates, editions
  1559, 9, 17, 33, 45, 47, 53, 62, 63, 65, 68, 71, 72, 81, 89, 95, 96, 98, 101, 109, 112, 113, 123, 127, 155, 199, 216, 231, 232, 233, 235, 236, 238
  1563, 1, 3, 8, 17, 53, 56, 62, 113, 122, 124, 147, 153, 170, 171, 181, 208, 238
  1563, second part, 28, 32, 233, 236, 237, 238, 239, 241
  1571, 3, 54, 55, 109, 112, 220
  1578, 10, 73, 104, 109, 112, 163, 218, 220, 224, 234, 237
  1587, 2, 3, 10, 126–7, 128, 129, 130, 131, 136–43, 164, 166, 186, 238
  1610, 4, 147, 165, 170, 176, 181, 182–3, 219
  Memorial, 3, 17, 18, 26, 28, 33, 37, 38, 46, 48, 53, 58, 59, 62, 63, 68, 72, 73, 112, 175, 220, 233
Misrule, Lord of, 41

Mistris Turners Farewell to all Women, 192
Monson, Thomas, 184, 187
Montague, Thomas, 37
More, Thomas, 29, 236
  History of King Richard III, 29, 170, 236, 238, 242
  Utopia, 9, 18, 44
Morpheus, 64, 65, 66, 129, 152
Mowbray, Thomas de, 28, 98, 99, 100
Mulcaster, Richard, 81
Munday, Anthony, 148, 218

Nashe, Thomas, 223
Nero, 137
Neville, Alexander, 211
  Oedipus, 11, 200, 210, 212
Neville, Anne, 242
Neville, Richard, 236
Newstok, Scott L., 49
Newton, Thomas, 135
Niccols, Richard, 4, 11, 102, 147, 164–76, 182
  A Winter Night's Vision, 11, 169–70, 182, 189, 191
  Beggar's Ape, 165, 166
  Cuckow, 182
  England's Eliza, 169, 170, 174–5, 219
  Expicedium, 165
  London's Artillery, 166, 167–9
  Mirror for Magistrates (1610), 9, 102
  Sir Thomas Overbury's Vision, 11, 166, 181–95
Niccols, Richard (snr)
  A Day Starre for Darke Wandring Soules, 172
Noah, 142
Norland, Howard B., 42
Norman Conquest, 3, 148, 152, 190, 216
North, Thomas
  Plutarch, 136
Northern Rising, 131
Norton, Thomas, 11, 132, 133, 154, 209
Norton, Thomas, and Thomas Sackville
  Gorboduc, 11, 41, 42, 128, 133, 140, 141, 154, 157, 200, 208–10, 211, 212
Nuce, Thomas
  Octavia, 136

Odysseus, 132
Oedipus, 210, 211
Omphale, 168
Orwin, Joan, 195
Orwin, Thomas, 195
Overbury, Thomas, 11, 166
  murder, 184, 188, 191, 194
  scandal, 181, 185
Ovid, 155, 156
  Metamorphoses, 156

Oxford
  university, 42, 71
    Magdalen Hall, 165
    St Andrew's Hall, 115

Painter, William
  Palace of Pleasure, 4
Parker, Matthew, 145
Parker, Patricia, 239
parliament, 123, 132, 203, 209
Parry, William, 137
Patten, William, 67–8
  Expedition into Scotland of the duke of Somerset, 66
Patterson, Annabel, 94, 170
Peele, George, 142
  Troublesome Reign of John, King of England, 135, 172
Persons, Robert, 137
Petrarch, Francesco, 25, 27, 28, 33
Phaer, Thomas, 6, 8, 95, 104, 155, 156, 163
  Natura brevium, 95
  New Book of Presidents, 95
  Seven First Books of the Aeneid, 156
Philip II of Spain, 122, 132, 133, 238
Pickering, John
  Horestes, 140
Pincus, Steven, 185
Pinkie Cleugh, Battle of, 67
Plotinus, 128
Plutarch, 128
poetics, 28, 49, 155
Pole, Margaret, 190
Polybius, 128, 152
Ponet, John
  Short Treatise of Politic Power, 212
Pontius Pilate, 111, 140
Preston, Thomas
  Cambises, 140
Priam, 132, 207
Princes in the Tower, 243
Propertius, 163
prosopopoeia, 39, 50, 61, 73, 77, 78, 79, 80, 82, 99, 116, 190–2
Puttenham, George, 41, 150
  Art of English Poesy, 4

Quintilian, 60, 79
Quintus Curtius, 128

Racine, Jean
  Phèdre, 61
Rainolde, Richard, 82
Ralegh, Walter, 220, 223
Rastell, William, 92

Raymond de Rouer
  Instructions sur le Faict de la Guerre, 152
rebellion, 36, 43, 84, 134, 135, 139, 144, 159, 172, 174, 202, 222, 223, 228, 238, 240, 242
Reformation, 6, 21, 71, 73, 74, 76, 78, 91, 100, 101, 116, 131, 140, 160
regicide, 138, 139
Renaissance, Northern, 18
republic, 5
  monarchical, 133
  Roman, 126, 136
Rhodes, Neil, 82
Richard I, 231
Richard II, 12, 28, 35, 36, 65, 66, 93, 123, 155, 194, 202, 203, 218, 227, 235, 236, 239, 240
Richard III, 12, 57, 120, 181, 190, 235, 239
Ridolfi Plot, 131, 134
Ringler, William, and Michael Flachmann
  Beware the Cat, 75
Robinson, Richard, 66
  Reward of Wickedness, 66, 148, 218
Rome, 111, 126, 129, 130, 131, 132, 135, 136, 137, 139, 141, 142, 152, 158, 175
Rutland, Earl of, 63, 64, 96, 199

Sackville, Thomas, 6, 8, 11, 29, 41, 66, 153, 154, 156, 157, 209, 234, 237
  Induction, 1, 29, 41, 66, 153, 189, 190, 208, 233, 241
Sampson, 47
satire, 8, 9, 24, 56, 67, 76, 78, 94, 149, 158, 159, 190
  Juvenalian, 189
  Menippean, 8, 67
Savile, Henry
  End of Nero and Beginning of Galba, 141
  Tacitus, 141, 142
Scaliger, Julius Caesar, 42
Scipio Africanus, 151, 152
Scott, Thomas, 183
  Robert Earl of Essex his Ghost, 183
  Sir Walter Raleigh's Ghost, or England's Forewarner, 183
  Vox Populi, or News from Spain, 183
Sejanus, 137
Seneca, 41, 42, 155, 156, 207, 211, 212
  Agamemnon, 205
  Medea, 206
  Oedipus, 200, 210
  Thyestes, 206
  Troas, 200, 205
Senecan tragedy, 128, 136, 156, 205, 207, 211, 212
Serjeantson, Richard, 99
Seymour, Edward, 37, 38, 46, 49, 73, 112

Index

Shakespeare, William, 2, 4, 8, 11, 12, 35, 37, 126, 142, 218, 226–8, 238
  Cymbeline, 161
  Hamlet, 45, 96
  Henry IV Part 1, 35
  Henry IV Part 2, 239, 240
  Henry V, 239, 240
  Henry VI, 239, 241
  Henry VI Part 1, 37
  Henry VI Part 2, 111, 231, 232
  history plays, 231–43
  Julius Caesar, 10, 142, 149
  King John, 96, 135, 172
  Lover's Complaint, 119
  Othello, 79, 242
  Rape of Lucrece, 109, 142
  Richard II, 11, 227–8, 238, 239
    deposition, 226
    John of Gaunt, 194
  Richard III, 170, 171, 239, 240–3
  Tempest, 240
  Titus Andronicus, 142
Sherry, Richard, 27, 150
  Treatise of Schemes and Tropes, 27, 150
Sidney, Philip, 4, 37, 41, 191, 220
  Apology for Poetry, 37
  Arcadia, 164
Singleton, Hugh, 221
Sinon the Greek, 132
Sir Thomas Overbury, his Wife, now a Widow, 184, 185
Skelton, John, 27, 47, 48, 94
  'Colin Clout', 94
  'On the Death of the Noble Prince King Edward the Fourth', 48
  Philip Sparrow, 27
Skura, Meredith, 8, 55, 131
Smith, Thomas
  De republica Anglorum, 133
Socrates, 158
Solomon, 47
Somnus, 129
Sorrow (personification), 66, 190
Spanish Armada, 222
speculum principis, 5, 205
Spenser, Edmund, 4, 8, 11, 126, 149, 155, 160, 165, 166, 168, 174, 176, 219, 220, 223, 224, 226, 228, 238
  Colin Clout, 165, 223
  Colin Clout's Come Home Again, 223, 225
  Complaints, 223
  Faerie Queene, 11, 168, 174, 177, 179, 219–22, 224, 225, 230, 244
    Anamnestes, 149
    Artegall, 168, 221, 225
    Britomart, 221, 223
    Duessa, 174, 225
    Eumnestes, 149
    Fidessa, 174
    Radigund, 168
    Red-Cross Knight, 174
  Mother Hubberds Tale, 165, 223
  Shepheardes Calender, 160, 221, 222
  Virgil's Gnat, 223
Stationers' Register, 182, 184
Steible, Mary, 119
Stenner, Rachel, 76
Stow, John, 3, 6, 151, 166, 169
Stubbes, John, 219, 221
  Discovery of a Gaping Gulf, 217, 219, 222
succession, 127, 132, 134, 135, 138–42, 218, 221, 222, 224, 239
Suetonius, 138
Surrey. *See* Howard, Henry

Tacitus, 141
  Agricola, 141
  Histories, 138, 141
Terence, 73
testimony, 10, 91–5, 96, 98, 99–101, 102, 105, 159, 186, 187, 190, 192, 194, 228
Thirty Years War, 183
Throckmorton, Nicholas
  conspiracy, 135
  trial, 38, 94
Tiberius, 137, 139
Tibullus, 155, 156
Tillotson, Kathleen, 148
Tillyard, E. M. W., 1, 89
topicality, 29, 32, 37, 46, 94–5, 98, 101, 103, 112–13, 123, 130, 132, 136, 139, 142, 158, 185, 186
Tottel, Richard, 1
  Songs and Sonnets, 8, 24
Tower of London, 190, 191
treason, 11, 36, 94, 101, 115, 116, 123, 127, 132, 134–6, 137, 138, 142, 155, 174, 190
Treatise of Treasons, 132
Trismegistus. *See* Mercurius Trismegistus
Trojan horse, 132
Trojan War, 168, 205
Tromley, Frederick, 25
Troy, 27, 132
  fall, 27, 207
  women of, 205, 206
Troy, new, 131, 132, 220
Turbervile, George, 8, 155, 156, 163
  Epitaphes, Epigrams, Songs and Sonets, 156
  Heroical Epistles, 156
Turner, Anne, 184, 185, 188, 191, 192–4

Tusser, Thomas
  Five Hundred Points of Good Husbandry, 4
tyranny, 38, 67, 126, 127, 136, 137, 138–40, 141, 158, 173, 179, 190, 191, 202, 212, 218, 228

Vallans, William, 166
Vergil, Polydore, 150, 157
  English History, 151
Virgil, 73, 155
  Aeneid, 66, 132, 144, 156, 222

Wall, Wendy, 181
Warner, William
  Albion's England, 142
Wars of the Roses, 63
Wayland, John, 2–3, 18, 26, 28, 71, 72, 74, 89, 90, 96, 234
  'The Printer to the Reader', 71

Webbe, William, 153
Webster, Richard, 147, 148, 182
Wentworth, Peter, 140
Weston, Richard, 184, 187, 188, 191, 194
Whetstone, George, 148
Whitchurch, Edward, 2, 71, 72, 74
William I, 152, 190, 234
William of Orange, 142
Wilson, Thomas
  Art of Rhetoric, 119
Wilson-Okamura, David, 222
Winwood, Ralph, 184
Womersley, David, 7
Woodbridge, Linda, 212
Worden, Blair, 227
Wroth, Thomas, 165
Wyatt, Thomas, 24–6

Zoilus and Momus, 160